ELTING MEMORIAL LIBRARY NEW PALTZ

3 2913 00003 3593

D1085013

301.58 Wallis, Roy.
WAL
        The road to total
        freedom

DATE			

Elting Memorial Library
93 Main St.
New Paltz, N. Y.

© THE BAKER & TAYLOR CO.

The Road to Total Freedom

A Sociological Analysis of Scientology

The Road to Total Freedom

A Sociological Analysis of Scientology

Roy Wallis

Elting Memorial Library
93 Main St.
New Paltz, N. Y.

NEW YORK   COLUMBIA UNIVERSITY PRESS   1977

36,025

Copyright © 1976 Roy Wallis

All rights reserved.

Printed in Great Britain

Library of Congress Cataloging in Publication Data

Wallis, Roy.
  The Road to Total Freedom.

  Bilbliography: p.
  Includes index.
  1. Scientology. I. Title.
BP605.S2W34   1976   131'.35   76–27273

ISBN 0–231–04200–0

PREFACE

There is a sense in which sociology is inevitably a subversive enterprise. The very act of reflecting on the behaviour of people and organizations entails that these activities do not bear their meaning and explanation on their face. The sociologist's pursuit of further or different knowledge after he has already been informed of the 'truth' of the matter by the individuals or organizations concerned, displays the fact that he does not accept the 'self-evident', and perhaps even that motivated by malice, he is prepared to tell some entirely different story.

Hence, the sociologist poses a threat to the rhetorics and legitimations employed by social groups and a potential challenge to their definition of reality, and to the definitions of themselves which they present for public consumption. He therefore risks calling down upon himself the wrath and opprobrium of groups which he studies. Generally, the groups examined by sociologists are relatively powerless and their complaints may do little more than prick his own conscience or the consciences of his more radical colleagues. In other cases, however, the group examined may not be without power and in such instances, depending on the nature of the power and the society in which it is exercised, the sociologist may risk more severe if not necessarily more serious, consequences,

I began my work on Scientology as a raw graduate student, fascinated by the relationship between beliefs, social organisation and society. While I had initially intended that Scientology be considered as one among a range of unorthodox system of belief to which I proposed to devote attention, I found myself increasingly interested by the rich body of material I was uncovering on this multifaceted movement. I have recounted at length elsewhere (in my contribution 'The moral career of a research project' to Colin Bell and Howard Newby, editors, *Doing Sociological Research*, Allen and Unwin, London, 1976) the history of my research on Scientology. It remains, however, to summarize a few points salient to the final production of this book.

As my opening remarks would suggest, the Church of Scientology was suspicious of my research. Having suffered at the hands of newspaper reporters, investigators for state and medical agencies, and government enquiries in many countries, my own work was readily placed by the leaders of the Church of Scientology into the category of hostile or critical commentary. My protestations that I had no axe to grind, and that I sought only to provide a coherent and as-nearly-objective account of Scientology as possible, were viewed with commendable scepticism by the church leadership.

The Church of Scientology is not known for its willingness to take what it construes as criticism without recourse. Indeed its record of litigation must surely be without parallel in the modern world. It therefore seemed almost inevitable that my own final work would be the subject of lengthy and expensive litigation. In such a situation, the writer faces a dilemma. Does he 'tell the truth, and damn the consequences'? Or does he, in the light of the extreme severity of the British law of libel, reflect that in over a hundred thousand words of text, anyone can make a mistake? There is a powerful tension between the threat of censorship and the possibility of enormous cost in time, effort and money for a single error.

But there is a further consideration. The sociologist has an *obligation* to the subjects of his research. Even if his relationship with them has sometimes approached open war, he owes them a duty not to misrepresent their activities and beliefs, the more so if they are in any respect a socially stigmatized or politically threatened collectivity. In my decision to make my manuscript available to the Church of Scientology, *both* of those considerations weighed heavily. Informing them in advance of what one intended to say had its dangers. Forewarned is, after all, forearmed for any legal battle. But the risk, in this case, paid off. It is my feeling that the church leadership appreciated the gesture, and while they remained adamant over a period of months that certain things should not be said, they were willing to compromise and to negotiate.

These negotiations, covering several reams of typescript were salutory. I came to appreciate that things which had initially sounded innocuous to me could be read as pejorative or even invective. In due course, I made various modifications to the text in this light. As an example, I amended my argument that Hubbard was 'obsessed' with communism, to read that he was 'preoccupied' by it. I also deleted a comparison with the Nazi party and the SS which seemed on reflection *unnecessarily* offensive to members of the Church of Scientology. I further incorporated into the text from various commentaries sent to me by the Church of Scientology, statements of their views on certain events on which we could not find common ground.

As a final gesture to the Church I offered to include in the work, as an appendix, a commentary commissioned by the Church, on my work as a whole. This seemed to provide what they claimed had been denied them in the past, i.e. an adequate right of reply, for which reason they had been forced to seek recourse in the courts. Dr Jerry Simmons was commissioned by the Church to write this reply. His interesting paper 'On maintaining deviant belief systems', has often been cited by sociologists working in the field of unorthodox collectivities of believers.[1]

As a believer himself in this case, Dr Simmons inevitably rejects my study.

[1] *Social Problems*, 11, Winter (1964), pp. 250–6.

His main argument is that my methods are not adequate in that they do not fulfil the criteria of traditional survey research, and that I therefore violate "the scientific method'. Dr Simmons fails to recognise that methods are tools and tools must be adapted to circumstances. The 'scientific method' is no more than an injunction to examine evidence dispassionately and critically. My study does not intend to be a piece of survey research. Dr Simmons' strictures are, there-fore, at best, misplaced. There are no 'sampling errors' since there is no 'sample'. My respondents are ethnographic informants not randomly sampled survey respondents. That many of them were not practising Scientologists and were openly hostile to Scientology only tells us that my information *may* be biased and not that it *is*. As it happens, information secured from informants, whether devoted adherents or active opponents, could be checked against other informants or against documentary sources. Dr Simmons suggests that I was offered permission to interview over 4,000 believers for my study. This offer was not, I'm afraid, ever as clear to me as it was to Dr Simmons. He accuses me again of bias in sampling statements from documents rather than performing a content analysis, but again his argument is misplaced. Had I wished for an analysis of the content of the documents, I would have conducted a content analysis. But something said only once in a body of documentation may have as much influence on organizational and individual behaviour as something said a thousand times. Hence I utilized documentation as any historian would, seeking to locate influential statements and to cite statements which information from other sources had indicated were important for behaviour, rather than to analyse as a whole the content of documents which, in the case of Scientology as of many other organizations and social movements, are often written for public relations purposes.

Ultimately, of course, which of us – Dr Simmons or I – is right on the quest-tion of the degree of bias in this book, is open to dispute. That is as it should be. I would be as foolish as Dr Simmons thinks me, if I believed I have said the last word on Scientology. It is right, and indeed exciting in its prospect, that debate about this movement will continue. I am hopeful that new information will continually come to light, and urge anyone with documentation on Scientology to send it to me, or to the Librarian of Stirling University, where an archive can be formed to preserve such material for future scholars. In the meantime, any-one hoping to resolve the matter can do no better than Dr Simmons suggests: begin your own investigation. Read Hubbard's *Dianetics: The Modern Science of Mental Health* and compare it, in terms of objectivity, the 'scientific method', etc., with my book.

CONTENTS

ACKNOWLEDGEMENTS

In a research enterprise of this kind innumerable debts are inevitably accumulated. For the first two years of the research I was fortunate to be a student at Nuffield College, Oxford. I am grateful to the Warden and Fellows for providing me with a home, facilities, and intellectual stimulation during this period. The Social Science Research Council generously provided me with a grant which enabled me to pursue this research. The Ofrex-Drexler Foundation also kindly provided me with a small grant at a crucial stage in my work. Professor Duncan Timms, Chairman of the Department of Sociology of Stirling University, greatly assisted my work by providing me with time, research funds and secretarial assistance.

Without the aid of Cyril Vosper, the study would never have begun. I am also grateful to him for many stimulating conversations and useful leads in the course of the research. Mr P. Hetherington made available to me material otherwise unavailable in Great Britain on the early days of the movement. On a research visit to America, Mr and Mrs Don Rodgers, Mr and Mrs Ross Lamoureaux, A. E. van Vogt and his late wife, Mayne, Perry Chapdelaine, Beau Kitselman, and Waldo Boyd kindly provided hospitality and much useful material. There I benefited from conversations with Paulette Cooper and Robert Kaufman. Among the interview and questionnaire respondents to all of whom I am grateful, Miss Shelia Hoad, and Miss Carmen D'Allessio provided much assistance. Mrs Nan Mclean and Dr Russell Barton provided useful information and documentation.

The Editors of the *News of the World*, *Mayfair*, the *Denver Post*, and of other newspapers and magazines too numerous to mention individually, and the management of Reuters, all made freely available copies of articles otherwise unobtainable, or provided me with facilities to examine their clipping files. I have benefited from discussions with Miss Mary Appleby, OBE, formerly secretary of the National Association for Mental Health (now the Mind Association); and with Mr David Gaiman, of the Guardian's Office of the Church of Scientology, who also arranged for me to interview students and staff at Saint Hill Manor. Dr Christopher Evans and Mr C. H. Rolph kindly showed me their manuscripts prior to publication.

Earlier drafts of Chapter 1 appeared as part of an article 'Scientology:

therapeutic cult to religious sect' in *Sociology*, 9, 1 (January 1975); and aspects of the theory were presented in 'The cult and its transformations' in *Sectarianism: Analyses of Religious and Non-Religious Sects* Roy Wallis, (Peter Owen, London, 1975). This latter work also contained an early formulation of sections of Chapter 7, under the title 'Societal reactions to Scientology: a study in the sociology of deviant religion'. For comments on earlier versions of Chapter 7, I am grateful to Professor Stanley Cohen, Dr David Downes, Dr Shelia Mitchell, and Dr Russell Dobash. The bulk of the manuscript has been read by Robert Kaufman and Richard Bland, and all of it by Professor David Martin and Dr Roderick Martin, whose comments and criticisms have been most helpful. Dr Bryan Wilson supervised my research for the doctoral thesis on which this book is based, and provided personal encouragement, sociological insight, and incisive editorial criticism. He has read many drafts of the manuscript and commented carefully and patiently upon each. I owe him a particular debt of gratitude. My wife and children have tolerated me throughout, a more difficult task than can easily be imagined.

Parts of the manuscript have been typed by Pam Drysdale and Marion Govan. To them and to Grace Smith who, with my wife, performed the bulk of the secretarial tasks connected with the preparation of this work, I wish to express my thanks.

Finally, I acknowledge a most profound debt to those who talked to me, completed my questionnaires, wrote letters, sent me information or otherwise assisted my research, but who must, for one reason or another, remain anonymous. None of those acknowledged here bear any responsibility for the final product.

This book is dedicated to the memory of my late father, John C. Wallis.

ABBREVIATIONS

OT	Operating Thetan
OTC	Operations and Transport Corporation
(OTS)	(Operations and Transport Services Ltd)
PTS	Potential Trouble Source
Q & A	Question and Answer
Sec	Secretary
Sec Check	Security Check
S.P.	Suppressive Person
Stats	Statistics
T.R.	Training Routine
WW	World Wide

OTHER ABBREVIATIONS

AJS	*American Journal of Sociology*
AMA	American Medical Association
ASR	*American Sociological Review*
BJS	*British Journal of Sociology*
FDA	Food and Drug Administration
JSSR	*Journal for the Scientific Study of Religion*
NAMH	National Association for Mental Health

INTRODUCTION AND
METHODOLOGICAL NOTE

A number of notable nineteenth-century rationalists held the view that the development of mankind resembled the development of the human individual. In his early, primitive state man was childlike in his mode of thought. His power of reason suffered severe limitations. It was said to be 'prelogical' in character.[1] Men believed that things once associated with each other continued to influence each other when apart; that words had the power to alter the course of nature; and that objects similar in one major respect were similar in others.[2] Primitive man was said to possess a magical world-view. Magic was held to have been born of man's ignorance of natural causation and his desire to influence and control the dangerous and threatening natural environment in which he found himself.

On some accounts primitive man gradually learned that his magical methods were inefficacious. The law-like generalizations hitherto employed were discerned not to hold in all instances. Consequently, this account runs, he began to predicate the existence of supernatural beings, like himself except for their superhuman powers, which might be mobilized to the good or to the detriment of mankind. Where formerly he had commanded events through the incantation of a formula regarded as inevitable in its consequences (other things being equal), he now propitiated these superior beings, seeking to cozen and cajole them into interfering in the course of nature and human society.[3] By this means the great world religions were said to have been born.

Although this religious world-view was to prevail for many centuries, the nineteenth-century rationalists believed that they could perceive a change overtaking the intellect of civilized western man. The prevailing view of the world was again being challenged. As religion replaced magic, so science was coming to replace religion. As Man 'came of age' in Victorian Britain, so he cast off less mature modes of thought. A cosmos inhabited by arbitrary and capricious spirits and deities was giving way to a cosmos governed by natural laws,

[1] Lucien Levy-Bruhl, *Primitive Mentality* (Allen & Unwin, London, 1923).
[2] James G. Frazer, *The Golden Bough* (Macmillan, New York, 1922).
[3] Ibid.

mechanical in their functioning, operating upon objects rendered visible by an advancing scientific technology.

This view was enshrined in the work of Sigmund Freud. Freud maintained that religion was an infantile obsessional neurosis born of anxiety and wish-fulfilment. Science marked, and provided the means to further, the maturation of man. Science broke through the illusion and infantile projection. Scientific thought was therefore not merely more mature than religious thought, it was on Freud's account, psychologically healthier.[1] Although both the logic and the empirical detail of these evolutionist accounts of the development of human thought have been challenged, a variant on this view remains incorporated in much contemporary thinking on the relationship between religion and social change. The spectacular advance of science in the nineteenth century is seen as one central feature of an account of the decline in the hold that religious beliefs have on man's actions, and the declining commitment displayed to religious institutions in most western societies.[2] In short, a prevalent view holds that with the development of science and its increasingly evident ability both to explain the world in which we live, and to modify that world in the direction of human desire, secularization is an inevitable concomitant of the development of industrial societies.

This view has its critics, of course, and we can here neither debate the conceptual problems incorporated in the notion of secularization,[3] nor the empirical case of persistent high levels of religious affiliation in the United States of America.[4] What is more central to the enterprise recorded in the following chapters is the fact that despite the enormous progress of science and the evident decline in religious commitment in most western nations, new religious movements have continued to appear at an apparently undiminished rate. Indeed since the end of the Second World War there has, if anything, been an increase in both the rate of formation of such movements and the rate of growth of their membership. This phenomenon is not restricted to western industrial nations. Japan too has experienced a rapid increase in the number of new religious movements, and the size of their followings.[5] The industrialization and rationalization of contemporary, technologically advanced societies appears to have

[1] Sigmund Freud, *The Future of an Illusion* (Hogarth, London, 1962).

[2] Bryan R. Wilson, *Religion in Secular Society* (Penguin Books, Harmondsworth, 1969), pp. 57–74.

[3] For discussions of these problems, see: Vernon Pratt, *Religion and Secularisation* (St Martin's Press, London, 1970); David Martin, 'Secularisation' in Julius Gould, ed., *Penguin Survey of the Social Sciences 1965* (Penguin Books, Harmondsworth, 1965); Idem, *The Religious and the Secular* (Routledge & Kegan Paul, London, 1969); Idem, *The Sociology of English Religion* (SCM Press, London, 1967).

[4] Wilson, op. cit., pp. 109–50.

[5] H. Thomsen, *The New Religions of Japan* (Tuttle, Rutland, Vermont, 1963); H. N. McFarland, *The Rush Hour of the Gods* (Macmillan, New York, 1967); C. B. Offner and H. van Straelen, *Modern Japanese Religions* (Brill, Leiden, 1963).

produced problems for their members with which science has yet proved incompetent to cope.

Rationalist and humanist intellectuals have tended to be puzzled by this flourishing of exotic new religious and quasi-religious movements in relatively secular societies. Many, viewing contemporary industrial society through sometimes unacknowledged evolutionary eyes, conceive such phenomena as 'regressive' in character. Resort to the occult and the supernatural is seen as a withdrawal from the realities of modern life, a retreat from the anonymity, the tensions, and the individualism of the modern world. For those with Marxist inclinations, the new religions are seen as a particularly bizarre form of 'false consciousness'. They have in general been regarded as peripheral to the central features of modern society. Since they are viewed as a fringe phenomenon, ephemeral, and even frivolous, they have not motivated any extensive sociological description or analysis. Published monographic studies of such movements by social scientists are rare.[1] Only if they maintained clear links with the prevailing religious tradition[2] or had political implications[3] have these movements been regarded as sufficiently important to merit any considerable sociological attention.[4]

While it may be the case, however, that some new religious movements in advanced industrial societies are more or less explicitly attempts to escape from the more unattractive features of modern life: its impersonality, atomization, materialism and bureaucratization;[5] or attempts to recast it in form, other

[1] Leon Festinger, Henry W. Rieken and Stanley Schachter, *When Prophecy Fails* (Harper, New York, 1964); John Lofland, *Doomsday Cult* (Prentice Hall, Englewood Cliffs, New Jersey, 1966); Allan W. Eister, *Drawing Room Conversion* (Duke University Press, Durham, North Carolina, 1950); H. T. Dohrman, *California Cult: the Story of Mankind United* (Beacon, Boston, 1958); Geoffrey K. Nelson, *Spiritualism and Society* (Routledge & Kegan Paul, London, 1969).

[2] Malcolm J. C. Calley, *God's People* (Oxford University Press, London, 1965); Richard Enroth, Edward Ericson and C. Breckinridge Peters, *The Story of the Jesus People* (Paternoster, Exeter, 1972); Luther P. Gerlach and Virginia Hine, *People, Power, Change* (Bobbs-Merrill, New York, 1970).

[3] Eric C. Lincoln, *The Black Muslims in America* (Beacon, Boston, 1961); E. V. Essien-Udom, *Black Nationalism: a Search for Identity in America* (Penguin Books, Harmondsworth, 1962); James A. Dator, *Soka Gakkai: Builders of the Third Civilisation* (University of Washington Press, Seattle, 1969); James W. White, *The Sokagakkai and Mass Society* (Stanford University Press, Stanford, California, 1970).

[4] The new religious movements in less developed societies have been better served. In part this must be due to the concern among anthropologists and sociologists to understand the mechanisms of social change in hitherto largely stable societies. Moreover since such societies were less secularized, religious phenomena could be seen as playing some central part in social change and adaptation. In 'secular' industrial societies, religion and its social-scientific study have been relegated to a very inferior position.

[5] Benjamin Zablocki, *The Joyful Community* (Penguin Books, Baltimore, Maryland, 1971); Thomas Robbins and Dick Anthony, 'Getting straight with Meher Baba', *JSSR*, 11, 2 (June 1972), pp. 122–40; Francine J. Daner, 'Conversion to Krishna

movements have thoroughly embraced the modern world. They accept rather than reject the values which prevail within it. They are bureaucratic and rationalistic in orientation, and sometimes thoroughly materialistic. They may be relatively impersonal and individualistic rather than communally based. They sometimes seek to incorporate science, or its rhetoric, into their legitimations.

Such movements, Bryan Wilson has termed 'manipulationist'.[1] Rather than a means of escape from the world, of attaining other-worldly salvation, or of achieving a radical transformation of the prevailing society, they offer the believer some superior, esoteric means of succeeding within the status quo. They offer knowledge and techniques to enable the individual to improve his 'life-chances'; the means of achieving the valued goals of this world. The manipulationist movements appear, in terms of numbers of recruits and income, to be among the more successful of the new religions in industrial societies. Within this category fall Christian Science, the Japanese movement Soka Gakkai, Transcendental Meditation, and the subject of the present work, Scientology.

Scientology is a movement which straddles the boundary between psychology and religion. It offers a graded hierarchy of 'auditing' (the quasi-therapeutic practice of the movement) and training, which will ultimately release fully all the individual's inner potential. Correct application of the knowledge purveyed by the movement will, it is claimed, lead to the freeing of the individual's superhumanly powerful spiritual nature. In the progress towards this desirable state, current human limitations – psychosomatic illness, psychological and physical disabilities, lack of confidence, or competence – will fall away, enabling the individual to cope more successfully with his environment.

Training and 'auditing' are provided primarily by the central organizations of the movement which are administered on highly bureaucratic lines. The services provided by these organizations are expensive to purchase, and have been marketed with all the more aggressive techniques of modern salesmanship. The size of Scientology's following is almost impossible to estimate, but substantial groups of followers exist throughout the English-speaking world; and smaller groups in Germany, Scandinavia, and France. The movement is able to command sufficient resources to maintain a large permanent staff and a fleet of vessels known as the 'Sea Org'. Scientology has aroused widespread controversy and occasional public hostility. It has been the subject of government

---

[1] Bryan R. Wilson, *Religious Sects* (Weidenfeld & Nicolson, London 1970), pp. 141–66.

Consciousness: the transformation from hippie to religious ascetic', in Roy Wallis, ed., *Sectarianism: Analyses of Religious and Non-Religious Sects* (Peter Owen, London, 1975; Robert Lynn Adams and Robert Jon Fox, 'Mainlining Jesus: the new trip', *Society*, 9, 4 (1972), pp. 50–6; Donald W. Peterson and Armand L. Mauss, 'The Cross and the Commune: an interpretation of the Jesus People', in Charles Y. Glock, ed., *Religion in Sociological Perspective* (Wadsworth, Belmont, California, 1973), pp. 261–79.

investigations in a number of states and legislative sanction in others (these are discussed in Chapter 7).

Scientology is of sociological interest for a number of reasons. Its recruits, as will be demonstrated in the following chapters, are not drawn from the categories of the traditionally dispossessed. They are not marginal individuals, but individuals who are members of groups and strata which are in many ways central to the character of industrial society. They are for the most part drawn from a relatively privileged, relatively comfortable, middle class. Analysis of this movement may therefore direct us to features of contemporary society which are a source of persistent alienation and anxiety, even to its most typical constituent groups.

Scientology is of theoretical interest also because although the nature of its doctrine and practice differs from them radically, Scientology shares a number of characteristics with movements such as Communism, the Nazi Party, and Jehovah's Witnesses. Scientology is a source of data and further insight into the tactics and dynamics of totalitarian and sectarian movements. Moreover, in the course of its development Scientology has undergone a transformation from a loose, almost anarchic group of enthusiasts for a lay psychotherapy, Dianetics, to a tightly controlled and rigorously disciplined following for a quasi-religious movement, Scientology. It therefore provides an opportunity to explore a little understood transformation, that of a cult into a sect.

The chapters which follow analyse the history, the membership, the beliefs and practices, the structure and functioning, and the changing nature of the relationship of this movement to the wider society. In chapter one, a typology of ideological collectivities is presented, and a theory of the development of cults into sects. Cults are presented as highly individualistic collectivities prone to fission and disintegration. The transformation of a cult into a sect is viewed as a strategy by means of which leaders seek to perpetuate and to enhance their status by arrogating authority in an attempt to create a stable and cohesive following.

Chapter two describes and analyses the emergence of Dianetics, exploring the origins, the nature and the development of its beliefs and practices, the character of its followers, and its mode of organization. In chapter three the strains and tensions which threatened the disruption of the movement are considered, and the processes by which the movement's leaders sought to resolve these problems. Chapter four presents the beliefs and practices of the new gnosis, Scientology, on the basis of which organizational transformation was carried through. The progressive rationalization of the practise and teaching of Scientology was an important component of the process by which the leader was enabled to secure unchallenged control of the movement. In chapter five the manner in which this control was exercised through an increasingly bureaucratic administration is discussed. Chapter six analyses the motivations of recruits to Scientology, and the process through which, as individuals become increasingly committed to the movement, they are transformed into deployable agents, available for mobilization in the pursuit of organizational ends. In chapter seven a model drawn from the sociology of deviance, the 'deviance-amplification' model, is employed to analyse the controversy and hostility in which this movement was involved during the 1960s, and the nature of the movement's response. In chapter eight Scientology is viewed as a deviant version of social reality, and a number of mechanisms are described by which this reality is sustained. In the concluding chapter Scientology is located within a view of secularization and its impact on the prevailing religious climate; and a number of the major themes explored in the work are summarized.

Methodology

The methodology of the study is eclectic. Since the aim of the research was primarily that of generating data concerning certain broad themes rather than testing a limited and defined set of hypotheses, various methods were employed in order to maximize the information available, and at the same time to provide a method of 'triangulation', whereby one data source could be checked against another.

The principal source of information has been documentary. L. Ron Hubbard was a prolific writer for some years before his creation of Dianetics, and the movement has, throughout the quarter of a century of its existence, been the source of many millions of words. Much of this material was of ephemeral interest, and much that was produced in the early years is no longer available. Fortunately, some individuals in England and America have retained collections of old documentation – a dusty reminder of an earlier enthusiasm – and these collections proved an invaluable source of historical information. Containing, as they often did, the works of schismatics and heretics, notebooks and letters, these documentary sources often fulfilled both methodological needs. Study was made of the now extensive, although by no means complete, collection of more recent material in the British Museum. In the United States, legal records and supporting documents were examined. Individuals made other documents and tape-recordings available to me, as did the Church of Scientology on certain occasions.

The second important source of information was from interviews. 83 individuals were interviewed, of whom 35 had become involved in the movement during its Dianetics phase[1] and 43 after the transition to Scientology. The remaining 5 individuals were never committed to the movement, but had

---

[1] Dianetics as a form of theory and practice is still employed by the movement. However, I use the term throughout, unless contextually indicated, to refer to *a phase of the movement*, prior to the development of Scientology. 'Dianeticist' usually refers to someone who joined the movement during this phase, or to someone who continued the practice of Dianetics independently of the official Scientology organization.

become involved with it or had information on it from some other point of view.

Interviews were principally occasions for respondents to talk freely on certain themes to which I sought to direct them. Usually, the interviews were tape-recorded, unless the informant objected on the grounds that some traceable record of our conversation might fall into hostile hands; or when the surroundings made recording difficult. The interviews varied greatly in length, from three-quarters of an hour to a total of over ten hours. The yield from these procedures was inevitably uneven in the quantity and quality of usable material produced.

Interview respondents were generated in a number of ways. Names of potential informants were originally supplied by a former member. These individuals in turn supplied further names, some former members, some still committed in various ways to the movement. Other interview respondents were generated as a result of a questionnaire which was circulated.

This questionnaire method was relatively unfruitful in terms of conventional survey criteria. Of some 150 questionnaires sent out over several months, only 46 completed schedules were returned. As well as sending questionnaires to individuals whose names were supplied by informants, questionnaire respondents also provided further names. A very dated mailing list of the Hubbard Association of Scientologists International was provided by one informant, and the names sampled. It was this which led to the low return-rate. The mailing list was some eight years out of date, and very few of the questionnaires sent to the sample from it were returned. Questionnaires were sent only to United Kingdom residents.

A very brief period was spent in participant observation. At an early stage in the research, the author went to the movement's headquarters, Saint Hill Manor, to take a Communications Course. Despite later claims by representatives of the movement that the author acted unethically by not revealing his sociological interest, the author was simply responding to widespread advertising inviting members of the public to take this course and at no point made any effort to conceal his identity. After two days, he found it impossible to continue with the course without having to lie directly about his acceptance of its content, and withdrew.

A number of other individuals and agencies have been contacted during the course of the research, and many sent long letters and other documents presenting aspects of their involvement with this movement.

While very little published material on Scientology was available when the study was begun, at the time of writing some seventeen systematic and lengthy accounts exist, ranging from the journalistic to the apologetic, including five lengthy government inquiries or sponsored studies.[1]

[1] Paulette Cooper, *The Scandal of Scientology* (Tower, New York, 1971); Cyril Vosper *The Mind Benders* (Neville Spearman, London, 1971); George Malko, *Scientology: the*

Now Religion (Dell, New York, 1970); Robert Kaufman, *Inside Scientology* (Olympia, New York, 1972); Maurice Burrell, *Scientology: What It Is and What It Does* (Lakeland, London, 1970); C. H. Rolph, *Believe What You Like* (André Deutsch, London, 1973); Christopher Evans, *Cults of Unreason* (Harrap, London, 1973); David R. Dalton, *Two Disparate Philosophies* (Regency, London 1973); Omar V. Garrison, *The Hidden Story of Scientology* (Arlington Books, London, 1974); Harriet Whitehead, 'Reasonably fantastic: some perspectives on Scientology, science fiction and occultism', in Irving I. Zaretsky and Mark Leone (eds), *Religious Movements in Contemporary America* (Princeton University Press, Princeton, 1974); John A. Lee, *Sectarian Healers and Hypnotherapy* (Queen's Printer, Toronto, 1970); Walter Braddeson, *Scientology for the Millions* (Sherbourne, Los Angeles, 1969); Helen O'Brien, *Dianetics in Limbo* (Whitmore, Philadelphia, 1966); Sir John G. Foster, *Enquiry into the Practice and Effects of Scientology* (HMSO, London, 1971); Kevin V. Anderson, *Report of the Board of Inquiry into Scientology* (Government Printer, Melbourne, 1965); Sir Guy Richardson Powles and E. V. Dumbleton, *Report of the Commission of Inquiry into the Hubbard Scientology Organisation in New Zealand* (Government Printer, Wellington, New Zealand, 1969); G. P. C. Kotzé, et al., *Report of the Commission of Enquiry into Scientology for 1972* (Government Printer, Pretoria, South Africa, 1973). It should be noted that of these works, that by Burrell was withdrawn shortly after it appeared, and the publishers of the works by Cooper and Malko have undertaken not to reprint them.

Part I

THE SOCIOLOGY
OF CULT AND SECT

1. CULT AND SECT: A TYPOLOGY AND A THEORY

Identification

Sects have been the focus of considerable research enterprise in the sociology of religion, and much of this endeavour has been directed to the issue of whether, or under what conditions, sects become transformed into denominations.[1] This dominating area of concern has distracted attention from other types of ideological collectivity and other possible processes. An analogous but different process, to which little attention has been paid, is that of the transformation of cults into sects.

Until recently, cults have been regarded as rather trivial social phenomena, unworthy of systematic sociological attention. More important perhaps, the process of transformation of cults into sects has, on some accounts, been rendered not merely empirically unlikely, but a priori impossible.

Consider, for example, Glock and Stark's definition. Cults they argue are

> religious movements which draw their inspiration from other than the primary religion of the culture, and . . . are not schismatic movements in the same sense as sects whose concern is with preserving a purer form of the traditional faith.[2]

Glock and Stark define cult and sect in terms of the *content* of belief. Cults have theologically alien beliefs, sects have more rigorous or more fundamentalist variants of the prevailing theology, and are schismatic in origin. On this basis there could be individual *conversion* from one to another, but not organizational transformation.

While Glock and Stark draw an impenetrable theological boundary between cult and sect, others such as Lofland and Dohrman blur any boundary between

[1] H. R. Niebuhr, *The Social Sources of Denominationalism* (Holt, Rinehart & Winston, New York, 1925); Bryan R. Wilson, 'An analysis of sect development', *ASR*, 24 (1959), pp. 3–15.
[2] Charles Y. Glock and Rodney Stark, *Religion and Society in Tension* (Rand McNally, Chicago, 1965), p. 245.

them at all. Lofland, in his definition of cults, describes them as 'little groups' which break off from the

> conventional consensus and espouse very different views of the real, the possible and the moral[1]

while Dohrman suggests that

> the concept of 'cult' will refer to that group, secular, religious, or both, that has deviated from what our American Society considers normative forms of religion, economics, or politics, and has substituted a new and often unique view of the individual, his world, and how this world may be attained.[2]

These forms of definition seem inadequate from a number of points of view:

1. If deviance is the identifying characteristic of cult beliefs as suggested by Lofland and Dohrman, Christian schismatic and heretical forms of belief, such as those of Christian Science, the Mormons, Jehovah's Witnesses, and even the Salvation Army, become the ideologies of cults. The distinction between cult and sect disappears.[3]

2. If, as Glock and Stark suggest, cults are to be identified by their alien 'inspiration', and sects by their concern to preserve the purity of the 'traditional faith' and their schismatic origins, cults and sects are types of ideological collectivity which bear no developmental relationship to each other. We cannot predicate of a cult its possible transformation into a sect. More important, however, this definition ignores a crucial sociological feature, that is the social organization of the collectivities concerned. The theological criterion of classification employed by Glock and Stark provides us with no insight into the similarities in mode of organization and methods of control over adherents of such theologically diverse movements as Christian Science, Scientology,[4] Jehovah's Witnesses, etc.

Deviance, it has been suggested, is a distinguishing feature of both cult *and* sect. Cult and sect are deviant in relation to the respectable, the normatively sanctioned, forms of belief prevailing at any time. Today they are deviant in comparison with prevailing indifference, agnosticism, or denominational Christian orthodoxy.[5] A feature which distinguishes between them is that, like

---

[1] John Lofland, *Doomsday Cult* (Prentice-Hall, Englewood Cliffs, New Jersey, 1966), p. 1.

[2] H. T. Dohrman, *California Cult: the Story of Mankind United* (Beacon Press, Boston, 1958), p. *xi*.

[3] As it does in the work of some theologians – for example, A. A. Hoekema, *The Four Major Cults* (Eerdmans, Grand Rapids, 1963).

[4] For a comparison of Christian Science and Scientology, see Roy Wallis, 'A comparative analysis of problems and processes of change in two manipulationist movements: Christian Science and Scientology' in *The Contemporary Metamorphosis of Religion?* Acts of the 12th International Conference on the Sociology of Religion (The Hague, Netherlands, August, 1973), pp. 407–22.

[5] On the prevailing religious climate in Britain and America, see Bryan R. Wilson, *Religion in Secular Society* (Penguin Books, Harmondsworth, 1969); Will Herberg, *Protestant–Catholic–Jew* (Doubleday Anchor, New York, 1960); Rodney Stark and

the church, the sect is conceived by its adherents to be *uniquely legitimate* as a means of access to truth or salvation. The cult, like the denomination, is conceived by followers to be *pluralistically legitimate*, one of a variety of paths to the truth or salvation.[1] This provides us with the following typology:

A Typology of Ideological Collectivities[2]

	Respectable	Deviant
Uniquely legitimate	Church	Sect
Pluralistically legitimate	Denomination	Cult

A theory of cult development

Although not all new religious movements go through any simple undirectional sequence of stages,[3] it is worth emphasizing that some do undergo transformation from one type of collectivity to another. The best known case, although less typical than was once believed, is the development of sects into denominations. It is argued here that some new religious movements emerge as cults, and of these, some develop into sects.

Colin Campbell has proposed the notion of the *cultic milieu* to refer to the cultural underground from which cults arise. This cultic milieu he describes as

> Much broader, deeper and historically based [*sic*] than the contemporary movement known as *the* underground, it includes all deviant belief-systems and their associated practices. Unorthodox science, alien and heretical religion, deviant medicine, all comprise elements of such an underground. In addition, it includes the collectivities, institutions, individuals and media of communication associated with these beliefs. Substantively it includes the worlds of the occult and the magical, of spiritualism and psychic phenomena, of mysticism and new thought, of faith

[1] The notions of unique and pluralistic legitimacy were first employed by Roland Robertson, *The Sociological Interpretation of Religion* (Blackwell, Oxford, 1970), p. 123, in slightly different fashion. David Martin has also drawn attention to the pluralistic legitimacy of the cult and the denomination. See the appendix, 'The denomination' in David Martin, *Pacifism* (Routledge & Kegan Paul, London, 1965).

[2] In the context of some ideological collectivities the label 'church' would be inappropriate, as indeed might some of the others. In the case of political movements, for example, what one has in mind here is the Nazi party in Germany after 1934, or the Bolshevik party in Russia after 1922. In terms of churches, Catholicism would typically fit this category, as would the Calvinism of Calvin's Geneva. Catholicism in contemporary America, however, is clearly denominational.

[3] The Quakers, for example, appear to have fluctuated between sectarianism and denominationalism, see Elizabeth Isichei, 'From sect to denomination among English Quakers' in Bryan Wilson, ed., *Patterns of Sectarianism* (Heinemann, London, 1967), pp. 161–81.

Charles Glock, *American Piety: the Nature of Religious Commitment* (University of California Press, Berkeley, 1968).

healing and nature cure. This heterogeneous assortment of cultural items can be regarded despite its apparent diversity, as constituting a single entity – the entity of the cultic milieu.[1]

This idea seems a helpful one in broadly characterizing the background from which cults emerge. Cults differentiate themselves from this background as more or less temporary associations of 'seekers' organized around some common interest, the researches or the revelations of an individual. The belief systems around which they are organized are typically broadly based syntheses of ideas and practices available within the cultic milieu and sometimes beyond, adapted, supplemented, and organized through the insights of their founders.[2]

Cults are generally described as exhibiting a number of typical features. They are depicted as oriented towards the problems of individuals, loosely structured, tolerant, non-exclusive, they make few demands on members, possess no clear distinction between members and non-members, have a rapid turnover of membership, and are transient collectives. Their boundaries are vague and undefined, and their belief systems are said to be 'fluctuating'.[3] These features of the cult can be accounted for in terms of a central characteristic of cult organization, which I shall refer to as 'epistemological individualism'.[4] By epistemological individualism I mean to suggest that the cult has no clear locus of final authority beyond the individual member. Unlike the sect, the ideal-typical cult lacks any source of legitimate attributions of heresy. Hence in movements such as spiritualism,[5] New Thought,[6] and much of the flying saucer movement,[7] so vague is the range of accepted teaching that 'heresy' is a concept

[1] Colin Campbell, 'The cult, the cultic milieu and secularization' in Michael Hill, ed., *A Sociological Yearbook of Religion in Britain*, No. 5 (SCM Press, London, 1972) p. 122.

[2] For some of the pseudo-scientific cults to have developed, see Martin Gardner, *Fads and Fallacies in the Name of Science* (Dover Publications, New York, 1957).

[3] See Geoffrey K. Nelson, 'The concept of cult', *Sociological Review*, 16, 3 (1968), pp. 351–62, for a review of the characteristics of the cults.

[4] David Martin has stressed that 'The fundamental criterion of the cult is . . . individualism', David Martin, *Pacifism* (Routledge & Kegan Paul, London, 1965), p. 194. However, in contrast to my own formulation, Martin regards the sect as exhibiting either 'authoritarianism or . . . almost total lack of authority' (Ibid, p. 185). He also employs an implicitly theological distinction. Cults are conceived to be theologically alien, while sects fall within the Christian tradition and are marked by the extremism with which they reject contemporary society.

[5] Geoffrey K. Nelson, *Spiritualism and Society* (Routledge & Kegan Paul, London, 1969).

[6] Charles S. Braden, *Spirits in Rebellion: the Rise and Development of New Thought* (Southern Methodist University Press, Dallas, Texas, 1963); J. Stillson Judah, *The History and Philosophy of the Metaphysical Movements in America* (Westminster Press, Philadelphia, 1967).

[7] H. Taylor Buckner, 'The flying saucerians: a lingering cult', *New Society*, 9 September 1965. An exception is the Aetherius Society, which has moved very much closer than Buckner's groups towards sectarianism. See Roy Wallis, 'The Aetherius

without clear application. The determination of what constitutes acceptable doctrine is a matter to be decided by the individual member.

Lacking any authoritative source of attributions of heresy there can be no clear boundaries between (1) cult ideology and the surrounding cultic milieu, nor, in the absence of authoritative tests of doctrine or membership, between (2) members and non-members. There are, therefore, few barriers to doctrinal adaptation and change. Since the determination of doctrine lies with the members, cults cannot command the loyalty of their membership which remains only partially committed. Commitment being slight, resources for the control of members are lacking. Members typically move between groups, and between belief systems adopting components to fit into the body of truth already gleaned. The loyalties of members are thus often shared between ideological collectivities, and this leads to tolerance. Membership changes rapidly as members move on from one group to another,[1] and the collectivities themselves tend to be transient as charismatic leaders emerge and attempt to control the activities of the following and this, in turn, leads to alienation; or as dissension arises due to the relatively limited basis of shared belief. Since any particular cult is only one among many possible paths to the truth or salvation, membership may decline through sheer indifference. In order to retain or bolster membership, appeal may be made to an ever wider range of interests, leading to ideological diffuseness and the reduced relevance of the cult beliefs for the individual's salvation.[2] Power lies in the hands of the consumer, and leaders may often be forced to cater for consumer interests rather than directing them, or risk membership decline.

Cults then, are fragile institutions. They typically face a problem of *doctrinal precariousness*, that is, the ideological distance between the cult doctrine and the cultic milieu from which it was derived is typically slight. Ideologically the cult is, therefore, poorly differentiated from its background. A membership primarily recruited from other cultic groups is liable to be selective in its acceptance of the doctrine and disposed to create a new synthesis of the cult's teachings with other belief-systems, thus threatening the reabsorption of the cult into the cultic milieu.

[1] Buckner suggests 'A typical occult seeker will probably have been a Rosicrucian, a member of Mankind United, a Theosophist, and also a member of four or five smaller specific cults. The pattern of membership is one of continuous movement from one idea to another. Seekers stay with a cult until they are satisfied that they can learn no more from it or that it has nothing further to offer, and then move on'. H. Taylor Buckner, 'The flying saucerians: an open door cult' in Marcello Truzzi, ed., *Sociology and Everyday Life* (Prentice-Hall, Englewood Cliffs, New Jersey, 1968), pp. 225–6.

[2] Buckner, op. cit. (1965), suggests such a process occurred in the flying saucer groups which he observed.

Society: a case study in the formation of a mystagogic congregation', *Sociological Review*, 22, 1 (1974), pp. 27–44. Reprinted in Roy Wallis, ed., *Sectarianism: Analyses of Religious and Non-Religious Sects* (Peter Owen, London, 1975).

Cults similarly face a problem of authority, deriving from two features of cultic movements. First, their membership is predominantly composed of seekers who see a variety of paths to the truth or salvation and who regard it as their right to select those ideas and practices which will lead towards this goal. Second, cults are typically service-oriented, purveying an experience, knowledge or technique through teachers and practitioners. Hence charisma tends to be dispersed towards the lower echelons. Membership (or clientele) loyalties are often centred on the local teacher or practitioner rather than on the movement as a whole. There is therefore a perennial threat of schism and secession as local teachers or practitioners assert their autonomy. Third, cults tend to face a problem of commitment. They are viewed as one among a range of paths to truth or salvation rather than a unique path. They typically dispense commodities of a limited and specific kind. The involvement of the membership tends, therefore, to be occasional, temporary and segmentary. Retaining, institutionalizing and enhancing membership commitment therefore presents a problem to cults which, if unresolved, may lead to passive and limited involvement, apathy, and declining adherence.

Sectarianism as strategy

In the face of these problems of organizational fragility, the possibility of developing a cohesive sectarian collectivity has had considerable appeal to some cult leaders.

Sects may emerge in a variety of ways, as schismatic movements from existing denominations, as a result of interdenominational crusades, or through a process of development from cults. The dimensions of the sect have been much debated.[1] Among those that have been advanced, characteristics, such as the eschatological nature of the sect stressed by Troeltsch, but also such characteristics as asceticism, the achieved basis of membership, an ethical orientation, and egalitarianism, seem in retrospect to have been features of the sect in particular socio-historical circumstances rather than timeless, or universal dimensions of sectarianism.[2] Those features advanced as central to the concept of sect which have stood the test of time, therefore, seem to centre on the right to exclusion, a self-conception as an elect or élite, totalitarianism, and hostility towards, or separation from, the state or society.

The suggestion advanced here is that these dimensions of sectarianism are

---

[1] Benton Johnson, 'A critical appraisal of the church-sect typology', *ASR*, 22 (1957), pp. 88–92; idem, 'On church and sect', *ASR*, 28 (1963), pp. 539–49; idem 'Church and sect revisited', *JSSR*, 10, 2 (1971), pp. 124–37; J. Milton Yinger, *The Scientific Study of Religion* (Collier-Macmillan, New York, 1970); Bryan R. Wilson, *Sects and Society* (Heinemann, London, 1961).

[2] I have argued this point in Roy Wallis, 'The sectarianism of Scientology' in Michael Hill, ed., *A Sociological Yearbook of Religion in Britain*, No. 6 (SCM Press, London, 1973), pp. 136–55.

related to the characteristic which underlies sect organization – 'epistemological authoritarianism'. Sects possess some authoritative locus for the legitimate attribution of heresy.[1] Sects lay a claim to possess unique and privileged access to the truth or salvation. Their committed adherents typically regard all those outside the confines of the collectivity as 'in error'. The truth must be protected from defilement or misuse and therefore extensive control is necessary over those to whom access is permitted, and the exclusion of the unworthy. Those who remain, therefore, believe themselves to have proven their superior status. Hostility to state or society readily follows. The state demands acceptance of its own version of the truth in some particulars. In those areas it defines as its legitimate concern it can brook no rivals – taxes must be paid, births registered, children educated, wars fought – whatever the revelation. Thus state and society may threaten, and even directly conflict with, the sectarian's notion of what constitutes the truth, sometimes forcing the sect to defend its vision by isolation and withdrawal.

The transition from cult to sect, therefore, involves the arrogation of authority. In order for a cohesive sectarian group to emerge from the diffuse, individualistic origins of a cult, a prior process of expropriation of authority must transpire. This centralization of authority is typically legitimized by a claim to a unique revelation which locates some source or sources of authority concerning doctrinal innovation and interpretation beyond the individual member or practitioner, usually in the person of the revelator himself.

Propounding a new gnosis and centralizing authority permits the exercise of greater control over the collectivity through the elimination or undermining of alternative loci of power and the transmutation of independent practitioners and teachers into organizational functionaries. It facilitates the establishment of clearer cognitive boundaries around the belief-system; the abandonment of elements which most closely link it to the cultic milieu; and the introduction of new doctrinal elements which effectively distinguish it from competitors. Doctrine may be expanded to incorporate a systematic metaphysics increasing its scope beyond the mere provision of a rationale for a specific and limited form of practice. Thus a wider and deeper commitment is encouraged. Since the new doctrine is endowed with unique salvational efficacy it provides a focus for more than segmentary and occasional involvement, and a rationale for insulating the believer, for example, by the denigration of alternative sources of ideology and involvement, and by endowing the world and competing belief-systems with formerly unsuspected danger. The emergence of a charismatic leader provides a

---

[1] Where such authority lies may not always be obvious, even to members. It may sometimes be shared between two or more loci, a situation liable to lead to conflict, and a power-struggle, as, for example, in the struggle between the prophets and the apostles in the Catholic Apostolic Church. See Kenneth Jones, 'The Catholic Apostolic Church: a study in diffused commitment' in Michael Hill, ed., *A Sociological Yearbook of Religion in Britain*, No. 5 (SCM Press, London, 1972), pp. 137–60.

focus of loyalty of a supra-local kind. Together these factors assist in the transmutation of a clientele into a following. A successfully implemented strategy of sectarianization, therefore, provides one viable and attractive solution to the cultic problem of institutional fragility.[1]

[1] Aspects of this theoretical structure have been developed in Roy Wallis, 'Ideology, authority and the development of cultic movements', *Social Research*, 41, 2 (1974), pp. 299–327.

Part II
THE CULT AND ITS TRANSFORMATION

2. THE CULT PHASE: DIANETICS

Background to the cult

The founder of Dianetics and Scientology, L. Ron Hubbard, is reported to have been born in 1911 at Tilden, Nebraska. His father was an officer in the US navy and appears to have seen service in the East, on which occasions his son may have spent vacations with him. He was raised for some years by his maternal grandfather who owned a ranch in Montana, and spent his early teens in Washington DC, where he graduated to George Washington University. According to the testimony of the Registrar of George Washington University, Hubbard attended the summer session in 1931, and the fall and spring sessions 1931–32. He was placed on probation in September 1931 and failed to return for the fall 1932 session.[1]

His early adulthood is somewhat difficult to trace. He appears to have led a mobile life, acquiring a number of skills and working in various jobs. Among the occupations in which he is reported to have been engaged during this period, are pilot, US Marine, radio entertainer, scriptwriter and explorer. Hubbard was also a prolific writer of pulp magazine adventure, phantasy, and science fiction stories and novels in the same genres.

Hubbard was commissioned into the navy before the outbreak of the Second World War and is reported to have spent some time in Oak Knoll, a military hospital. There he is reported – and his own statements lend some credibility to this account – to have interested himself particularly in the patients suffering from mental or emotional disorders to whom he talked, and to have sought out books dealing with the subject.[2]

Following the war, Hubbard parted from his first wife and two children to go

[1] In the light of Hubbard's later claims to competence in physics it is worthy of note that in a course on dynamics – sound and light – he achieved a grade E, in a course on electricity and magnetism a grade D, and in a course on modern physical phenomena – molecular and atomic physics – he was awarded a grade F. *Stenographic Transcript, Founding Church of Scientology v. U.S.A.*, in US Court of Claims, No. 226–61, Washington DC.

[2] For example, in a story reported in the *Wichita Eagle*, 24 April 1951.

to Hollywood as a scriptwriter. What success he may have had at this vocation is uncertain, but during the following three years Hubbard became a major writer for *Astounding Science Fiction*, acquired an expert knowledge of the practice of hypnosis, and became briefly involved with Jack Parsons, a follower of Aleister Crowley in Pasadena.[1] During his period in Hollywood, Hubbard claims

> I got a nurse, wrapped a towel around my head and became a swami, and by 1947 achieved 'clearing'.[2]

Probably some time during 1948 Hubbard wrote a book outlining his ideas for a new form of psychotherapy, later published in revised form as *The Original Thesis*, for which he was unable to find a publisher at the time. By 1949, Hubbard was living in Bay Head, New Jersey, where he appears to have interested John W. Campbell Jr, editor of *Astounding Science Fiction*, in his therapeutic ideas, and indeed to have relieved him, at least temporarily, of chronic sinusitis.[3, 4]

Gaining John W. Campbell as a disciple was indeed fortunate. Campbell was an established editor of a respected science fiction magazine with a considerable following. He was acquainted with doctors, scientists, publishers and others who could lend their support to Dianetics, Hubbard's new psychotherapy, and commanded access to an important medium of communication within and beyond the cultic milieu.

Campbell succeeded in interesting a Michigan general practitioner who occasionally contributed to *Astounding*, Dr J. A. Winter. After some correspondence with Hubbard, Winter visited Hubbard's house in Bay Head, New Jersey, where the latter had a small clientele on whom he was practising and developing his technique. Winter relates:

> I arrived in Bay Head, N.J. on October 1, 1949, and immediately became immersed in a life of dianetics and very little else. I observed two of the patients whom Hubbard had under treatment at this time, and spent hours each day watching him send these men 'down the time-track'. After some observation of the reaction of

[1] Alexander Mitchell, 'The odd beginnings of Ron Hubbard's career', *Sunday Times*, 5 October 1969, p. 11; correspondence with members and former members of the Ordo Templi Orientis; and interviews with acquaintances of Hubbard at this time. See also Chapter 4. It should be noted that the *Sunday Times* article contained errors for which its publishers rendered an apology and paid an out of court settlement.

[2] L. Ron Hubbard, 'The story of dianetics and scientology', *Lectures on Clearing* recorded at the London Congress 1958 (Hubbard Communications Office, London 1958).

[3] Martin Gardner, *Fads and Fallacies in the Name of Science* (Dover Publications, New York, 1957), p. 264.

[4] Much of this account of Hubbard's life is based on George Malko, *Scientology: the Now Religion* (Dell, New York, 1970), pp. 27–41, and Gardner, op. cit., modified in the light of interviews with early colleagues and acquaintances of Hubbard. See also Christopher Evans, *Cults of Unreason* (Harrap, London, 1973). While the account offered here is not to my knowledge inaccurate, it should be noted that Malko's book has been withdrawn by its publishers who also paid a legal settlement.

others, I concluded that my learning of this technique would be enhanced by submitting myself to therapy. I took my place on the couch, spending an average of three hours a day trying to follow the directions for recalling 'impediments'. The experience was intriguing; I found that I could remember much more than I had thought I could, and I frequently experienced the discomfort which is known as 'restimulation'. While listening to Hubbard 'running' one of his patients, or while being 'run' myself, I would find myself developing unaccountable pains in various portions of my anatomy, or becoming extremely fatigued and somnolent. I had nightmares of being choked, of having my genitalia cut off, and I was convinced that dianetics as a method could produce effects.[1]

Having experienced these effects in therapy and discovering that he could produce them in others, Winter moved to New Jersey to work with Hubbard. There with Campbell and Hubbard he worked on a systematic formulation of the theory and practice, modifying nomenclature. A paper giving a 'resumé of the principles and methodology of dianetic therapy' was submitted by Winter to the *Journal of the American Medical Association*, but was rejected. A revised version including case histories supplied by Hubbard was submitted to the *American Journal of Psychiatry*, but again rejected.[2] Winter was also unsuccessful in his attempts to persuade other medical practitioners to try out the therapy.

Hubbard therefore decided to write a book directed to the laity rather than the medical profession, and Campbell commissioned an article from him on Dianetics for *Astounding*. This article was previewed by Campbell in his editorials in extremely enthusiastic terms:

in longer range view . . . the item that most interests me at the moment is an article on the most important subject conceivable. This is not a hoax article. It is an article on the science of the mind, of human thought. It is not an article on psychology – that isn't a science. It's not General Semantics. It is a totally new science called *dianetics*, and it does precisely what a *science* of thought should do. Its power is almost unbelievable; it proves the mind not only can but does rule the body completely; following the sharply defined basic laws dianetics sets forth, physical ills such as ulcers, asthma and arthritis can be cured, as can all other psychosomatic ills. . . . It is, quite simply, impossible to exaggerate the importance of a true science of human thought.[3]

I assure you of two things: you will find the article fascinating, and it is of more importance than you can readily realise.[4]

And finally:

Next month's issue will, I believe, cause one full-scale explosion across the country. We are carrying a sixteen thousand word article entitled 'Dianetics . . . An

[1] Joseph A. Winter, *A Doctor's Report on Dianetics: Theory and Therapy* (Julian Press, New York, 1951), p. 11.

[2] Ibid., p. 18.

[3] John W. Campbell, 'In times to come', *Astounding Science Fiction*, 44, 4 (December 1949), p. 80.

[4] John W. Campbell, *Astounding, Science Fiction*, 45, 1 (March 1950), p. 4.

Introduction to a New Science', by L. Ron Hubbard. It will, I believe, be the first publication of the material. It is, I assure you in full and absolute sincerity, one of the most important articles ever published. In this article, reporting on Hubbard's own research into the engineering question of how the human mind operates, immensely important basic discoveries are related. Among them:

A technique of psychotherapy has been developed which will cure any insanity not due to organic destruction of the brain.

A technique that gives a man a perfect, indelible, total memory, and perfect, errorless ability to compute his problems.

A basic answer, and a technique for curing – not alleviating – ulcers, arthritis, asthma, and many other nongerm diseases.

A totally new conception of the truly incredible ability and power of the human mind.

Evidence that insanity is contagious, and *is not hereditary*.

This is no wild theory. It is not mysticism. It is a coldly precise engineering description of how the human mind operates, and how to go about restoring correct operation tested and used on some two hundred and fifty cases. And it makes only one overall claim: the methods logically developed from that description *work*. The memory stimulation technique is so powerful that, within thirty minutes of entering therapy, most people will recall in full detail their own birth. I have observed it in action, and used the techniques myself.

I leave it to your judgement: Will such an article be of interest to you? It is not only a fact article of the highest importance; it is the story of the ultimate adventure – an exploration in the strangest of all *terra incognita*; the human mind. No stranger adventure appeared in the Arabian Nights than Hubbard's experience, using his new techniques, in plowing through the strange jungle of distorted thoughts within a human mind. To find, beyond that zone of madness, a computing mechanism of ultimate and incredible efficiency and perfection! To find that a fully sane, enormously able and altruistic personality is trapped deep in every human mind – however insane or criminal it may appear on the outside![1]

These editorial previews attracted inquiries from individuals seeking therapy and training, and in April 1950, the Hubbard Dianetic Research Foundation was established to provide the services for which a demand was appearing.

Theory and practice of Dianetics

The eagerly awaited article appeared in the May issue of *Astounding*.[2] There

---

[1] John W. Campbell, 'In times to come', *Astounding Science Fiction*, 45, 2 (April 1950), p. 132.

[2] L. Ron Hubbard, 'Dianetics: the evolution of a science', *Astounding Science Fiction*, 45, 3 (May 1950), pp. 43–87. Reprinted with some minor modifications as *Dianetics: the Evolution of a Science* (Publications Organisation World Wide, 1968), hereafter referred to as *ES*. An earlier article on Dianetics had appeared in a publication of the New York Explorers Club, L. Ron Hubbard, 'Terra incognita: the mind', *The Explorer's Journal*, 28, 1 (Winter–Spring 1950), pp. 1–4, 52. This article presents

Hubbard presented a model of the mind as a computer. The 'optimum' mind, Hubbard argued, would have perfect recall of all sense-impressions which had ever impinged upon it, and vastly improved mental agility beyond that of the normal brain. Since this level of optimum functioning is potentially available to every mind, Hubbard called this the 'basic personality':

> the basic personalities contacted were invariably strong, hardy, and constructively good! They were the same personalities as the patients had in a normal state minus certain mental powers, plus electronic demons and plus general unhappiness.[1]

The basic personality was also called a 'clear'. This term was derived from the operation of a calculating machine, in which depressed numbers are released. If left unreleased, the depressed numbers will result in a systematic inaccuracy in future computations. Since the 'normal' mind fell far short of the heights postulated by Hubbard for the basic personality, he argued that like the computer with a 'held down seven', the normal mind was operating under the constraints of severe 'aberrations' which limited its capacities and caused mis-computation.

These aberrations resulted from pain. Pain was a threat to survival (which Hubbard argues is the basic principle of existence). Therefore the mind – the sane, analytical mind – sought to avoid it. Evolution had provided a mechanism which made this possible. The 'Reactive Mind' had evolved as a means of protecting the sensitive computing machinery of the 'Analytical Mind' from damage in the face of threats to survival.

> The reactive mind thinks in identities. It is a stimulus-response mind. Its actions are exteriorly determined. It has no power of choice. It puts physical pain data forward during moments of physical pain in an effort to save the organism. So long as its mandates and commands are obeyed it withholds the physical pain. As soon as the organism starts to go against its commands, it inflicts the pain.[2]

In moments of pain, unconsciousness or emotional trauma, the analytical mind shuts off and the reactive mind comes into operation. The reactive mind operates on the basis of information stored in the reactive memory banks. The contents of these reactive banks are 'engrams' and 'locks'.[3]

An engram is a recording of the full perceptic content of a moment of pain, unconsciousness, or emotional loss. Hence, Hubbard argued that while it was

[1] *ES*, p. 30.
[2] Ibid., p. 62.
[3] Ibid., p. 63. In part of the original *Astounding* article, the term 'norn' was used instead of 'engram'.

Dianetics as an aid to expedition commanders with unbalanced personnel. It had little or no impact. Dianeticists and Scientologists do not in general know of its existence, and it is of interest solely because it employs the term 'comanome' rather than the earlier term 'impediment', or the later term 'engram'. This lends some support to Winter's version of the derivation of Dianetic terminology, and hence to his claim that the work of Richard Semon was unknown to Hubbard at this time. See below, page 38.

believed by orthodox psychology that during periods of unconsciousness, nothing was perceived, he had discovered that there was no period when the organism did not perceive. Perception, however, was performed by different components of the mind – the analytical mind during periods of normal consciousness, the reactive mind during periods of 'analytical attentuation' ('anaten'), that is what were otherwise believed to be periods of unconsciousness. At some future date should the individual enter an environment which contained any of this perceptic content, the analytical mind would begin to shut off, the reactive mind would come into operation and the individual would experience some of the pain originally contained in the engram, as a warning to leave the situation of danger. For example:

> Here's how an engram can be established: Mary age 2, knocked out by a dog, dog bites. Content of engram: anaten; age 2 (physical structure); smell of environment and dog; sight of dog jaws gaping and white teeth; organic sensation of pain in back of head (hit pavement); pain in posterior; dog bite in cheek; tactile of dog fur, concrete (elbows on pavement), hot dog breath; emotion; physical pain plus endocrine response; audio of dog growl and passing car.
> What Mary does with the engram: she does not 'remember' the incident but sometimes plays she is a dog jumping on people and biting them. Otherwise no reaction. Then at age 10 similar circumstances, no great anaten, the engram is restimulated. After this she has headaches when dogs bark or when cars pass that sound like *that* car, but only responds to the engram when she is tired or harassed otherwise. The engram was first dormant data waiting just in case. Next it was keyed-in – stuff we have to watch out for. Then it was thereafter restimulated whenever any combination of its perceptics appeared while Mary was in slight anaten (weary). When forty years of age she responded in exactly the same way, and still had not the slightest conscious understanding of the real reason![1]

If in the formation of the engram words are spoken, these words may have a later effect similar to that of a post-hypnotic suggestion. If the words are subsequently repeated, the engram is 'keyed-in' or partially restimulated, and if 'the individual is slightly anaten – weary, ill, sleepy' the engram will be fully restimulated, leading him to behave in aberrated ways.

The purpose of Dianetic therapy, therefore, was to gain access to and locate engrams, and 'erase' them from the reactive mind, thus eradicating their effects in the form of psychosomatic illness, emotional tension, or lowered capability, by permitting the analytical mind to operate unimpeded.

Hubbard claimed to have a technique which would remove an engramic 'memory' from the reactive mind, refiling it in the memory of the analytical mind where it no longer had engramic effects.[2] Exhausting the reactive mind of engrams hence has a number of highly desirable consequences. The individual becomes 'self-determined' rather than having his actions determined by his

[1] *ES*, pp. 65–6.
[2] Ibid., p. 70.

engrams. The analytical mind being a perfect computer would always supply the correct answer from the information fed in, when relieved of the engrams which lead to error.[1] The individual's IQ would rise dramatically. He would be free of all psychological or psychosomatic illness, his resistance to physical illness would be vastly improved, and he would be able to cure himself of other illnesses or injuries much more rapidly. His memory would vastly improve. He would, in short be a 'clear'. As Hubbard describes it:

> The experience of his entire life is available to the *clear* and he has all his inherent mental ability and imagination free to use it. His physical vitality and health are markedly improved and all psycho-somatic illnesses have vanished and will not return. He has greater resistance to actual disease. And he is adaptable to and able to change his environment. He is not 'adjusted'; he is dynamic. His ethical and moral standards are high, his ability to seek and experience pleasure is great. His personality is heightened and he is creative and constructive. It is not yet known how much longevity is added to a life in the process of clearing, but in view of the automatic rebalancing of the endocrine system, the lowered incidence of accident and the improvement of general physical tone, it is most certainly raised.
>
> As a standard of comparison, a clear is to the contemporary norm as the contemporary norm is to a contemporary institutional case. . . . A clear, for instance, has complete recall of everything which has ever happened to him or anything he has ever studied. He does mental computations, such as those of chess, for example, which a normal would do in half an hour, in ten or fifteen seconds. . . . He is entirely self-determined. And his creative imagination is high. He can do a swift study of anything within his intellectual capacity, which is inherent, and the study would be the equivalent to him of a year or two of training when he was 'normal'. His vigor, persistence and tenacity are very much higher than anyone has thought possible.[2]

The only obstacle to this desirable state was that while 'locks' – severe restimulations of engrams – could be released by 'returning' the individual to the restimulating situation, releasing engrams and hence clearing the reactive mind required that the earliest engram (the 'basic-basic') be located and cleared.

Then the therapy could move on to later engrams. Hubbard, claimed in his *Astounding* article that his 'pre-clears' (patients) had first been found to have engrams resulting from birth, but even these did not turn out to be the earliest. The earliest engrams turned out to occur in the period shortly after conception.[3] Hubbard's radical claim therefore was that the source of much human illness and incapacity lay in 'pre-natal' engrams. The commonest source of pre-natal engrams Hubbard claimed was attempted abortions.[4]

[1] *ES*, p. 76.

[2] L. Ron Hubbard, *Dianetics: the Modern Science of Mental Health* (Hubbard College of Scientology, East Grinstead, 1968; first published by Hermitage House, New York, 1950), pp. 170–1. This book will be referred to hereafter as *MSMH*.

[3] In the *Astounding* article (p. 81) Hubbard states that the earliest engram he had found occurred twenty-four hours *after* conception. In the version of this article printed subsequently as *ES*, p. 86, this had been amended to read '*Shortly before conception* . . .'

[4] *ES*, p. 88.

Therapy proceeded in the following manner:
The pre-clear lay on a bed or couch in a quiet room.

The auditor tells him to look at the ceiling. The auditor says: 'When I count from
one to seven your eyes will close'. The auditor counts from one to seven and keeps
counting quietly and pleasantly until the patient closes his eyes. A tremble of the
lashes will be noticed in optimum *reverie*.[1]

Hubbard insisted that this process of inducing 'Dianetic reverie' was quite
different from hypnosis. To ensure against hypnotic suggestion, however, a
canceller is installed. That is, the pre-clear is told:

In the future, when I utter the word *Cancelled*, everything which I have said to you
while you are in a therapy session will be cancelled and will have no force with you.
Any suggestion I have made to you will be without force when I say the word
cancelled. Do you understand?[2]

The pre-clear is assured he will be aware of everything that happens. When the
pre-clear has entered the state of reverie he is requested to return to childhood,
to an incident involving a pleasant experience and to go through it from the
beginning recounting all the perceptual detail involved in the incident. This is
to give the pre-clear the idea of what is expected. If he cannot recall (or
'relive' in Hubbard's view) such an early incident, he is returned to a more
recent incident. After further preliminaries the auditor directs the pre-clear to
return to 'basic-basic'. He does this by directing the 'file-clerk' (a hypothetical
entity which 'monitors' the memory banks and selects appropriate material on
request by the auditor)[3] to return to the incident necessary to resolve the case.
Generally, the basic-basic is not located so simply, however, and other engramic
material will be brought up. This has to be 'reduced', that is the pre-clear is
asked to return to the beginning of the incident and recount all the perceptual
detail involved in the incident. The pre-clear is directed to recount this incident
until all the emotion involved in it is discharged.[4]

---

[1] *MSMH*, p. 159.

[2] *MSMH*, p. 200.

[3] Ibid., p. 198.

[4] The criteria for what counts as the reduction or erasure of an engram are given by
Hubbard as follows:

'To reduce means to take all the charge or pain out of an incident. This means to
have the pre-clear recount the incident from beginning to end (while returned to it
in reverie) over and over again, picking up all the somatics and perceptions
present just as though the incident were happening at that moment. To reduce
means, technically, to render free of aberrative material as far as possible to make
the case progress.

'To "erase" an engram means to recount it until it has vanished entirely. . . . If
the engram is early, if it has no material earlier which will suspend it, that engram
will "erase". The patient, trying to find it again for a second or sixth recounting,
will suddenly find out he has no faintest idea what was in it'. *MSMH*, p. 287.

The 'file-clerk' is then asked for 'the next incident required to resolve this case', and the process is repeated. Ideally, basic-basic would be located and erased and the pre-clear then progressively cleared of all subsequent engrams and locks. Often, however, this would not occur and it would therefore be necessary to end the session at some convenient point, usually after the reduction of an engram. (The modal length of a Dianetics session was generally around two hours, but when the pre-clear was 'stuck in an incident', that is, an engram, it might occasionally last several hours.)

The pre-clear would be told to 'come up to present time'. The auditor might then question him as to the time, location, etc., to ensure that he was 'in present time'. He would then say 'Cancelled' and end the session.

> . . . (work continues until the auditor has worked the patient enough for the period) . . . Come to present time. Are you in present time? (Yes) (Use canceller word). When I count from five to one and snap my fingers you will feel alert. Five, four, three, two, one. (snap).[1]

The thrust of the auditing activity was to get the pre-clear to return to the 'basic area', that is, the area of pre-natal experience, contact the basic-basic engram and erase it, and then move along the 'time-track' erasing later life engrams until the individual was cleared. In order to reach the basic-basic, however, it was generally believed necessary to reduce, or discharge the painful emotion from later life trauma which blocked access to it.

In the course of therapy the pre-clear was often unable to contact an earlier engramic incident and would verbalize this inability with a phrase such as 'I can't go back at this point'.[2] Such a phrase is an engramic command, which must be overcome by means of 'repeater' technique. This technique simply involves getting the pre-clear to repeat the phrase over and over again, similar phrases, and anything else the pre-clear might add. For example:

Woman: All I get is 'Take her away'.
Auditor: Go over that again.
Woman: Take her away [repeated three times].
Auditor: Go over it again.
Woman: Take her away.
Auditor: Go over it again.
Woman: No, no, I won't.
Auditor: Go over it again.
Woman: I won't, I won't, I won't, I won't.
Auditor: Go over it again – take her away. Go over the phrase again. Take her away.
Woman: Take her away [crying] No, no.

.   .   .   .

[1] *MSMH*, p. 202.
[2] *MSMH*, p. 124.

Auditor: Go over the phrase, take her away.
Woman: Take . . . take [crying], no, no.
Auditor: Go over the words 'no, no'.
Woman: No, no, no.
Auditor: Go over it again.
Woman: No.

. . . .

Auditor: Go over it again.
Woman: [Moaning] . . . don't . . .
Auditor: Go over it again, go over 'don't'.
Woman: [Crying].

. . . .

Auditor: Go over the word 'don't'.
Woman: Don't, don't, don't, don't, [Etc.][1]

Repetition of such phrases, Hubbard argues 'sucks the patient back down the track and into contact with an engram which contains it',[2] sometimes facilitating the reduction of that engram, or otherwise releasing emotional charge from the reactive bank.

Another important technique was that of securing a 'flash answer'. This technique was typically employed to discover where on the time-track the pre-clear was stuck, that is when an engram had occurred which had since been a major source of aberration, and to discover the nature of the incident.[3]

In the first case, the auditor would tell the pre-clear,

'When I count to five . . . a phrase will flash into your mind to describe where you are on the track. One, two, three, four, five!' 'Late pre-natal', says the pre-clear, or 'yesterday' or whatever occurs to him.[4]

Counting was later replaced by snapping the fingers, in order to discover the nature of an incident about which the pre-clear, unaided, was not forthcoming:

The auditor asks a series of questions which will identify the incident and receives flash answers on a yes–no basis. The auditor says, 'When I snap my fingers you will answer yes or no to the following question': 'Hospital?' (snap!), and the pre-clear answers yes or no. Such a series of questions and answers might run as follows: 'Accident?' 'Yes' 'Hospital?' 'No' 'Mother?' 'Yes' 'Outdoors?' 'No' 'Fall down?'

[1] This example is taken from an actual auditing situation, a recording of a public demonstration of Dianetic auditing, given by L. Ron Hubbard on 28 September 1951. For further illustrations of repeater technique in Dianetics sessions, see Walter Braddeson, *Scientology for the Millions* (Sherbourne Press, Los Angeles, 1969), pp. 83–5, 87–9, 91.

[2] *MSMH*, p. 215.

[3] *MSMH*, p. 296; L. Ron Hubbard *Science of Survival* (Hubbard Dianetic Foundation Inc., Wichita, Kansas, 1951), I, pp. 104–5; II, pp. 57–8. All references are to the Tenth Printing, published by Hubbard College of Scientology, East Grinstead, Sussex, 1967. Hereafter referred to simply as *Science of Survival*.

[4] *MSMH*, p. 296.

'No' 'Cut?' 'Yes' 'Kitchen?' 'Yes'. And suddenly the pre-clear may remember the incident or get a visio of the scene or remember or get a sonic recall of what his mother said to him . . .[1]

The background to the theory and practice of Dianetics

Dianetics was a form of abreaction therapy, with strong similarities to a variety of techniques then in use. Since Hubbard himself has asserted the originality of the entire theory and practice and acknowledges having been influenced only in a most general way by other writers, it is difficult to be certain of the sources of his synthesis. Ideas which approximate to many aspects of the theory and practice of Dianetics were currently available in orthodox and fringe psychology, although it is not certain how much Hubbard may have derived from them, and it is clear that he added many entirely original elements of his own.

The theory that aspects of human behaviour might be explained as responses to traumatically (and, of course, other) conditioned stimuli was prominent in psychology following the work of Pavlov and Watson. Pavlov's work on the induction of 'experimental neuroses' in dogs was taken up by psychiatrists impressed by the correspondence between his clinical descriptions of these neuroses and the acute war neuroses they observed in evacuated soldiers.[2] The therapy developed to treat these neuroses was an abreaction therapy, described as follows by Sargant:

> A drug would be administered to a . . . patient . . . and as it started to take effect, an endeavour would be made to make him re-live the episodes that had caused his breakdown. Sometimes the episode, or episodes, had been mentally suppressed, and the memory would have to be brought to the surface again. At other times it was fully remembered, but the strong emotions originally attached to it had since been suppressed. The marked improvement in the patient's nervous condition was attributed to the releasing of these original emotions.[3]

The technique of suggesting quite imaginary situations to a patient under drugs, leading to abreaction of fear or anger was found to be as equally effective in the restoration of mental health, as getting him to re-live actual traumatic experiences.[4]

The therapeutic role of abreaction had been systematically explored first by Breuer and Freud,[5] whose investigations revealed that the root of many hysterical symptoms lay in the experience of psychological trauma:

[1] *Science of Survival*, II, pp. 57–8.
[2] William Sargant, *Battle for the Mind* (Pan Books, London, 1959).
[3] Ibid., p. 17.
[4] Ibid., pp. 17–18.
[5] Joseph Breuer and Sigmund Freud, *Studies in Hysteria*, Vol II of the Standard Edition of the Complete Psychological Works of Sigmund Freud (Hogarth Press, London, 1955).

> Any experience which calls up distressing affects – such as those of fright, anxiety, shame or physical pain – may operate as a trauma of this kind. . . .[1]

The affect associated with the traumatic situation is repressed rather than discharged when the individual is unable to react due to social circumstances or because it involved something he wished to forget, or when the experience occurred while the patient was in a 'dissociated' or 'hypnoid' state of mind, that is, when under conditions of:

> severely paralysing affects, such as fright, or during positively abnormal psychical states, such as the semi-hypnotic twilight state of day-dreaming, auto-hypnoses, and so on.[2]

The memory of the traumatic experience is either partially or completely out of normal consciousness but can be aroused 'in accordance with the laws of association . . . by a new experience which sets it going owing to a similarity with the pathogenic experience'.[3]

The aim of therapy was therefore to bring the original experience with its associated affect into consciousness, and get the patient to describe the event in detail, thereby arousing and discharging the accompanying affect:

> We found . . . that each individual hysterical symptom immediately and permanently disappeared when we had succeeded in bringing clearly to light the memory of the event by which it was provoked and in arousing its accompanying affect, and when the patient had described that event in the greatest possible detail and had put the affect into words . . .[4]

Although Freud first employed hypnosis as a means of locating traumatic material and bringing it to consciousness, he shortly found that some patients could not be effectively hypnotized. This led him to the creation of a new technique for extending the patient's memory. He would ask his patients if they recalled what occasioned the symptoms. He assured them they *did* know:

> After this I became still more insistent; I told the patients to lie down and deliberately close their eyes in order to 'concentrate' . . . I then found that without any hypnosis new recollections emerged which went further back and which probably related to our topic.[5]

Should the patient still prove recalcitrant, Freud would then apply manual pressure to the patient's head, assuring him that when he did this a recollection would come to mind.[6]

The parallels with early Dianetic practice are quite striking. With only minor modifications in practice and terminology Dianetic theory and practice might

[1] Ibid., p. 6.
[2] Ibid., p. 11.
[3] Ibid., p. 16.
[4] Ibid., p. 6, emphasis omitted.
[5] Ibid., p. 268.
[6] Ibid., p. 270.

have been adapted from that of early Freud. That this is more than merely a possibility is suggested by John W. Campbell's letter to Dr Joseph Winter in July 1949 telling of Hubbard's discoveries, 'His approach is, actually, based on some very early work of Freud's, some work of other men, and a lot of original research'.[1]

The process of engram formation resembles the mechanism of repression elaborated by Freud, and Hubbard's distinction between the analytical and the reactive mind loosely fits Freud's distinction of the conscious and unconscious. There are even hints in Freud's discussion of the analysis of hysteria which strongly suggest an origin for Hubbard's notion of the 'file-clerk', for example:

> consequences of the [manual] pressure give one a deceptive impression of there being a superior intelligence outside the patient's consciousness which keeps a large amount of psychical material arranged for particular purposes and has fixed a planned order for its return to consciousness.[2]

or yet more directly,

> it was as though we were examining a dossier that had been kept in good order. The analysis of my patient Emmy von N. contained similar files of memories . . . These files form a quite general feature of every analysis and their contents always emerge in a chronological order . . .[3]

although the order was the reverse of the actual experiential order. Hubbard's 'file-clerk' did not always deal with matters in such a systematic fashion.

In one published comment, Hubbard admitted a considerable psychoanalytic influence on early Dianetics:

> In the earliest beginning of Dianetics it is possible to trace a considerable psychoanalytic influence. There was the matter of ransacking the past; the matter of believing with Freud that if one could talk over his difficulties they would alleviate and there was the matter of concentrating on early childhood. Our first improvement on psycho-analysis itself consisted of the abandonment of talk alone and the direct address to the incident in its own area of time as a mental image picture susceptible to erasure. But many of the things which Freud thought might exist, such as 'life in the womb', 'birth trauma', we in Dianetics and Scientology confirmed and for them provided an adequate alleviation. The discovery of the engram is entirely the property of Dianetics. Methods of its erasure are also owned entirely by Dianetics, but both of these were pointed to by early Freudian analysis and Hypnotism.[4]

Despite the fact that Freud had abandoned the practice, hypnotic abreactive therapy was widely developed during the 1930s and 1940s.[5] The phenomena of

---

[1] Cited in Winter, op. cit., p. 3.

[2] Breuer and Freud, op. cit., p. 272.

[3] Ibid., p. 288.

[4] L. Ron Hubbard, 'A critique of psycho-analysis 3', *Certainty*, 9, 7 (1962), p. 4.

[5] See the discussion of, and reference to, earlier work in Jacob H. Conn, 'Hypnosynthesis: III Hypnotherapy of chronic war neuroses with a discussion of the value of

spontaneous and induced regression had also been explored under hypnosis,[1] and it was known that age regression could be induced by suggestion in a non-hypnotic state.[2] Moreover, the phenomenon of hypnotically age-regressed patients reporting details of intra-uterine life, on being told they were at an appropriate age, had been observed.[3]

In the practice of hypnosis a distinction was sometimes drawn between *regression*, described as a 'half-conscious dramatisation of the present understanding of that previous time', and *revivification*, described as 'the type of time regression in which the hypnotic situation itself ceases and the subject is plunged directly into the chronological past'.[4]

The term *regression* was generally used for both kinds of phenomena, and some doubt was thrown on the status of such a process of returning to early periods of childhood, when Young in a controlled experimental study showed that a sample of controls requested to simulate the performances of three-year-olds as measured by a series of tests were able to approximate such performances more accurately than hypnotized subjects ordered to regress to their third birthday. Young felt the results of his experiment better supported an explanation in terms of which the hypnotized subjects 'were unwittingly playing a role, and playing it less skilfully than the controls by virtue of having voluntarily surrendered their critical attitudes during the trance . . .' than an explanation in terms of any actual return, or recovery of actual memories of the time in question.[5]

Hubbard was clearly familiar with some of this work. He was an experienced practitioner of hypnosis, and in *MSMH* carefully distinguished returning and reliving in Dianetics from regression and revivification in hypnosis.[6]

Although the 'recalling' of the experience of birth and prenatal life had been

[1] Milton H. Erickson, 'Hypnotic treatment of acute hysterical depression: report of a case', *Archives of Neurology and Psychiatry*, 46 (1941), p. 176; Merton M. Gill, 'Spontaneous regression on the induction of hypnosis', *Bulletin of the Menninger Clinic*, 12, 2 (1948), pp. 41–8.

[2] Leonard T. Maholick, 'The infant in the adult', *Psychosomatic Medicine*, 11 (1949), pp. 295–337.

[3] J. H. Masserman, 'The dynamics of hypnosis and brief psychotherapy' *Archives of Neurology and Psychiatry*, 46 (1941), pp. 176–9.

[4] Milton H. Erickson and Lawrence S. Kuble, 'Successful treatment of a case of acute hysterical depression by return under hypnosis to a critical phase of childhood', *Psychoanalytic Quarterly*, 4 (1941), pp. 585–609.

[5] Paul Campbell Young, 'Hypnotic regression – fact or artifact?' *Journal of Abnormal and Social Psychology*, 35 (1940), pp. 273–8.

[6] *MSMH*, p. 12. The reason given for the terminological substitution is that 'regression' had pejorative connotations, and 'revivification' was something that happened under hypnosis. As Dianetics did not employ hypnosis, 'reliving' was more appropriate.

abreaction, regression, and revivification', *Journal of Clinical and Experimental Hypnosis*, 1 (1953), pp. 29–43; Lewis R. Wolberg, *Hypnoanalysis* (Grune & Stratton, New York, 1945).

noted in hypnotized subjects, it was little explored in the main streams of psychology. Experimental work had been conducted on the possibility of conditioning the unborn child with considerable success during late pregnancy,[1] but the influence of the experience of birth and pre-natal life on later psychological development was most actively explored by Otto Rank and his followers. Rank held that the origins of neurosis lay not in the Oedipus complex, but in the trauma of birth.[2] Phyllis Greenacre developed this theory further, suggesting that events in intra-uterine life, particularly after the seventh month of pregnancy when responsiveness to sound begins to appear, might have a traumatic effect on the foetus leading to reactions akin to anxiety and influencing later psychological development.[3] Finally, Nandor Fodor, in a book published by the publishers of *MSMH* only the year before Hubbard's book, also argued that pre-natal traumata were the cause of later life neuroses, and, curiously presaging Hubbard's thought, argued that

> . . . nature left the unborn child unprotected against the violence of parental intercourse in the advanced stages of gestation, and thus exposed it to an ordeal the traumatic nature of which is clearly traceable in dreams through-out our lives.[4]

and that

> accidents suffered by the mother may expose the unborn to physical shocks through the protective amniotic cushion. . . .[5] [6]

The need to 'relive' the repressed memory of birth and pre-natal trauma stressed by Fodor,[7] also appears in a book by an English healer.[8] There Eeman discusses pre-natal memory and the successful treatment of a number of cases of apparently organic disability by a non-hypnotic abreactive therapy based on re-living traumatic experiences.

[1] David K. Spelt, 'The conditioning of the human foetus *in utero*', *Journal of Experimental Psychology*, 38 (1948), pp. 338–46.

[2] Otto Rank, *The Trauma of Birth* (Harcourt Brace & Co, New York, 1929).

[3] Phyllis Greenacre, 'The predisposition to anxiety', *Psychoanalytic Quarterly*, 10 (1941), pp. 66–94.

[4] Nandor Fodor, *The Search for the Beloved: a Clinical Investigation of the Trauma of Birth and Pre-natal Conditioning* (Hermitage Press, New York, 1949), p. 309.

[5] Ibid., p. 304.

[6] For a resumé of Rank, Greenacre and Fodor, see J. A. C. Brown, *Freud and the Post-Freudians* (Penguin Books, Harmondsworth, 1964), pp. 52–5. The publisher of *MSMH*, a member of the Bay Head circle, assured me that Hubbard did not know of Fodor's work published in that first year before the public appearance of Dianetics. This may, of course, have been the case. However, Fodor suggests that the unborn child may have knowledge of what is going on outside the womb by means of telepathy. Hubbard takes pains to rebut the thesis of telepathically derived knowledge, without mentioning Fodor, *MSMH*, pp. 320–1.

[7] *Fodor*, op. cit., p. 193.

[8] L. E. Eeman, *Co-operative Healing* (Frederick Muller, London, 1947). pp. 102–24.

The practice of securing 'flash answers', known as a technique of induced association also existed in the practice of hypnotherapy. Brenman and Gill refer to such a technique, which was employed if a patient was unable to answer a question in therapy, or if the answer was unenlightening:

> the general formula applied was: 'I will count to a certain number and when I reach that number you will tell me the first thing that occurs to you in connection with so-and-so.'[1]

The notion of 'reverie' is referred to in the work of Baudouin[2] but not as a state to be induced for therapeutic purposes. The notion of the 'engram' also need not have been sought far.[3] It was a commonly current term used to designate a memory trace, or an altered condition in tissue or neural structure as a result of excitation or stimulus and was employed by a number of psychologists.[4]

Hubbard's theories regarding the operation of the reactive mind, which 'computes in identities' may owe something to Count Alfred Korzybski, whose General Semantics located the source of many of Man's ills in a misguided tendency to think in terms of identification,[5] or to his follower Hayakawa.[6]

How much Hubbard's theories derived from Richard Semon's work is now

---

[1] Margaret Brenman and Merton M. Gill, *Hypnotherapy: a Survey of the Literature* (International Universities Press, New York, 1947), p. 84.

[2] Charles Baudouin, *Suggestion and Autosuggestion* (Allen & Unwin, London, 1920), p. 130.

[3] Winter claims the search went no farther than *Dorland's Medical Dictionary* (W. B. Saunders & Co, Philadelphia, 1936). See Winter, op. cit., p. 18.

[4] Richard Semon, *The Mneme* (Allen & Unwin, London, 1921); K. Koffka, *Principles of Gestalt Psychology* (Harcourt & Brace, New York, 1935); Charles K. Ogden and I. A. Richards, *The Meaning of Meaning* (Kegan Paul, London, 1946); and Karl S. Lashley, 'In search of the engram', *Society of Experimental Biology Symposium No. 4: Physiological Mechanisms in Animal Behaviour* (Cambridge University Press, Cambridge, 1950), pp. 454–82.

[5] S. I. Hayakawa, 'From science-fiction to fiction-science', *ETC*, 8 (1951), p. 285; Paul Kecskemeti, 'A review of General Semantics', *New Leader*, 38, 17 (25 April 1955), pp. 24–5; Alfred Korzybski, *Science and Sanity* (International Non-Aristotelian Library Publishing Co, New York, 1933); Gardner, op. cit., Chapter 23. Some Dianeticists saw clear parallels: 'Korzybski's . . . work is implicit in Hubbard's', '. . . Hubbard [is] obviously an old and expert student of general semantics . . .' *Dianotes*, 1, 5 (December 1951), p. 11. In some of his later works, Hubbard does credit Korzybski along with Aristotle, Isaac Newton, Confucius, etc. as 'source material', e.g. the 'Foreword' to L. Ron Hubbard, *Scientology 8–8008*, 5th edn (Hubbard College of Scientology, East Grinstead, Sussex 1967).

[6] S. I. Hayakawa, *Language in Thought and Action* (Allen & Unwin, London, 1965). The first US edition appeared in 1949. This book is also notable in this context for its emphasis on the role of *survival* as a motivating principle, an idea prominent in Hubbard's writing.

difficult to determine. Semon's 'mnemic psychology' certainly appears to have anticipated some Hubbardian ideas. Semon proposed the existence of a mnemic property, that is, a tendency for organic tissue to be modified as a result of stimulation. This modification produced by the stimulus, Semon called an engram.[1] This stimulus impression could be reactivated, or in Semon's terminology, 'ecphorised', by the complete or partial recurrence of 'the energetic conditions which ruled at the generation of the engram'.[2] Under conditions of the strongest 'ecphoric effect',

> the mnemic state of excitation reproduces the original excitation in all its proper proportions, inclusive of time values.[3]

Semon describes such an engram and its ecphory from his own experience:

> We were once standing by the Bay of Naples and saw Capri lying before us; near by an organ-grinder played on a large barrel organ; a peculiar smell of oil reached us from a neighbouring 'trattoria'; the sun was beating pitilessly on our backs; and our boots in which we had been tramping for hours, pinched us. Many years after, a similar smell of oil ecphorised most vividly the optic engram of Capri, and even now this smell has invariably the same effect.[4]

In his later *Mnemic Psychology*, Semon stresses the vividness of 'mnemic sensations':

> When associatively . . . there is ecphorised the mnemic image of some old teacher whose stupid grammatical contentiousness and general pedantry made him the chief object of our boyhood hatred thirty years ago we do not merely 'remember' this person, dead for fifteen years past, but we *see* him in the flesh.
>
> Thus the whole simultaneous stratum of the engram-complex to which he belongs in our dream, and which has 'ecphorised' him as its central figure, gains reality, appearing not as the ecphory of an old stratum, but as that of a present one . . . We are ourselves thirty years younger; we are again going to school and having to pass our final examinations.[5]

This is, of course, all highly reminiscent of Hubbard's theory. The engram is substantially the same in each case, and indeed in his early work Hubbard suggested that the engram was retained as a cellular recording.[6] Ecphory and restimulation are exact parallels and both are evoked through association. Hubbard goes very much further than Semon, however. Hubbard's engram is created during periods of unconsciousness, pain, or emotional loss, while Semon's is created during normal consciousness. When restimulated, it takes

---

[1] Richard Semon, *The Mneme* (Allen & Unwin, London, 1921).

[2] Ibid., p. 145.

[3] Ibid., p. 149.

[4] Ibid., p. 92.

[5] Richard Semon, *Mnemic Psychology* (Allen & Unwin, London, 1923), p. 221. Semon planned a further work *Pathology of Mneme* which would treat the subject of the disappearance of engrams. However, as far as I can discover, this work was never written.

[6] For example, *MSMH*, p. 71.

complete command of the individual, rather than being a further, albeit sometimes powerful, stimulus. There is no suggestion in Semon's work that engrams are a cause of psychosomatic illness, nor practices for the elimination of engrams. If Hubbard was influenced by Semon's work, little more was derived from this source than the notions of the engram and its restimulation, ideas which were available elsewhere, as I have indicated.[1]

Unfortunately, the fact that 'engram' was not the first choice of terminology for Hubbard's published work does not altogether settle the matter. Hubbard first used the term 'impediment', then 'norn' and 'comanone' (the latter at Winter's suggestion[2]), and not until then was 'engram' publicly used. Hubbard may have begun with the notion of engram derived from Semon (or elsewhere) and sought an alternative terminology to distinguish his own ideas from those other conceptualizations which employed the term. Winter is, however, emphatic that during the Bayhead period, '. . . Semon's work was unknown to our group'.[3] In the absence of any stronger evidence. Winter's word must be accepted.

Developments in theory and practice

Dianetics theory and practice developed rapidly. By the end of 1950 in a series of lectures in California, Hubbard introduced a distinction that formed the basis of further theoretical change, between 'MEST' and 'theta'. MEST (Matter, Energy, Space, Time) was Hubbard's acronym for the material or physical universe, while theta stood for the universe of thought.[4] Hubbard also introduced the notion of the A–R–C (Affinity, Reality, Communication) triangle. This involved the idea that these three components were mutually related so that 'when reality is low, affinity and communication will be low. When communication is high, affinity and reality will be high'.[5] Moreover, Hubbard established a fundamental principle of the movement's epistemology:

> Reality is that upon which we agree. If I say there are twelve black cats on the stage and you don't agree someone is insane. The prime insanity is not to agree with another's reality.[6]

> Agreement and reality are synonymous. We agree upon something: it becomes reality. We don't agree. There isn't reality.[7]

[1] See Koffka, op. cit., Ogden and Richards, op. cit., and Lashley, op. cit.
[2] Winter, op. cit., p. 17–18.
[3] Winter, op. cit., p. 18.
[4] L. Ron Hubbard's *Notes on the Lectures of L. Ron Hubbard*, Edited by the Staff of the California Foundation (Hubbard Communications Office Ltd, Saint Hill Manor, East Grinstead, 1962). From lectures delivered late 1950. First published 1951. Hubbard's predilection for acronyns and contractions to form new words probably dates from his naval days. The practice is particularly prominent among U.S. military personnel.
[5] Ibid., p. 9.   [6] Ibid., pp 17–18.   [7] Ibid., p. 57.

THE CULT PHASE: DIANETICS

In *MSMH*, Hubbard had identified four 'dynamics':

The dynamic principle of existence – SURVIVE!

Survival, considered as the single and sole Purpose, subdivides into four *dynamics*. By symbiote is meant all entities and energies which aid survival.

DYNAMIC ONE is the urge of the individual toward survival for the individual and his symbiotes.

DYNAMIC TWO is the urge of the individual toward survival through procreation; it includes both the sex act and the raising of progeny, the care of children and their symbiotes.

DYNAMIC THREE is the urge of the individual toward survival for the group or the group for the group and includes the symbiotes of that group.

DYNAMIC FOUR is the urge of the individual toward survival for Mankind or the urge toward survival of Mankind for Mankind as well as the group for Mankind, etc., and includes the symbiotes of Mankind.[1]

By the end of 1950 these had increased to seven:

Fifth Dynamic – Life
Sixth Dynamic – MEST
Seventh Dynamic – Theta[2]

By August 1951 a further dynamic had been added and some of the others modified

DYNAMIC FIVE is the urge to survive as a life organism and embraces all living organisms.

DYNAMIC SIX is the urge to survive as part of the physical universe and includes the survival of the physical universe.

DYNAMIC SEVEN is the urge toward survival in a spiritual sense.

DYNAMIC EIGHT is the urge toward survival as a part of or ward of a Supreme Being.[3]

The optimum solution to any problem, Hubbard argued was the 'solution which brings the greatest benefit to the greatest number of dynamics'.[4]

At this point Hubbard had not developed the theory of Dianetics beyond a concern with the current lifetime. However, the period in which engrams could occur had been pushed back so that 'now, they have found an aberrative sperm and ovum series. Normally, however, the earliest engram is one day after conception.'[5]

[1] *MSMH*, pp. 37–8.
[2] Hubbard, *Notes on the Lectures*, pp. 95–6.
[3] *Science of Survival*, I, p. xi.
[4] Hubbard, *Notes on the Lectures*, p. 96.
[5] Ibid., p. 131. Winter also comments on this period: 'Investigation of the "past death" – or the "last death" in less imaginative patients – had only a brief popularity. It was replaced by the "sperm–ovum" sequence, which was defined as the "recollections" of occurrences at the moment of a person's conception.' Winter op. cit., p. 189.

A definite public commitment by Hubbard to 'past lives' did not occur until after Hubbard's break with Don Purcell and the Wichita Foundation,[1] in 1952, although he made reference to past lives and deaths in *Science of Survival* published in August 1951.[2]

The concept of 'theta' was expanded to incorporate not only thought, but 'life-force, elan vital, the spirit, the soul ...'[3] Theta, Hubbard argued, was constantly becoming entangled with MEST. When they came together 'forcefully' and 'intermingled "permanently"' an engram was formed.[4] Theta and MEST became 'enturbulated' in the reactive mind. Processing therefore involved releasing the theta held in the reactive mind as 'entheta' (enturbulated theta) and restoring it to the analytical mind.

Science of Survival was organized around the 'Tone Scale'. This scale purported to indicate a range of characteristics associated with the amount of 'free theta' available to the analytic mind. Locating a pre-clear in terms of key criteria on the scale permitted the prediction of other characteristics possessed by that individual (or group). Hence, being at 1·1 on the tone scale meant one was in a state of 'covert hostility' and therefore psychotic.[5] Among the other features of such an individual are that he is 'incapable, capricious, irresponsible'.[6] Point 4·0 on the tone scale meant that the individual was a MEST clear, he would be 'Near accident proof. No psycho-somatic ills. Nearly immune to bacteria' and he would have a 'high courage level'.[7] The tone scale also provided the basis for political observations by Hubbard. In *Science of Survival*, for example, liberalism is identified as 'higher-toned' than fascism, which is 'higher-toned' than communism.[8]

One major innovation in technique was that of 'straight-wire' processing, or 'straight memory':

[1] The history of Hubbard's relationship with and secession from Don Purcell and the Wichita Foundation is detailed below (pp. 77–95).

[2] *Science of Survival*, I, p. 61, Hubbard states: 'The subject of past deaths and past lives is so full of tension that as early as last July [1950–Ed.] the board of trustees of the Foundation sought to pass a resolution banning the entire subject.' He would only commit himself to the view that some past life and past death experiences 'seem to be valid and real ...' He also insisted these experiences should be run as normal engrams, and not invalidated or neglected. *Science of Survival*, II, p. 35.

[3] Ibid., I, p. 4.

[4] Ibid., I, p. 8.

[5] Hubbard was wont to describe those who disagreed with him as '1.1'. In the light of the later campaign in Scientology for civil rights for the institutionalized mental patient, it is interesting to observe that in *Science of Survival* individuals below 2.0 on the tone scale are identified as 'psychotic' and Hubbard argues 'any person from 2.0 down on the tone scale should not have, in any thinking society, any civil rights of any kind ...' *Science of Survival*, I, p. 131.

[6] 'Hubbard Chart of Human Evaluation and Dianetic Processing' supplied as a loose sheet with *Science of Survival*.

[7] Ibid.

[8] *Science of Survival*, I, p. 124.

Straight memory consists of the pre-clear's staying in present time with his eyes wide open and being asked to remember certain things which have been said to him and done to him during his life time. He is not asked to return to these incidents. He is asked only to recognise their existence.[1]

It was specifically directed at the pre-clear who 'has difficulty remembering' but seems to have been used as a tacit coaching device to instruct pre-clears who had difficulty contacting incidents in auditing.

If the pre-clear says bluntly that he cannot remember things, it is up to the auditor to encourage and validate this pre-clear's memory. If the pre-clear says 'I can't remember names', the auditor says, 'Well, what is the name of your business associate? The pre-clear says, 'Oh, his name is Jones!' The auditor has proven to the pre-clear that the pre-clear can remember at least one name.[2]

Coaching the pre-clear may have had an important part in the effective running of Dianetic auditing. For example:

There is a trick of reaching conception in a case . . . The auditor asks the pre-clear to run a moment of sexual pleasure, and then when his pre-clear, who does not have to recount this moment aloud appears to be settled into that moment, *the auditor demands that the pre-clear go immediately to conception.* The pre-clear will normally do so . . .[3]

In this case, Hubbard is auditing a woman and has returned her to infancy:

Woman : I'm imagining being a baby.
Hubbard: All right. What do you see there. What's your visio as you're lying there being a baby?
Woman : I guess there was a crib.
Hubbard: Let's take a look at it.
Woman : All I can see. Just holding on to the side of the crib.
Hubbard: You're holding on. How you feel lying there in the crib?
Woman : I'm sitting.
Hubbard: You're sitting in the crib. And who comes into the room?
Woman : [unclear, possibly a name].
Hubbard: What does he look like?

   .   .   .   .

[Mother enters]
Hubbard: [. . .] All right, now what's her voice sound like?
Woman : I don't understand it.
Hubbard: What's she saying. What language? Is it a different language?
Woman : Yes.
Hubbard: Well what language is it? All right, pick up the first word she says, how's

[1] Ibid., II, p. 68.
[2] *Science of Survival*, II, p. 69.
[3] Ibid., II, pp. 173–4. (My emphasis.)

it sound? Go to the moment of the first word she says. How does it
sound?

Woman : [Laughs]
Hubbard: What is it?
Woman : Maboushka.[1]

A further major technical change was the introduction of 'lock scanning'.
Locks and engrams were held to form chains of similar kinds of incident – for
example, all occasions when the pre-clear suffered a break in affinity, or an
enforced agreement. It was claimed that to run each of these incidents in early
Dianetic fashion would be far too lengthy a process, but that an equally effective
and far speedier procedure was simply to get the pre-clear to 'scan' in his mind
similar types of incidents from the earliest to the latest.

> The auditor asks the file clerk if there is a type of incident which can be scanned in
> the case. The file clerk, at a snap of the auditor's fingers, answers yes or no. The
> auditor requests the name of the type of incident. The file clerk gives the name of the
> type of incident. The auditor then tells the pre-clear to go to the earliest available
> moment on this chain of locks . . . the auditor tells the pre-clear to scan from this
> earliest moment to present time through all incidents of the type named.[2]

Scanning such chains several times, Hubbard argued, was an effective way of
converting entheta into theta (that is freeing theta).

Hubbard's next major work after *Science of Survival* marked a turning point in
the development of the theory and practice of the movement. While Dianetics
had hitherto maintained that engrams were a result of what had been *done to*
the pre-clear, *Advanced Procedure and Axioms* presented the idea that the individual
was responsible for his engrams:

> Everything which is wrong with [the pre-clear] he has selectively and particularly
> chosen to be wrong with him.[3]

[1] L. Ron Hubbard, Recording of a public demonstration of Dianetic auditing,
September 1951. For a clear case of coaching see the auditing session reported by
Joseph Winter, reprinted in Gardner, op. cit., pp. 276–8. The following account of a
reporter's unsuccessful auditing session reported in a magazine also seems apposite:

> 'The experiment by one of the foremost practitioners in the new science was not
> a success. My "engrams" were playing hard-to-get, or my pre-natal recording
> device was faulty. After two hours of attempting to recall the phrases heard in
> childhood or before, Schofield switched on the lights and said: "You should read
> The Book [*MSMH*] more carefully".'

Roland Wild, 'Everyman his own psychoanalyst', *Illustrated* (30 September 1950), p. 18.
It is not my intention to suggest that 'coaching' was consciously carried out by auditors
rather, as many investigations into psychotherapy and psychological experiment show,
the therapist or experimenter may give many unconscious cues as to what he wants or
expects from his patient or subject.

[2] *Science of Survival*, vol. 11, pp. 124–5.

[3] L. Ron Hubbard, *Advanced Procedure and Axioms* (hereafter *AP&A*) (Central Press,
Wichita, Kansas, 1951), p. 7. Quotations are from the fourth edition, 1962, published
by Hubbard Communications Office Ltd, East Grinstead, Sussex.

Each individual at some time in the past chose some means of securing sympathy or 'co-operation on the part of the environment'[1] which seemed at the time necessary for his survival. This was called the 'service facsimile'.[2] Thereafter, the individual became subject to the service facsimile, believing it essential to his continued survival. Restoring the individual's self-determinism therefore required the release of the service facsimile.[3]

This volume also contained the 'Definitions, Logics and Axioms', a set of numbered assertions described as 'logics', 'corollaries', 'axioms' and 'definitions', for example:

> Axiom 68 – The single arbitrary in any organism is time.
> Axiom 69 – Physical universe perceptions and efforts are received by an organism as force waves, convert by facsimile into *theta* and are thus stored.
> Definition: Randomity is the mis-alignment through the internal or external efforts by other forms of life or the material universe of the efforts of an organism, and is imposed on the physical organism by counter efforts in the environment.[4]

Hubbard's next significant book, although first issued at the Wichita Foundation made a clear commitment to immortality and employed the term 'scientology', providing the vehicle for his secession from the Wichita Dianeticists on the basis of a new 'science'.

Social organization and development

With the publication of *MSMH* and the article in *Astounding*, Dianetics emerged organizationally in two forms. Organized around L. Ron Hubbard was the Hubbard Dianetic Research Foundation [hereafter referred to as the Foundation, the Elizabeth Foundation, or HDRF], incorporated in April 1950 in Elizabeth, New Jersey. The Foundation had a board of directors, presided over by Hubbard. Branches of the Foundation had also been established in other major American cities, so that by November 1950 there were branches in Los Angeles, New York, Washington, Chicago and Honolulu. The Foundations in Elizabeth and Los Angeles were offering an 'intensive, full-time course, lasting four weeks for professional auditors',[5] as well as courses of therapy, while the other Foundations mainly provided therapy.

The board of directors was composed of five others apart from Hubbard and his second wife Sara, including John W. Campbell, Joseph Winter, the publisher of *MSMH*, Arthur Ceppos, and a lawyer, C. Parker Morgan. Each Foundation had a staff of professional auditors and instructors, and those in New Jersey and Los Angeles had a small research staff employing Dianeticists and trained

[1] Ibid., p. 7.
[2] It is the means he uses to excuse his failures.
[3] The term 'engram' was largely replaced by 'facsimile' from this point.
[4] L. Ron Hubbard, 'Definitions, logics and axioms', *AP&A*, p. 35.
[5] Advertisement in *Astounding*, 46, 3 (November 1950), back cover.

psychologists. The Elizabeth Foundation employed some thirty people on its staff. Numbers at the other Foundations fluctuated.

While an organizational structure was emerging within the Foundations, however, 'grass-roots' organizations of a rudimentary kind had emerged spontaneously. With the appearance of Hubbard's article and book, individuals all over America and in Great Britain began practising the technique. Many began with members of their own family or with friends, co-auditing each other, and enthusiastically proselytizing among their acquaintances. Some publicised their activities through advertisements in newspapers and magazines,[1] or through newspaper stories.[2] Some wrote to booksellers, or the Foundations to locate others in their area interested in the practice.

In this fashion, numerous small groups rapidly appeared with names such as: The Bristol Dianetic Group, The Connecticut Valley Dianetic Association, The Central London Group of Dianeticists, etc. With one or more enthusiasts organizing group activities, arranging meetings and contacting members, these groups had a fluctuating membership, and little formal structure. They generally met one or two evenings a week. The 'senior' Dianeticist present (senior in the sense that he had been practising longest or, less frequently, because he had taken some official training), would normally give a lecture, a demonstration, or conduct group-auditing. After a break, members would then team up in pairs for co-auditing.[3]

Communication between the groups, between isolated individual followers, and between followers and the Foundations was initially largely by letter. The early followers were prolific correspondents. The more enthusiastic among them kept up correspondence with as many as a dozen others, detailing in their letters the cases they were running (or auditing) at the time; the activities of their group; new developments in theory and practice (whether retailed from official Dianetic sources or their own innovations) and rumours of administrative or political developments at the Foundations; as well as social and personal news. As some of these groups became established, however, mimeoed news-sheets were produced, along the lines of the 'fanzines' which link together science-fiction enthusiasts. Cheaply produced, they provided a means for the leading independent figures and groups practising Dianetics to remain in contact with a dispersed and growing list of correspondents. These mimeoed bulletins were an important feature of Dianetics, providing the sense of a Dianetic community[4] for the

---

[1] See for example, *Life Preserver*, 1, 1 (June 1953), pp. 5–6; 1, 2 (July 1953), n.p.

[2] See for example, *The People*, 24 February 1952, p. 3.

[3] The organisational model for these groups was, I think fairly evidently, the clubs of science fiction enthusiasts. Kingsley Amis refers to these clubs and their 'fanzines':

> 'groups in a score of major cities and dozens of others. . . . Many clubs will meet weekly, have a hierarchy of officials, hold organised discussions, and mimeograph or even print a magazine.'

Kingsley Amis, *New Maps of Hell* (New English Library, London, 1963), p. 49.

[4] Among the distinctive symbols of the Dianetic community was the practise of

amateur following, as well as a later focus for, and a medium through which to express, discontent at the redirection of the movement by Hubbard.

The usual amateur bulletin would contain one or more articles on the theory or practice of Dianetics; discussions of cases audited; details of group meetings; information on innovations in theory and practice by recent graduates of Foundation courses or members of other groups; social information concerning figures in the Dianetic world; letters of encouragement or complaint; notices of recent publications; etc.[1] The Foundation also issued a publication,[2] in a slightly more sober style, containing articles by Hubbard and Foundation staff, and details of courses, tape-recordings and books available.

Individuals within the Dianetic community rapidly became well-known through letters, articles and personal stories in the group bulletins, and enthusiasts would make a point of visiting each other while in the neighbourhood of other Dianeticists on holiday or on business, often stopping off a while to try out each other's auditing techniques.[3]

As the Foundations began training and certifying 'professional' auditors, other elements were added to the structure of the Dianetic community. Some trained auditors gravitated to leadership positions in the local amateur groups, virtually transforming the membership into a private clientele. In the Dianetics period this was, however, quite exceptional. Some set up entirely new private practices. Others were absorbed into the staff of the Foundations themselves. Some adopted a peripatetic form of practice, travelling around and engaging in a period of practice in one area before moving on to another.

A picture of how the professional practice of Dianetics was ideally envisaged is presented in one of the American newsletters:

> A Dianeticist has his shingle out and a lady enters the waiting room. She has been troubled with her problems for some time now and feels that she may not be operating as optimum as she would like. Still she does not feel that a 'Nut Doctor, [psychiatrist] is the answer. She has heard that Dianetics has helped cases like hers, and after much mental hash and re-hash, she has decided to investigate. What's there to lose?
>
> A pleasant girl, in a simple street dress has received her, has asked the usual questions, and then instructed her to have a seat after telling her that the counselor would see her shortly. There is a buzzing and the receptionist rises and motions her

[1] During late 1951 to early 1952 there were at least seventeen of these bulletins or newsletters in America. There were probably never more than five in Britain.

[2] That of the Elizabeth Foundation was called *The Dianamic*, but this was ephemeral and *The Dianetic Auditor's Bulletin* became the established Foundation periodical.

[3] See, for example, *Life Preserver*, 1, 3 (September 1953), p. 8; Interviews.

signing letters to other members 'In ARC' instead of 'Best wishes' (ARC standing for Affinity, Reality and Communication, the 'Communication Triangle', all the elements of which must be present for adequate communication to occur, according to Hubbard.) See, for example, correspondence in *Dianotes*, 1, 5 (December 1951).

to the door, politely shows her into the counselor's office and then leaves. The Auditor addresses the case in such a manner as to ascertain the problem and at the same time relax the patient as much as possible. There is no sales talk on Dianetics, no appeal at this time to assimilate its concepts. This would have nothing to do with the woman's problems. She has come to the Auditor for help as if he were a doctor, and in a sense that is exactly what he is. If he can help her he does, if not he lets her know and she goes her way. There is no converting, sales talk, or education. Treatment is what she wanted and treatment she should have, nothing more.[1]

Practitioners trained by the Foundation were eligible for Associate Membership in the HDRF, as were others interested in the practice of Dianetics, for a $15 annual fee. In return for this fee they were entitled to receive *The Dianetic Auditor's Bulletin*, the Foundation periodical publication, in which they learnt of advances in theory and technique, and notification of new books, and lecture or demonstration tapes by Hubbard. There was, however, little or no control over those who graduated from the Foundation courses. They received a certificate as an HDA (Hubbard Dianetic Auditor) and were henceforth entitled to practice their new-found profession wherever they chose. This was a source of concern to some board members of the Foundation.[2]

The emergence of Dianetics in Britain

In Britain, the problem of adequate contact with the central organization was further compounded by the relative expense of Foundation courses and the cost of travel, which considerably restricted the number of British Dianeticists who took professional training at this period. Foundation and other publications were difficult to secure due to currency exchange control restrictions. Copies of amateur group newsletters were sometimes obtained on an exchange basis between editors, and many of the American newsletters had a policy of supplying their publications in exchange for a written contribution of some kind either technical, theoretical or merely social. Hence there was some transatlantic contact between amateur groups, but relatively little between British amateur groups and the Foundation. This became particularly the case as the Foundations were beset by immediate and local problems which drew attention away from the outlying Dianetic groups.

Dianetics in Britain developed spontaneously as the result of interest aroused in readers of *Astounding* and their acquaintances, by Campbell's editorials and Hubbard's article. Imported copies of *MSMH* became available in mid-1950 and several Dianetic groups were started, five in London, others in Bristol, Chorley, Hull, Glasgow and elsewhere. A correspondence network emerged as individuals contacted each other through booksellers. Early Foundation materials were retyped by hand and circulated, and enthusiasts made personal

[1] *Dianotes*, 1, 12 (June–July 1952), p. 2.
[2] Winter, op. cit., p. 30.

visits to other Dianeticists to learn more of auditing.[1] Later one or two were to visit the American Foundations for training, but by the end of 1950 there were only three Associate Members of the Foundation in Britain.[2] These three individuals organized a 'postal group' called the British Dianetic Association (BDA) to reproduce and distribute Foundation materials. Some eighty to ninety people joined the BDA for a small subscription but it went into voluntary liquidation in June 1951.

Access to Foundation materials and their distribution was the prime problem facing the British Dianetic groups. In January 1951 a Central London Group of Dianeticists was formed and joined by some forty members of the BDA living in or near London 'to give people a chance to get together and exchange views and to find potential co-auditors',[3] and to encourage the formation of further local groups.[4]

The liquidation of the BDA led to attempts to establish a national Dianetic association on a sounder legal and financial footing. In November 1951 the Dianetic Association Ltd was incorporated to facilitate the distribution of material and establish a Dianetic library. A British edition of *MSMH* was produced.[5] Many groups and local leaders felt that communication nevertheless remained a problem, hampering the development of the movement and one of the larger London groups, the Dianetics Study Group, sought to bring about a federation of Dianetic groups throughout the country:

> With a view to creating an organisation which would be consonant with Hubbard's democratic and humanist principles [sic], in which the voice of every minority would be given full, fair and balanced representation, and would steadily work up to professional standards.[6]

A meeting was held in June 1952, with representatives of a number of local amateur groups, at which a Dianetic Federation of Great Britain was formed.[7] Subsequently the DFGB absorbed the Dianetic Association Ltd.[8] Thus the only organization for the movement as a whole in Britain was a loose federation of amateur groups, the role of the central organization being primarily the distribution of material from America. The American Foundations similarly provided a weak central organization for the amateur groups in the USA, with little or no control over the membership and practitioners at large.

---

[1] Interviews.

[2] *The Dianeticist*, uncertain date and issue no. probably 1952, p. 4; *Dianotes* 1, 7 (Jan–Feb 1952), p. 8.

[3] *The Dianeticist*, uncertain date and issue no. probably 1952, p. 4.

[4] *Dianotes*, 1, 7 (Jan–Feb. 1952), p. 9.

[5] This was a somewhat edited version.

[6] Letter from Secretary Dianetic Study Group, N.W.3, to other Dianeticists, n.d. – probably early 1952.

[7] Anon 'Dianetic Federation of Great Britain (Preliminary Report)', n.d., typescript.

[8] *Life Preserver*, 1, 1 (June 1953), p. 2.

In its origins and form of organization, based primarily around local groups of amateur enthusiasts, with professional or semi-professional practitioners some-times at their head, Dianetics closely resembled spiritualism. The spiritualist movement which emerged after the publicity given to the Fox family and the Rochester Rappings in 1848 rapidly spread throughout the United States and beyond. Mediumship was believed to be a gift which many or most people possessed, and local circles of enthusiasts grew up around those in whom this gift was manifested.[1]

Emergence of organizational crisis

Since local groups varied in composition or orientation, some leaders were unprepared to co-operate to any great extent with others whose methods, promotion, or personality were a source of friction. The democratic basis of the movement was manifested in the suspicion with which local groups viewed any loss of autonomy or any attempt to vest a central organization with more than a minimum of authority.

In this respect there is a strong resemblance between Dianetics and such cultic movements as spiritualism and New Thought. These two movements were, like Dianetics, composed of a variety of groups which shared a number of ideological themes but were otherwise heterogeneous. The 'epistemological individualism' of these movements is manifested in their democratic ideologies:

> . . . the special characteristic of the Spiritualist movement from the beginning has been its democratic character. There has been neither recognised leader nor authori-tative statement of creed. This characteristic . . . gave breadth, tolerance, and expansiveness to the movement . . . and rendered it possible for the new belief to combine with almost any pre-existing system of doctrine.[2]

The individualistic and democratic nature of New Thought was founded on a belief that knowledge of God

> is ultimately a highly personal, intuitive, experiential matter, how [then] can it submit to any limitation upon its freedom of expression?[3]

Both spiritualism and New Thought emerged around multiple leaders who shared only a limited basis of belief and practice. Leaders of the spiritualist movement synthesized its beliefs with socialism, free love, and oriental philoso-phy, while New Thought leaders differentially emphasized the strands of

---

[1] Geoffrey K. Nelson, *Spiritualism and Society* (Routledge & Kegan Paul, London, 1969); Frank Podmore, *Modern Spiritualism: a History and Criticism* (Methuen, London, 1902); Roy Wallis, 'Ideology, authority and the development of cultic movements', *Social Research*, 41, 2 (1974), pp. 299–327.

[2] Podmore, op. cit., p. 299.

[3] Charles Braden, *Spirits in Rebellion: the Rise and Development of New Thought* (South-ern Methodist University Press, Dallas, Texas, 1963), p. 20.

Phineas Quimby, Warren Felt Evans, Transcendentalism, Swedenborgianism, and traditional Christianity, from which the movement's beliefs had developed, or introduced new strands from Theosophy or Rosicrucianism.

Many spiritualists had an aversion to formal organization:

> Many local societies failed to survive as a result of the individualistic attitude of Spiritualists and the casual and ineffective type of organisation these societies were forced to adopt in order to appease the libertarian and anarchistic views of their members.[1]

Many New Thought leaders had taken up their vocation after alienation from the authoritarianism of Christian Science and refused to establish more than minimal, formal organization or to attempt to exercise any far-reaching control over their following. After more than half a century only a very loose International New Thought Alliance, commanding little loyalty, has been established.

Dianetics, spiritualism and New Thought emerged as 'spontaneous' cults[2] which came into existence in many places more or less simultaneously. From the very beginnings of these movements there had been many local autonomous leaders, and they were almost invariably opposed to the attempts of any individual to arrogate authority.

The central organizations of Dianetics were poorly administered. Hubbard was lecturing in various parts of the country and commuting between Los Angeles and New York during late 1950 and early 1951, giving little direction to either of these Foundations in day-to-day administration, and progressively alienating other board members by his practice of initiating developments without consulting them, and by what some of them viewed as his increasingly evident authoritarianism.

Large numbers of staff were recruited in the early months, without adequate supervision. Foundation income was expended on the assumption that the Dianetics boom would long continue. However, by the beginning of 1951 applications for training and therapy began to drop off and income correspondingly fell. In part, the decline in new recruits to Foundation services was precipitated by attacks on Dianetics by doctors and psychiatrists in the press and scathing reviews of Hubbard's book. Recruitment may, to some extent, have been affected by the publicity given to Hubbard's second wife, Sara Northrup Hubbard, who in her suit for divorce claimed to have psychiatric evidence that Hubbard was a severe paranoid. (She lost her suit, Hubbard winning a counter suit. Sara Northrup Hubbard later signed a statement to the effect that the 'things I have said about L. Ron Hubbard in the courts and the

[1] Geoffrey K. Nelson, 'The analysis of a cult: Spiritualism', *Social Compass*, 15, 6 (1968), p. 475.

[2] Geoffrey K. Nelson, 'The Spiritualist movement and the need for a redefinition of cult', *JSSR*, 8 (1969), p. 156.

public prints have been grossly exaggerated or entirely false'.)[1] In particular, however, the decline in numbers was due to the failure of Dianetics to live up to its early promise in the eyes of the public.

The 'clear' who would emerge after only twenty hours of auditing had not made his appearance. The clears proclaimed by Hubbard did not seem to live up to expectations. One of these indeed was Sara Northrup Hubbard. Another was a Miss Sonya Bianca whom Hubbard exhibited before a large audience in Los Angeles, but who failed the simplest tests of memory.[2] Many individuals who had been working at the technique found their cases had improved little or not at all, and gave up.

The Elizabeth Foundation moved towards a financial crisis. Hubbard saw the need to take some action to cope with this situation,[3] but Joseph Winter and Hubbard's publisher resigned from the board of directors in October 1950 – Winter to set up a private Dianetic practice in New York. C. Parker Morgan resigned in January 1951 and John W. Campbell in March 1951. Creditors began to demand payment of their bills and Hubbard, faced with financial disaster and threats of commitment by his wife Sara, resigned in April 1951 and departed to Cuba.[4, 5]

Don Purcell, a Wichita businessman, offered to assist the Foundation out of its difficulties. The Foundation was centralized and its assets moved to Wichita, Kansas in April/May 1951, where Purcell made funds and a building available. Purcell became President of the Foundation and Hubbard its Vice-president and Chairman of the board of directors on his return from Cuba. The other branches were closed down and the number of staff drastically reduced. The New Jersey creditors, however, pressed for settlement of the Elizabeth Foundation's debts, and a court decision declared the Kansas operation its successor

[1] Statement by Sara Northrup Hubbard, 11 June 1951, copy made available by the Church of Scientology.

[2] Interviews.

[3] 'Various memoranda from L. Ron Hubbard were read and discussed which indicated extreme urgency in . . . forwarding and executing plans for centralisation in a favourable place . . .' HDRF, New Jersey, Executive Management Committee of the Board of Trustees, Minutes of 22 January 1951.

[4] John W. Maloney, a member of the board of directors of both the Elizabeth, N.J. and the later Wichita Foundations, asserts in a letter to Dianeticists titled, 'A factual report on the Hubbard Dianetic Foundation', 23 February 1952: 'In November of 1950, the combined income of the Hubbard Dianetic Research Foundations did not quite total one-tenth of its payroll.' It is clear that a number of staff members had not been paid for some time since many were listed as creditors in the ensuing bankruptcy action.

[5] Christopher Evans asserts that Hubbard went to Puerto Rico. Since Purcell arranged for Hubbard's return from Cuba, and Sara Northrup Hubbard produced a letter in court from Hubbard in Cuba, I believe Evans to be mistaken. The point is, however, not of any importance. See Christopher Evans, *Cults of Unreason* (Harrap, London, 1973).

and liable for its debts.[1] A receiver was appointed. A compromise settlement of the claims was negotiated, but new claims were filed by other creditors.[2]

In February 1952 Hubbard resigned as Chairman and Vice-president and sold his stock in the corporation for a consideration of $1 and an agreement to the effect that he would be allowed to set up an independent school, Hubbard College, in Wichita, and receive assistance in establishing it. Don Purcell then entered the Foundation into voluntary bankruptcy.

Shortly after Hubbard's resignation, it was alleged that:

> . . . certain articles mysteriously disappeared from the Foundation's offices. Those things which vanished were the mailing list, the addressograph plates, tapes bearing the recorded lectures of Mr Hubbard, typewriters, sound recorders, sound trans-cribers and other equipment. At a preliminary hearing held in March, 1952, Mr [J] Elliott [a personal associate of Hubbard] testified that he inadvertently re-moved these articles from the premises. The tapes were in three boxes, each of which weighed more than twenty-five pounds.[3]

A restraining order was issued against Hubbard and Elliott, and the tapes and mailing lists were eventually returned to the Foundation, although it was alleged that the tapes had been mutilated.[4] (Officials of the Scientology organi-zation dispute this account of what transpired. They argue that Don Purcell had permitted all the items concerned to be removed to the new school, Hubbard College. They allege that Don Purcell then went back on this agreement that Hubbard could establish Hubbard College.)

Late in 1952 a warrant was issued ordering Hubbard to appear before a Federal Court for failing to return $9000 wrongfully withdrawn from the Wichita Foundation. A compromise was again negotiated, Hubbard agreeing to pay $1000 and return the car originally supplied by the Foundation.[5]

In April 1952 assets of the Wichita Foundation were auctioned under the auspices of the Bankruptcy Court. Purcell entered a bid of $6124 and, as the highest bidder, was granted possession of these assets including the publishing rights on *MSMH*, the copyrights outstanding in the Foundation's name, and the sole right to the title 'Hubbard Dianetic Foundation'. Hubbard, had meanwhile moved to Phoenix, where he established Scientology.

Membership and motivations

The circle around Ron Hubbard at Bay Head, New Jersey, contained in micro-cosm the characteristics that typified much of the following of Dianetics after its

[1] *Hubbard Dianetic Foundation Inc. In Bankruptcy No. 379–B–2*, District Court of the United States for the District of Kansas.

[2] Including Joseph Winter's sister, who had subsequently married John W. Camp-bell. She and Winter had each put up $5000 to finance the Elizabeth Foundation.

[3] Letter from Owens, Moore and Beck, attorneys acting for Purcell, to Dianeticists, 20 May 1952.

[4] *Hubbard Dianetic Foundation Inc. In Bankruptcy*, op. cit.

[5] Ibid.

public presentation. Campbell suffered from chronic sinusitis. He had a wide, if sporadic, knowledge of modern natural-scientific developments and an acute ignorance of the social sciences and psychology. His model of science was pragmatist and technological. He was prone to sudden enthusiasms for new ideas which led to a profound suspension of his critical faculties.[1]

Winter was a doctor of medicine with little knowledge of psychiatry and psychology. He was unhappy with the trend in medicine towards greater specialization and compartmentalization, with the consequent absence of a vision of the patient as a whole. He had earlier sought this holism in General Semantics, 'and while I agree with Korzybski that "the word is not the object", I found no satisfactory explanation for how such a confusion between levels of abstraction had arisen in the first place.'[2]

He sought answers to questions that medical science was unable to provide:

> I became aware again of the perplexity which plagues all doctors – the 'why' of human behaviour. I thought of all the questions which had gone unanswered or which had been answered in a tentative or equivocal manner – of questions which were frequently unasked because of their presumed unanswerability. Why did Mr M attempt to commit suicide? Why was it that Mrs E began to hear voices telling her to kill her new-born baby? Why did an intelligent man like Mr P find it necessary to drink a quart of whiskey every day? Why did Mrs T have coronary occlusion?
>
> The list of questions beginning with 'why' could be extended indefinitely. They all had one element in common: I knew of no satisfactory answer for any of them. The 'answers' and explanations which I had learned in medical school and which I passed on to my patients were superficial, taking into account only the preceding link in the chain of causality. A patient would ask me, 'Why does a person get coronary occlusion?' and I would answer glibly, 'Because there is a narrowing of the lumen of the coronary arteries'. And with that answer he would appear to be satisfied.[3]

Dr Winter, however, was not. He wanted to know why it had happened *in this particular* case,[4] and how it could be treated or prevented. Others in that

---

[1] Gardner, op. cit., pp. 346–7. Brian Aldiss observes of him:
    'Even the hardheaded Campbell, who saw in science and applied science "the salvation, the raising of mankind", even Campbell believed that the impossibility of getting something for nothing might be transcended by a formula of incantation – hence his extraordinary notion that seventy-five per cent of the brain (and the most powerful part) lay unused, his belief in psionics, and his pursuit of cults such as Dianetics . . . [etc]'.
Brian W. Aldiss, *Billion Year Spree* (Weidenfeld & Nicolson, London, 1973). p. 238.
[2] Winter, op. cit., pp. 7–8.
[3] Winter, op. cit., p. 6.
[4] It has, of course, not escaped us that this was a question of some importance to the Azande. E. E. Evans-Pritchard, *Witchcraft, Oracles and Magic among the Azande* (Clarendon Press, Oxford, 1937).

early circle led to Hubbard by Campbell, were conscious of the possibility of improvement in their lives. One had suffered trauma in childhood and had long experienced a sense of social isolation, and social inadequacy, for which he had sought a cure in the literature of hypnosis and suggestion, and in psychotherapy:

> So before Dianetics arrived, I was looking for something that would get the anguish out of me and speed up the therapeutic process so I could be comfortable . . . I had learned to chart my path very cautiously and carefully through a lot of shoals, through things that were like this – there were certain people . . . I couldn't approach, or certain people on certain subjects, because I would burst into tears – now I'm talking about me as an adult . . . 40 years old. There were things I couldn't go and ask my boss for or about because I would burst into tears. That's not acceptable behaviour, so I learned how to stay off of subjects so that wouldn't happen. And I was a very – the modern word is 'uptight' – kind of person just from being unable to do so many things like that for various reasons. I had very little freedom in relating to other people. So I was ready for Hubbard when he came along [. . .]
>
> Well I think the reason that it seemed so important is basically that I wasn't happy, and there was happiness here. There was a promise . . . that I could bypass all my troubles and come out in the clear without having to face them. And there was an absolution . . . the engram is something that has been done to you which determines your behaviour.[1]

Others had been involved in a variety of psychotherapeutic practices.

The early circle at Bay Head was white, and primarily engaged in professional or semi-professional occupations. Although as the movement gained a mass following it was to spread both up and down the social scale, it remained pre-eminently middle class.

Information on the following of the Dianetic movement is, of course, very limited, but a number of clues are available. Early in 1952, for example the editors of one prominent Dianetic newsletter organized a survey of their readership (mainly, but not exclusively in the United States). It is uncertain how many questionnaires were distributed, but 198 replies were received.[2]

The age distribution of their respondents was as follows:

Age	Number
21–26	20
27–40	100
44–51 [sic]	37
51+	17
	174

[1] Interview: early Dianeticist and member of the Bay Head circle.
[2] *The Dianews*, 1, 23 (15 June 1952).

The average age, they estimated, was about 38.

The sex distribution of the respondents showed a marked male over-representation – 140 men, 59 women.[1] As would be expected from the age distribution, most were or had been married.

Marital status	Number
Single	42
Married	126
Widowed	3
Separated	8
Divorced	5
	184

Of those who were married, most had children.

Number of children	Number
1	38
2	44
3	27
4	6
	115

It is not clear how many of the remaining 27 had more than 4 children, and how many had none.

The religious affiliations of the respondents showed the largest proportions to be Protestant and 'agnostic'.

Religious affiliation	Number
Agnostic	69
Protestant	68
Christian [sic]	12
Catholic	8
Quaker	4
Jewish	3
Other[2]	16
	160

An attempt was also made to determine the occupations of subscribers.

[1] Clearly either the number of replies received or that of the number of men or women among the respondents is an error. Since it is not clear which, I simply report the figures given.

[2] Those in the category 'other' belonged to diverse cults, occult groups or marginal sects – Mormon, Baha'i, Religious Science, Rosicrucian, etc.

	Occupation	Number
'Psychological'	Dianetic Auditors	20
	Psychologists	6
	Related work	3
'Technical'	Engineers	25
	Physicists	2
	Chemists	2
	Research scientists	3
	Other technical	11
'Medical and	MDs	3
Health'	Nurses	2
	Other[1]	10
'Professional'	Teachers	11
	Professor	1
	Lawyers	2
	Clergy	2
	Armed Forces	3
	Artists	3
	Writers	4
	Others	5
	'Business'[2]	30
'Miscellaneous'	Homemakers [sic]	21
	Students	8
	Children	2
	Retired	1
	Total	180

The education level of respondents was claimed to be well above average.

Educational attainment	Number
Ended with grammar[3] school	17
Ended with high school	53
Had one or more years of college	24
Held one or more degrees	89
Bachelors of Science	46
Bachelors of Arts	42
Masters of Science	7
Masters of Arts	7
Ph.Ds.	3
MDs	3
DD	1
DSc	1
Miscellaneous Doctors [sic]	5

[1] Those listed in the 'other' category belonged to various limited, marginal or quasi-therapeutic professions: pharmacist, osteopath, chiropractor, dietician, naturopath, etc.

[2] In such occupations as 'newspaper work', manufacturer, manager, mechanic, truck driver, clerical, salesman, etc.

[3] That is, elementary.

The editors found that 135 of their respondents were readers of science fiction. They also found that 91 had read the speculative philosophical work of Count Alfred Korzybski and 102 that of his popularizer, S. I. Hayakawa.

The general picture that emerges is of a following of white,[1] young to early middle-aged, adults, mainly married with families, from predominantly Protestant backgrounds and with Protestant or no religious affiliation, white-collar occupations and a high school or college education. They were predominantly consumers of science-fiction literature,[2] and many had already ventured into the 'cultic milieu', having acquainted themselves with at least one quasi-philosophical-psychological system. Despite the obvious limitations of these figures, they remain the only ones available from the period. The broad conclusions to which they lead can, moreover, be supplemented by further observations.

A similar picture emerges from the nine respondents to my questionnaire who had been associated with Dianetics during its first two years in Britain. Among these, the average age at which they took up Dianetics was 38 years, with a range of between 28 and 55 years of age.[3] Six were married, two separated or divorced and one was single. Parents were overwhelmingly Anglican. Seven were employed in white-collar occupations, self-employed or of independent means, and only two were employed in manual occupations. Educational levels were above average for Britain with only three having left school before 15 years of age, three having attended university. At least six had first heard of Dianetics through the article in *Astounding Science Fiction*. Of the thirty-one Dianeticists

[1] Although there may have been one or two others, the only non-white individual I have ever heard of in the context of Dianetics practice was the chauffeur of a pre-clear, who received a brief course of auditing.

[2] In many respects they are close to the characteristics of science-fiction fans as described by Kingsley Amis:

> 'Males greatly predominate over females . . . As regards age, the average would come somewhere in the later twenties, with a sprinkling of school-children and a number of veteran fans . . . As for occupation, not unnaturally there is a pronounced technological or scientific bias, with engineers, chemists, research workers, and so on accounting for perhaps forty per cent of readers . . . Other groups mentioned as numerically important are the non-scientific professions, college students, and the armed forces.'

Kingsley Amis, *New Maps of Hell* (New English Library, London, 1963), p. 50. Unfortunately Amis cites no sources for these views. The average age of Dianeticists is probably higher due to the appeal of a therapeutic cult to the older and more illness-prone, otherwise these observations reflect the characteristics of Dianeticists, as we would expect.

[3] The twenty-four individuals in Colbert's study had an average age of 36 years. The educational achievement of this group was distributed as follows: below high school, 1; high school, 5; high school graduate, 9; beyond high school, 5; college degree and higher education, 4. John Colbert, *An Evaluation of Dianetic Therapy*, Thesis for the degree of Master of Science in Education, School of Education, The City College, New York, 1951, p. 32.

interviewed in Britain and America, from whom this information was secured only two had manual occupations at the time of their entry into Dianetics, and most when queried commented on the predominantly middle-class composition of the movement. Over half of them had prior involvement in marginal religious, philosophical or therapeutic practices, Rosicrucianism, Theosophy, Christian Science, Baha'i, General Semantics, Krishnamurti, hypnosis, or Jungian analysis.[1] A number of others had experience of more orthodox psychotherapies.

It is possible to gain a fuller picture of the backgrounds and motivations of those who entered Dianetics from the interview material, and biographical sketches or other details in Dianetic newsletters and other publications.

One mode of entry into Dianetics seems to have been through a process of 'drift', in which individuals in search of answers to the problem of meaning passed through a variety of metaphysical groups or marginal healing movements before locating an answer, at least temporarily, in Dianetics. An example of this pattern is provided in a biographical sketch by a New Zealand Dianeticist. Presenting his concern as a question of 'what made people tick?', he read widely in religion and psychology for the answer. Religion and medicine seemed too limited in what they could offer, or insufficiently practical. Even psychology

> . . . while having exciting possibilities, seemed very narrow in viewpoint with a lot of varying theory but very little to offer which had practical application. There was little here which one could use confidently, knowing that it would lead to improvement for the other individual or oneself.[2]

He at first planned to be a minister, until the Depression forced him into other work,

> but my interest in healing, religion and psychology continued unabated. There were not many orthodox or unorthodox methods of healing which did not attract my attention, nor indeed, were there many religions which I did not investigate.
> At the age of seventeen I became very interested in mysticism. Aldous Huxley and Evelyn Underhill became my mentors and the Hindu, Buddhist and Taoist Scriptures, along with the Christian Mystics, my text books.
> Reluctantly I dropped all idea of psychology delivering an answer . . . Psychology was no longer concerned with the psyche or soul of man, it was dealing with trivialities.
> Shortly after this period I became interested in Ouspensky and Gurdjieff, men who had much to contribute, much to offer by way of original thought and knowledge.
> I was excited too by an Australian, F. M. Alexander. Here, at last, was someone who had derived knowledge from direct observation of man. Here was someone who had very practical advice backed up by solid theory and practice. . . .[3]

[1] Possibly by asking the wrong question, the *Dianotes* readership survey may have underestimated the degree of prior marginal religious, healing or occult involvement of the sample.

[2] Marcus Tooley, *People are Human* (Graham Ltd, Aukland, N.Z., 1955). This and the following quotations are taken from pages 1–7.

[3] Ibid.

He later came into contact with a healer expelled from the BMA for his unorthodox methods, at that time practising dietary and faith healing in New
Zealand, and another man who proved adept at hand reading:

> I was amazed at the accurate character analysis and physical diagnosis which he
> gave. I had not imagined that anyone could be so accurate in depicting my various
> idiosyncracies, emotional traits and medical history! Furthermore he was able to tell
> me of various things which had happened to affect my life and the age when these
> had occurred. Here was knowledge which had wide possibilities and it was not long
> before I was reading books by . . . psychologists and medical authorities . . . and
> others who were experts in this study.[1]

He began practising a form of therapy based on hand-reading, getting his clients
to talk about painful incidents which he located in their hands. He found that
after talking them out, and often re-experiencing much of them, their condition
generally improved. In 1952 he read *MSMH* and found there a statement of all
his earlier beliefs and suspicions about the mind, and workable techniques for
therapeutic success.

This typical 'seeker' pattern is also apparent in the origins of one Dianetics-
Scientology newsletter:

> The Ghost was started as a personal letter from Clem and Lois Johnson to their
> friends in Dianetics, Scientology, Huna, Spiritualism and other occult fields
> including herbs and medicine.
>
> [The] editor has taken 'yogi', Spiritualism and Huna in his stride toward the
> TRUTH, accepting them all as so much data, and rejecting them as more data was
> received.[2]

This seeker pattern is exhibited in the descriptions of their development given
by two other Dianeticists, later to achieve prominence as heretics of Scientology:

> In high school my primary interest lay in the sciences. I followed through with this
> interest in college and then worked for a time in physics. During this time and after,
> I searched fervently through many religions, not only all the major ones, but a
> goodly number of esoteric cults that are so numerous in Southern California. In
> addition to that, I practised various forms of exercises, and invested numerous hours
> in the meditations of sundry groups. Though I could demonstrate ability in music
> and art, I ultimately abandoned the serious pursuit of these fields, for I found no
> final answers to Life in them.[3]

---

[1] Ibid.

[2] *The Ghost of Scientology*, 9 (1 March 1953), p. 7. Clem Johnson elsewhere indicated
that he also belonged to, or had passed through: the British Society of Dowsers, the
Borderland Science Research Association ('all borderland sciences including spiritu-
alism and the riddle of the flying discs'), Institute of Mentalphysics ('Edwin C.
Dingle's school of "metaphysics" or Yoga'), and the Brotherhood of the White Temple.
Ghost of Scientology, 11 (15 June 1953), p. 4.

[3] Charles Berner, 'Preface: a self-introduction and some acknowledgements' in H.
Charles Berner and Richard Williams, *Abilitism: a New Religion* (Adams Press,
Chicago, 1970), p. 3.

Thruout [sic] these many years, I had merely gone thru [sic] the motions of being an engineer. It was with difficulty that I was able to keep my attention from the constant gnawing feeling within me, that I should be doing something other than what I was doing. Just what I 'should' be doing, I did not know. This became acute, in 1948. For six weeks I suffered a nervous breakdown. Now, I know – I simply was not 'doing my own thing'.

I constantly investigated, sampled every different religion, cult, ism I could find. They all seemed to, in their own flavour, try to explain Spirituality in terms of agreements upon solids. They took a partial truth, centred upon it, created a limited, local frame of reference, represented it to be total and ultimate truth.

[. . .]

It is an understatement to say that I was merely lonely. I beheld the specter of other so-called 'truth-seekers', who so ardently sought some solid, infinite system of truths which would overwhelm them – and would precisely fit the present hangups which owned them. I wondered if I were such.

Psychology was of no interest to me, as it posited that man was nothing more than a complex meat mechanism. It seemed to me that most psychiatrists should be in the patient's chair, rather than acting as therapist.

[. . .]

In July, 1950, my dentist casually remarked that a friend of his, another dentist, was experimenting with a new fad, called Dianetics. As I left the chair, I felt the imperative urge to get the book. I drove seven miles out of my way, to the nearest book store, bought it. I read it thru [sic].[1]

Shortly after, he began co-auditing with a colleague at work.

Others came into the orbit of Dianetics as some member of an amateur psychology or philosophy discussion group with which they were associated drew their attention to this development:

Well, we work away here on Dianetics. . . . Dianetics seems quite the best thing yet . . . although Jung's Analytical Psychology did give us more vivid inspiration.[2]
The original Houston Dianetics Society grew directly out of the local General Semantics Society . . .[3]

The search for therapeutic efficacy was a prominent source of motivation for many Dianeticists. Although none of my interviewees claimed any physical illness at the time of their entry, at least six were suffering from severe illnesses which they recognized to have a primarily mental or emotional origin. A number sought a means of curing others, usually other members of their own family, of conditions as diverse as cancer, schizophrenia or agoraphobia. For example:

My attention was called to a newspaper ad. in San Francisco, I think it was around 1951. There was a big ad. in the paper about Dianetics and about L. Ron Hubbard,

[1] Frank S. Sullivan, *Adventures in Reincarnation* (CSA Press, Clayton, Georgia, 1971), pp. 17–19.
[2] Letter from the Australian Psychology Center, *Dianotes*, 1, 9–10 (March–April 1952), p. 8.
[3] Correspondent, *The Aberree*, 2, 4 (July–August, 1955).

who was going to lecture in Oakland. I happened to have at the time a big problem with my son who had been hospitalised . . . He was out of the army several years and he was not getting any better. So when I saw this ad. I got very interested and I thought, well this might be helpful . . . I decided to go in for it, and I went to hear L. Ron Hubbard lecture.[1]

The case of Don Purcell who financed the transition to Wichita is typical of many who were experiencing diffuse psychosomatic illness or a sense of lowered efficiency:

In 1948 I was in pretty sad shape, My energy level was so low that I was unable to do more than half a day's work and the work I did do was pretty ineffective. My condition became so serious that I finally went to a Doctor friend of mine, a Fellow of the Mayo Clinic. He gave me a thorough examination and suggested that I see a psychiatrist. This I did.
The final prescription of the psychiatrist was a long rest at the hospital with insulin shock treatment. This may give you some idea of my general condition at that time. However, for some obscure reason, I decided to decline the prescription of the psychiatrist and to go on a good fishing vacation instead. When I returned I felt quite a bit improved.
About this time my father and I, who had been in partnership for many years, decided to dissolve our partnership. As soon as the partnership was dissolved I began to improve remarkably. Within a couple of months I was putting in a full day, although I still experienced quite a bit of nervous and physical upsetment.
In May 1950 I read about dianetics and immediately went to Elizabeth to learn more about it. I had high hopes of becoming a 'clear' in a couple of months or so. I knew, somehow, that within the framework of dianetics was the thing I wanted. . . .[2]

A similar story is told by a correspondent to a Dianetics magazine:

Having been always very emotional and nervous, there were so many 'buttons' in my environment that I was constantly bothered by strange feelings in my stomach, my heart action was irregular and my throat was irritated or there was a choking sensation. Even after years of metaphysical studies and various courses in psychology, mental healing, etc. those conditions persisted. After my first session with her [a Dianetic auditor] I began to feel happier, and more free of all those disturbing things.
During April and May I had read *Dianetics: The Modern Science of Mental Health* and *Science of Survival*, and had gone over the handbook twice, just reading it and doing a few locks on my own. The auditor took me through birth and even through my 'Service Facsimile'. Many crises in my life were recognised for what they were worth and I have not had any of the old emotional reactions since.[3]

A large number of Dianeticists, although it is impossible to say what proportion they comprised, had a strong sense of capacities latent within them

[1] Interview: American Dianeticist.
[2] Don G. Purcell, 'Starting Point', *Dianetics Today*, 3, 9 (September 1954), n.p.
[3] *Dianetic Auditor's Bulletin*, 3, 3 (September 1952), p. 250.

which could be brought to the surface if only a method could be found. John W. Campbell, for example, had argued in 1937 that we are only using a quarter of our brain capacity.

> The total capacity of the mind, even at present is to all intents and purposes, infinite. Could the full equipment be hooked into a functioning unit, the resulting intelligence should be able to conquer a world without much difficulty.[1]

It was not for a further twelve years that he was to be offered by Hubbard a convincing means of achieving this end. From my interviews, it is clear, however, that this was a goal widely, if vaguely, aspired to:

> It had always been, for many years, a feeling of mine that one – specifically myself and by inference other human beings – don't perform with 100% efficiency, either mentally or physically, but mentally particularly. Hubbard's thesis of the 'held-down seven' and so on seemed to be a rational and satisfying explanation, and from that, the immediate urge was to try and do something about it.[2]

> We were basically a group of musicians, one was a writer, another a painter. . . . [What was it that attracted you to something of this kind?] I had been looking for something that gave a step by step . . . a methodology that was workable, that you could use to help yourself or somebody else . . . I used to put it in terms of: Why is one person more creative than another . . . what was the creative drive, what was the difference and how could you bring it out in each one? How could you increase it? I guess all of us had pretty well read the Kansas City Library dry, and found nothing in the scientific, psychological, the mystical, or the religious. Nothing seemed to 'click'. There's a lot of methodologies, and 'we've got the answers', but nothing 'clicked' and this sort of clicked with all of us. It was something we could all do to each other.[3]

Or, as in this case, a sense of faculties not fully utilized combined with a general sense of purposelessness and meaninglessness:

> In 1947 I was really at very loose ends. You see, I have a very high IQ and I knew it. I'd had my IQ tested by the Veterans Administration when I came back from overseas. My first question to the psychometrist was: What the hell good is it? I'm miserable, I don't know what to do with it. What do you do with a gift like this, it's never done any good for me? I was very near suicide at the time, because I couldn't make head or tail out of what's the use . . . what's life all about? I didn't have any particular mental problem which even today I recognise. It was just: why am I here, where am I going, what's it all about, and why am I singled out for a high IQ and what the hell good is it? But that was incidental really, because I said, well, if you have a high IQ you ought to be able to figure this out in nothing flat. All the answers ought to come to you, but they don't. . . . I was seriously considering

[1] John W. Campbell, 'The story behind the story', *Thrilling Wonder Stories* (August 1937) as cited in Aldiss, op. cit., p. 241.
[2] Interview: British Dianeticist.
[3] Interview: American Dianeticist.

suicide. So along came Dianetics. Everything fell into place, smack! I knew then here is a possibility of getting all these answers.[1]

An English questionnaire respondent indicated that he had hoped Dianetics would prove to be the solution to his 'sense of frustration at not being able fully to use talents I possess'. Others admitted to a deep sense of inferiority or in-security before they heard of Dianetics, which they hoped that it would enable them to overcome.

Colbert's sample of American Dianeticists indicated the following range of personal problems: interpersonal relationships, 15; disturbing subjective states (nervousness, anxiety, irritability, self-consciousness, lack of concentration), 15; intellectual and memory disturbances, 7; vocational adjustment, 3; family relationships, 3; alcoholism, 2; psychosomatic symptoms, 14; lack of drive-energy, 1; sexual adjustment and male–female relationship problems, 5; miscellaneous problems, 4.[2]

These accounts permit a typification of the motivation of Dianetics recruits. The three categories of motivation which can be distinguished are: (1) the problem-solver; (2) the truth-seeker; and (3) the career-oriented. Since the last two types seem to involve fewer Dianetics recruits, than the first, we shall begin with these.

The career-oriented

Dr Joseph Winter is close to being a paradigm case of this type of motivation. As a medical practitioner he was dissatisfied with the inability of medicine to provide solutions to all the problems which his patients presented. He was growing aware of the role of psychological factors in physical illness and hoped to find in Dianetics a set of tools which would enable him more adequately to carry out his therapeutic role. A former clinical psychologist whom I inter-viewed displayed predominantly the same motivation. He had been employing a method of group psychotherapy on a Freudian basis in his hospital work and was profoundly dissatisfied with its efficacy. At a period when psychopharma-cological treatment was only just beginning on any scale, and when the only alternatives to lengthy and only sporadically successful psychotherapy were custodial care and psychosurgery which he regarded as misconceived, Dianetics offered a revolutionary new therapeutic tool.

The truth-seeker

Many individuals were attracted to Dianetics when they came upon it at some point during a life-long search for meaning and truth. During the course of this search they had often examined the literature of popular philosophy and psychology, of religion, metaphysics and occultism. Science fiction, with its panoramic vision of man, time, and the cosmos, also provided many with an insight into the meaning of life and human behaviour. Dianetics, with its

---

[1] Interview: American Dianeticist.

[2] Colbert, op. cit., p. 100. Subjects indicated more than one problem each.

assertive claims to infallibility offered to answer many of the questions which puzzled such individuals, albeit in a rather mechanistic manner; and moreover offered a practical and easily operationalized technique to put into effect the truths which it had uncovered.

The motivation of many was, it should be stressed, multi-determined. Although the previous two types of motivation appear to have been important for a number of recruits, many, perhaps most, also sought solutions to concrete problems.

The problem-solver

The problem-solver was an individual with a concern for self-improvement based upon an acute awareness of his failure to attain the standards of achievement normatively approved and culturally reinforced in the society around him. While rendered significant by their social meaning, his failures might be either physically, mentally or socially based. His concern might be for *physical improvement* and oriented towards recovery from ill health, overcoming physical disability, or eradicating a stigmatizing physical characteristic. His concern might be for *psychological improvement* of a more or less extensive character. At its most severe the problem would be an acute or chronic mental illness of a disabling psychotic or neurotic kind. Less drastically, it would be an awareness that certain mental attributes were inadequately controlled or ineffective – poor memory, persistent minor guilt or anxiety, unwanted behaviour patterns or habits. His concern might be for *social improvement,* based on failure to achieve personal ambitions or social expectations, or on difficulties in interpersonal relations.

These three classes of disability and hence sources of concern for improvement are likely to coincide in the same individual. A highly typical case was the combination of physical and psychological disability in the form of psychosomatic illness, incapacity which had, or was believed by its sufferer to have, an emotional basis. All three types of disability bear the sociological feature of a recognized failure to achieve expected and normatively valued standards of role performance or status attainment. They involve a disparity between the level of status and competent role-performance to which the individual aspired and that which he had actually achieved, a disparity generally conceptualized in terms of 'relative deprivation'.

The appeal of Dianetics in modern society

Thomas Luckmann and Peter Berger have pointed to general features of advanced industrial societies which would account for this sense of failure and 'relative deprivation'. They have argued that personal identity becomes particularly precarious in urban industrial society.[1] Increased social and

[1] Thomas Luckmann and Peter Berger, 'Social mobility and personal identity', *European Journal of Sociology,* 5 (1964), pp. 331–43.

geographical mobility produce a blurring of the class structure and of criteria for locating the social status of others in interaction, and relative uncertainty concerning one's own status location. The existence of multiple criteria for status ranking gives rise to the possibility of *status inconsistency*. As Luckmann and Berger suggest,

> If status is relatively uncertain and relatively inconsistent, conditions are created that are unfavourable for the consistency and stability of the self.[1]

Rationalization of production shifts emphasis from ascribed to achieved bases of status placement. Individual achievement becomes a major means of status placement, increasing social mobility. Increased mobility in turn creates an *expectation* of mobility, and the inculcation of general mobility aspirations which cannot, however, be realized by all. Standards of adequate achievement are no longer defined by traditional status groups in which most people live out their lives and which establish an horizon on expectations of achievement. Standards are established rather by the status groups in which membership is sought, and since achievement is valued intrinsically, there can be no clear horizon of expectations. There can, therefore, also be no clear criterion of adequate achievement, resulting for many in a persisting sense of failure.[2]

Moreover, increased mobility, the breakdown of established status groups, and the disappearance of cohesive communities in which relationships are personal rather than role-articulated, results in a precariousness of social interaction.[3] In the absence of clear means of identifying others and traditionally established means of conducting social intercourse, social interaction has a fragility and unpredictability which makes any social interaction a potential source of embarrassment and threat to the identity which actors proffer for recognition. Social interaction in anonymous urban industrial societies has to be negotiated without the aid of elaborate formulae of civility and identity markers typical of pre-industrial societies.[4] The skills required for such negotiations are inadequately acquired by a proportion of the population.

In societies with a democratic ethos, stressing the equality of members and a mobility ethos in which:

> Mobility is no longer a means to an end, but becomes an end in itself and thereby a yardstick for other values in the life of the individual[5]

[1] Ibid., p. 335.

[2] Jacob Tuckman and Robert J. Kleiner, 'Discrepancy between aspiration and achievement as a predictor of schizophrenia', *Behavioural Science*, 7 (1962), 443–7 suggest that frustration, caused by a discrepancy between actual and desired group membership, may be a cause of schizophrenia.

[3] For graphic accounts of this 'interpersonal precariousness' see the works of Erving Goffman, particularly his *Presentation of Self in Everyday Life* (Doubleday Anchor, New York, 1959), and *Behaviour in Public Places* (Free Press, New York 1963).

[4] See Erving Goffman, 'Symbols of class status', *BJS*, 2 (1951), p. 295.

[5] Luckmann and Berger, op. cit., p. 340.

THE CULT PHASE: DIANETICS

Failure to achieve the levels of mobility, wealth, or even sexual access aspired to, are defined as failures *of the individual* rather than a consequence of socially structured constraints on opportunity, or of an unrealistic ideology in the light of opportunities available.

Luckmann and Berger suggest two broad patterns of adaptation to such failure – withdrawal and mobility Machiavellianism.[1] At their most extreme, these patterns may be represented by withdrawal into psychosis and isolation, and Machiavellianism of a kind in which any means to mobility are construed as appropriate, for example, crime. Less extreme forms of adaptation would be, for example, legitimating failure through movement into the sick-role, or seeking additional or superior means of securing mobility. The latter might include securing further educational qualifications which lacked any intrinsic interest to the individual, simply as a means of 'getting ahead'; seeking training in the presentation of self through Dale Carnegie courses or books on 'how to win friends and influence people', or seeking esoteric means of securing mobility through the acquisition of hidden knowledge.

Dianetics was presented as a means of improving the individual's chances of status mobility, a means of achieving normatively established levels of aspiration. It offered a rationale for failure in social mobility and in social interaction. It provided an explanation in terms of traumatic incidents in which the individual had been unwittingly involved, and thereby relieved him of responsibility for his failure. All the past mistakes, failures and sources of guilt could be wiped out.[2] Most important, it offered a means of eradicating the persisting causes of his failure, and thus of attaining the level of achievement to which he aspired. The theory of Dianetics assured its follower that his 'true self', his conception of what he believed he was really capable of achieving, was indeed as he conceived it. It reaffirmed this idealization of self and promised a means of eliminating the barriers to its fulfilment, of eradicating the gap between his 'true self' and the identity that was typically confirmed in social interaction. Moreover, Dianetics provided a means of understanding not only oneself, but also others, a way of categorizing and accounting for their behaviour, and a guide to appropriate responses.[3]

The further question remains, however, of why Dianetics was seen as an

---

[1] Ibid., p. 341.

[2] Helen O'Brien, a prominent early Dianeticist suggests:

'The tremendous appeal of dianetics came from Hubbard's apparent certainty that you could easily clear yourself in present time of the heritage of woe from past misadventures.'

Helen O'Brien, *Dianetics in Limbo* (Whitmore Publishing Co, Philadelphia, 1966), p. 72.

[3] Dianetics literature and the letters and recollections of Dianeticists are full of commentary on others in terms of Hubbard's 'tone scale'. Locating them on the tone scale provided a way to account for their behaviour, explaining its occurrence, and providing prescriptions for reaction to it.

acceptable and legitimate solution to the problems with which recruits were faced. The answer to this question would seem to be that they had either tried alternative systems of belief and practice and found them unsuccessful, or they had rejected such alternative systems as inappropriate to their situation.

Many of those interviewed claimed an acquaintance with the literature of psychology, and expressed dissatisfaction with it. Psychology as far as they could see in the 1940s was split between behaviourism and psychoanalysis. Behaviourist psychology seemed to have little or no relevance to man in general and no solution to their problems in particular. Psychoanalysis, while addressing many of the problems which they faced and offering solutions to them, had two major drawbacks. Firstly, analysis seemed an inordinately lengthy process, often lasting several years. Secondly, it was too expensive for most to consider it as a practical proposition.

Those who were suffering physical ills or disabilities had generally tried medical means of overcoming them, but found little satisfaction from medical professionals, few of whom recognized the essentially psychological or social basis of many of the complaints presented to them. Ill-equipped through lack of training to cope with the needs of such patients, they resorted to pharmacological or surgical treatments which, while successful in some cases, left others feeling the need for a treatment practice which took greater account of man as a whole. Others, suffering chronic illnesses for which medical treatment had proved unsuccessful or from illnesses for which effective therapeutic interventions had not yet been discovered, had exhausted all the resources that orthodox medicine could offer. In the case of those suffering both physical and mental problems, the individuals concerned had generally sought solutions in a variety of other therapeutic practices before they came in contact with Dianetics.

Bureaucratization and the scale of modern urban society produce a context in which many individuals experience a lack of control over their destiny and environment, a sense of being moved and constrained by forces beyond their control. Many of those who did not conceptualize their situation in medical or psychological terms experienced the world in which they lived as more or less unpredictable, chaotic, or meaningless. They sought some means of greater control over their environments and their reactions to it. Related to this, a small proportion were engaged in therapeutic work of a limited or marginal kind, and saw considerable limitations in the tools they had available. A further small proportion claimed a simple intellectual curiosity, which had earlier led them to other systems of self-improvement, metaphysics or occult knowledge.

While science held great promise, having delivered technological 'cargo', and having proved a powerful tool in the improvement of material conditions, it had done little to solve perennial and increasing problems of psychological well-being, to provide cures for certain forms of illness, or to equip man better to cope with his social environment. Dianetics followers tended to conceptualize appropriate solutions to such problems as being 'scientific' in form. Their conception of science was, however, a lay conception (albeit a lay conception which has from time to time been offered as an academic account in the form of Pragmatism). It was technological and instrumental in form. What constituted a science was a body of knowledge which appeared to explain some set of phenomena in a rational and consistent way and which provided a means of intervening in the processes involved so as to achieve successful or desired outcomes. Their test of standing of any body of knowledge was: does it work? That is, do interventions of the prescribed form issue in desired outcomes? When, after a Dianetic session, they felt better than before, they concluded that it worked.[1]

They tended to expect that new and important scientific developments would appear through media or institutions marginal to the scientific community. Their conception of this community was one of an élitist group with vested interests in the promotion of particular theories and practices, unwilling to accommodate new ideas or even to give them a fair hearing. Hence the innovator would generally need to find a more marginal institutional base in order to get his revolutionary new thoughts heard.

Dianeticists appear to have held a belief in the *immanence of knowledge* – that it was freely available and anyone who applied himself might expect to secure radically new or deeper insights into the nature of the world. They also held a belief in the *élitism of science*[2] – that scientists had arrived at their own views to which they were unwilling to permit any radical challenge. Since orthodox science was so conservative on this account, the intellectually curious might seek truth in less orthodox realms – metaphysical or occult groups, marginal healing, philosophical or psychological movements, or science fiction. Science fiction provided all that science lacked, filling in the lacunae of scientific knowledge or competence with fictional or speculative detail, and blurring the distinction between the empirical and the desirable.[3] Converts to Dianetics were mobilized to accept an unorthodox system of belief and practice by the urgency of their need, which orthodox systems had been unable to meet, or by a conviction that radical developments in knowledge were to be anticipated outside the domain of the institutions of orthodoxy, which lacked the vision to generate them.

John W. Campbell was an influential figure in the science-fiction world and neighbouring regions of the cultic milieu. His readership saw him as a man of vision, willing to give any idea a hearing. When Campbell gave his support to

[1] For a fuller treatment of this conflation of science and technology in popular culture, see Oscar Handlin, 'Science and technology in popular culture' in Gerald Holton, ed., *Science and Culture* (Beacon, Boston, 1967), pp. 184–98.

[2] On this point, one of the clear attractions of Dianetics was that anyone could do it. Although esoteric, it did not require lengthy and rigorous training. 'Ordinary' people could do it for each other. See for example, *Life Preserver*, 1, 1 (June 1953).

[3] And of course, the undesirable and horrific. See Kingsley Amis, *New Maps of Hell* (New English Library, London, 1963).

Dianetics, interest was aroused on the basis of his prestige and his enthusiastic acclaim of this new science of the mind. On the publication of Hubbard's Dianetic writings, the idea of 'clear' like that of 'flying saucer' became a kind of Rorschach blot,[1] a vague and amorphous image upon which any individual could impose his aspirations. Being clear, however Hubbard might define it, meant being able to do all those things which one currently could not do, and to which one aspired so desperately.[2]

The self-improvement and healing cults

Dianetics has a place in a continuing tradition of self-improvement movements in the recent history of the United States. Enormously accelerated social mobility and an ideology of individual achievement led to the emergence of a concern for infallible techniques that would ensure success for the mobility-oriented. This was a particularly pressing concern for those who had failed in, or failed to gain access to, the major channels of mobility in modern industrial societies, the institutions of higher education. The late nineteenth and early twentieth centuries saw the appearance of various movements and organizations which offered access to advanced, occult, metaphysical, or otherwise esoteric knowledge, and some which, more cynically, merely offered certification that access to such knowledge or training had been obtained. The 'diploma-mill' became an established, if derogated, institution. Movements such as New Thought suggested that prosperity and success were available to everyone. The use of a few simple techniques would enable anyone to overcome the limitations which he believed held him back.[3]

Dianetics also found a place in the continuing tradition of healing movements in the United States. Indeed, the two traditions overlapped to a very high degree, movements within this domain offering both healing and self-improvement, and certifying 'professional' competence in the practices purveyed.[4] The development of science, particularly medical science, during the nineteenth century, led, it has been argued, to increased expectations regarding physical health and comfort. These expectations were in excess of what medicine could actually achieve.

[1] See H. Taylor Buckner, 'The flying saucerians a lingering cult', *New Society* (9 September 1965).

[2] For a sensitive and illuminating appraisal of the relationship between Dianetics and Scientology and occultism, psychoanalysis, science, pseudo-science, etc., see Harriet Whitehead, 'Reasonably fantastic: some perspectives on Scientology, science fiction and occultism' in Irving I. Zaretsky and Mark Leone, *Religious Movements in Contemporary America* (Princeton University Press, Princeton, 1974).

[3] A. W. Griswold, 'New Thought: a cult of success', *AJS*, 40, 3 (1934), pp. 308–18.

[4] For an account of a number of such 'diploma-mills', healing and 'psychological' practices, see Lee R. Steiner, *Where Do People Take Their Troubles?* (Houghton Mifflin, Boston, 1945).

The great breakthroughs in medical research by Lister, Pasteur and many others had created a new level of expectation that medicine could defeat man's age-old enemies of pain and disease. New accomplishments in engineering, agriculture and public sanitation brought the hope of a healthier, more comfortable life to the lowest citizen. But it was a long time after many of these advances became theoretically possible that they were actually realised for the average person . . .[1]

From about 1860 to at least 1900, in the experience of all but the wealthiest classes, there was a very real gap between the ultimate promise and the actual performance in medicine and public health measures. The medieval resignation to disease and pain was gone, but the modern means of accomplishing general health and well-being for the whole population were not yet fully mobilized.[2]

The new healing movements such as Christian Science and New Thought offered means of overcoming this gap between expectation and performance in the realm of physical healing. While medicine became increasingly specialized and compartmentalized and allopathic medicine directed attention to the disease rather than the individual, leading to a depersonalization of the practitioner–client relationship, the new healing movements retained a personal orientation, a concern for the 'whole man'.[3] Hence it has been argued that the role of the practitioner in such movements is closer to that of the psychotherapist than of the medical practitioner.[4] The thereapeutic success claimed by such movements is generally attributed to mistaken diagnosis,[5] the 'placebo effect',[6] spontaneous remission, and the mobilization of the patient's expectation of healing.[7] This expectation can be heightened and directed by the therapist in subtle, and often unconscious ways, particularly if his own belief in the efficacy of the practice is strongly held. The 'non-directive' or 'evocative' therapies employed afford a strong temptation to the therapist

> to induce the patient to express material that confirms his theories, because he can regard it as independent evidence for them; and the patient is induced to accept the therapist's formulations because he believes them to be his own.[8]

The therapist's very determination not to direct his patients may itself create

> an ambiguous situation that may increase the patient's suggestibility, and also arouse his anxiety and resentment, which . . . may act as an incentive to change.[9]

[1] John A. Lee, *Sectarian Healers and Hypnotherapy* (Queen's Printer, Toronto, 1970), p. 7.
[2] Ibid.
[3] Ibid., p. 5.
[4] R. W. England, 'Some aspects of Christian Science as reflected in letters of testimony', *AJS*, 59, 5 (1954), pp. 448–53.
[5] Ibid.
[6] E. Th. Cassee, 'Deviant illness behaviour: patients of mesmerists', *Social Science and Medicine*, 3 (1970), pp. 389–96.
[7] Jerome D. Frank, *Persuasion and Healing* (Johns Hopkins Press, Baltimore, 1961).
[8] Ibid., p. 168.
[9] Ibid.

Even in the absence of conscious or unconscious 'coaching', the patient generally arrives for therapy with a fairly clear idea of the performance that he will be expected to produce. From material he has read, stories he has heard, or from generally available cultural stereotypes, he will construct an anticipatory image of the appropriate performance. In the case of Dianetics, reports of the practice were so widely published in newspapers and magazines that few pre-clears can have presented themselves for auditing without some knowledge of what experiences, were the session successful, they would undergo.

As, through the early twentieth century, medical practice became more competent to deal with physical illness, expectations of health and well-being became increasingly centred on the psychological domain and the difficulties of interpersonal relations. Movements like Christian Science and New Thought which had claimed efficacy in handling physical illness lost ground, while others arose offering psychological well-being; release of mental and emotional tensions; cures for psychosomatic and neurotic illness; techniques for releasing hidden inner abilities; and means of 'making friends and influencing people'.[1] In such areas science has yet achieved little concrete progress, and the market remains open to cultic groups offering knowledge and techniques produced by more mystical, occult, or pseudo-scientific means. Whatever the source of such knowledge the prestige of science has become such as to require that almost every new movement entering this field claim scientific legitimacy and authority,[2] if by no other means than that of incorporating 'science' in its title.[3]

Societal reaction and social involvement

While the response of the book-buying public rapidly placed *MSMH* in the best-seller lists,[4] it was not everywhere received with enthusiasm. Reviews by psychologists and psychiatrists were almost uniformly unfavourable. Rollo May objected to Hubbard's oversimplified monocausal determinism and regarded his grandiose promises as potentially harmful to mentally and emotionally troubled people.[5] Others objected to his repeated claims 'of exactitude and of scientific experimental approach, for which every trace of evidence is lacking',

[1] Among others, Pelmanism, Transcendental Meditation, and Encounter Groups.

[2] As Robert Merton has observed, 'Partly as a result of scientific achievements . . . the population at large becomes susceptible to new mysticisms expressed in apparently scientific terms. The borrowed authority of science bestows prestige on the unscientific doctrine.' Robert K. Merton, *Social Theory and Social Structure* (Free Press, New York, 1957), p. 560.

[3] Science of Mind, Christian Science, the Science of Creative Intelligence, *Dianetics: the Modern Science of Mental Health*.

[4] According to its publisher and others: interviews.

[5] Rollo May, 'How to back-track and get ahead', *New York Times Book Review*, 2 July 1950.

and suggested that patients might waste time in Dianetic therapy before seeing a doctor, time that might in severe cases prove fatal.[1]

More sympathetic reviewers suggested that Dianetics was harmless enough and might possibly even be of help to socially isolated individuals:

> The close relationship between the two people who 'audit' each other can become a bridge from the isolated person to the outside world. The person gets encouragement from another, no matter what kind, and thus achieves a feeling of connectedness with other people, and consequently succeeds where he has previously failed.[2]

The benefits of a sympathetic listener while the pre-clear ventilated his problems were recognized by some reviewers who nevertheless remained concerned at the effects this might have, in untrained hands, in the case of severe mental disorder.[3] Although some of these reviews may have attracted people to Dianetics, it was the view of some Dianeticists that the reviews in the larger circulation periodicals and newspapers were generally so unfavourable that they had led many to fall away.[4]

Apart from numerous marginal, limited and quasi-medical converts, Dianetics was received coldly by the medical, psychiatric and psychological professions. Dr Gregory Zilboorg publicly attacked Dianetics before a forum at the New York Academy of Medicine,[5] and the American Psychological Association was widely reported for its resolution calling on psychologists not to employ Dianetic techniques in therapy:

> While suspending judgement concerning the eventual validity of the claims made by the author of 'Dianetics', the association calls attention to the fact that these claims are not supported by the empirical evidence of the sort required for the establishment of scientific generalisations. In the public interest, the association, in the absence of such evidence, recommends to its members that the use of the techniques peculiar to Dianetics be limited to scientific investigations to test the validity of its claims.[6]

Attempts were subsequently made to carry out such scientific investigations. In a laboratory test, a Dianetic pre-clear was rendered unconscious by the administration of sodium pentathol, and a passage read to the pre-clear from a physics text, during which pain was inflicted, at the suggestion of the representative of the Dianetic Research Foundation, Los Angeles. Six months of auditing by a trained auditor failed to recover any part of the passage read.[7]

[1] Martin Gumpert, 'The dianetics craze', New Republic, 132 (14 August 1950), pp. 20–1.

[2] Willard Beecher and Calder Willingham, 'Boiled engrams' American Mercury 73 (August 1951), p. 80.

[3] Anonymous, 'Dianetics', Consumer Reports (August 1951), pp. 378–80.

[4] Dianotes, 1, 5 (December 1951).

[5] 'Dr Zilboorg attacks dianetics', New York Times, 101, 30 March 1951, p. 15.

[6] 'Psychologists act against Dianetics', New York Times, 9 September 1950, p. 7.

[7] Jack Fox, Alvin E. Davis and B. Lebovits, 'An experimental investigation of

An earlier study by Harvey Jay Fischer had attempted to test the claims made for Dianetic therapy in terms of improved mental functioning and mathematical ability, and lessened personality conflict.[1]

Securing a sample of applicants to a Dianetic centre in an American city, he divided them into three groups, controlling for educational status and age. Standardized psychological tests were administered before and after a sixty-day period, alternate forms of the tests being used. The first group received two sessions of auditing each week for one hour each session. The second group received two sessions of auditing each week for two hours each session. The third group received no auditing. The three groups therefore received respectively eighteen, thirty-six and zero hours of auditing during the experimental period at the Dianetic centre.

From an analysis of the test results, Fischer concluded:

> For the population of disturbed persons who applied for dianetic therapy, and who were between the ages of 22 and 47 years, and who had at least some high school education, regardless of the sex of these persons, it was concluded that:
>
> 1.   dianetic therapy does not exert a systematic influence either favourably or adversely upon intellectual functioning;
> 2.   dianetic therapy does not exert a systematic influence either favourably or adversely upon mathematical ability; and
> 3.   dianetic therapy does not exert a systematic influence either favourably or adversely upon the degree of personality conflicts.[2]

John Colbert conducted a study which attempted to determine the effect of Dianetic therapy on the basis of tests administered before and after a course of auditing, although he did not utilize a control group.[3]

In a pilot study, Colbert claims that 'the people who applied for dianetic therapy were found to be above average in intelligence, education and income'.[4] To an 'unselected' sample of 24 applicants for Dianetic auditing at the New York City and Elizabeth, New Jersey Hubbard Dianetic Research Foundations, Colbert administered Rorschach, IQ and other tests, and a questionnaire. Colbert found no significant changes in IQ before and after auditing.[5] Clinically, on the basis of the Rorschach data, Colbert's findings were that 'fifteen individuals were believed to have undergone changes that tended in the

[1] The derivation of Fischer's hypothesis that Dianetic therapy reduced personality conflict, is obscure.

[2] Harvey Jay Fischer, 'Dianetic Therapy: an Experimental Evaluation', Unpublished PhD dissertation, School of Education, New York University, 1953, p. 42.

[3] John Colbert, 'An Evaluation of Dianetic Therapy', Thesis for the degree of Master of Science in Education, School of Education, The City College, New York, 1951.

[4] Ibid., p. 15. Unfortunately no adequate details of this pilot study are supplied.

[5] Ibid., p. 104.

Hubbard's engram hypothesis (dianetics)', *Psychological Newsletter*, 10 (1959), pp. 131–4.

negative direction, but these changes were in all but one case not unequivocally negative'. Six individuals were believed to have undergone no change, while the overall pattern of change in the remainder was in doubt.[1] The Rorschach pattern displayed by the group lent itself in his view 'to a description of the group in terms of its prominent hysteroid and infantile-suggestible features'.[2] (Various tests produced under the auspices of Dianetic and Scientology organizations, however, show considerable improvements as a result of Dianetic auditing. See, for example, the test results included in *Science of Survival*.)

Winter, as medical director of the first Foundation, attempted to interest his colleagues in Dianetics, but with little success. A meeting was arranged in Washington DC, at which Hubbard lectured to a group of 'psychiatrists, educators and lay people'. Winter comments on this meeting:

> I did not feel that the Washington venture was a successful one – at least, not from the medical point of view. It was noteworthy that most of the people whose interest in dianetics had been augmented by this presentation were members of the laity, rather than the profession, and I thought that I could detect in their attitudes the fervor of the convert, rather than the cool, objective interest of the scientist. The professional people evidenced an interest in the philosophy of dianetics; their interest was repelled, however, by the manner of presentation of the subject, especially the unwarranted implication that it was necessary to repudiate one's previous beliefs before accepting dianetics.[3]

Dr Morris Fishbein, a spokesman for the American Medical Association, was widely reported for his castigation of Dianetics as yet another 'mind-healing cult'.[4]

Some sectors of the medical profession clearly took the view that there was a need for more active steps to be taken to deal with what was seen by some doctors as a form of quackery. In January 1951, it was reported in a *Bulletin* of the Elizabeth Foundation that:

> Because no teaching license was ever procured for New Jersey despite reports that it had been in June, Elizabeth is under suit from the State for teaching without a license.[5]

The New Jersey Board of Medical Examiners[6] had initiated an injunction against the Elizabeth Foundation, later vacated, for conducting a school of medicine without a license. It was almost certainly as a result of the publicity given to this action that creditors of the Foundation began to demand settlement, leading to reorganization and centralization of the Foundation at Wichita.

[1] Ibid., p. 96.
[2] Ibid., p. 56.
[3] Winter, op. cit., pp. 29–30.
[4] See 'Poor Man's Psychoanalysis', *Newsweek* (16 October 1950), pp. 58–9.
[5] *Bulletin* (21 January 1951). See also *The Dianamic*, HDRF, Elizabeth NJ, 13 (8 February 1951), p. 3.
[6] Interviews; George Malko, *Scientology: the Now Religion* (Dell, N.Y. 1970), p. 58; Morris Fishbein, 'Editorial', *Medical World News* (7 January 1972), p. 68.

Possibly as a result of this response from the established therapeutic professions, Hubbard has since demonstrated a marked antagonism to medical practitioners, and to psychiatrists in particular. Hubbard brushed aside all criticism, attributing it to the ignorance of the critic and his vested interests in the income from and the prestige of practices threatened by Dianetics; his engramic condition;[1] and to professional incompetence:

> There is a direct ratio between the brilliance of a mind and its ability to understand and work dianetics – we have proven that continually; a person highly successful, for instance, in the field of psychoanalysis can be counted upon to grasp dianetics quickly – the second rater, whose practice is unsuccessful, whose security is already small, may have difficulty in understanding dianetics and even be savage about it.[2]

The social involvement of Dianetics was severely limited by its individualistic character and its monocausal theory. Dianetics was oriented to the alleviation of social and economic ills by individual improvement rather than social or political change. The root of man's social, economic and political misfortunes was held to lie in the formation of engrams which led individuals – politicians in particular – to acts that were detrimental to the survival of the individual and society. Erase the engrams, and social and political ills and injustices would disappear.

However, until everyone was able to experience the benefits of Dianetic processing, it might be necessary for an élite of clears to guide the destiny of the world. Hubbard foresaw the emergence of 'an aristocracy of the mind' from those who had the understanding required to accept Dianetics and undergo clearing:

> There will be many of these. But they will have to carry, on their own energy, so to speak, those they wish to benefit. Below this will be the persons whose insanity or criminality has made them a menace to society and who will be given a *release* in dianetics at state cost and those persons who have money enough to buy a release. . . . On a lower strata [sic] there will be those who, for various reasons, do not undertake clearing and for whom no clearing is done. A wide gulf is thereby established. On the adage that them as has gits [sic], one sees with some sadness that more than three quarters of the world's population will become subject to the remaining quarter as a natural consequence and about which we can do exactly nothing. The saving part of this is that the good will of the upper quarter will inhibit their exploitation of the less fortunate.[3]

One area of social concern was of immediate importance to Hubbard. Like many others in post-war America, Hubbard was exercised by the threat of

---

[1] L. Ron Hubbard, 'Homo Superior, here we come!' *Marvel Science Stories*, 3, 3 (May 1951), p. 112.

[2] L. Ron Hubbard, letter in 'Brass Tacks', *Astounding Science Fiction* 45, 6 (August 1950), p. 155.

[3] Ibid.

communism and, as its concomitant, the threat of nuclear war. While his Allied Scientists of the World scheme was in some measure a fund-raising device, like many later, similar schemes, it was consistent with, and probably partly motivated by, other principles which guided his behaviour.

Allied Scientists of the World was based on a plan to establish an atom-bomb-proof archive for scientific information, collected from all over the world, in Arizona. Hubbard established an office in Denver which he staffed with personnel associated with the Wichita Foundation. Letters were sent to scientists and technicians whose names were secured from mailing lists. The letters informed the recipients that they had been awarded fellowships in the organization in recognition of their scientific achievements, and asked for $25 annual dues. Accompanying literature described the plan to establish a bomb-proof archive, and to band scientists together to protest against the use of atomic energy in future war. Hubbard had planned to approach scientists of little repute first, and then, when he had secured their support, to move on to the more prestigeous. Had any considerable support been generated, he planned to set up an anonymous committee to issue books sponsored by the organization, but in fact written by Hubbard.[1] (In a comment upon the manuscript provided by officials of the Church of Scientology, an American Dianeticist, who is said to have been privy to these events, is reported to have indicated that there was no plan to issue books sponsored by the organization, but written by Hubbard.)

In the event, however, the scheme led to investigation by postal authorities and other State and private agencies; the response from those who received the mailings was negligible; and Allied Scientists of the World was abandoned.

The cultic characteristics of Dianetics

In terms of the types outlined in Chapter I, Dianetics can be unambiguously located as a cult. It was defined as deviant by the mass media and by most established professional bodies and their spokesmen. The movement's following in general conceived it as providing one of many possible paths to the truth or salvation. Dianetics emerged from the 'cultic milieu' of self-improvement and healing cults, science-fiction, and popular psychology. Its beliefs and practices appear to be a synthesis of strands drawn from this milieu and from more orthodox psychological research and psychotherapeutic practice, supplemented and adapted by the researches and insights of its founder.

The movement was loosely organized. Dianetic groups were linked to each other and to the Foundations by largely informal means. Little loyalty was owed to the central organizations, which had few means of enforcing commands. Practitioners and followers were tolerant of other practices or beliefs. Dianetics was seen as one contribution to the sum of esoteric knowledge leading

[1] Interview; see also *Denver Post* 60, 178 (27 January 1952); Letter from Don Purcell, *The Dianews*, 1, 22 (31 May 1952), p. 10.

to salvation, but by no means the only available path, nor a completed and closed revelation. Followers eagerly sought to improve and extend the beliefs and practices of Dianetics, drawing eclectically on other traditions and belief systems within the cultic milieu.

The movement's 'epistemological individualism' is displayed in the following statements by the editor of a Dianetic newsletter, and a prominent Dianetic practitioner:

> There is no reason to take what I say as the 'truth', as the 'right way'. Your way is the best for you.[1]

> ... there are many, many roads to a higher state of existence ... no man can say, 'This is the road for all to follow' ...[2]

The movement was non-exclusive. Membership was loose and flexible as was the belief-system. An enthusiasm for, or interest in, Dianetics was the only important criterion of membership for most of the following. While the more sectarian sections of the movement's leadership made efforts to exlude some practitioners and practices, these attempts were resisted by the following, which was prepared to listen to any innovation from no matter what source. Membership changed rapidly as followers lost interest, solved their problems, or found a new enthusiasm.

Finally, Dianetics lacked any clear and unambiguous locus of authority. While Hubbard was recognized and acclaimed as the founder of this science of the mind, the following in general did not agree that this gave him any exclusive right to determine what should or should not constitute acceptable doctrine and practice, or who should or should not be accepted as a member of the Dianetic community. Except for a small minority who were prepared to submit to Hubbard's authority, the Dianetics following recognized no authoritative source of attributions of heresy within the movement. They alone, as individuals, had the right to determine who or what should be accepted.

---

[1] *Dianotes*, 1, 9–10 (March–April 1952).
[2] Jack Horner, 'Jack Horner Speaks', Transcription of a lecture at the New York Dianetic Association, November 1952, The Eidetic Foundation, Alabama, 1952.

3. CRISIS AND TRANSITION

Sources of the crisis

The developments that took place in the ideology and organization of Hubbard's following emerged partly as the resolution of a variety of strains and conflicts in the Dianetics community, which existed between Hubbard and other leaders; between Hubbard's desire for a strong central organization and the amateur groups keen to retain their independence; and between Hubbard and other innovators of theory and practice. They were also, in some measure, a response to external vicissitudes: a hostile environment, and a declining market.

The break between Hubbard and Purcell was the culmination of a series of strains in their relationship and even earlier difficulties with other co-leaders of the movement. Winter, for example, had broken with Hubbard over a number of issues, of which the financial precariousness of the Elizabeth Foundation was only one. Firstly, Winter found

> a difference between the ideals inherent within the dianetic hypothesis and the actions of the Foundation in its ostensible efforts to carry out these ideals. The ideals of dianetics, as I saw them, included non-authoritarianism and a flexibility of approach; they did not exclude the realization that this hypothesis might not be absolutely perfect. The ideals of dianetics continued to be given lip-service, but I could see a definite disparity between ideals and actualities.[1]

He had growing doubts about the possibility of achieving the state of 'clear', and was concerned at the extent to which the effects of Dianetic therapy were simply the results of suggestion. He felt that the effect of the techniques might not always be beneficial to the pre-clear, and that it might sometimes be positively dangerous in the hands of poorly trained auditors without adequate medical knowledge. The increasing disparagement of 'the medical profession and the efforts of previous workers in the field of mental health' disturbed him, as well as the absence of scientific research – for the purpose of which the Foundation had supposedly been established.[2] The research which was being conducted was

[1] Joseph A. Winter, *A Doctor's Report on Dianetics: Theory and Therapy* (Julian Press, New York, 1951), p. 30.

[2] Ibid, p. 40.

directed to 'investigating the possible therapeutic benefits of "recalling" the circumstances of deaths in previous incarnations'[1] and Winter did not regard this as likely to result in acceptance by the medical profession. Finally, he objected to the uncontrolled administration of a vitamin and glutamic acid compound known as 'Guk', as an aid to therapy.[2] His protests concerning these matters met with sharp rebuff 'and I was led to infer that I was acting as a deterrent to the progress of the Foundation'.[3] Winter resigned from the Foundation and established a private psychotherapy practice in Manhattan where he combined Dianetics with psychoanalysis and General Semantics.[4] In due course, Dianetics dropped from his practice.[5]

John W. Campbell in retrospect also criticized the increasing dogmatism and authoritarianism of Hubbard.[6] The relationship between Hubbard and Purcell followed a similar pattern. After a short period of co-operation, Hubbard began to feel that Purcell was constraining his control over the development of Dianetics. Purcell attempted to establish the Foundation on a sound business footing, but Hubbard rapidly began generating new techniques faster than students could be trained in them. More money was being spent than was being earned as experimentation continued with vitamin compounds and later started with electropsychometers.

When Purcell insisted that expenditure be reduced to meet income, Hubbard began initiating independent fund-raising schemes[7] which were a source of embarrassment to other Foundation directors, and a source of further expense.[8] Finally, Hubbard insisted on pursuing the matter of past-lives in spite of the protests of other leaders of the Dianetics movement, including Purcell.[9]

[1] Ibid, p. 189.

[2] On 'Guk', see L. Ron Hubbard, *Science of Survival*, 11, p. 260.

[3] Winter, op. cit., p. 190.

[4] 'Departure in dianetics', *Time*, 58, 10 (3 September 1951), p. 39.

[5] See his later book: Joseph A. Winter, *Are Your Troubles Psychosomatic?* (Messner, New York, 1952).

[6] Letter in *The Arc Light*, 25 (May 1952), pp. 6–8.

[7] Such as the Allied Scientists of the World, discussed in the previous chapter.

[8] Letter of Don Purcell, 19 April 1952 in *The Dianews* 1, 21 (April 1952); Letter of Don Purcell, 21 May 1952 in *The Dianews* 1, 22 (31 May 1952), pp. 9–12; 'Foundation Story', *Dianetics Today*, 3, 1 (January 1954), pp. 1–3; interviews with leaders of the Dianetic movement.

[9] A footnote in *Science of Survival* indicates that past-lives had been an early source of strain:

> 'The subject of past deaths and past lives is so full of tension that as early as last July (1950-ed) the board of trustees of the Foundation sought to pass a resolution banning the entire subject. And I have been many times requested to omit any reference to these in the present work or in public for fear that a general impression would get out that Dianetics had something to do with spiritualism.'

(*Science of Survival* I, footnote, p. 61).

Purcell, like Winter and Campbell before him found Hubbard attempting to secure sole authority:

> Ron's motive has always been to limit Dianetics to the Authority of his teachings. Anyone who has the affrontry [sic] to suggest that others besides Ron could contribute creatively to the work must be inhibited.[1]

In the later bankruptcy action, it was alleged that:

> . . . Hubbard completely dominated the affairs of the corporation and dominated the meetings of the Board of Directors to such an extent that only those matters which he approved were discussed at the Directors' meetings and other matters were not considered. During such periods of time, said Hubbard exercised complete control over the employees of the bankrupt, to the extent that from time to time he countermanded the orders of the other officers and directors and ran the business of the bankrupt according to his own whim and choosing.[2]

By the time this action took place, it was clear to Hubbard that any future organization would have to be based on his sole leadership.

While Hubbard was facing challenges to his authority at the centre of the movement in the Foundations, challenges were also appearing from the grass roots. These took a number of forms.

The dispersed amateur groups which formed the main active body of support for Dianetics exhibited a considerable independence. They tended to view with suspicion attempts to create more than a loose central organization and the possibility of the infringement of their autonomy. The attitude most prominent in the publications was one of independent, democratic individualism. One description of the movement by a Dianeticist represented it as:

> processing of ordinary cases by ordinary people. It means ordinary people getting together for study and practice. It means little groups of dianeticists up and down the country.[3]

While others saw Dianetics as moving towards a professional rather than an amateur basis they retained a preference for a democratic form of organization. When Dianeticists proposed to set up a national organization in Britain, three possible models were envisaged.

1. There might be one central organisation, tending to paternal authoritarianism, with individual auditors relatively unqualified . . .
2. A state of affairs might be reached in which individual members would be sufficiently highly qualified to be able to look after themselves legally, professionally, etc., and so need from the central organisation the minimum of

---

[1] *Dianetics Today*, 3, 1 (January 1954).

[2] *Hubbard Dianetic Foundation Inc. In Bankruptcy No. 379–B–2*, District Court of the United States for the District of Kansas.

[3] *The Dianeticist*, 1 (April 1952), p. 3.

authority compatible with the maintenance of those standards which the individual members would eventually be adopting. Thus Dianetics would be safeguarded from exploitation by any biassed section by ensuring the competence of each individual auditor, so ensuring maximum individual freedom.

3.   Or there might be a central organisation whose functions were so limited that it could not claim the authority to take much responsibility, with individual members and local groups left largely autonomous to feel their own way towards the sort of standards which will eventually become necessary if they are to have safety as well as freedom as dianeticists.[1]

Model one was totally rejected, and while model two was seen as the form of organization towards which Dianetics would eventually move, three was seen as the only viable interim form of organization. The Dianetic Federation of Great Britain followed such a model, with no control over affiliated groups, and little responsibility beyond the circulation of information.

Hostility was frequently expressed in the independent Dianetics literature for 'authorities' of any kind:

> In working with advanced cases we have discovered much that is not in accordance with Hubbard's teachings. For example, Reality. There is only one reality for each of us and we destroy it by accepting the realities of others . . . Dianetics is Hubbard's reality. Christianity is Jesus' reality, Theosophy is Blavatsky's reality, etc. All of these must be given up before a person can go optimum.[2]
>
> In a healthy and growing science, there are many men who are recognised as being competent in the field, and no one man dominates the work [. . . .]
>
> To the extent dianetics is dependent on one man, it is a cult. To the extent it is built by many minds and many workers, it is a science.[3]

As early as mid-1951, at the time of the much publicized divorce case between Hubbard and his second wife, Sara, it was argued that the movement could well proceed without Ron Hubbard:

> . . . Dianetics no longer revolves wholly around Hubbard. He developed it, and gave it to the world – and the world has taken it and gone on from there. Other groups besides the Foundation are carrying on research and processing.
>
> As for the Hubbard affair, we dianeticists do not have to either explain or deny it. Dianetics does not depend on their actions – and if they choose to disqualify themselves as leaders, we now have others.[4]

On the occasion of the split between Hubbard and the Wichita Foundation, a section of the movement took the view that there was no reason to identify Dianetics with Hubbard, and that as . . . .

[1] Letter from Secretary, Dianetics Study Group, to Dianeticists n.d. (probably early 1952).
[2] Letter from Jim Welgos, *The Preclear*, 1, 7 (5 June 1952), p. 12.
[3] Letter from John W. Campbell, *The Arc Light*, 25 (1 May 1952), pp. 6–8.
[4] *Dianews*, 1, 3 (15 April 1951).

Physics is a science independent of Newton; Dianetics is a science independent of Hubbard . . . Hubbard is not the only original thinker in Dianetics – many others are thinking and producing ideas, some, elucidations of Hubbard's ideas, some ideas that Hubbard has never mentioned.[1]

Dianetics would progress, they argued, 'with or without Hubbard'.[2] This attitude of independence and individualism led many practitioners to generate new Dianetic techniques and theoretical rationales. Some felt their innovations to be so far reaching as to have become a completely new practise deserving a separate name and recognition, and set up institutes, schools and foundations of their own to propogate the practice. This diversification was deplored by some Dianeticists:

The dianetic population, though of unknown size, certainly is small compared to the total world population. Even so, there have already appeared many vectors of effort (factions) among this relatively small group. Recriminations, name-calling, denials of other's reality . . . are a part of the scene.

Some of the vectors involved are Kitselman's Institute of Integration, and Automatic Scan Clearing; Altman's Examiner Theory and Techniques; Fisher's Integrator Therapy; Naylor's PCMA techniques; Winter's modification of 'classical' (1950) dianetics, Home Work techniques, Hubbard's 1950 theory and techniques, recent developments in theory and technique now coming from Wichita, and many others; the Hubbard Dianetic Foundation, as a commercial institution . . . HDF as a school; Power's Function Processing; the HDAA–I, a society of professional auditors with their own individually varying attitudes; and all the individuals and groups throughout the country who act to any degree along any of these vectors, or along one of their own.[3]

It was, however, applauded by others:

Each of these cell-divisions accomplished something positive. Hubbard built more wisely than he knew when he insisted on a principle of non-authoritarianism for now we have dianetics, we have E therapy, we have ER, we have Naylor's PCM, we have . . . analytical procedure and nexology, and humanics, and, as an adjunct, gestalt therapy [Etc].

We have all these things and I, for one, believe the whole is worth while. These cell divisions have made possible our survival. More important, they have made our potentialities limitless – as compared to those of our cousins, the psycho-analysts – because of our essentially non-authoritarianistic structure.[4]

Such innovators often believed their own developments to have greatly surpassed those of Hubbard:

[1] *Dianews*, 1, 22 (31 May 1951), p. 2.
[2] Ibid., p. 3.
[2] Editorial, *Dianotes*, 1, 5 (December 1951), pp. 2–3.
[4] Art Coulter, 'Cell Division and Growth', *Dianotes*, 3, 34 (July 1954), p. 9; for an amusing account of the factionalism in Dianetics, see Vox Populi, 'Origin and development of Psychoreligion', *Dianotes*, 3, 31 (April 1954), pp. 8–10.

... we have progressed beyond Dianetics ... Now we are promulgating teachings of greater depth, 'Eidetic Psychology'. ... We find agreement with all techniques in part, but it seems that the higher goals produce greater results.[1]

while admitting their basis in Dianetics:

only one third or less of the total process is based on Dianetic Procedure ...[2]

One former Dianeticist who established his own foundation even had the temerity to offer for sale a book entitled *Dianetics Perfected*.[3] Others, while not extensively developing independent theories and procedures, eclectically combined Hubbardian theory and practice with those of other psychological and philosophical schools: Carbon Dioxide Therapy,[4] New Thought affirmations,[5] nutritional regimes,[6] Orgone Therapy,[7] etc.[8]

A widely prevailing view was that any theory or technique which could help gain the ends sought through Dianetics should be employed. Thus one Dianetics newsletter editor reviewing a book on Huna (Hawaiian magic), Max Freedom Long's *The Secret Science Behind Miracles*, suggests:

Open-minded Dianeticists might do well to consider much of this data [sic] in the light of blending some of the suggested techniques into our present procedures. If they will simplify and speed up processing, they are well worth a trial.[9]

Some practitioners became extremely eclectic, one describing a technique derived from

Krishnamurti, Henshaw Ward, Gestalt Therapy, Analytical Procedure, and Karen Horney.[10]

A few moved towards more occult realms, one group even began delving into alchemy in order to create gold.[11]

For many others, however, the direction in which they wished Dianetics to

---

[1] John B. Lewis, 'A report on the investigation of dianetic phenomena', *The Arc Light* (15 April 1952), pp. 5–7.

[2] Ibid.

[3] James Welgos, *Dianetics Perfected* (Human Engineering Inc, Fairhope, Alabama, 1955).

[4] *Dianotes*, 3, 26 (November 1953).

[5] *Dianotes*, 4, 45 (June 1955), p. 6. For example, 'I will not gain (or lose) weight anymore ... Food can be fattening or not, as I wish it to be ...'

[6] *California Association of Dianetic Auditors Journal*, 1, 5 (May 1951).

[7] *The Arclight* (26 January 1952).

[8] Of 27 professional Dianetic auditors in Southern California in a 1955 Dianetic publication, 14 were listed as practising and offering other techniques as well as Dianetics and Scientology – including General Semantics, Nutritional Therapy, Gestalt Therapy, Psycho-analysis, Rogerian Therapy, Concept Therapy, etc. *CADA Bulletin*, 1, 11 (1955), pp. 8–9.

[9] *Dianotes*, 2, 15 (December 1952).

[10] *Dianotes*, 3, 28 (January 1954), p. 5.

[11] Letter in *The Ghost of Scientology*, 10 (April–May 1953), p. 8.

proceed, was towards a rapprochement with the medical and psychological professions. They viewed Dianetics explicitly as a form of psychotherapy, tended to reject the occult and spiritual aspects of the theory that developed out of the notion of *theta*, such as past lives, and restricted themselves to the form of practice presented in Hubbard's early Dianetic works. The shift towards more mechanistic procedures of rote processing, on the basis of lists of auditing commands, alienated them further.

Some of those who possessed a model of Dianetics as a therapeutic art advocated the assimilation of elements of orthodox healing theory and practise:

> . . . we should not hesitate to carefully examine and integrate into Dianetics, where applicable, any and all of the techniques which are in common use in psychological and psychiatric practise. Certainly these practices work to a certain extent; in so far as they are useful and safe, they will have to be integrated into Dianetics eventually. If they are not, then Dianetics will not develop into the complete, well-rounded and comprehensive science of the mind that it now *potentially* is.[1]

Finally, a number expressed a commitment to the notion of Dianetics as a science, independent of the medical or psychological professions, but rejecting Hubbard's occult developments.

All such views were reported in the independent Dianetics media. New techniques were presented and new theories discussed with considerable tolerance:

> Mr Powers has his ideas about this . . . others have other ideas . . . and Dianetics has room for all.[2]

The newsletters and bulletins reflect the tolerance and eclecticism of many of their readers and correspondents:

> I feel in dianetics we have a segment of the truth . . . but in order to get this segment of truth in perspective, we need to compare it to other truths. If so indicated, we can then individually decide whether or not we wish to add to the original segment.[3]

What constituted the truth was held to be an individual affair, up to each member of the Dianetics community to determine. As one E-therapist stressed:

> In discussing the psychic aspects of E, I wish to state, first of all, that whatever I may say is only my truth. By this I mean that what may be true for me, may not be true for anyone else in the world.[4]

Hubbard himself did not view such attitudes and developments favourably. From the time of the Elizabeth Foundation he had called developments of Dianetic techniques which he did not sponsor 'Black Dianetics'[5], and declared

[1] *Introductory Bulletin of the Central Pennsylvania Dianetic Group* (August 1951), pp. 2–3.
[2] *The Dianews*, 1, 22 (May 1952), p. 10.
[3] *CADA Bulletin*, 1, 19 (1955), p. 18.
[4] *Dianotes*, 3, 33 (June 1954), p. 4.
[5] L. Ron Hubbard, 'Suggested Changes in the Organisation of the Foundation', mimeo (Elizabeth, New Jersey, 1950).

the mixing of Dianetics with some other therapy to be the source of many problems with students.[1]

A severe challenge to Hubbard's standing in the movement came when independent auditors began to proclaim that they had produced 'clears'. Such auditors were eagerly sought for guidance, training and auditing, and rapidly moved into positions of leadership in the Dianetics community. However, it was one of those declared 'clear', Ronald B. Howes, rather than his auditor, who presented the gravest potential challenge to Hubbard's leadership within the Dianetic community.

Howes was a Dianeticist in Minneapolis. Like many others, he had got into the movement as a result of the article in *Astounding*. He had previously been briefly a convert to Catholicism, and was declared clear in January 1952. A close associate at this time described him before he had attained the state of clear, as tending to be a 'promoter with his feet off the ground' and having 'big ideas which didn't work due to other people's lacks'.

Howes had been audited by a man who had been associated with the Wichita Foundation. As a result of processing and conversation with this auditor, Howes went through what appears to have been an intense mystical experience which convinced him and many others that he was clear. Many Dianeticists hurried to Minneapolis to meet him, and later to Colorado Springs where he established the Institute of Humanics. Tape-recordings and transcripts of his conversations with other members of the Minneapolis group, and visitors were widely circulated. They convey an attitude of considerable awe on the part of his associates, who regarded him as capable of displaying miraculous powers:

> We have in Ron the validation for the vision of 'Perfect Man' which has haunted mankind through the centuries.
>
> Ron will demonstrate the absence of galvanic reflexes to the most extensive and exhaustive questioning, the absence of body tremors or other waste motion such as occulomotor jerks. He will be completely relaxed save for the particular activations required for particular requirements. He can induce cellular proliferation at any point in the body, grow cancerous or other tissue and make it disappear at will. His sleep requirements are reduced to an optimum for him of four hours to five hours per night, with full alertness on awakening. His 'psychic' activities are phenomenal; he can read other's thought-feelings as though they were an open-book . . . His mental calculations are with extreme speed and precision.

He was believed to be engaged on projects such as:

> further development of his conquest of gravity and space . . . explorations into the mechanics and manipulability of life and behaviour towards more optimum human beings and societies.[3]

[1] L. Ron Hubbard, 'Instruction Protocol, Official', mimeo (20 November 1950, Elizabeth, New Jersey).

[2] Grace Krausy, 'Meet Mr Ron B. Howes', *Dianotes*, 1, 11 (May 1952), p. 11.

[3] Dwight H. Bulkley, 'Introduction' to Gordon Beckstead, ed., *Prologue to Survival*, Part III (Psychological Research Foundation, Phoenix, Arizona, 1952) .

It is extremely difficult to convey the banality and pontifical style of Howes' pronouncements during this period without extensive quotation,[1] but as a sample:

Q. What is your reading speed compared to what it was?

A. It's mighty fast and improving steadily every day. I noticed and my wife remarked upon it, that I seemed to be turning the pages about three times as fast. My comprehension of printed material has gone up enormously compared to the past. The most difficult paragraphs in technical reading are very easy now. No confusion, no identity, no failure. My ability to pick out errors in judgement of other people on paper is much higher.

Q. How do you find the field of physical chemistry now?

A. I have never discovered a cave with aboriginal drawings in it but when I opened my physical chemistry text book I did. The child has more intuitive knowledge about the world than the adult scientist, if the child is reasonably high toned. At one time I was in that state for a period of approximately two years. There were peaks, of course, and there were valleys. There were moments when I as an individual was higher than I am right now, and certainty was absolute. There were no goals impossible to achieve. I was right. My ability to solve a problem was complete. I could do it. I was me. I was a strong force. My heart sang and the stars were alive – and then I went to school – it may sound like a jest, but it is not. Our educational system is one of the finest methods of controlling society of which I know, and the most insidious.

Q. Can you be affected by bacteria?

A. I still believe there are bacteria which I can't resist, but there must be many bacteria which I can resist now that I could never resist before.

Q. What do you contemplate as your duration of life?

A. In chronological years, if my anti-gravity plan works, I would assume approximately another four hundred years. Under present circumstances, one hundred and a quarter.

Q. How much concern have you at this time over income?

A. None. No fear, worry, anxiety. All my postulates on losing my job disappeared; about being successful, disappeared. I can do more for any particular person who employs me than any other person possibly could. And I find it very easy to talk them into giving me money if I so desire – no difficulty.

Q. What experiments have you performed on yourself?

A. . . .

I've also tried to see if I can regenerate teeth. For the moment I've got some very sore gums but no teeth. Perry suggested to me, in a roundabout way that I should regenerate teeth. Sunday, Monday, Tuesday, Wednesday, I got extremely sore gums. Teeth were pulled out. I've regenerated tissue to the maximum extent I can. The soreness is now disappearing. The gums are much more healthy. Next point is what constitutes a seed tooth? I think it's possible to construct them again.

[1] See Appendix I.

Incidentally, I haven't decided what I am going to look like yet. It's variable and to a large extent subject to one's pleasure.[1]

Although other auditors also announced that they had produced clears[2] none of these was to cause the excitement in the field of Dianetics aroused by Howes. He rapidly gained a reputation second only to Hubbard himself. His theories and practices were widely taken up, and the question was raised whether with Hubbard apparently leaving the field, Howes might be 'A new leader in the making?'[3] When Hubbard began publicizing Scientology, some Dianeticists felt the community had split into two 'apparently conflicting camps of "thought": the Howes ideas and the Hubbardian ideas'.[4]

Many Dianeticists pilgrimaged to the Institute of Humanics in Colorado Springs to receive processing from him, but he made no attempt to organize his clientele, and his prestige received a shattering blow when police investigation of the Institute was widely reported, and Howes was found to have been claiming a doctorate which he did not possess. Howes closed the Institute, and although a small personal following remained associated with him, his influence on Dianetics was thereafter negligible.[5]

While the Dianetics community was splitting into competing factions, it was also suffering a considerable attrition of membership. *MSMH* had, according to its publisher, sold 150,000 copies during its first year of issue. Many thousand people had tried out the practice, and a proportion had actively pursued their interest in Dianetics by taking courses at the Foundation, or by joining amateur groups. A tailing-off of interest had appeared, however, as early as the beginning of 1951. The income of the Elizabeth Foundation had dropped from $28,160 in January to $20,620 in February of 1951.[6] After the initial boom, a slump had begun to set in. By mid-1952 it was clear to one newsletter editor that:

> The public, it would seem, does not want to participate in Dianetics, but rather they want to benefit by it. . . . They want, in Dianetics, to be able to purchase the resultant end product without actively doing the constructive work that it requires, like buying an automobile without helping the assemblage.[7]

[1] Gordon Beckstead, ed., *Prologue to Survival*, Part II (Psychological Research Foundation, Phoenix, Arizona, 1952), pp. 5–6.

[2] See 'Jack Horner' in Ibid., pp. 14–15.

[3] *Dianotes*, 2, 14 (November 1952), p. 2.

[4] *The Communicator*, 1, 9 (November 1952), p. 1.

[5] Howes appears to have had less interest in founding a movement, than in establishing a self-supporting community. He continued in this attempt after his 'exposure', founding among others the St Eloi Corporation where a small group of followers worked with him on various research and development projects, including a 'rare-earth' separation plant. The community appears eventually to have foundered, and Howes and some of his followers were received [back] into the Catholic Church. Interviews.

[6] Documents made available to me by a former Foundation director.

[7] *Dianotes*, 1, 12 (June–July 1952), p. 2.

As another Dianeticist observed in retrospect, 'Whilst dianetics reached the proportions of a national craze in 1950, by late 1951 it had largely collapsed'.[1] A number of groups had disappeared, and many had experienced a decline in active membership.

Dianeticists had a number of hypotheses concerning this decline. The most important reason for the loss of interest, many believed, was that the promise had been very great but that it had not been fulfilled:

> The promise made in *Dianetics: the Modern Science of Mental Health* was a very definite and simple one. It was stated that the application of the approach described in the book would within a few hundred hours of auditing time produce a cleared individual, free of all aberration. It was also stated that as auditing continued, progress toward 'clear' became consistently more easy.
> The reason that dianetics did not retain its original impetus and, in fact, rapidly lost almost all the ground it had gained at first, was due simply to the fact that, when dianetics was put into practice, it was observed that none of these statements was correct.[2]

Many Dianeticists had become 'disappointed because we weren't clears after one hundred hours of processing.'[3] This disappointment was heightened by the apparent failure of those declared 'clear' to perform in a manner regarded as appropriate – Sonya Bianca, Sara Betty Hubbard, Ron Howes; and the failure of the two hundred or so individuals, Hubbard maintained that he had cleared before the publication of his book, to manifest themselves in any way. Hubbard's own behaviour between 1950 and 1952 had given some cause to doubt the efficacy of his 'science'. Others had abandoned Dianetics in the face of attacks upon it by psychiatrists and psychologists.[4] Yet another reason for attrition was the presentation of Dianetics as a psychotherapy. Whatever their feelings about the state of clear, many people had gone into Dianetics to solve relatively specific problems of illness or psychological handicap. Whether through spontaneous remission, the hope given them by Dianetics, the attention they received as pre-clears, or the therapeutic validity of the practice, a number had felt improved in consequence. Having secured what they had wanted from Dianetics, some discontinued involvement.[5]

---

[1] James H. Schmitz, 'What happened to the tens of thousands?', *International Dianetic Society Letter*, 1 (1957).

[2] Ibid.

[3] Milt Carland, 'Remember that bridge?', *Dianotes*, 1, 5 (December 1951), p. 1.

[4] That people had drawn away from Dianetics because of bad reviews of L. Ron Hubbard's *Dianetics: the Modern Science of Mental Health*, by psychologists and psychiatrists, was certainly believed by Dianeticists themselves – *Dianotes*, 1, 5 (December 1951), p. 4.

[5] Interviews with former group leaders and Dianetic auditors.

Adaptations

From the earliest days of the movement, Hubbard had attempted to assert control over its direction and development. He first sought to control the theory and practice of the movement, attempting to prevent the submergence of his own ideas under the weight of synthesis, or ideological or technical innovation.

While technical innovations by others were permitted, such developments only received publicity in official media if they were approved by Hubbard:

> Our subject is standard procedure, a routine of auditing devised by James E. Hurt in July of 1950. It had become obvious by that time that many people, who had studied the book only, were running into problems which their knowledge of dianetic procedure would not resolve. When this became apparent to Jim, he sat down one evening and outlined a procedure for dianetic processing which would eliminate these apparently irresolvable situations. His plan was studied by Mr Hubbard and then adopted by the Foundation for general use.[1]

Other theoretical or technical innovations of which Hubbard did not approve, or which had not been submitted for his approval, were attacked in official publications:

> E-therapy is an outgrowth of an amalgamation between dianetics and a system of opinion held by an individual. The advice of the Foundation is: Don't use it. At best, it is another wild variable in an area which already has too many variables. At worst, it can be actually dangerous. Dianetics should not be diluted.[2]

As early as *MSMH*, Hubbard had attempted to protect the practice against compounding:

> Don't mix gasoline and alcohol, or dianetics and other therapy except purely medical . . .[3]

Crossing Dianetics with an older therapy was considered one source of troubles with students in training[4] and a dangerous practice.[5] The term 'Black Dianetics' had come into use at the Elizabeth Foundation with the meaning of any form of, or variation on, Dianetics, or any use of it, of which Hubbard disapproved. The dangers of 'Black Dianetics' became a part of the course

[1] Anonymous, 'An Outline of Dianetic Standard Procedure', mimeo transcription of tape, n.d., probably 1951. For a general statement of this policy, see L. Ron Hubbard, 'A definition of standard procedure', Appendix Two, *Science of Survival*, 1st edn (Hubbard Dianetic Foundation, Wichita, Kansas, 1951).

[2] *Dianetic Auditor's Bulletin*, 1, 8 (February 1951). See also L. Ron Hubbard, 'A definition of standard procedure', op. cit., p. 308, where an attack is made on a doctor who can be no other than Joseph Winter, for his attempts 'to develop, without facilities or experience, certain techniques of application'.

[3] *MSMH*, p. 298.

[4] L. Ron Hubbard, 'Instruction Protocol, Official', op. cit.

[5] *MSMH*, p. 165.

curriculum at the Wichita Foundation, although it was not a widely publicized idea until Scientology was launched.[1]

Having established the existence of heresy, Hubbard had also to establish machinery for locating and managing it. This remained rudimentary during the Dianetics period. A *Board of Ethics* was established at the Elizabeth Foundation in November 1950 with the brief of 'checking on alignment with Standard Procedure',[2] but the activities of this Board do not appear to have had any great influence on the Dianetic community at that time.

An attempt was also made to constrain the free use of the term 'Dianetics' and to exercise some control over independent and competing professional schools:

> Dianetics has encountered its greatest difficulty with those who have tried to jump on the bandwagon for personal gain. It has had to resort to legal measures against unqualified persons who style themselves professional dianeticists, those who mis-represent the name of dianetics by opening unauthorised schools and clinics and others who attempt to publish plagiarised or fraudulent dianetic literature.[3]

Hubbard and his associates also sought to distinguish Dianetics from what its detractors in the press had seen as its principal sources, hypnosis and psycho-analysis. Dianetics was distinguished from hypnosis by a number of factors. In Dianetic auditing, the pre-clear retained full consciousness of his environment, and of what occurred. No form of positive suggestion was used, it was argued. Indeed post-hypnotic suggestion was regarded as aberrative in Dianetics, and a form of engram.[4] Hypnosis was held to be dangerous since while in the trance state, anything said by the therapist would be engramic.[5]

Psychoanalysis was held to differ from Dianetics in that the former was con-cerned primarily with sex, while this was only one among four dynamics in Dianetics. Psychoanalysis sought to recover unconscious memories only from childhood (or in the Rankian variant, from the birth trauma) while Dianetics returned to the pre-natal period. While psychoanalysis stressed *insight* as an

---

[1] L. Ron Hubbard, 'Danger: Black Dianetics', *Journal of Scientology*, 3G, n.d. (1952), p. 7. The term had been employed publicly before in reference to A. L. Kitselman's E-Therapy. Alan A. Engelhardt 'An analysis of E-Therapy' in Waldo Boyd, ed., *Supplement No. 2 to 'Science of Survival'* (Wichita, 1951), p. 41. There are, of course, close parallels between 'Black Dianetics' and 'Malicious Animal Magnetism' which Mrs Eddy accused her apostate and heretic students of employing to evil ends.

[2] John Maloney, 'Organisational Memorandum', mimeo (6 November 1950, Elizabeth Foundation).

[3] *The Dianamic*, 1, 16 (30 March 1951), p. 2. It is unlikely these 'legal measures' ever went beyond attorney's threats, though a progress report issued by the Foundation in August 1951 indicated that suit had been filed against one individual who, although not a qualified auditor, was advertising courses in Dianetics, and giving the degree of Dianetic Auditor upon graduation. Reported in *The Dianews*, 1, 15 (December 1951), pp. 6–7.

[4] *MSMH*, p. 66.

[5] Ibid., p. 124.

essential therapeutic agent, Dianetics stressed the recounting of incidents to the point where they were erased. The Dianetic auditor, unlike the psychoanalyst, never interpreted or evaluated material, but only acknowledged it.[1]

Hubbard's most important reaction to the crisis within Dianetics, however, was its abandonment, and the promulgation of Scientology as a separate system of beliefs and practices. It was around this ideological innovation that all other adaptations were based.[2]

As early as the Elizabeth Foundation, Hubbard had found that pre-clears produced material which seemed to have no relation to their experience in this life. It appears that he briefly resisted the notion that this material emanated from past lives,[3] but shortly became reconciled to this view and began experimentation on the running of past-life engrams.[4] It is not hard to see how a conviction of past lives would develop out of Dianetic technique. Since the location of the basic-basic and its erasure would quickly result in clearing the case, it followed that if individuals were not cleared there *must* necessarily be an earlier incident to resolve.[5] When pre-clears had returned to conception without clearing as a consequence, they began to produce material prior to conception of the 'sperm-dream' variety.[6] When even this did not solve the problem, some began recalling past deaths. Hubbard had also early noted the phenomenon of 'exteriorization',[7] but in Dianetics this was seen as a matter to be handled by releasing 'moments of painful emotion' before turning to the process of engram running.[8] In Scientology, exteriorization was a state to be sought. Both past-lives and exteriorization were predicated on the assumption of the 'thetan', the entity which could exteriorize from the body, the essential persistent individuality that formed the continuity between various past lives.

[1] Donald H. Rogers, 'Dianetics and psychoanalysis', *Dianetic Auditor's Bulletin*, 1, 8 (February 1951). Hubbard later wrote a 'critique' of psychoanalysis along largely these lines, L. Ron Hubbard, 'A critique of psycho-analysis', Part One, *Certainty*, 9, 7 (1962); Part Two, *Certainty*, 9, 8 (1962).
[2] Dianetics again became part of the corpus of Scientological theory and practice after the return of the Hubbard Dianetic Research Foundation to Hubbard's control in late 1954. See p. 95 below.
[3] Students of the Elizabeth Foundation have claimed that the first person to 'run a past-life' was expelled from the course. I have been unable to verify this, although reference is also made to this story by George Malko, *Scientology, the Now Religion* (Dell Publishing Co, New York, 1970), p. 57, and certainly up to and including August 1951 and the publication of *Science of Survival*, Hubbard's public pronouncements on past-lives were extremely cautious.
[4] Winter, op. cit., p. 189.
[5] L. Ron Hubbard, *Dianetics: the Original Thesis*, Scientology Publications Organization (Copenhagen, 1970), p. 116. First published HDRF, Wichita, Kansas, 1951.
[6] Winter, op. cit., p. 189.
[7] A dissociated state in which the individual believes himself to be outside his body. It is a familiar symptom in psychiatry, and has had an important role in occult and religious experience as 'astral travel'.
[8] *MSMH*, p. 256.

Scientology was a new revelation entirely transcending the limitations of Dianetics. While Dianetics had been a form of psychotherapy concerned with eradicating the limitations on the achievement of full human potential, Scientology was heralded as the 'Science of Certainty' concerned with rehabilitating the thetan to its full spiritual capacity.

While Hubbard's theory and techniques had been moving increasingly in this direction, it was not until his break with Purcell and the Wichita Foundation that Hubbard established Scientology in Phoenix, Arizona. Phoenix had a flourishing Dianetics community, organized under the auspices of the Psychological Research Foundation, and an independent auditing practice, which provided an immediate clientele on which Hubbard could draw. (As the Scientology organization correctly point out, however, Hubbard's parents lived in Phoenix at this time. This may have influenced his decision to settle there briefly.) In Phoenix, Hubbard established the Hubbard Association of Scientologists (HAS), and a *Journal*, which announced that he had discovered 'The source of life energy'[1] and the reason for the existence of matter, energy, space, time and thought.[2]

On the basis of his new revelation Hubbard sought to establish control over the Dianetics community. His publications roundly attacked the Wichita Foundation which had continued to operate under Purcell's ownership. He hinted broadly that receipts from the sale of his books had found their way into private pockets (other than his own) rather than into furthering the purposes of the Foundation. It was asserted that the directors of the earlier Foundations had been motivated solely by a desire for profit.[3] The Wichita Foundation was classed as an 'unauthorized' group and it was argued that

the enormous change in Scientology in the last year and the great advance in its effectiveness . . . have rendered unimportant organisations which falsely offer certification in Dianetics or Scientology.[4]

Purcell found it necessary to defend himself against the charge that he aimed to destroy Dianetics or Ron Hubbard, and that he had received half a million dollars from the American Medical Association to put the Foundation into bankruptcy.[5]

Hubbard appealed to the amateur following, seeking to secure its support

[1] *Journal of Scientology*, 3G (1952), p. 1.

[2] Ibid., p. 2.

[3] *Journal of Scientology*, 4G (1952), p. 1. Later Hubbard would refer to 'money mad millionnaires, crooked, dishonest and incompetent management . . .' *Professional Auditor's Bulletin* 1 (May 1953), p. 1.

[4] *Journal of Scientology*, 9G (1952).

[5] Letter from Don Purcell, *The Dianews*, 1, 22 (31 May 1952), p. 12. On the split between Hubbard and the Wichita Foundation, see also Helen O'Brien, *Dianetics in Limbo* (Whitmore Publishing Co, Philadelphia, 1966), pp. 49–51.

against the Wichita Foundation, placing many Dianeticists in a considerable dilemma:

> While the Foundation has not asked us to renounce Hubbard in order to work with the Foundation, Hubbard has insisted that we follow only him and reject all others. If we do not do this, he replies by rejecting us.[1]

This appeal was supported by changes in organizational practice. Those who adopted Scientological theory or techniques were at first urged to join the HAS, but by late 1954 more forceful methods were employed to secure support.

Amateur groups were notified by the Hubbard Association of Scientologists International (to which the HAS had been changed) that:

> ... only a member ... of the HASI or its affiliated organisations shall have the right to possess and use the information of Scientology.[2]

As a result, a new policy for amateur groups was to be enforced. To qualify as affiliated groups all group members were to hold HASI memberships and monthly reports of activities were to be submitted to the HASI. Those groups which did not comply would be regarded as inactive and have their certificates revoked, and would become ineligible for Scientology materials.

A similar policy was also applied to independent practitioners. A Committee of Examination, Certification and Services had been established by the HASI to secure conformity from practitioners. Practitioners who had manifested a consistently independent line of thought were informed that their right to practice Dianetics and Scientology, and their certificates as professional auditors, were revoked.[3]

A former member of the Committee of Examination, Certification and Services expressed the direction of policy at this time.

> A lot of other things came out, ideas and -ologies, and some people halted at the split and some ... took off in their own direction ... Ron was trying to get a codified procedure and a set of ethics ... and a standard group activity ... But this is pretty hard when there are people calling it psychology, or a guy is still being a psychologist, or a Rosicrucian, or a 'Mixologist'. We were trying to be a Scientologist, be a group ... It was trying to define, to differentiate Scientology from other -ologies. This was the basic effort of that time and it did come out in revocation of certificates.[4]

These policies aroused protest from those sectors of the Dianetic community which had not followed Hubbard unquestioningly, and saw this as an attempt on Hubbard's part to secure a monopoly of Dianetics and Scientology,[5] and as authoritarian.[6]

---

[1] *The Dianews*, 1, 22 (31 May 1952), p. 1.
[2] Letter from HASI Group Secretary to Group Members, 9 October 1954.
[3] *Dianotes*, 4, 37 (October 1954).
[4] Interview with former member of CECS.
[5] 'Poor Man's Psychiatry', *Dianotes*, 4, 39 (December 1954).
[6] *Bristol Dianetic Review*, 3, 31 (October 1954), pp. 170–1.

Since his removal to Phoenix, Hubbard had sought to secure the support of some of the Dianetic newsletters and magazines, and through them, of the Dianetic community. In a letter published in one of these newsletters he expressed his dissatisfaction with the factional state of Dianetics and Scientology: 'these splinter groups and copyists are holding back the entire movement of Dianetics and Scientology . . .'[1] Only one of the many newsletters responded by adopting a totally Hubbardian line. The editor of *The Ghost of Scientology* attacked deviation from Hubbard's policy, and supported him in his attempt to gain control of the field:

> If you are not a Hubbardian Scientologist, then you are not a 'scientologist' at all, as Hubbard coined that word to fit HIS Science.[2]

This publication attacked other newsletters which did not follow the same practice and individual practitioners who continued to adopt, sponsor, or promulgate non-Hubbardian theory and technique.[3]

Hubbard's own publications followed a similar practice, advocating the harassment of groups which appeared to be engaged in any activity remotely connected with Dianetics and Scientology, but not approved by the HASI:

> if you discovered that some group calling itself 'precept processing' had set up and established a series of meetings in your area . . . you would do all you could to make things interesting for them. In view of the fact that the HASI holds copyrights for all such material . . . the least that could be done . . . is the placement of a suit against them for using materials of scientology without authority . . . The purpose of the suit is to harass and discourage rather than to win.
>
> The law can be used very easily to harass, and enough harassment on somebody who is simply on the thin edge anyway, well knowing that he is not authorised, will generally be sufficient to cause his professional decease. If possible, of course, ruin him utterly.[4]

Independent newsletters were also threatened with legal action if they persisted in 'defaming' Scientology.[5] It was suggested that one editor had practised fraud[6] when he had earlier worked for the HASI, and a detective agency was commissioned to investigate another editor 'to disclose any criminal past or connections . . .'[7]

An attempt was made to force organizations of independent practitioners to disband. The California Association of Dianetic Auditors, for example, was informed that its charters, certificates and permissions to employ Dianetics

[1] Letter from L. Ron Hubbard, *The Ghost of Scientology*, 10 (April–May 1953), p. 2.

[2] *The Ghost of Scientology*, 11 (15 June 1953), p. 4.

[3] Ibid., 11 (15 June 1953), pp. 10, 15, 16; 14 (20 November 1953), pp. 5, 7; 17 (25 June 1954) passim.

[4] 'Dissemination of material', *Ability Major*, 1, n.d. (late 1954/early 1955), p. 7.

[5] Ibid., p. 12.

[6] 'Aberee [sic] – you said it', *Ability Minor*, 3, p. 3.

[7] 'Detective Hired', Ibid., p. 11; *Bristol Dianetic Review*, 4, 37 (April 1955), p. 6; *The Aberree*, 1, 6 (October 1954), p. 13; *The Aberree*, 1, 7 (November 1954), p. 1.

were withdrawn.[1] Since it was an independent corporation, however, its members declined to disband and refused to observe the requirement of the HASI that all CADA members also become members of the HASI.[2]

Hubbard sought to move Scientology away from the amateur practitioner basis of Dianetics. Group processing had been extensively promoted during 1954, but an increasing distinction was emerging between the certified auditor and the ordinary member. The latter was permitted only limited access to information. Training became a prerequisite for access to advanced materials.[3] Advanced training and certification were centralized in the HASI and its associate schools, and an attempt was made to require practising auditors to contract to pay a percentage of their fees to the HASI, and to sign promissory notes for $5000 as a bond of good behaviour.[4] This attempt to control practitioners met with little success and the policy was abandoned.[5]

While Hubbard sought to exert control over practitioners and other followers in the field, he also tightened control over his central organization, dismissing officers who failed to perform precisely in accordance with his requirements.[6] Executive officers in Hubbard's organizations typically enjoyed only brief tenure in office. In 1954 during an absence in England, for example, Hubbard directed the leaders of his Philadelphia Associate School to move the HASI from Phoenix to Philadelphia; fire various officers; and tighten up control on the flow of information to members of suspect loyalty. On his return from America, in the face of a barrage of protest from followers against the actions of his Philadelphia lieutenants, Hubbard disclaimed all responsibility for the actions they had taken and expelled them from office.[7]

Hubbard progressively gained complete control over Scientology, its membership, ideology, practices and organizations. The development of those sectors of the Dianetics movement which did not follow Hubbard was very different. The Wichita Foundation continued to operate after Hubbard's departure, but its membership and clientele declined rapidly in the absence of Hubbard. By 1954 the active membership of the Foundation was down to 112. While originally aiming to remain within the field of Dianetics, new theories and techniques were developed at the Foundation, leading to an increasing diffuseness of its ideological base and a decline in the immediacy of its appeal.[8] Don Purcell had become disillusioned with Dianetics, and increasingly interested in a new development produced by one of the HDRF members, 'Synergetics':

[1] *Ability Major*, 2, n.d. (early 1955).
[2] *Dunbar's ARC* (11 April 1955), p. 2.
[3] 'Dissemination of material', *Ability Major*, 1, p. 11.
[4] *The Aberree*, 3, 1 (April 1955), p. 9.
[5] Interview with former members of CECS.
[6] Letter from Reg Gould, ex-director, HAS London . . . *The Ghost of Scientology*, 15 (January 1954), p. 11.
[7] Interviews. Also see Helen O'Brien, op. cit., pp. 68–77.
[8] *Dianetics Today*, 3, 7 (July 1954).

In synergetics Art Coulter has created a new scientific approach to the solution to the problem we are dealing with. Synergetics includes much that is included in dianetics and a great deal that is not.[1]

Late in 1954, Purcell announced that he would support Dianetics no longer, but would devote his resources in future to Coulter's Synergetics. After taking a 'straw vote' among the membership concerning disposal of the Wichita Foundation, Purcell advised Hubbard that he would hand over to him the Hubbard Dianetic Research Foundation – whose principal assets were the copyrights to *MSMH*, and a mailing list. Hubbard accepted gladly, and announced that 'the entire and complete control without contest of Dianetics, as well as Scientology . . .' was vested in the HASI.[2] It was undoubtedly the return of Dianetics to Hubbard's control which led to the more rigorous attempts to end fringe practices, exclude practitioners who compounded Dianetics or Scientology with other practices, and force critical newsletters to cease publication.

Some of the remaining amateur groups and newsletters allied themselves with one of the leaders who had emerged from the Dianetic community to found their own Institutes – Coulter's Synergetics, Howes' Humanics, Welgos' Institute of Integration.[3] Others moved toward an increasingly eclectic position, or shifted their ideological loyalties to other systems of thought. Minneapolis Dianetics Inc and the Minnesota Scientology Council, for example, had united in 1954 as a result of the reuniting of Dianetics and Scientology in Hubbard's hands. By 1955, however, they had split again because of conflict between the two groups. The Dianetic group which controlled the newsletter, *The Dianotes*, moved under the auspices of the Institute of Humanics.[4] It later printed an increasing number of articles promoting the practice of Yoga. Another prominent newsletter, *The Aberree*, moved progressively further from Dianetics and Scientology, becoming after 1956 an open forum in which followers of any cultic belief could present their ideas. During the following years articles appeared on astrology, atlantis, Totology, Yoga, New Thought, mystic Christianity, hypnosis, numerology, Subud, etc. By 1961 it had become a general occult-metaphysical magazine with only one small article on Dianetics in its July–August issue.

The founder of E-Therapy, A. L. Kitselman, attempted to found an eclectic colony devoted to self-improvement:

. . . the Pyramid Lake Project is a resort-community specialising in the human mind and its functions.

[1] Don G. Purcell, 'Special Announcement', *Dianetics Today*, 3, 10 (October 1954).

[2] 'Dianetics and Scientology organisations united again', *Group Newsletter* (September 1954).

[3] Only Synergetics and E-Therapy appear to have survived through the 1950s, and Synergetics disappeared early in the 1960s.

[4] See *Dianotes*, volume 4, nos 47 (August 1955), 48 (September 1955); and volume 5, nos 51 (December 1955), 52 (January 1956), etc.

> The Project was started on October 1st of 1956 by A. L. Kitselman, developer of a form of lay psychotherapy known as 'E-Therapy'. It was Kitselman's wish, however, to establish a project not dominated by any one man or doctrine, and, accordingly, the Pyramid Lake Project is being used by many persons who have little interest in E-Therapy.
>
> Now that the Project has completed its first year there is nothing spectacular to report. The enterprise is slowly growing in size, and persons who are strongly interested in self-improvement are becoming permanent residents at Pyramid Lake. Others visit the Project regularly whenever free to do so.[1]

The project shortly failed, however, although Kitselman continues to write on, and practice, E-Therapy and appears to have a small, unorganized following.[2]

Only scattered individuals remain in the United States who maintain a loyalty to early Dianetics. As far as I can ascertain there are now no full-time Dianetic practitioners in America practising only the Dianetics of the early years. Only one independent organization remains to foster the practice of traditional Dianetics, the California Association of Dianetic Auditors, with a persistently declining membership.

In England, after the establishment of the Dianetic Association Ltd, and the Dianetic Federation of Great Britain, as loose national organizations to facilitate communication between Dianetic groups, and between them and the American organizations, Hubbard announced that he would visit England, and proposed the establishment of a Hubbard Dianetic Foundation in Great Britain as a subsidiary of the HAS. Some leading British Dianeticists favoured the establishment of a Foundation but felt that his 'proposal re control would not necessarily be acceptable to all British Dianeticists'.[3]

Hubbard was not prepared to accept the attempts by some British Dianetics leaders to limit his authority. He approached a Dianeticist outside the leadership echelons of the movement and asked her to establish a Hubbard Association of Scientologists in Britain, as a profit rather than non-profit corporation, and under his complete control. As he made clear in his letters to her, he blamed the failure of the Dianetic Foundations on the fact that he lacked complete control over them, and had no desire for members or co-directors with voting rights in Scientology organizations. He saw no virtues in the factional independent groups around which Dianetics was organized in Britain and sought to establish a strong central organization which would eliminate them.[4] The HAS was established in London. When Hubbard made his first visit to England in late 1952 groups rapidly flocked to affiliate with the HAS, and independent Dianetics

---

[1] Anonymous mimeo sheet, 'News from Pyramid Lake', c. 1957.

[2] Among his writings are, for example: A. L. Kitselman, *Hello Stupid!* (Translator's Press, La Jolla, California, 1962); *E-Therapy* (Institute of Integration, New York, 1953); *What Integration is About* (Institute of Integration, La Jolla, California, 1960).

[3] 'British dianetics – the present position', *Epicentre: Bulletin of the Dianetic Federation of Great Britain*, 2 (September 1952), p. 1.

[4] L. Ron Hubbard, Letters to M—— D——, August–September 1952.

groups almost entirely disappeared. The last remaining independent group finally disbanded and ceased publication of its newsletter in 1955[1] in the face of increasing hostility from the HAS.[2]

The personal paths of those involved in Dianetics during the early 1950s provided the pattern for the development of the groups, organizations, and publications. It is not possible to calculate how many of the initial following remained with Hubbard during the transition to Scientology. A number experienced no difficulty in making this transition. Some do not seem to have noticed any major change:

> I wasn't too aware of that [the transition from Dianetics to Scientology] . . . I went to Phoenix with the idea that I was going to study Dianetics, but when I came there they gave us some Dianetics and then it was already Scientology and I just couldn't see too terrible big a difference between Dianetics and Scientology. It all dealt with communications and getting a person to trace back his experiences. I wasn't unhappy about that [the notion of past lives] as a matter of fact I am very fascinated with it. . . . I found it very absorbing.[3]

Some lost interest as their own problems seemed to be resolved; as a result of domestic or occupational pressures on their time; as a result of alienation from Hubbard's progressively more overtly metaphysical pronouncements; or through some combination of these factors. Others left from hostility to Hubbard's organizational changes.

Among the early Dianeticists from whom interviews were obtained, many of those who objected to what they thought was a developing authoritarianism in Hubbard's organization, passed on from Dianetics to other forms of cultic belief:

> We did a period of research with something connected with something they do in California, and also other types of Dianetic techniques. Benefit came when we went on to study Ouspensky & Gurdjieff. We became interested in Indian stuff, Hindu and meditations. We've been interested in meditative techniques. I find meditation of tremendous benefit. I've gone on to Krishnamurti . . . I personally consider I've reached the end with Krishnamurti because the things he teaches are so true to life . . . so concrete . . . I'd come across Krishnamurti before Dianetics and found him very difficult to understand, but after Dianetics I really began appreciating him.[4]

Some continued the practice of early Dianetics, paying little or no attention to Hubbard's later developments, although introducing modifications of their own. A number of others made a point of indicating to me that they had later joined MENSA.[5]

[1] *Bristol Dianetic Review*, 4, 40 (August–September 1955).
[2] *Bristol Dianetic Review*, 3, 27 (June 1954); 3, 32 (November 1954).
[3] Interview: American Dianeticist.
[4] Interview: English Dianeticist.
[5] While MENSA is not a self-improvement organization it seems to have a clear status-conferring and ego-enhancing function for individuals who are convinced they

Institutional fragility and the strategy of sectarianization

The origins and early development of Dianetics bear a close resemblance to those of a number of other cultic movements. Mary Baker Eddy claimed a new revelation which led her to move away from the ideas of Phineas P. Quimby which she had earlier taught under the name Moral Science. Aspects of the healing practice most closely associated with Quimby, such as manual manipulation of the patient's head, were dropped, and new doctrines such as that of malicious animal magnetism and a radically idealist metaphysics were introduced. Mrs Eddy's developing system drew heavily on Quimby's work as well as owing a lesser debt to other currents of thought then prevalent in New England: Transcendentalism, Swedenborgianism and spiritualism.[1] When faced by challenges to her authority both from members of her Church, and from former students who had established their own Institute and Colleges and had begun developing new ideas of theory and practice, or combining Christian Science with Theosophy or even orthodox medical practice, Mrs Eddy dissolved or suspended the operation of the movement's organization. In their place she erected the highly centralized Mother Church, administered through a personally appointed bureaucracy. She drastically reduced the authority of local leaders by limiting their duration of office; of teachers by permitting them to teach only the preliminary levels of doctrine and by restricting the frequency of their classes; and of practitioners by making their continued practice depend on their good standing with the central organization.

Members were forbidden to join more than a limited range of voluntary associations; constrained from seeking medical assistance or advice; and forbidden to read other occult or metaphysical literature. Mrs Eddy's preoccupation with the influence of malicious animal magnetism sensitized her followers to the dangers of the world outside the safety of the Church.[2]

[1] Bryan R. Wilson, 'The Origins of Christian Science: a survey', *The Hibbert Journal*, 57 (1959), pp. 161–70.

[2] Roy Wallis, 'Ideology, authority and the development of cultic movements', *Social Research*, 41, 2 (1974), pp. 299–327. Roy Wallis, 'A comparative analysis of problems and processes of change in two manipulationist movements: Christian Science and Scientology', in *The Contemporary Metamorphosis of Religion?* Acts of the 12th International Conference on the Sociology of Religion (The Hague, Netherlands, 1973), pp. 407–22; Ernest S. Bates and John V. Dittemore, *Mary Baker Eddy: the Truth and The Tradition* (George Routledge & Sons, London, 1933); Edwin Franden Dakin, *Mrs Eddy: the Biography of a Virginal Mind* (Charles Scribner's & Sons, London 1929); Charles S. Braden, *Christain Science Today* (Southern Methodist University Press, Dallas, Texas, 1958); Bryan R. Wilson, *Sects and Society* (Heinemann, London, 1961).

have greater capabilities than their other status attributes would suggest. It provides a conviction of hidden powers, talents and abilities for individuals who lack clear sources of such conviction in their other achievements. It perhaps provides a functional alternative for those who sought psychological and social improvement through Dianetics.

Unity School of Christianity was much influenced by the diffusion of Christian Science teaching. Its founders, Charles and Myrtle Fillmore appear to have been active in the cultic milieu of Kansas City. Charles Fillmore had been a follower of spiritualism for many years and had a clear acquaintance with various metaphysical schools, as well as having contact with a number of Christian Science schismatics and teachers in the emerging New Thought movement. The sources of Unity teaching have been traced in New England Transcendentalism, Theosophy, Christian Science, spiritualism, and New Thought.[1]

The movement was organized primarily through the medium of a number of magazines produced by the Fillmores. While early editions of their magazines exhibited an eclectic orientation, containing articles on Christian Science, Theosophy, spiritualism and Rosicrucianism, they progressively moved toward a more rigid and intolerant editorial policy, and a less open doctrinal system. Elements derived from Christian Science and the New Thought Movement became more prominent, although Unity was distinguished from these movements by the extent to which it incorporated features of traditional Christian doctrine. Unity broke with the loose International New Thought Alliance because of the 'open-platform' policy of that body, which permitted lecturers from all affiliated groups to lecture at centres of other members. The Fillmores began to resent this freedom to present ideas at variance with their own at Unity centres, particularly when they discovered that in some centres teachers were holding spiritualist seances and practising numerology.[2]

A 'Statement of Faith' was drawn up, to which followers were required to subscribe, and greater controls over ministers and centre leaders implemented. Formerly autonomous centres were required to use textbooks and other literature published by the central organization, and to eliminate all literature and teachings not approved by the leadership.[3]

Dianetics, Christian Science and Unity illustrate in their early years the problem of institutional fragility faced by the leaders of cultic movements. Their belief-systems were precarious in that they were liable to selective acceptance and synthesis by seekers recruited often from other cultic groups. Authority within the movement was open to challenge by practitioners, teachers and leaders of local followings. The commitment of members was limited because the doctrine and practice offered was not seen as having any unique salvational efficacy, and hence the loyalty of members was often shared with other groups and practices.

[1] James Teener, 'Unity School of Christianity', Unpublished PhD dissertation, University of Chicago, 1939.

[2] J. Stillson Judah, *The History and Philosophy of the Metaphysical Movements in America* (Westminster Press, Philadelphia, 1967), p. 244.

[3] Roy Wallis, 'Ideology, authority and the development of cultic movements', op. cit.

These features of cultic movements provide a set of environmental and structural contingencies with which the movement leadership is faced. They pose a threat to the persistence of the collectivity. In the face of such a threat, a strategy of *sectarianization*, the arrogation and centralization of authority and control, appears to have had a considerable appeal to cult leaders. If successfully implemented – as in the cases of Dianetics, Christian Science, and Unity – such a strategy may result in the emergence of a distinct ideology which only the leadership may interpret or extend; a reduction in the autonomy of members and practitioners; and the emergence of a stable and cohesive collectivity organized around the leader.

Elting Memorial Library
93 Main St.
New Paltz, N. Y.

Part III
THE SECT: SCIENTOLOGY

4. THEORY AND ITS TRANSMISSION

Several million words have been written on the theory and practice of Scientology, for the most part by Hubbard himself. While the basis of the theory has changed relatively little since 1952, the techniques employed to secure the ends specified by the theory have changed frequently as one thing after another was tried in an effort to find the set of techniques which would routinely achieve these ends. A full account of the theory and practise of Scientology and their vicissitudes over the past twenty-two years or so would be tiresome and unenlightening, perhaps even to the committed adherent. Moreover, much of the material to provide such an account consists of confidential documents and tape-recordings available only to the thoroughly initiated. However, published materials do permit the presentation of an outline of the theory of Scientology and a description of some of the techniques that have been prominently employed. It is hoped that the following account will convey the 'flavour' of both practice and doctrine, although it must necessarily fall short of being a complete set of recipes for the attainment of the state of 'Operating Thetan'.

Cosmologica
The theory and practice of Scientology is underpinned by a cosmology. Hubbard's notion of 'theta' began life as 'thought' or as an impersonal life-force, but became in the course of several re-workings an animate entity, the 'thetan'. The thetan according to Hubbard is

> A Static with the ability to consider, postulate, and have opinions, that has, through postulates and considerations, developed a differentiation from the static theta. The thetan is the 'I' the individual that force, not a part of the physical universe, which is directing the organism.[1]

The thetan is immortal, 'omniscient and omnipotent'.[2] the true self of each individual, which has existed since before the beginning of matter, energy, space,

[1] L. Ron Hubbard, *The Creation of Human Ability* (Scientology Publications, London, 1955), p. 286.
[2] Robert H. Thomas, Guardian of the Church of Scientology in the USA, quoted in Omar V. Garrison, *The Hidden Story of Scientology* (Arlington Books, London, 1974), p. 53.

and time. These latter are merely the creations of thetans bored with their existence. 'Life' Hubbard assures us, 'is a game'.[1] To enliven the game, thetans permitted limitations upon their abilities. They began to create matter, energy, space, and time (MEST), to form universes and worlds with which, and in which, they could play. These worlds might take any variety of forms, but gradually the thetans became increasingly attracted by the universes they had created. Progressively they became absorbed into the games they were playing, permitting further limitation of their abilities, imposing limitations upon other thetans, forgetting their spiritual nature, and becoming more dependent upon the material universes that they had created. While the MEST universe began as the postulation of thetans it gradually acquired an overwhelming sense of reality. The thetans became so enmeshed in their creation they forgot their origins and true status, lost the ability to mobilize their spiritual capacities, and came to believe that they were no more than the bodies they inhabited.[2]

Hubbard therefore claims that each thetan has taken on many millions of MEST bodies during the trillions of years of its existence. During this time it has been subjected to many traumas, such as the loss (through death) of the MEST body with which it has come to identify itself entirely; attacks by other thetans or other life forms (in which 'implants' are received); and the psychic damage to itself which accrues when the thetan, or the body which it was inhabiting, harmed or sought to control another. The techniques of Scientology aim to restore to the thetan his original capabilities:

> Almost the entirety of Scientology consists of the discovery and refinement of methods whereby the Thetan can be persuaded to relinquish his self-imposed limitations.[3]

Having relinquished them, the individual achieves the state of 'Operating Thetan', a state, the exalted nature of which, is indicated by the following:

> Operating Thetan has not before been known as a state of being on Earth. Neither Lord Buddha nor Jesus Christ were OTs according to the evidence. They were just a shade above Clear.[4]

The methods employed in the process of achieving the states of clear and OT, have taken a number of forms.

Incidents on the 'whole track' or the recordings of events possessed in the form of 'facsimiles' or mental image pictures by each thetan, may be 'run' (that is, audited or processed) as engrams. *Have You Lived Before This Life?* is a collection

[1] L. Ron Hubbard, *Scientology 8–8008* (Hubbard College of Scientology, East Grinstead, Sussex, 1967), p. 107.

[2] Christopher Evans, *Cults of Unreason* (Harrap, London, 1973), pp. 43–5; Cyril Vosper, *The Mind Benders* (Neville Spearman, London, 1971), pp. 28–31; Garrison, op. cit., pp. 49–53.

[3] Vosper, op. cit., p. 31.

[4] *Ability*, 81 [c. 1959], p. 6.

of reports by auditors and pre-clears of the processing of whole-track (or past-life) engrams. For example:

Scientologist's Report
Located the incident with the command 'Have you ever died?' The E-meter needle dropped. 'Was it more than 100 years ago?' Needle dropped . . . Carried on like this and finally located it at 55,000,000,000,000,000,000,000 years ago . . .
'Be in that incident'. 'What part of that incident can you confront?' and we were away. First picture that came was of the sea, great deal of unreality but by discussion and continuing the question 'What part of that incident can you confront?' various other pictures and sensations uncovered which eventually added up to a section of the incident concerning a giant Manta Ray type of acquatic creature which the preclear had seen while underwater . . . the engram started on [a] spaceship. The ship had needed an outside repair. On going outside, the preclear had been hit by a meteorite particle which had not punctured the suit. At this point an acute pain under the arm where the meteor had struck, occurred. The Pc clambers back into the space-ship. Later the atomic engines of the ship break down and the Pc has to repair these and apparently receives radio-active burns. He finds that he has to leave the ship and so falls from a ladder into the sea where he encounters the Manta Ray.[1]

Another report recounts how the

. . . Pc, after a period of 440 years without a body, arrives in error on a planet which is being taken over by 'Black Magic' operators who are very low on the ethical scale and using electronics for evil purposes. Having come originally from a 'good' planet he battles for a long, long time against the forces of 'black magic', which, like a fifth column, are subverting the originally 'white magic' populace. It is a losing battle, implant after implant gradually weakening his ability and control by causing hallucinated perceptions. Eventually after a period of spiritual torment and grief he abandons his former high goals and goes over to the 'Black Magic' faction, not having entirely given up the idea of outwitting it from within. This occurs some 74,000 years after his first arrival on this planet.
He now goes to another planet by space ship. A deception is accomplished by hypnosis and pleasure implants (rather like opium in their effects) whereby he is deceived into a love affair with a robot decked out as a beautiful red-haired girl who receives all his confidences for a period of 50 years [Etc.][2]

The other incidents reported in this work range across lives as a supporter of the Pretender after the '45, a Tibetan nobleman in the sixteenth century, the captain of a space-ship, a space pilot with a robot body over a million years ago, etc.

[1] L. Ron Hubbard, *Have You Lived Before This Life?*, *A Scientific Survey* (The Department of Publications World Wide [Church of Scientology, East Grinstead], 1968), pp. 53–4.
[2] Ibid., pp. 156–7.

Running past-life incidents as engrams is not, however, typical of contemporary Scientology technique. Unlike Dianetics, Scientology does not seek to erase the causes of limitations on the individual's full capacity, since with the development of the belief in the whole-track, this would be far too lengthy and arduous a process. The aim of Scientology is therefore to free the thetan from the limitations of MEST and the control of the facsimiles he has recorded, and to increase his awareness of his spiritual capacities to such an extent that he becomes the cause and not merely the effect of his environment and his life (and of course, his past lives).[1]

Central themes in Scientological theory

While Scientological theory is underpinned by a cosmology and extensive metaphysics, little of this is initially transmitted to the following in an overtly dogmatic fashion. There is a recognition that the theory of the origins of the universe and the space-operatic scenarios of some of the more distant past-lives may 'have very little reality' for some adherents. These aspects of the ideology are referred to as 'para-Scientology', a category variously defined – for example:

> that large bin which includes all greater or lesser uncertainties. Here are the questionable things, the things of which the common normal observer cannot be sure with a little study . . . Some of the classified bodies of data which fall in Para-Scientology are: Dianetics, incidents on the 'whole-track', the immortality of Man, the existence of God, engrams containing pain and unconsciousness and yet all perception, pre-natals, clears, character, and many other things which, even when closely and minutely observed, still are not certain things to those who observe them. Such things have relative truth. [. . .]
> Also under the heading of Para-Scientology one would place such things as past-lives, mysterious influences, astrology, mysticism, religion, psychiatry, nuclear physics and any other science based on theory.[2]

The para-Scientological is held not to be required belief, and indeed Hubbard has frequently expressed the view that new followers or potential converts should not be exposed to it at too early a stage. 'Talking whole track to raw meat' is frowned upon,

> Now, in talking to a group, steer off from para-Scientology. Lay off the whole track stuff, huh? Lay off the fantastic. If you have some chap around who insists on telling people about these things, just note him down; he isn't working for us, fellahs. The quickest way to lose a beset person or group is to load him down with phenomena. Talk, instead, about the fact that there is a spiritual side to Man. Talk about the fact that Scientology solves social problems. When they are very initiate and it's all

[1] L. Ron Hubbard, *Dianetics 55!* (Department of Publications World Wide, East Grinstead, 1968), p. 18.

[2] L. Ron Hubbard, *The Creation of Human Ability* (Scientology Publications, London, 1955), pp. 188–9.

in good fun and they've also got their HPA or HCA, do what you like with the whole track. Or use it in private sessions. Don't hand it out to the public raw. It's too strong.[1]

This policy is also reflected in the relative dearth of published information on this aspect of Scientological belief. Past-lives are discussed in only three of the movement's books in any detail, and there is no systematic account of the cosmological doctrine in any publicly available documents.

Most published work deals with those aspects of the doctrine which have a practical relevance, and it is to these that Scientologists themselves seem to have strongest commitment. Many of these derive directly from earlier Dianetic practice. The notion of ARC and the tone-scale, for example, were carried over into Scientology with only minor modification. With the transition to Scientology, however, a number of new elements were added or differently stressed. While 'exteriorization' had been seen as a state in need of remedy in Dianetics, it was now seen as a state to be aimed for:

> The usual residence of the thetan is in the skull or near the body. A thetan can be in one of four conditions. The first would be entirely separate from a body or bodies, or even from this universe. The second would be near a body and knowingly controlling the body. The third would be in the body (the skull) and the fourth would be an inverted condition whereby he is compulsively away from the body and cannot approach it.
> ... one of the many goals of processing in Scientology is to 'exteriorise' the individual and place him in the second condition above, since it has been discovered that he is happier and more capable when so situated.[2]

Recovering the thetan's ability 'to confront' his environment is also an important goal.

> That which a person can confront he can handle. The first step of handling anything is gaining an ability to face it.[3]
> Problems start with an inability to confront anything.[4]

Not confronting things one has done leaves one 'in mystery' about them and subject to their impact. Being able 'to confront', to face up to, and take responsibility for, things one has done would erase their power. One might illustrate this as follows: a man who causes an accident which injures others might repress his part in the incident and in his future interactions with these others behave in an aberrated fashion – for example, attacking them for their clumsiness and causing further trauma out of fear of being found out. Were he able to confront

[1] L. Ron Hubbard, *Professional Auditor's Bulletin*, 61 (16 September 1955), p. 2.
[2] L. Ron Hubbard, *The Fundamentals of Thought* (The Publications Organisation World Wide, Edinburgh, 1968), pp. 57–8.
[3] L. Ron Hubbard, *Scientology A New Slant on Life* (The American St Hill Organisation, Los Angeles, California, 1965), p. 85.
[4] Ibid.

his part in the incident and take responsibility for it, the situation might improve rather than continue to deteriorate.

The theory of 'confronting' has a number of ramifications. In this life and in past lives we have all performed a number of 'overt acts'.[1] Generally we justify such acts by means of a 'motivator'[2] and they become 'withholds'.[3] Having withholds against some person or group leads to guilt and fear about being found out which in turn leads one to perform further overt acts against them. It is by means of this theory that Scientologists explain attacks upon them by press, politicians, doctors, and psychiatrists, and other 'enemies' of Scientology.[4] The notion of the withhold became particularly prominent in the practice of 'Sec Checking'.[5]

A further fundamental concept in Scientology theory is that of communication. The individual spends most of his time out of communication with his environment (out of present time). He is held at some point on the 'time-track' as a result of trauma or 'misemotion' and lives out his present involvements from a point of view in the past. Scientology aims therefore to bring the individual 'up to present time'.

> When we say that somebody should be in present time we mean that he should be in communication with his environment. We mean further that he should be in communication with his environment as it exists, not as it existed.[6]

Many psychosomatic ailments are held to be the result of the individual, the thetan, being out of communication with a particular part of his body, and living, in relation to that body part, at some point in the past when it suffered pain. Techniques have been developed which seek to bring him into communication in present time with that body part.[7]

[1] 'OVERT ACT (Overt): Harmful or contra-survival act. Precisely, it is an act of commission or omission that harms the greater number of dynamics', Anonymous, *Scientology Abridged Dictionary* (Scientology Publications Organization, Copenhagen, 1970).

[2] 'The consideration and dramatisation that one has been wronged by the action of another or a group, and which is characterised by constant complaint with no real action undertaken to resolve the situation'. Ibid.

[3] 'WITHHOLD: Undisclosed contra-survival act; a no action after the fact of action, in which the individual has done or been an accessory to doing something which is a transgression against some moral or ethical code consisting of agreements to which the individual has subscribed in order to guarantee, with others, the survival of a group with which he is coacting or has coacted towards survival'. Ibid.

[4] See Chapter 8, below.

[5] For the practice of 'Sec Checking', see Chapter 5, below; Paulette Cooper, *The Scandal of Scientology* (Tower, New York, 1971), pp. 85–92.

[6] L. Ron Hubbard, *Dianetics 55!* (The Department of Publications World Wide, East Grinstead, 1968), p. 62.

[7] These techniques of an informal kind are known as 'assists', on which see L. Ron Hubbard, Jr., George Richard Halpern and Jan Halpern (compilers), *ACC Prepara-*

Improving the individual's ability to communicate therefore improves his ability to handle his body and his environment, bringing him to present time, and releasing him from points on the time track at which he has become stuck. Improving communication therefore means improving the individual's abilities in general.

The notion of control is important in Scientology theory. The thetan has permitted itself to become 'an effect' of the universe. It has allowed itself to believe that it has no spiritual powers and that it is merely the body it inhabits. Having denied its spiritual powers it has become prey to its creation, suffering the traumas and injuries of its bodies, the guilt and fear of its overt acts, reacting to its environment on a stimulus – response basis, obsessively holding on to MEST and facsimiles out of confusion and insecurity. One aim of Scientology processing is therefore to increase the thetan's ability to control the body it inhabits and its environment, to be willing to have and 'not-have' MEST, postulates, facsimiles, etc. That is, to overcome the stimulus-response reaction and increase the self-determinism of the thetan; to restore its ability to be 'at cause' over its environment.

> CLEAR: (noun) A thetan who can be at cause knowingly and at will over mental matter, energy, space and time as regards the First Dynamic (survival for self).[1]
> O.T. (Operating Thetan): A Clear who has been familiarised with his environment to a point of total cause over matter, energy, space, time and thought, and who is not in a body.[2]

The final aspect of the theory of Scientology which I wish to discuss is that of its metatheoretic assumptions. Hubbard has defined Scientology in a variety of ways. In his early formulations, he stressed the scientific status of the enterprise.

> Scientology is defined as the science of knowing how to know.[3]

Hubbard developed the principle that in contrast to the fields generally termed 'sciences' which were full of 'maybes' Scientology was 'the science of certainty'.[4]

> You aren't a scientist, and you don't have to be wishy washy and indefinite about what you say.[5]

Scientology was the study of knowledge, dealing in 'stable data'. 'Knowledge is certainty'[6] and moreover 'Certainty is *sanity*'.[7] This conception of what issued

---

[1] Anonymous, *Scientology Abridged Dictionary*, op. cit.

[2] Ibid.

[3] L. Ron Hubbard, *Scientology 8-8008*, 2nd edn (HASI, London, 1953), p. 5.

[4] *Journal of Scientology*, 166, n.d.

[5] *Professional Auditor's Bulletin*, 16 (September 1955), p. 3.

[6] L. Ron Hubbard, 'The three universes', *Certainty*, unnumbered issue, n.d. (transcription of a lecture delivered by Hubbard at Birmingham Town Hall in 1953), p. 5.

[7] Ibid., p. 4.

tory Manual for Advanced Students in Scientology (The Academy of Scientology, [Washington DC], 1957), pp. 30–45.

from the mouth of Hubbard as certain knowledge seems to stand in contradiction to the distinction drawn elsewhere between Scientology and para-Scientology, and the principle often quoted to show the non-dogmatic nature of the movement, that 'If it's true for you, then it's true.' Since Hubbard's science is a matter of knowledge and certainty, certainty is sanity, and reality is agreement, it would seem to follow that those who decline to agree with Hubbard's conception of what constitutes knowledge are out of touch with reality; and that those who reserve their judgement, or who retain some uncertainty as to the truth of his claims, are insane.

This impression is strengthened elsewhere. In his volume *Scientology 8–80*, for example, Hubbard argues:

> Neither you nor a preclear need accept 'whole track' or the identity of the thetan as described fully in *What To Audit*. Not to begin. You'll very rapidly make up your own mind about it when you start to process 'Black and White'.[1]
> As for 'whole track' and thetans, I wouldn't dare say a word if 'Black and White' didn't show them up with alarming velocity.[2]

In the same volume Hubbard provides a technique 'to separate the preclear from bodies and discover *why* he thinks he is only the current body . . .'[3] and in one of his recorded lectures he states:

> Those who do not believe in past lives do not have to believe in past lives . . . but don't get audited![4]

There can, therefore, be no doubt about how Hubbard intended his followers to make up their own minds.

Influences on Scientology theory

A number of sources have been suggested for aspects of Hubbard's theory and presentation. George Malko suggests that Hubbard may have found some inspiration in an early work by R. Buckminster Fuller, called *Nine Chains to the Moon*. Apart from one passage in which Fuller argues that 'the sum-total of human desire to survive is dominant over the sum-total of the impulse to destroy', and his propensity to utilize upper-case type for emphasis, I can discover no convincing links between the work of Fuller and that of Hubbard.[5] Dr A.

---

[1] L. Ron Hubbard, *Scientology 8–80* (The Distribution Center, Silver Springs, Maryland, 1952), p. 22.

[2] Ibid.

[3] Ibid., p. 31.

[4] L. Ron Hubbard, 'The skills of clearing', Lecture 2 of the *Lectures on Clearing*, London Congress, 1958 (Hubbard Communications Office, London, 1958).

[5] R. Buckminster Fuller, *Nine Chains to the Moon* (Southern Illinois University Press, 1938); George Malko, *Scientology: the Now Religion* (Dell Publishing Co., New York, 1970), pp. 119–21.

Nordenholz, whom Malko also suggests as an important influence on Hubbard, seems an initially more plausible candidate.

Nordenholz, in a thoroughly opaque work of philosophical speculation published in 1934,[1] presents the notion of 'scientology' as a science of knowledge to be developed on the basis of a set of axioms. Apart from the name of the 'science', its concern with knowledge and how to grasp it, and the idea of erecting a set of axioms as the basic formulation of the science, it is not evident that Nordenholz provided much that became incorporated into Hubbard's Scientology.[2]

It has also been suggested that Hubbard secured some of the material incorporated into Scientology from Jack Parsons, a follower of Aleister Crowley and briefly the head of a Lodge of Crowley's Ordo Templi Orientis in Pasadena.[3] That Hubbard was associated with Parsons early in 1946 is not in doubt, although a press release issued by the Church of Scientology after the appearance of Alexander Mitchell's article offers a different interpretation of the facts,[4] claiming that he was sent to live with Parsons by 'certain agencies [which] objected to nuclear physicists being housed under the same roof'.[5] There is no evidence that Hubbard's system of Scientology owes any great debt to that of Crowley, Parsons or the O.T.O. Indeed none of the four members of Crowley's order whom I have contacted in England and America has been able to confirm

[1] A. Nordenholz, *Scientologie, Wissenschaft von der Beschaffenheit und Der Tauglichkeit des Wissens* (Ernest Reinhardt, Munich, 1934).

[2] It is also a mystery how Hubbard could have come into contact with Nordenholz's work. Hubbard did not, as far as I have been able to discover, read German, nor have I been able to locate a translation of this book by Nordenholz prior to the version produced by a former Scientologist in 1968 (A. Nordenholz, *Scientologie 1934*, trans. Woodward R. McPheeters, Causation Press, Lucerne Valley, California, 1968). It is on the basis of this translation that Malko suggests Hubbard was indebted to Nordenholz (Malko, op. cit., pp. 116–19) but McPheeters was a Scientologist of many years standing who left the movement for a schismatic offshoot, and in an atmosphere of mutual hostility. It is at least a possibility that this may have influenced the translation. An independent translation which I commissioned, of some pages from the original, seems to bear this out. The possible parallels with Hubbardian formulations are very much less evident.

[3] Although he does not refer to Hubbard by name, I think there can be no doubt that this is the implication to be drawn from Kenneth Grant's remark that an unnamed associate of Parsons after the death of the latter 'is still at large, having grown wealthy and famous by a misuse of the secret knowledge which he had wormed out of Parsons'. Kenneth Grant, *The Magical Revival* (Muller, London, 1972), p. 107. The context makes it quite clear that Hubbard is the man referred to. The same implication is to be found in a newspaper feature by Alexander Mitchell, 'The odd beginning of Ron Hubbard's career', *Sunday Times*, 5 October 1969, p. 11.

[4] Which are misreported or misunderstood in some particulars by Mitchell.

[5] This press statement was for the most part reproduced in the *Sunday Times*, 28 December 1969. The newspaper also paid the Church of Scientology a small sum in settlement of an action initiated by the Church in respect of Mitchell's article. (Parsons was a research chemist working at the California Institute of Technology.)

any significant points of similarity.[1] The only apparent similarities are those which are common to a number of systems of magical and occult practice – for example, the belief that the individual has supernatural abilities such as telepathy, teleportation, and telekinesis, which can be achieved or regained through mental and spiritual exercises. In the case of many magical and occult systems these practices and their goals have been absorbed from Yoga.

In Yoga a number of parallels with Scientology are evident. Yoga offers a system of metaphysical knowledge leading to 'rebirth to a non-conditioned mode of being'.[2] The aim of the earliest philosophy of Yoga, *sāmkhya*, was to dissociate the spirit from matter.[3] In Yoga the world is real not illusory, but its endurance is the result of the ignorance of spirit. When 'the last self shall have found its freedom, the creation in its totality will be reabsorbed into the primordial substance.'[4] The source of the soul's suffering is held to be man's solidarity with the cosmos, his participation in nature (the enturbulation of theta and MEST?).[5]

The conception of Spirit in Yoga is remarkably close to that of the thetan:

> Vedānta . . . regards Spirit as a unique, universal and external reality, dramatically enmeshed in the temporal illusion of creation (*māyā*). Samkhya and Yoga deny Spirit (*purusa*) any attribute and any relation; according to these two 'philosophies', all that can be affirmed of *purusa* is that it *is* and that it *knows* . . .[6]

Elements of the cosmology appear similar (although Yoga seems to have only a very rudimentary cosmology).

> From all eternity Spirit has found itself drawn into . . . illusory relation with psycho-mental life (that is, with 'matter'). This is owing to ignorance . . .[7]

While Yoga accepts the existence of God, the work of Patanjali, like that of Hubbard, did not accord him very much importance.[8] Yoga also contains the notion of the transmission of the 'subconscious' through Karmic transmigration.[9] After penetrating normally inaccessible areas of consciousness and reality, the yogin was believed to acquire *siddhis*, or miraculous powers – knowing one's previous existences, invisibility, great physical power, the power of rising in the air, of controlling and dominating any being, etc.,[10] although wanton use of

---

[1] The author, John Symonds, also paid a sum in settlement after his book on Crowley, *The Great Beast*, suggested a connexion between Crowley's 'tenet's of black magic' and 'the principles of Scientology' (*The Guardian*, 22 November 1974).

[2] Mircea Eliade, *Yoga: Immortality and Freedom* (Routledge & Kegan Paul, London, 1958), p. 4.

[3] Ibid., p. 8.   [4] Ibid., p. 9.   [5] Ibid., p. 10.

[6] Ibid., p. 16.   [7] Ibid., p. 27.

[8] Ibid., p. 29. God or the Supreme Being is mentioned in Scientological works, (see, for example, *The Background and Ceremonies of Church of Scientology of California, World Wide* (Church of Scientology, East Grinstead, 1970), p. 22), but does not figure greatly in either theory or practice.

[9] Ibid., p. 42.   [10] Ibid., pp. 85, 129.

them was believed to preclude further advance to the ultimate goal of yogic practice, immortality.[1]

Eliade even gives some ground for believing that the nature of the practice, while updated and elaborated in Scientology, may have had common features with Yoga:

> The scholastic Buddhist texts give us some details of the technique employed. It is the faculty that consists in retracing in memory the days, months and years until one arrives at one's time in the womb and finally at one's past lives . . .[2]

This is, however, clearly more reminiscent of early Dianetics than of current Scientology practices. Hubbard has credited the Vedic Hymns as one source of his inspiration[3] and the claim that Scientology has been most strongly influenced by such ancient eastern sources is one that might perhaps be taken more seriously. Certainly on the basis of Eliade's account of the theory and practice of Yoga, impressive similarities are to be found with the theory and practice of Scientology and Dianetics.

Auditing

Thousands of techniques to be used in auditing have appeared, although many are no longer in use and only a practising Scientologist would be able to say what currently constituted 'standard technology'. Many techniques are

---

[1] Hubbard has also counselled against the misuse of occult abilities regained on the path to Operating Thetan. These are also similar to the abilities of the Buddha to which monks aspire as earnests of their progress to *Neikban* (*Nirvana*).

'1. Knowledge of previous life (that is, total recall of all of his existences and of anyone else's).
2. Power of great sight (not only to see great distances but also to see through, over, and under objects. To see anything in the world at any time).
3. Complete absence of sexual desire (indicating fulfillment and complete satiation).
4. Ability to change his size (to any largeness or smallness).
5. Power of great hearing (to hear any sound anywhere at any time).
6. Power to cause events (if he wants a thing to happen, to will it).
7. Power to be where he wants (by an act of will to transport himself to where he wishes to be).
8. Power to be invisible.
9. Power to walk on air.
10. Power to know all that is known.'

Manning Nash, *The Golden Road to Modernity* (Wiley, New York, 1965), p. 149. Scientologists have claimed all but items 3, 5, and 10. I have not known Scientologists anxious to achieve item 3, and since Scientology is the science of knowing how to know, the achievement of item 10 must ultimately be a goal, although I have not known any Scientologist to claim that he possessed this ability.

[2] Eliade, op. cit., p. 184.

[3] L. Ron Hubbard, *Scientology 8–8008*, op. cit., 'Foreword'. Eliade, (op. cit., p. 102) suggests, however, that 'only the rudiments of classic Yoga are to be found in the Vedas . . .'

directed to the goal of giving the pre-clear a 'subjective reality' on his abilities as a thetan. One of the most basic is that of asking the pre-clear (the thetan) to give up the (self-imposed) need to be in a body, by 'exteriorizing' from that body:

> Ask preclear to be three feet behind his head. If stable there, have him be in various pleasant places until any feeling of scarcity of viewpoints is resolved. Then have him be in several undesirable places, then several pleasant places; then have him be in a slightly dangerous place, then in more dangerous places until he can sit in the center of the Sun.[1]

A development along these lines was known as the 'Grand Tour'.

> The commands of the Grand Tour are as follows: 'Be near Earth', 'Be near the Moon', 'Be near the Sun', 'Earth', 'Moon', 'Sun', giving the last three commands many times. Each time the auditor must wait until the preclear signifies that he has completed the command. The preclear is supposed to move near the bodies or simply be near them, it does not matter which. The Grand Tour continues with 'Now find a rock', 'Be inside of it', 'Be outside of it', 'Inside', 'Outside', 'Inside', 'Outside', 'Be in the centre of the Earth', 'Be outside of Earth', 'Inside', 'Outside', and back and forth until the preclear is able to do this very rapidly. Then the Grand Tour continues, 'Be near Mars' [Etc].[2]

Another purely mental technique much employed in Scientology's early days was a technique known as 'holding anchor points'. The purpose of this technique was held to be that of enabling the thetan 'to tolerate or make space'.[3] The preclear while seated would be told

> . . . 'Close your eyes', 'Locate an upper corner of the room behind you'. When he has done so, 'Now locate the other upper corner behind you', 'All right, hold on to these two corners, and don't think' . . . At the end of 15 minutes the auditor says, 'Now, find the third corner behind you', . . . When the auditor is assured the pre-clear has done this, he says, 'Now hold on to the same two you had before and the new one'. When the preclear has all three corners at once, the Auditor says, 'Now hold on to those three corners and don't think'. . . . The auditor then has the pre-clear locate all eight corners of the room and says, 'Now hold on to all eight corners of the room, sit back and don't think' . . . the Auditor has the preclear do this for at least fifteen minutes.[4]

Some thetans have allowed themselves to become so overwhelmed that they are no longer even able to control their bodies. A series of processes was designed to put the thetan back into communication with and control of his body. The first of these processes, known as CCH 1, involves the auditor and preclear sitting

---

[1] L. Ron Hubbard, 'This is Scientology: the science of certainty', *Journal of Scientology*, issue 16G, n.d. (some time in 1953), p. 12.

[2] L. Ron Hubbard, *The Creation of Human Ability* (Scientology Publications, London, 1955), p. 37, emphasis omitted.

[3] Ibid., p. 95.

[4] Ibid., pp. 95–6.

facing each other. The auditor commands, 'Give me that hand'. If the preclear gives him the hand the auditor gives it a slight pressure then returns it to the preclear's lap. If the preclear does not proffer the hand, the auditor takes it and does the same. This process may be run for several hours.[1]

CCH 6 took the following form:

> (auditor takes a book and bottle, placing them some distance apart on tables so that the preclear doesn't have to bend). 'With that body's eyes look at that book'. 'Thank you'. 'Walk that body over to that book'. 'Thank you'. . . . . 'With that hand pick up that book'. 'Thank you'. 'Put that book down in exactly the same place'. 'Thank you'. 'Turn that body round'. 'Thank you'. 'With that body's eyes look at that bottle'; etc.[2]

A further technique of some prominence in the 1950s was known as 'Waterloo Station' (or 'Union Station' in America).

> In a populated area (park; RR Station, etc) have pc tell auditor something he wouldn't mind not-knowing about persons or the persons not-knowing about him which auditor spots for him.
> Commands: Auditor: 'Do you see that (man, woman, described slightly)?'
> Pc: 'Yes'. [. . .]
> Auditor: 'Tell me something you wouldn't mind not-knowing about that person'.
> [. . .] the pc selects things he already can know to not-know. He does not give things he does not know anyway. This stress is the willingness to Not-Know things one already knows [sic]. Otherwise pc will become confused.
> [. . .] When . . . run flat or to a dope-off, reverse to:[3]
> Auditor: 'Tell me something you wouldn't mind that person not knowing about you'.
> [. . .] Run one side for hours then the other side in ordinary use.
> [. . .] The goal of Waterloo Station is not to make the pc make *one* thing vanish. That phenomenon is just the start. Auditor's have been quitting when the pc made somebody's hat disappear. When the pc can make the whole universe wink on and off at his consideration to know or not know it, you're getting somewhere – so don't stop at a hat.[4]

One basic aim of Scientology auditing is therefore to make the preclear aware that reality is a matter of his considerations, and changing his considerations will change the nature of reality. The theory and practice of Scientology is radically idealist in orientation.[5]

[1] L. Ron Hubbard, 'Procedure CCH', *Professional Auditor's Bulletin* 133 (1 April 1958).

[2] L. Ron Hubbard, 'Procedure CCH continued', *Professional Auditor's Bulletin*, 135 (1 May 1958).

[3] That is, a process is flat when it no longer produces change; dope-off is a sensation of drowsiness.

[4] L. Ron Hubbard, 'Six levels of processing', *Professional Auditor's Bulletin*, 69 (6 January 1956).

[5] L. Ron Hubbard, *Dianetics 55!* (The Department of Publications World Wide, East Grinstead, 1968), p. 67.

The E-Meter

Most current auditing (or processing, the terms are synonymous) is conducted with the aid of the E-meter.[1] The E-meter is a technological aid which has been developed to assist the process of auditing. It is a form of skin galvanometer operating on the principle of the Wheatstone Bridge which measures resistance to a current passing between two terminals. The terminals usually employed in Scientology auditing and training are ordinary tin cans. In the auditing situation, a slight current is transmitted through the pre-clear from one terminal to another, the resistance being measured on a dial. The needle on the dial moves in response to a variety of factors such as an increase in skin salinity resulting from sweat, skin surface area in contact with the terminals, pressure, etc. It is the view of the Scientologists that they are able to detect what are known to them as 'body-reads', and therefore are able to isolate readings which reflect changes in the state of the thetan. The E-meter is held to be infallible. It 'sees all, knows all. It is never wrong.'[2] A complex terminology is associated with 'needle action' on the E-meter – 'theta bop', 'rock slam', 'floating needle', etc., each of which indicates particular characteristics of the pre-clear, his mental and spiritual state.[3] Although the E-meter was first introduced into Dianetics by Volney G. Mathison in 1951, it was little employed until the emergence of Scientology in 1952. Mathison continued to mix Dianetics and Scientology with other practices. For a time he formed an alliance with the leaders of a therapeutic movement known as Concept Therapy, and marketed his meters to Concept Therapists and Chiropractors. Later Electropsychometry seems to have become an independent, if rather insignificant, movement in North America.[4] Mathison's incorrigible eclecticism led to a break between him and Hubbard, after which, for some time, the E-meter fell out of use in Scientology. By 1957, however, Hubbard and his associates had developed their own transistorized version of the machine and it returned to favour.[5]

[1] 'The E-meter is essential for all modern auditing with but a few exceptions'. Cyril Vosper, *The Mind Benders* (Neville Spearman, London, 1971), p. 83.

[2] L. Ron Hubbard, *Electropsychometric Auditing Operator's Manual* (HASI, London, n.d. [c. 1953–4]), p. 57.

[3] On the E-meter, see: L. Ron Hubbard, *E-Meter Essentials 1961* (Hubbard Communications Office, East Grinstead, 1961); L. Ron Hubbard, *The Book Introducing the E-Meter* (The Publications Organisation World Wide, Edinburgh, 1968); Mary Sue Hubbard (Compiler), *The Book of E-Meter Drills* (Hubbard College of Scientology, East Grinstead, 1967). Also see Kevin V. Anderson, *Report of the Board of Inquiry into Scientology* (Government Printer, Melbourne, 1965), Chapter 14; Cooper, op. cit., Chapter 18; Evans, op. cit., pp. 63–6.

[4] See John A. Lee, *Sectarian Healers and Hypnotherapy* (Queen's Printer, Toronto, 1970), Chapters 5 and 6.

[5] Anonymous, *The Story of Dianetics and Scientology Training*, (*The Auditor*, Supplement 6), SPO A/S, Copenhagen, 1969.

Contemporary processing

Processing or auditing is organized on the basis of a strict progression of pro-cedures. Each level or 'grade' has set processes associated with it which aim to produce different abilities. Passing through this progression of levels is known as 'getting your grades'. The first of these, Grade O, seeks to release the pre-clear from inhibitions about communication. When successfully completed, one becomes a 'communications release'.[1]

The auditing commands (questions) are: 'What are you willing to tell me about?'; 'What are you willing to tell me about it?' The pre-clear, holding the cans of the E-Meter, answers each of these questions in turn until the auditor spots a 'floating needle'. This indicates that the pre-clear has achieved a 'cognition' or insight concerning communication (or whatever he is being audited on) and should be accompanied by 'good indicators', a bright, aware, happy expression. In the course of such a process the pre-clear may offer many hundreds of answers to the auditing question. As may readily be seen, the nature of these answers may become very intimate, personal, even obscene. This feature of auditing has sometimes disturbed investigators of Scientology prac-tices,[2] but in this respect, opposition to the techniques would seem to be no more rationally based than earlier opposition to Freudian revelations, particularly with respect to the sexuality of children and infants.[3]

Grade I is Problems Release. The auditing commands are, 'Tell me a problem' and 'How would you solve it?'[4] Grade II is Relief Release, which deals with 'Overts' and 'Withholds', with the commands: 'What have you done?'; 'What haven't you said?'. Several further levels have to be negotiated before the pre-clear can undertake clearing and then the processes for the OT levels. Since some of these more advanced levels are self-audited (the pre-clear, employing a specially designed E-meter attachment, himself reads the E-meter and gives himself the auditing commands, or undertakes the other technical requirements for the process), the pre-clear who wishes simply to achieve the goals of auditing for himself has to undertake only the minimum amount of training required for him to be able to conduct self-auditing. This is known as the 'Processing Route'. The pre-clear is, however, strongly encouraged to take the 'Training Route', that is to become an expert auditor, able to carry out auditing upon others as well as himself. By this means, the pre-clear is encouraged to seek clearing, etc., not only for himself but also for others. The client of Scientology

[1] L. Ron Hubbard, 'Classification gradation and awareness chart of levels and certificates' (Athena Publications, Denmark, 1970).

[2] For example, Anderson, op. cit., passim.

[3] For a reconstruction from his own experience of auditing sessions see Robert Kaufman, *Inside Scientology* (Olympia Press, London, 1972), passim. Grade O may sometimes be preceded by Straight Wire Release in which the auditing commands are: 'Recall a communication'; 'Recall something real'; 'Recall an emotion'; repeated (or 'run') until a 'floating needle' appears. See Malko, op. cit., p. 133.

[4] Kaufman, op. cit., p. 14 et seq.

is thereby transformed into an agent of the movement whose personal goals in Scientology become closely bound to his successful dissemination of the belief-system to others.[1] The lower levels of both auditing and training can be secured at a 'Franchise' or 'Mission' of the movement. These are semi-autonomous organizations which may be run by a single professional auditor, or in partnership. After completion of Grades I to IV, more advanced auditing (and all but the lowest levels of training) must be secured from a central organization. A fixed price-list exists for auditing and training. A franchise is not permitted to charge less than the central organization. In 1972 the Grades cost a total of around £200 for the levels from O to IV.[2] Additional auditing may be purchased as a block of hours – typically twenty-five hours – at a time. According to a price list issued in 1972, twenty-five hours of auditing could be bought for £150 with reductions for larger blocks purchased at one time and with discounts for various kinds of member (for example, someone both an International and local member could secure a discount of 20 per cent).[3]

Training

Training in Scientology usually begins with the HAS (Hubbard Apprentice Scientologist) Course. With this, as with most other levels of training, successful completion of the course is signified by an impressive certificate, and members often affect the initials of the successfully completed courses as honorific appellations to their names – John Smith HPA, for example. It is not unknown for individuals who have been awarded a Book Auditor's certificate, after reading and successfully applying the principles and practices indicated in one of Hubbard's texts, to employ the style B.A. after their names.[4] At one time 'degrees' were issued permitting the individual to employ the styles B.Scn, D.Scn, D.D., and even 'Freudian Analyst' after their names.

The HAS or Communications Course inculcates the basic training routines (TRs) which a successful auditor should employ. A well-trained auditor will always 'have his TRs in'. The purpose of the TRs is to train the student to confront the pre-clear without extraneous behaviour or habits getting in the way; to direct commands at the pre-clear in a clear and authoritative manner; and to ensure that the pre-clear replies or follows the command without allowing him to distract the auditor from carrying out the process; to acknowledge the pre-clear's communications, etc.

The first routine, TR O requires the student and the coach (typically a fellow student, each taking turns at the two roles) simply to sit facing each other, neither

---

[1] This is taken up in detail in Chapter VI.
[2] *The Auditor*, 77 (1972).
[3] Leaflet sent to book purchasers.
[4] See the letter signed Frank E. Walker B.A. (Book Auditor) in *Certainty*, 1, 9 (n.d.), p. 13.

making any conversation or effort to be interesting. Have them sit and look at each other and say and do nothing for some hours. Students must not speak, fidget, giggle or be embarrassed or anaten. It will be found the student tends to confront with a body part, rather than just confront, or to use a system of confronting rather than just be there. The drill is misnamed if Confront means to do something to the pc. The whole action is to accustom an auditor to being there three feet in front of a pre-clear without apologising or moving or being startled or embarrassed or defending self. After a student has become able to just sit there for two hours 'bull baiting' can begin.[1]

'Bull baiting' involves the coach seeking to provoke a reaction from the student by actions, other than touching the student, or by 'treading' on the students 'buttons', that is referring to subjects about which the student is likely to be sensitive and to which he might react. Kaufman details amusingly a bull baiting session.

Most coaches found it most convenient to try to make the auditor-in-training laugh. Morton described to me one such session. He and his coach sat in chairs facing each other, the coach almost on top of him, with his knees tightly pinning Morton's. The coach then set out to find Morton Morvis's *buttons* – subjects which broke him up and diverted his attention from his auditing. He began by investigating the possibility that Morton had a 'Jewish button' which needed *flattening* (the majority of Jewish people happened to have such a button).
'Mishter Morvish' crooned the coach, 'mosht pipple leff et me ven I tzing – but you von't leff et me ven I tzing will you, Mishter Morvish?' With that he cleared his throat and went into repeated choruses of *Tzum golly golly golly*. Other Scientologists took up the refrain until the tune reverberated in various voice registers throughout the room. An ingenious girl added as counterpoint *Theme from Exodus*: 'Dai dai . . . dai dai . . . dai dai dai dai dai DAIEE. . .'. The org resounded with the music and Morvis's gasps of laughter. Just as he had calmed down a stranger stepped into the room and announced 'I've just come from the planet Sholom in the galaxy of Sheket. Did you ever see a thetan wearing a yarmulka?' and they were off again. All told it took six hours to 'flatten' Morvis's Jewish button.[2]

The more advanced training courses require the reading of 'packs' of bulletins and policy letters by Hubbard, duplicated and stapled in folders. Each course has a particular pack. There are also voluminous tape-recordings of Hubbard's lectures to which the student must listen. The student may also be required to demonstrate his understanding of the material by producing a model in clay at the Clay Table, which illustrates the point of what he has learned. Students on courses are normally paired off to test each other in their knowledge of the course materials and to carry out training in auditing techniques. Each course pack has a 'check-sheet' indicating what has to be done to complete the course successfully. Each item on the check sheet has to be initialled by the coach or course instructor when the student has acquired the knowledge or skill required.

[1] L. Ron Hubbard, 'Modernized training drills', *HCO Bulletin*, 29 April 1963, cited in Anderson, op. cit., p. 81.
[2] Kaufman, op. cit., pp. 4–5.

At each level in training, the student acquires the ability to audit pre-clears on the corresponding processes. An auditor may only process pre-clears up to the level for which he has received training. Part of the course requirement is therefore to find one or more pre-clears to audit through the necessary levels to demonstrate one's proficiency.[1] In this way, training further mobilizes the student as an agent for the dissemination of Scientology. While one may find one's pre-clears among friends, since the pre-clear goes to a central organization for training he may often not know anyone whom he can ask,[2] and he therefore has to secure 'raw meat' through dissemination on the street, or at his lodgings.

On commencing a course the student is introduced to the others en masse, who warmly applaud him. Similarly, on the completion of any level of auditing or training the individual is congratulated by his auditor or his classmates. At the central organizations a student or pre-clear will be brought to the room where study is in progress. The instructor tells the students to stop work and announces the individual's achievement. The student/pre-clear then gives a short speech indicating his 'gains' from auditing or from the course, and is applauded by those present. On completion of auditing the pre-clear is taken to the Qualifications Division of the 'Org' where he is briefly checked on the meter to make certain that he has been released on the grade. At more advanced levels, 'attestation' that one has achieved the grade is generally all that is required. Similarly, having completed training, the student will 'attest' to his successful completion. He is then taken to the Success Department, where he is asked to write a 'success story', a few lines indicating his gains from the auditing or the course. These success stories are frequently printed in Scientology publications and provide an indication of what various levels of training and auditing meant to those who had undertaken them.

> I am no longer afraid of causing an unwanted effect on another being. This Grade has cleared out such a lot of garbage that I knew was there – but could never put my finger on, and so was therefore the effect of it. I feel great now that it's gone!
>   Expanded Grade 2 Clive Nichol.[3]
> It's really great not to be constantly worrying and bogging myself down with a burden of PROBLEMS. Another great win I have had from this level is that my eyesight has improved a lot, and it was good before!
>   Expanded Grade 1 Clive Nichol.[4]
> I am now beginning to get freedom from my compulsions which I have had for twenty years or more. These compulsions have always blunted my intentions. I now see myself becoming free and expanded. It means the restoration of life to me.
>   Quintin McDougall.[5]
> Before Scientology I didn't know what I wanted in life or what to do with my life.

[1] See ibid., p. 186.
[2] Moreover, most students and pre-clears will have passed the level he is on and are not permitted to go through the lower level auditing again.
[3] 'Auditing Successes', *Change* 59 (1973), no pagination.
[4] Ibid.   [5] Dianetic Successes', leaflet (1971).

I depended a lot on other people and their opinions. Since being in Scientology I know just what I want to do and I am getting it done.

Jenny Good.[1]

What a perfect gradient these Expanded Grades are. I no longer feel afraid of anything. I feel calm and very stable. I can grant more beingness to others. I like myself a lot better too. Ron has given man a terrific thing with the Expanded Grades. It's great to see the things that have been bothering me for years disappearing for good.

Robin Youngman.[2]

For the first time for a long time I feel free to communicate. It is really great and I know I can do it

Shirley Pyle.[3]

Right after Clear I hit a keyed out OT state and could change my body size about 1 to $1\frac{1}{2}$ inches in height by actual measurement. Some people swore it was 2 to 3 inches, which it might have been, but it was 1 inch difference the time I measured. The ability was under control and I could do it at will.

Fred Fairchild OTvi Clear No 49.[4]

Duplication of data often brings interesting abilities into view. I'm OT 1. While studying with intention in the privacy of my bedroom, I heard a noise in the adjoining den. I looked around to 'see' what it was, and behold, I looked right through the wall into the next room as though no wall was there. When your intention is very strong you can do what you intend to do. Wow! Do you intend to go CLEAR? And O.T.?

Herb Stutphin, OT1 Clear No 2313.[5]

Yesterday I was walking down the main street. A woman ahead of me coming in the opposite direction was coughing badly. I put across to her – telepathically – 'Are you OK?'.

When she got beside me she beamed and said 'Yes, that is a lot better now, thank you'. Well? The secret is on the OT Courses – come and get it too.

Viki Dickey OT[6]

Today was fantastic. I walked downstairs to get some coffee and the coffee machine was buzzing. So I put my hands out and moved them around the machine putting out beams to bounce back and thereby I could tell by watching the particle flow exactly where the error in the machine was. I found it and corrected the molecular structure of that area in the machine and the buzzing stopped.

Then I heard my air conditioner rattling so I looked at why it was rattling and it stopped.

I'm becoming much more at cause. I love it – like Superman!

Michael Pincus OT[7]

Thank you, Ron, for immortality.[8]

---

[1] 'Wins every day with Scientology!', leaflet (1971).

[2] Ibid.   [3] Ibid.

[4] 'Success beyond man's wildest dreams!', *Clear News*, 6 (12 December 1969).

[5] Ibid.   [6] 'OT Phenomena Successes', *Advance!* Issue 17 (1973), p. 14.

[7] Ibid., pp. 16–17.

[8] A—— S——, after Class Ten auditing. Original source unknown, but cited in an affidavit to the South African Commission of Enquiry into Scientology shown to me by its author.

Religious practices

Despite its stridency in the proclamation of Scientology as a church in recent years,[1] the religious practices of the movement other than processing, and training, are quite rudimentary. The central organizations of the movement usually have a chapel at which a Sunday service is given. This service generally takes the form of a lecture by the minister on some basic principle of Scientology. Part of a recorded lecture by Hubbard is sometimes played. There may be a question and answer period.[2] At one time a session of group auditing might be conducted.[3] Weddings are solemnized with full legal recognition in America and, following recent legislation, in Australia; or after a civil ceremony in Britain. Funerals and naming ceremonies are also performed and the movement, from time to time, holds Prayer Days which are well supported by its followers. It is difficult to see these as more than peripheral aspects of the practice of Scientology. The theory and practice is highly individualistic in orientation and has little communal significance which might be recognized and celebrated through public ceremonial. The chaplain has a rather marginal role within the organizational structure of the movement; he acts as a marriage guidance counsellor, and as an arbitrator for interpersonal disputes between members on matters of a non-organizational and non-ideological kind. Scientology auditors must undergo 'ministerial training' before practising professionally. Press photographs in recent years have usually shown Scientology Ministers attired in clerical collars.

Conclusions

Scientology theory and practice seems to be oriented to goals that have been traditional in the realms of the occult and to derive this orientation and some of its philosophical rationale from Yoga. The abilities to which Scientologists lay claim parallel the *siddhis* of the yogi. In their techniques, Dianetics and Scientology depart radically from the meditative techniques of earlier occult practices. The largely passive meditation and the exercises for physical, mental, and spiritual control have been replaced by highly directive, activist techniques. The use of the E-meter clothes these exercises in a scientific garb and provides an aura of technological precision and contemporaneity.

In the years since 1952 and the transition to Scientology, a clear direction is visible in the development of the practice and training. Dianetics, for all its pretentions to be 'an engineering science of the mind' was essentially an art,

---

[1] On the historical and organizational aspects of which, see Chapter 5.

[2] Anonymous, *Ceremonies of the Founding Church of Scientology* (Department of Publications World Wide, East Grinstead, 1967), pp. 7–8.

[3] Testimony of Joseph Charles Belotte in Founding Church of Scientology v. U.S.A. in U.S. Court of Claims, No. 226–61, Washington, D.C. 1967, stenographic transcript, pp. 244–5.

dependent upon the ingenuity, inventiveness, and charisma of the practitioner. It therefore contained a number of fundamental dangers. The practitioner in the therapeutic situation, with only general guidelines to the correct practise of auditing at his disposal, was thrown upon his own resources. In such circumstances many practitioners independently developed methods of their own which finally diverged so far from Dianetics as to challenge Hubbard's practice. The clientele became attached to a particular practitioner rather than to the movement as a whole, or to Hubbard as its leader. Moreover, given the relatively limited aims of Dianetics practice and the nature of its techniques, many of the clientele, regarding it purely as a psychotherapy, departed when they achieved (or sometimes when they failed to achieve) some concrete psychological or psychosomatic benefit.

Hubbard sought to control the movement by ideological and technological as well as organizational means. First, he generated very rapidly numerous new techniques. The practitioner, wishing to satisfy a clientele which desired the best and therefore the newest techniques, was forced to resort to the central organization much more frequently to keep abreast of developments. He was thus rendered more dependent upon the organization. Second, Hubbard sought to standardize practice. Only certain techniques might be used, and used only in the precise manner established by the organization. From the diffuse skills required in Dianetics auditing, processing with the E-meter particularly took the form of stereotyped delivery of standardized commands and acknowledgements. The potential charisma of the practitioner was thus considerably restricted as his role was changed from that of an intuitive therapist to that of a machine-operative who had simply to determine the appropriate process, deliver the commands from lists prepared by Hubbard, and observe needle action on the E-meter. Auditing became a semi-skilled occupation. Skill depended not on tacit professional knowledge of the auditor but on his ability precisely to duplicate the auditing technique established by Hubbard. Training was directed to this end of securing exact duplication of technique. Since anyone could be trained to carry out the highly standardized forms of practice, the individual practitioner was thereby rendered far less important than formerly. Practitioners became highly substitutable, limiting their autonomy. The likelihood of schism and fission, while not eliminated, was greatly undermined by limiting the practitioner's independent authority. The practice of Scientology was considerably de-personalized by these measures. (The Scientologists advise me that: 'The requirements for certification of auditors have risen as time has gone by . . . graduates of the Saint Hill Special Briefing Course are required to study the entire evolution of auditing in all its facets and to demonstrate their ability to apply this data.')[1]

Through the management of theory and practice, Hubbard sought not only to control practitioners, but also to mobilize pre-clears. A highly differentiated

[1] Personal communication, Guardian's Office, November 1974.

programme of auditing and training was made available, leading to esoteric occult goals rather than to mere psychological improvement. Only the lowest levels were available from practitioners and teachers not employed by the organization. Thus, rather than fully competent professionals, the franchise operator and field auditor became largely recruiting agents. Courses were organized on a continuous production-line basis. Since the material for the courses were available in standardized form through the duplicated course 'packs' written by Hubbard and the tape-recordings of his lectures, the student could begin at almost any time rather than wait, as in normal academic practice for the beginning of the academic year or term, or, as in other forms of training, until there were enough students to make it worthwhile. The authority of the teacher or instructor was also undermined by forbidding him to 'evaluate the data' for the student. Rather than a teacher the course instructor became little more than an index whose role was only to refer the student with doubts or confusions to the appropriate location in the material provided by Hubbard for their resolution.

The theory itself became differentiated into what we may refer to as an esoteric and an exoteric ideology. The exoteric ideology is presented in most of the movement's publications, the works for publication of Scientologists other than Hubbard, and sympathizers of the movement. Such works present Scientology as concerned with the spiritual nature of man (the thetan); with increasing communication; understanding of others; ability to control oneself, one's interactions with others, and the surrounding environment.[1]

Most of these works deal with the value of Scientology in handling everyday problems and situations; how to bring up children;[2] how to manage organizations;[3] or the application of Scientology theory and technique to education.[4]

The esoteric ideology develops a cosmological doctrine of the origin and development (or degeneration) of the thetan,[5] and manifests far greater concern with past lives,[6] and the supernatural abilities that the individual can acquire through the practice of Scientology.

[1] See, for example, the following works by L. Ron Hubbard: *Dianetics 55!*, op. cit.; *The Fundamentals of Thought*, op. cit.; *Scientology A New Slant on Life*. See also J. F. Horner, *A New Understanding of Life* (Hubbard Communications Office, Auckland, New Zealand, 1961); Ruth Minshull, *Miracles for Breakfast* (Scientology Ann Arbor, Ann Arbor, Michigan 1968), and idem, *How to Choose Your People* (Scientology Ann Arbor, Ann Arbor, Michigan, 1972); Walter Braddeson, *Scientology for the Millions* (Sherbourne Press, Los Angeles, 1969); Omar V. Garrison, *The Hidden Story of Scientology*, op. cit.

[2] Ruth Minshull, *Miracles for Breakfast*, op. cit.

[3] L. Ron Hubbard, *How to Live Though An Executive* (Department of Publications World Wide, East Grinstead, 1953).

[4] Victor Silcox and Len Maynard, *Creative Learning: a Scientological Experiment in Schools* (Scientology Publications, London, 1955); Muriel Payne, *Creative Education* (William Maclellan, Glasgow, 1958).

[5] L. Ron Hubbard, *A History of Man* (HASI, London, n.d.).

[6] L. Ron Hubbard, *Have You Lived Before This Life*, op. cit.

This division between the esoteric and exoteric ideology is displayed in other areas of Scientology's operation. The movement currently maintains an extensive public relations apparatus, part of the function of which is to ensure that exoteric interpretations are available and publicized for organizational activity.

Scientology developed a transcendental doctrine, or theodicy, to explain the individual's current condition. This doctrine incorporated an elaborate metaphysics based around a theory of reincarnation. It was thereby greatly broadened from a 'do-it-yourself' psychotherapy to a cosmology, endowing the universe and individual human life with meaning. The belief-system of the movement became increasingly esoteric, and a 'hierarchy of sanctification' emerged. Members could locate themselves on levels of initiation into the movement's mysteries through 'the grades', 'clear,' and the 'OT levels'.

The charismatic nature of the revelation, the gnosis, is evident in the power which it is conceived to have. Viewing the materials of a higher level than one has yet achieved, even by accident, is held to be dangerous. Hence, the 'advanced materials' are kept secret from the uninitiated. The doctrine and practices of the movement therefore became available as a means of control, since access to higher levels could be denied to those who deviate from its norms.[1]

With the promulgation of Scientology, Hubbard was able to claim the new gnosis as a revelation into which he had privileged insight, heightening his authority over the movement, and inhibiting competing claims to revelation. Aspects of the theory and practice most closely linking the belief-system to the cultic milieu were abandoned. Dianetic 'reverie' with its clear links to hypnosis, and the concern with the trauma of early childhood and birth, with clear links to psychoanalysis and its developments, were abandoned. New elements of doctrine and practice – the thetan and the E-meter, for example – were introduced. Training and auditing were thoroughly routinized, inhibiting the development of any claim to charismatic legitimacy on the part of instructors and practitioners, minimizing their autonomy and power and heightening their substitutability.

The strategies employed in coping with the doctrinal precariousness of the movement bear strong similarities to those employed by Mary Baker Eddy. Mrs Eddy claimed that her writings, in particular *Science and Health*, were inspired revelations. Some aspects of the teaching became a hidden doctrine available only to those undergoing special instruction. Students of the Normal Course were carefully vetted for their loyalty to the Church and forbidden to take notes while undergoing instruction (as is still the case today). Mrs Eddy became the sole source of doctrinal innovation, adaptation and interpretation. Until the establishment of the Board of Education, she alone could claim to

---

[1] Seven OT levels are currently available (1974), although Hubbard has indicated that 'there are perhaps 15 levels above OT VII fully developed but existing only in unissued note form . . .' which he threatens to release in due course. See *Advance*, issue 20 (August/September 1973), p. 6.

teach the advanced levels of Christian Science. Students were required not to indulge in writing on Christian Science or in reading other metaphysical literature, and heretical teachers who persisted in teaching despite being excommunicated were pursued by Mrs Eddy in the press and lawcourts for infringements of her copyrights. There had to be a clear ideological boundary between Christian Science and any other metaphysical system, and this boundary was heightened by the fear instilled in her students of malicious animal magnetism – held to be the real nature of the practice of heretics, apostates, and imitators.

The authority of local teachers was undermined by constraints on teaching beyond the preliminary levels of doctrine. Teaching and practice became increasingly standardized and depersonalized. After 1895 the only 'pastors' permitted in Christian Science churches were *Science and Health* and the Bible. Preachers were reduced to Readers, whose performance was controlled to the extent of standardizing even the emphasis with which passages were read. Their expository task was taken over by a Board of Lecturers, appointed by the Directors and obliged to submit the text of their lectures in advance to the Mother Church. The technique of healing became standardized on the basis of Mrs Eddy's textbook. The annual re-election of Lecturers by the Directors and the requirement that Readers could hold office for three years only, precluded the development of these offices as a source of independent authority that could be directed against the Church leadership. Teachers were brought under increased control by permitting them to hold a class only once a year, for no more than thirty students, and forbidding gatherings of teachers and their students on other occasions.[1]

Christian Science thus provides an earlier example of a process later followed in Scientology, in which an attempt was made to manage the problem of institutional fragility faced by the cult leadership. The beliefs and practices of the movement, and their mode of transmission and application, were mobilized in the process of arrogating and centralizing authority, and maximizing control. One aim of these adaptations was to eliminate challenges to the authority of the leader, and to secure a disciplined and cohesive following.

---

[1] Roy Wallis, 'A comparative analysis of problems and processes of change in two manipulationist movements: Christian Science and Scientology' in *The Contemporary Metamorphosis of Religion?*, Acts of the 12th International Conference on the Sociology of Religion, The Hague, Netherlands, August 1973.

5. SOCIAL ORGANIZATION AND SOCIAL CONTROL

Historical background

After Hubbard moved his headquarters to Phoenix in 1952, Scientology went through a period of considerable organizational flux. The Hubbard Association of Scientologists (HAS, later the Hubbard Association of Scientologists International, HASI) was incorporated as a 'religious fellowship' under Hubbard's direct control. Hubbard travelled a great deal during the following years, particularly to England to consolidate and promote the growth of Scientology in Britain.

In his absence, he became dissatisfied with the way things were being conducted at Phoenix. The financial situation there had apparently deteriorated,[1] and the editor of the *Journal of Scientology*, Alphia Hart, employed a rather liberal policy in the conduct of the periodical. While lauding Hubbard and his practice, he printed letters critical of the movement and its beliefs and probably maintained too great an independence of his leader.[2]

Accordingly, Hubbard instructed the loyal organizer of an independent Scientology school, Helen O'Brien, to fly to Phoenix, sack Alphia Hart and remove the HAS to Philadelphia. There a new corporation was established, much of the running costs of which were covered by the Philadelphia practitioners,[3] and the *Journal* began appearing under Helen O'Brien's editorship. Hubbard, however, appears not to have been greatly reassured that his organization was now in safe hands.

He was a strange partner in business, because he seemed determined to undermine us. He airmailed our U.S. subscriber lists offers of books for sale from England, but

[1] Helen O'Brien, *Dianetics in Limbo* (Whitmore Publishing Co., Philadelphia, 1966), p. 68.
[2] Helen O'Brien, who despite her own later fall from grace remained loyal to Hubbard's interpretation of many events at this time, complains that he had 'hired an editor who never really understood the subject and who for several months injected his personal viewpoint in Hubbard's American communication line'. Helen O'Brien, op. cit., p. 61.
[3] At least according to their own account, Helen O'Brien, op. cit., p. 69.

reneged repeatedly on promises to ship us a supply, after we'd backlogged orders to the ceiling by advertising them on his instruction. He said that all letters should be forwarded to him for his reply, and then, when they went unanswered, dubbed us the 'Philadelphia Incommunicators'. When I hired a secretary, he wrote directly to her, with pages of instruction about how I should be conducting the operation![1]

On his return to Philadelphia late in 1953 for a Congress, Hubbard was able to appear as if responding to complaints from 'the field' present at the Congress that O'Brien and her partner had refused to communicate new information.[2] He dismantled the Pennsylvania corporation and excommunicated O'Brien and her partner.[3] The headquarters of the movement were moved a short distance to Camden, New Jersey.

There, late in 1953, three churches were incorporated. Only two of these, the Church of American Science (represented as a Christian Church) and the Church of Scientology (represented as non-denominational) were activated. The third corporation (which appears to have been called the Church of Spiritual Engineering [!]) was never utilized. Early in 1954 Hubbard removed the functioning corporate superstructure back to Phoenix, Arizona, and began 'franchizing' independent churches of Scientology in other states.[4] In 1955, Hubbard again moved his organization, this time to Washington DC, where William Young had built up a thriving practice. (The Scientology organization argues that Hubbard moved to Washington DC because of local attacks on Scientology, and Hubbard deemed it safer to be under the jurisdiction of Federal rather than State courts, in order to guarantee the Church's constitutional rights.) In 1959, Hubbard purchased Saint Hill Manor in East Grinstead, Sussex, which became the movement's headquarters until the establishment of the 'Sea Org' in 1966.

It is no easy matter to provide a clear picture of the corporate involvements of Hubbard and his movement. Hubbard was well aware of the value of corporate structures as weapons in the control of both his movement and its environment.[5] A complex corporate structure maximizes the difficulty of surveillance, or investigation of the movement's affairs, and also maximizes the number of public images through which the movement can be promoted. These exoteric 'faces' to the movement can then be differentially stressed (at different times) depending on public receptivity at any given time to any given image. The letter-paper of the Founding Church of Scientology of Washington DC in 1957 listed seventeen organizations which the movement leadership owned or controlled. These included the Congress of Eastern Scientologists, the American

[1] Helen O'Brien, op. cit., pp. 74–5.
[2] *Journal of Scientology*, 22G, n.d.
[3] *Journal of Scientology*, 24G (31 January 1954), p. 2.
[4] A Church of Scientology was 'franchized' to J. Burton Farber in California and another to William Young in Washington DC.
[5] Philip Selznick, *The Organizational Weapon* (Free Press, Glencoe 1960).

Society for Disaster Relief, Scientology Consultants to Industrial Efficiency, and the Distribution Center Inc. From 1954 Hubbard also promoted a Freudian Foundation of America. After Hubbard's re-acquisition from Purcell of the legal rights in the Wichita Dianetic Foundation in 1954, there were also among the list of corporations of the movement various Dianetic organizations, such as the Hubbard Dianetic Research Foundation. Sundry other legally incorporated organizations had been established in England.[1]

Most of the organizations were ad hoc and temporary. The movement was largely organized, during the 1950s, through the HASI. The HASI provided public services through the Hubbard Guidance Centre (HGC) which offered individual auditing; the Academy of Scientology which offered training; and later the Personal Efficiency Foundation which offered the free or inexpensive introductory courses designed to draw in new recruits.[2] The HASI also published various magazines and other promotional materials. A separate organization was the Hubbard Communications Office Ltd (HCO) which was Hubbard's direct administrative machine. Throughout the 1960s, considerable re-organization of the corporate structure took place as more of the corporate operation of Scientology was brought under the legal auspices of the Church of Scientology of California.

'Field' organization

During the 1950s, despite a progressive tightening of control over the movement as a whole in comparison with the days of Dianetics, organization of the following of Scientology in the field remained somewhat loose. By requiring affiliation of amateur groups with the HASI, Hubbard sought to control the grass-roots following. New information on theory and technique was now less readily available through public documents. Instead, practitioners were encouraged to take professional courses at considerable cost. The HPA course cost $500 and Advanced Clinical courses which led to the conferring of the 'Doctorate of Scientology' cost $800. Only those who had taken advanced indoctrination were permitted to teach and certify competence beyond the most basic levels.[3]

These developments led to a rapid 'professionalization' of field practice. Amateur groups could not secure the training or access to the material that had formerly made their existence worth while. The professional auditors and their organizations began to dominate the field. Amateur groups gradually disappeared. Those who remained committed to the movement affiliated with and became absorbed into the clientele of a local or central organization. The possibility of opposition to the leadership from the grass roots was thereby rendered virtually impossible. Members had no formal and few informal

---

[1] Sir John G. Foster, *Enquiry into the Practice and Effects of Scientology* (HMSO, London, 1971), pp. 29–33.
[2] *Certainty*, 19, 11 (1963), pp 9, 11.
[3] *Journal of Scientology*, 22G, n.d.

'horizontal' relationships with each other. The movement was transformed from an almost federal association of independent, autonomous groups into a 'mass' movement, with few ties other than those of an almost entirely 'vertical' kind between the central (and to a lesser extent, local) organization and individual members.

Professional practitioners might operate as independent 'Field Auditors' with a minimum of organization, or establish 'franchises' which received direct assistance, preferential discounts, and other concessions from the central organization, and in return were expected to send 10 per cent of their receipts to the Hubbard Communications office. Some of the more ambitious practitioners organized Churches of Scientology in their local area.

During 1954 various strategies were employed to tie practitioners more closely to the central organization. 'Bonding of auditors'[1] proved unsuccessful, but auditors were required to remain 'in good standing' with the central organization and to purchase annual professional membership of the HASI at a fee of $25.00 a year in order to ensure that their certificates remained valid.[2] The names of auditors who were not in good standing were published in movement periodicals,[3] and the membership were enjoined to have no dealings with non-approved practitioners. Various publications carried advertisements for local practices approved by the central organizations, and lists of approved franchises were occasionally published.

Practitioners were encouraged to recruit new members and to maximize their involvement in the movement. Group processing gradually fell from favour as Hubbard found it did not lead to increasing the involvement of members. One source reports a lecture by Hubbard in 1954 in which

> Ron told the assembled auditors that group processing was proving valueless – both from the standpoint of help to the audience and in revenue. Those helped weren't bad off to begin with, he said, and when these get past whatever may be bothering them at the moment they go on their way – and that's that.[4]

(The Scientology organization express the view that this statement appeared in an apostate's publication, and that it is not true. However, Hubbard's own words cited on p. 159 below have much the same substance.)

After the mid 1950s, practitioners were encouraged to attract recruits by means of a Personal (or sometimes Personnel) Efficiency Course, an Anatomy of the Mind Course, or some other introductory series of lectures and basic practices, from which recruits could be secured for more advanced training and auditing.

[1] Discussed in Chapter 3.

[2] *Journal of Scientology*, 37G, n.d., p. 1.

[3] For example, *Ability*, mimeoed edition, no number, no date, warns on its rear page, 'Marcus Tooley of Australia: all certificates and memberships HASI, HDRF suspended pending retraining'.

[4] *The Aberree*, 1, 7 (November 1954), p. 8.

While practitioners in the field were permitted to train and audit the less advanced levels of Scientology, Hubbard restricted certification to the central organizations. Currently even the lower grades have to be verified and certified at the 'Org'.[1] On completion of the lower levels, practitioners are encouraged to send pre-clears and students on to the Org by commission payments on the amount spent at the Org by the pre-clear. Independent practitioners are not permitted to charge less for their services than the charge made for equivalent services by the Org.

During the 1950s Hubbard encouraged the establishment of franchise operations,[2] but after the secession of a number of independent practitioners late in 1959 and early 1960, Hubbard became increasingly disenchanted with the idea of 'private practice'.

The idea of 'One Organisation and That's Scientology' is receiving much commendation everywhere. The idea of 'the private practitioner' has never set well on us as it's borrowed from organisations with few answers. You don't have to become 'private practice' if you've got the answers. There's enough action and money in sight to include everyone in. A united Scientology alone can stand up to the buffets of world clearing.[3]

Franchise holders were encouraged to set up as City offices owned and controlled by Hubbard rather than remaining independent.[4] During the secessions of the late 1950s/early 1960s, Hubbard had continually to reassure himself of the loyalty of practitioners. A Field Auditor Ethical Committee appears in Scientology publications in 1959, to investigate irregularities in the practise of these professionals,[5] and the certificates of a suspected practitioner would be suspended until he came into an Org for a check that he had 'Clean Hands'.

Hubbard controlled training and practice through ownership of copyrights to material, ability to certify practitioners and their clientele, and through control over the communications of the movement.[6] He was therefore able to determine whether or not an individual was recognized as an auditor in good standing and to publicize this fact to the field. By these means, Hubbard was able progressively to reduce the autonomy of practitioners, transmuting them from

[1] See, for example, Robert Kaufman, *Inside Scientology* (Olympia Press, London, 1972), p. 27 et seq. 'Org' is a Scientology abbreviation for the Scientology organization.

[2] See, for example, *Ability Major*, 104 (c. late 1959).

[3] L. Ron Hubbard, 'Ron's Journal', *HCO Information Letters*, 27 October 1962.

[4] Various *HCO Information Letters*, 1962.

[5] *Certainty*, 6, 6 (1959), p. 5.

[6] There is no clear evidence that independent publications were frowned on, but only one periodical publication independent of the Org appeared, as far as I can trace, after the disappearance of the various Dianetics newsletters and other similar circulars, which was sponsored by a practitioner in good standing with the Org. This was the *Auditor and Philosopher*, which ran for only 2 or 3 issues during 1956. Independent communications media were clearly not encouraged.

independent professionals to functionaries and recruiting agents for the central organizations.[1]

The Org

The founders of many social and religious movements, while bearing the charisma necessary to mobilize a large following and convey an innovatory message, not infrequently lack the administrative ability to establish an enduring organizational structure which will continue to promote that message after their demise. Hubbard, however, is an extraordinary administrator. Developed in its present form largely during the years after establishing his headquarters in East Grinstead, the Org is an elaborate and imposing bureaucratic machine.

Max Weber detailed the following characteristics of bureaucracy: fixed official jurisdictional areas ordered by rules; the distribution of regular activities as official duties; the stable and strictly delimited distribution of the authority of officials; and the restriction of office to those appropriately qualified. Bureaucracy rests on an ordered hierarchy of office and authority with the lower offices supervized by the higher; the extensive use of written documents preserved as 'the files'; specialized office management with expert training; and an elaborate body of general rules, knowledge of which constitutes part of the technical expertise possessed by officials.[2] As we shall establish below, in many respects the Scientology organization approximates very closely to this ideal type.

The structure of the Org is established by an organizational chart generally known as 'The Org Board'. The Org Board divides the organization into seven Divisions: Executive; HCO; HCO Dissemination; Treasury; Technical; Qualifications; and Distribution – each, as will be evident from their titles,

[1] Most books on Scientology by individuals within the movement other than Hubbard are copyrighted in Hubbard's name. When a writer falls from favour they are withdrawn from circulation. Thus when Reg Sharpe, a prominent aide of Hubbard in the mid-1960s fell from grace in 1967, the following order was published:

> Executive Directive
> ED 716 WW   November 7th 1967
> HCO SECS
> FRANCHISE
> FSMS
> Cancellation of Issue Authority
> LRH Issue Authority is hereby cancelled on the book 'This is Life' by Reg Sharpe. This book can no longer be issued, sold or displayed by Scientology orgs, FSMs, Franchise or Scientologists.
> Issue Authority WW
> For the
> LRH Communicator WW for
> Board of Directors of the Church
> [Seal]   of Scientology of California, UK.

[2] Max Weber, 'Bureaucracy', Chapter 8 in Hans H. Gerth and C. Wright Mills, eds, *From Max Weber: Essays in Sociology* (Routledge & Kegan Paul, London, 1970), pp. 196–8.

having distinct functions. Below these with yet more specialized functions are twenty-seven Departments. The chain of command culminates in L. Ron Hubbard, currently shown as 'Founder', below whom is ranged his (third) wife Mary Sue Hubbard as 'The Controller', and the Executive Directors of each organization. Beneath 'The Controller' lies the office of 'The Guardian' and the HCO side of the organization, which deals among other things with external relations; communication to and from Hubbard; general communication within the organization; personnel; and internal social control of the movement. The Org Executive Directors have responsibility for the operating divisions of the organization – processing, training, accounting, etc.

Each department has a particular function and jurisdiction as established in Hubbard's *Policy Letters*. These documents specify the grounds for the operation of each unit within the organization, the responsibilities of its officers, and the organization's goals and procedures. Many of them are collected in a series of eight volumes as an 'Encyclopedia of Scientology Policy', which collectively form *The Organisation Executive Course*.[1] Org executives are required to have an operating knowledge of these volumes, and an executive is expected to be able to legitimate his actions by reference to relevant policy.

The Org maintains extensive files. Policy now demands that *all* orders be written down and copies kept by the Department of Inspection and Reports.[2] Every post within the organization has associated with it a 'hat' file.[3] The hat file contains the relevant policy for the operation of that post, plus memoranda from its former incumbents which will aid a newcomer in 'wearing the hat' – that is, operating the post effectively. Hat files are written up with such specificity that theoretically any individual could take over and operate the post after simply learning the file. The 'Org Exec Course' provides executive training for higher echelon personnel.

The Org Board provides the model for all Scientology organizations. In small organizations which lack sufficient personnel to staff every post separately, one staff member may 'wear several hats'. However, the Org Board is presented not merely as an appropriate structure for Scientology organization; rather it is taken to be the perfect organizational form, applicable from the level of the individual (who could operate, it is argued, on the same functional model) to that of the world. As Scientology expands, its followers believe the whole world will gradually get 'pulled in under the Org Board'.

[1] L. Ron Hubbard, *The Organisation Executive Course* (Scientology Publications Organisation, Copenhagen, 1970). This volume will hereafter be cited simply as *OEC*. I was initially permitted to purchase only the first two of these volumes, which alone comprise some 1000 pages of policy letters. The Scientology publishing company did not agree to sell me the other six volumes until too late to utilize them for the purposes of this research.

[2] *OEC*, Vol. O, p. 296.

[3] Posts in Scientology orgs are known as 'hats', from the phrase 'wearing his—— hat', meaning acting in his such-and-such role.

The virtues of the Org Board derive particularly from the fact that it is held to be a practical representation of the basic scheme of Scientology theory:

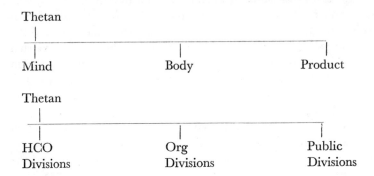

Thetan
|
Mind   Body   Product

Thetan
|
HCO   Org   Public
Divisions   Divisions   Divisions

Hubbard and his direct subordinates are the guiding spirit, the thetan, of the Org operating through its 'mind', the HCO Divisions including the Guardian's Office and the Ethics Officers.[1]

Pugh and Hickson in their analysis of the structure of fifty-two organizations found none which showed the kind of profile to be expected from Weber's model of bureaucracy, that is one which

> would appear as highly specialised with many narrowly defined specialist 'offices', as highly standardised in its procedures, and as highly formalised with documents prescribing and recording all activities and available in the files as precedents. If everything had to be referred upwards for decision, then it would also score highly centralised. In configuration it would have a high proportion of 'supportive' or administrative or 'non-work-flow' personnel.[2]

They suggest that such 'extreme total bureaucracy' may only exist among the bureaux of central government. Yet the Scientology organization appears to fit this model singularly closely. While not every decision could conceivably be referred upwards, few need to be in the Org, since most decisions can be made on the basis of the centrally prepared policy documents, which specify in great detail how operations are to be carried out.[3] Only in the event of ambiguity or unprecedented circumstances need matters be referred upward for decision.

While the organization has become highly bureaucratized, it departs from the classic Weberian model over the position of 'the official'. Staff posts are presented

---

[1] Ibid., p. 252.

[2] D. S. Pugh and D. J. Hickson, 'The comparative study of organisations' in Graeme Salaman and Kenneth Thompson, eds, *People and Organisations* (Longman, London, 1973), p. 59.

[3] When he lived at Saint Hill, for example, Hubbard wrote a lengthy memorandum detailing the proper way to wash the Hubbard family cars. This is still printed in *OEC*, Vol. 1, pp. 295–6.

as fulfilling a duty in assisting Ron to 'clear the planet',[1] and enjoy a measure of social esteem, particularly in the more specialized and executive positions.[2] Posts are filled by appointment[3] and the hierarchy of offices might be said to provide a career, and will no doubt increasingly provide an established ladder of advancement as the movement becomes more thoroughly institutionalized. However, the concept of career is only loosely applicable, since many staff members join the organization only temporarily, working out contracts of specified length (typically two and a half years) in return for free auditing and training.[4] Many therefore see their staff membership as of limited duration. It is doubtless in part because of the rapid turnover in staff engendered by the contract system that the highly formalized machinery of staff hats, etc., has been instituted, to equip an individual to cope with a post after minimal training. Moreover, even the executive officials of Scientology Orgs do not enjoy security of tenure. Security of tenure, as Weber has indicated, enhances, even if it does not ensure, the independence of the office holder. Such independence is entirely contrary to the spirit of Scientology's organizational practice.

The Org bureaucracy departs from the Weberian model in two further particulars. While Weber specified that 'official activity demands the full working capacity of the official, irrespective of the fact that his obligatory time in the bureau may be firmly delimited',[5] Scientology personnel are utilized as disposable agents by the leadership to an extent far beyond that usual in bureaucratic organizations. In periods of organizational or departmental crisis, personnel may be required to remain at the Org working, except for brief periods of rest snatched on the floor or wherever is available, for forty-eight or more hours at a time,[6] or sent off with case-loads of books to be sold in distant towns after a normal day's work at the Org.[7] The extent to which the organization may encroach on the 'private' time and activities of its personnel is a function of the ideological commitment of its staff, a personal involvement that departs from the impersonal aura of Weber's bureaucrat.

Secondly, Weber's official 'receives the regular pecuniary compensation of a normally fixed salary and the old age security provided by a pension'.[8] As far as I can learn no pension provision is made by the Scientology organization, and staff are not, for the most part, paid a fixed salary. Remuneration in the

---

[1] 'A post in a Scientology Org isn't a job. It's a trust and a crusade', *OEC*, Vol. O, p. 34.

[2] Incumbents of lower posts are often regarded with pity, even by staunch adherents, rather than respect, but that is probably true of bureaucracy everywhere.

[3] The more important posts are appointed only by Hubbard himself. See *OEC*, Vol. 1, pp. 2, 100, 127.

[4] See, for example, *OEC*, Vol. O, p. 48.

[5] Weber, op. cit.

[6] Cyril Vosper, *The Mind Benders* (Neville Spearman, London, 1971), p. 9.

[7] Interviews. See also Kaufman, op. cit., p. 103.

[8] Weber, op. cit., p. 203.

organization is based on gross receipts. Fifty-five per cent of the gross income for a particular Org is transferred to a Salary Account. Each post within that Org has a certain number of 'units' allotted to it, each unit entitling the staff member to a certain proportion of the salary fund. Hence, as Org income fluctuates so, accordingly, will individual salaries.[1] The Anderson Report indicates that the resulting salary levels achieved by staff of the Victoria Organization were relatively low, often less than the state's basic wage level.

For example, for the week ended 17th May 1962 where the unit appears to have been 5s 6d, a person on 16 units received as little as £4 8s for 40 hours work. Other instances for that week were:-

No. of units	Hours worked	Gross salary £ s d		
25	40	6	17	6
19	42½	5	4	6
28	42½	7	14	6
20	40	5	10	0
13	32½	3	11	6
3	7½	0	16	6
33	47	9	1	6

The highest paid employee in the HASI in this week was the cleaner, who was paid at the rate of 10s per hour. HCO staff fared a little better than the HASI, two of them getting £16 17s 6d and £16 respectively.[2]

Interviews with former employees of the Org in England and America confirm the low average level of pay and its fluctuations, although there may have been some improvement in recent years.

Two of the factors which normally play an important part in recruitment to bureaucracy, job and income security, are thus dispensed with in the Scientology organization. Personnel are attracted to Org posts as a result of ideological commitment, and the fact that contracting to work for the Org permits access to training and auditing they could otherwise ill afford. Dispensing with these two aspects of bureaucracy also facilitates greater control by the leadership of the incumbents of staff posts.

The Org is a highly bureaucratized structure although it retains distinctive patrimonial characteristics.

It is decisive for the specific nature of modern loyalty to an office that, in the pure type, it does not establish a relationship to a *person*, like the . . . disciple's faith . . . in patrimonial relations of authority.[3]

[1] Kevin Victor Anderson, *Report of the Board of Enquiry into Scientology* (Government Printer, Melbourne, Australia, 1965), pp. 26 et seq.

[2] Anderson, op. cit., p. 27.

[3] Weber, op. cit., p. 149.

The employees of Hubbard's Org are not merely officials, but also *disciples*. Hence commitment of staff to the Org is secured by ideological means, replacing the need for the attractions of tenure, secure salary and orderly promotion through a work hierarchy. Moreover, the movement leadership seeks to proscribe the development of an independent basis of authority within the movement, even in its own bureaucratic structure. The absence of tenure and the considerable substitutability of employees even at the highest levels, enhances the dependence of the bureaucracy on the authority and direction of the leader, and the maintenance of ultimate control in his hands.

Statistics

An important element of the organization's bureaucratic practice is its 'statistics', or 'stats'. Statistics provide both a measure of organizational efficiency and a means of control. The development of statistics was one major aspect of the bureaucratization of the movement and the shift in administration from a purely patrimonial, personally directed staff of disciples to impersonal control through formal rules and procedures.

> An org today is *not* run on personalities. It's run on statistics. All orders are based on statistics.[1]

The statistic is a measure of operating efficiency based on some readily available indicator. Each Org, division, department, and hat is assigned a statistic which indicates 'normal operation'. The statistics are indicated by the gross income of the facility; number of letters mailed out with promotional material; gross book sales; number of students enrolled; number of 'success stories' written; or some similar objective indicator.[2]

Weekly statistics reports are transmitted up the organizational chain of command and provide a ready means of checking the productivity of lower echelon departments and personnel. 'Up statistics', that is a level above the arbitrary norm set for normal operation indicate that the individual occupying the post, or the department concerned is in a 'higher condition'[3] and therefore eligible for various awards. An individual in a condition of 'Power' on his post receives

> Pay and full bonuses. Awarded $25.00 credit for Org Services at own org or is payable by Org as credit against services in a higher Org. Has top priority on Org service lines. Gold star on Comm basket and on Org Board.[4]

[1] L. Ron Hubbard, *HCO Policy Letter*, 1 February 1966, p. 2.
[2] L. Ron Hubbard, 'Statistics for divisions', *HCO Policy Letter*, 30 September 1965, in *OEC*, Vol. 1, pp. 328–9.
[3] See Ethics section below.
[4] 'Conditions, awards and penances', *HCO Policy Letter*, 16 November 1971.

On the other hand, 'down statistics', that is, below normal operation, indicate that the individual or Org is in a 'lower condition' and becomes liable to various penalties. In 'Liability' an individual receives

> Pay, but no bonuses. Must submit and execute a 10 hour Amends Project in own time. Is off all training and auditing except for Cramming, Word Clearing or hatting actions necessary to handle own post. Minimal meal breaks. Austere working uniform or clothing. May not have time off or receive vacation while in this condition. A gray ribbon is placed on their Comm basket and a gray flag by their name on the Org Board. Must wear a gray armband on left arm.[1]

The leader

At least until recent years, Hubbard indisputably controlled the Scientology organization. Until 1966, he and members of his immediate family occupied the more important directorship positions of the various Scientology organizations. During 1966 he was said to have resigned from all directorships of such organizations. While Hubbard appears to have relinquished direct legal control, he retained certain rights as 'Trustee' and signatory to various international bank accounts of the movement until at least 1969.[2] According to the Guardian's Office of the Church, Hubbard is not currently a signatory on any Church of Scientology bank account, nor does he have any 'Trustee' status.[3]

While policy documents are now often issued over other names than Hubbard's, many are still issued over Hubbard's name. The Guardian's Office advise me that Hubbard has 'sold his name' to the Church, which they indicate means that the right to append Hubbard's name to policy is vested in the Board of Directors of the Church of Scientology World Wide.[4] This may indicate that Hubbard has relinquished direct administrative control over Scientology. It may, however, indicate that like Mary Baker Eddy, Hubbard found it convenient not to appear to be directing the Scientology organizations. Until her death, Mrs Eddy actively supervised the administration of the Christian Science Church, although she had nominally relinquished control to the Board of Directors.

The policy of the movement states that Hubbard is the source of all Scientological theory and practice – in the sense that even where he did not invent a particular practice, only his approval legitimates its use – and is often referred to in Scientology publications as the 'Source'. The Guardian's Office claim,

---

[1] Ibid.

[2] Testimony of Herbie Parkhouse, Church of Scientology of California Inc. v. Bernard Green and Barbara Ferraro, etc., 60 civ 5745 before Hon. Richard H. Levet, District Judge, U.S. District Court, Southern District of New York, Stenographer's Minutes, October 4, 5, 6, 1972, pp. 577–609.

[3] Letter from David Gaiman, Guardian's Office, Church of Scientology, 21 March 1974.

[4] Ibid.

however, that ownership of all Hubbard's philosophical and technical materials is now vested in the Church.

Evidence tendered by officers of the Washington Founding Church of Scientology in legal actions in 1967 also indicated that, whatever the legal position, Hubbard remained in ultimate control of the movement, and could reassume day-to-day operational control without difficulty.

He still issues ou[r] policy letters as the founder which are applicable to Scientologists everywhere.[1]

. . . I think it is fair to say that from the viewpoint of all Scientologists, we accept Ron Hubbard as the final authority and the source of Scientology.[2]

Q. Let me ask you this. Is it within Mr Hubbard's power at any time to assume the control of the Founding Church and all other Scientology organisations?
A. Only by the agreement of Scientologists.
Q. If Mr Hubbard tomorrow were to issue a memorandum where he was to state that he was taking back what he had said last year and he was again to be put on the board of directors of all organisations, would the Scientologists allow him to be put back?
A. May I answer that in two parts?
Q. Please answer yes or no and then explain.
A. The answer is yes, and I will elaborate on that by saying that theoretically, or better said, as a point of practicability, the boards of all churches could actually refuse that, but in actual fact, I know that would never happen.[3]

Moreover, as Hubbard has apparently withdrawn from operational direction of the movement, other members of his family have come to play a larger role. His wife, Mary Sue, is 'The Controller' to whom the Guardian is responsible. The Guardian directs the operations of the Assistant Guardians based in each organization. The Assistant Guardian is the senior and most powerful executive in every local organization.[4]

[1] Testimony of John Bevis Fudge, Founding Church of Scientology v. USA in US Court of Claims, No. 226–61, Washington D.C. 1967, transcript, pp. 217–18.
[2] Ibid., p. 218.
[3] Ibid., p. 291. In his deposition, Bevis Fudge, Legal Officer and Assistant Guardian of the Founding Church of Scientology also makes this point clear:
'Q. Does Ron Hubbard have, let's say, the power within the organisation to influence its activities and operations since he resigned his directorships in 1966?
A. Definitely.
Q. So there has been no real change then in his control over the organisation?
A. No, not to my knowledge.'
('Deposition of Bevis Fudge' in Founding Church of Scientology v. U.S.A., 3 January 1967, stenographic transcript, p. 12.) Documents made available to me by a recently defected Sea Org member make it quite clear that there remains a direct chain of command from Hubbard through the Sea Org to all Scientology organizations.
[4] Deposition of Anne L. Ursprung, in Founding Church of Scientology v. The Washington Post Co, Civil Action No. 214 1–68, U.S. District Court for the District of Columbia, 1968. Miss Ursprung testified that as Assistant Guardian she was superior

Hubbard's daughter, Diana, and son, Quentin, are assuming a progressively more important place in the affairs of the movement, figuring prominently in recent publications, and acting as Hubbard's proxies at major gatherings of the movement. As Hubbard has withdrawn from the direct public control of the movement, other members of his family have moved into leadership roles.

The Sea Org

A relatively recent addition to the organization of Scientology is the Sea Org. Shortly before the British Home Office advised Hubbard that he would no longer be permitted entry to the United Kingdom, he acquired, with considerable foresight, a sea-going vessel, the avowed purpose of which was to enable Hubbard to explore ancient civilizations.[1] By 1971 the Sea Org fleet contained some six ships.[2]

Its purpose has been variously presented.

The Sea Org was formed to compose a superiorly disciplined, elite group working directly under Ron to aid the creation of a new civilisation on this planet.[3]

The Sea Organisation operates on a high standard of mobility and confront. Its end product is Ethics and Order. Its purpose is to get ETHICS IN.

The Sea Organisation is the most powerful organisation in the world. It works with the primary rod of Ethics.[4]

The Sea Organisation is composed of the 'aristocracy' of Scientology.[5]

The Sea Organisation (the research and management branch of the Church of Scientology) . . .[6]

The Sea Org has no separate corporate status, but comprises an elite order of Scientologists, with a broad authority to intervene in the affairs of Scientology organizations.[7]

[1] See, for example, the letter from David Gaiman to Sir John Foster cited in Foster, op. cit., p. 34. This is one clear example of the exoteric versus the esoteric presentation of Scientology. While it may be true that Hubbard desired to explore ancient civilizations, this can have been only a very minor part of the Sea Org's purpose.

[2] Foster, op. cit., p. 350.

[3] *Advance*, 7, n.d., n.p.

[4] Diana Hubbard, 'What is the Sea Org?', mimeo (15 March 1968).

[5] Leaflet, no publisher (1972).

[6] *The New Civilization*, 12 (1972), p. 3.

[7] The ownership of the vessels of the Sea Org is something of a mystery. Herbert Parkhouse, a senior Church executive, testified in Church of Scientology of California Inc. v. Bernard Green, etc., op. cit., that the vessels of the Sea Org were owned by a corporation known as Operations and Transport Services Ltd, which also receives fees paid by students for Sea Org and other advanced courses. Parkhouse testified that

in the Washington Church to the HCO Exec Sec, the Org Exec Sec and the Public Exec Sec, the Board of Trustees, whose decisions she could veto, the President of the Executive Council, and that she had ultimate authority in administrative matters.

The Sea Org sends its officers to individual orgs with *unlimited powers* to handle
   a. Ethics
   b. Tech
   c. Admin.[1]

The vessels of the Sea Org are surrounded with an aura of mystery and secrecy. The whereabouts of the Flag Ship on which Hubbard resides is kept a closely guarded secret even from rank and file Scientologists.[2] 'Missions' are despatched from the Sea Org to take command of organizations with 'down-statistics', to remedy the situation. Among their 'unlimited powers' is that of superior authority to the land organization executives. For example:

> ... as per HCO POL 20 June 1968, the senior Ethics Officer on the planet is the International Chief Ethics Officer WW. OVER THE CHIEF E/O ARE THE MASTERS AT ARMS OF THE SEA ORG.[3]

The services of the Sea Org Missions are paid for at far from meagre rates by the organizations concerned.[4]

Advanced organizations, that is those that provide upper-level training and OT courses, are located aboard Sea Org vessels or otherwise staffed by Sea Org personnel. The members of the Sea Org are completely committed followers of Hubbard. Recruits are required to sign a 'billion year contract' on entry,[5] are paid little more than pocket money,[6] and are subject to more severe discipline

---

[1] L. Ron Hubbard, *HCO Policy Letter*, Issue II, 8 February 1968 (my emphasis).

[2] Interview.

[3] Tom Moore, Master of Arms, AOLA, 'Subject: *Conditions Orders*' (mimeo), Department of the Master at Arms, The Advanced Organisation, Los Angeles, A Mission of the Sea Organisation-Flag, 12 August 1968.

[4] This is evident, for example, from the following (despite the confusion as to who is to pay whom):

> 'There has been a rumor started to the effect that AO [Advanced Organisation] owes $5000 to the L.A. [Los Angeles] Org for a Sea Org Mission which declared 2 Liabilities, 2 Doubts and 1 Enemy [Ethics Conditions, See pp. 142–8 below]. These were said by the S.P. [Suppressive Person] to be wrong conditions. These were in fact 100% correct as out Tech and out Ethics were found in L.A. The L.A. Org does in fact owe the Advanced Organisation $4,500 for an Ethics Mission and $20,000 as an order from Flag.'

Fran Deitsch, Supercargo, Flag Mission, Sea Org, 'Malicious rumor mongering-S.P.', *HCO Ethics Order Master at Arms Dept*, 14 August 1968.

[5] 'Sea Org requirements changed', leaflet, n.d.; and Foster, op. cit., p. 35.

[6] 'A Sea Org member draws only about four pounds a week and his room and board'. *The Auditor*, 51 (1970). He also receives a maritime uniform which while 'optional when they are on land' (David Gaiman cited in Foster, op. cit., p. 34) is usually worn as a mark of status in Scientology circles.

---

various Orgs charter vessels from Operation and Transport Services for training and other purposes. Ibid., pp. 567–71.

than ordinary followers or staff members.[1] They also receive all training and auditing free.[2]

Sea Org personnel are generally trained on the most advanced procedures and constitute a powerful elite, commanding widespread respect within the movement.[3] Officially, individual Sea Org members are employees of the various Churches of Scientology, and are subject, like all other employees, to the Board of Directors. My impression is, however, that the Sea Org, whether formally or informally, has a considerable commitment to Hubbard personally, and provides an executive force mobilizable by Hubbard to maintain his authority and carry out his policy anywhere in the world.[4] It is also mobilized in public relations exercises to provide a good image for Scientology, or for OTC Ltd (one designation for the company owning the Sea Org vessels), which is represented as a management training organization in various Mediterranean and Latin American countries. In some of these, no link between OTC Ltd and Scientology is publicized. The public relations exercises include an 'open-house programme', in which members of the public are given a tour of Sea Org vessels and 'V.I.P.s' are entertained. The purpose of this programme is detailed in a Sea Organization Flag Order

> Production target No 1 : Increased number of allies.
> Production target No 2 : Existing allies more firmly allies.
> Production target No 3 : Many well-handled visitors who leave the ship with an excellent reality on it and its operation, officers and crew, who will spread this affinity and reality widely.[5]

Ethics

The Scientology leadership has developed, over the history of the movement, an extensive system of social control. In essence, of course, all organization is a form of social control in that it establishes limits on what may or may not be done, where, and when. Hence, everything that has gone before in this chapter is germane to the question of how the employees and followers of the movement are controlled.

Beyond these practices, however, Scientology employs a formal machinery of control, the Ethics system of the movement. The Ethics system is based upon a

---

[1] *HCO Policy Letter*, 26 September 1967.

[2] *OEC*, Vol. 1, p. 88. Subject of course to the proviso that they are charged for everything should they decamp.

[3] 'If almost any person in the Sea Organisation were to appear in a Scientology Group or Org he would be lionized, red-carpeted and Very-Important-Personed beyond belief', L. Ron Hubbard, 'The Sea Organisation', pamphlet, [Church of Scientology] n.d.

[4] We are unlikely to learn the true extent of Hubbard's control over the organization of Scientology, and the Sea Org, until well after his death.

[5] 'Ship Open-House Programme', *Sea Organisation Flag Order*, 2910, 2 August 1971.

list of 'Conditions' which could be said to indicate the state of grace of any individual or organization. The following Conditions are specified:

Power
Power Change
Affluence
Normal Operation
Emergency
Danger
Non-Existence
Liability
Doubt
Enemy
Treason.[1]

Below Normal Operation, the individual or organization is liable to penalties, while above it they may receive rewards. The Condition of Liability, for example, is assigned when

The being has ceased to be simply non-existent as a team member and has taken on the colour of an enemy.
It is assigned where careless or malicious and knowing damage is caused to projects, organisations or activities. It is adjudicated that it is malicious and knowing because orders have been published against it or because it is contrary to the intentions and actions of the remainder of the team or the purpose of the project or organisation.[2]

An individual assigned to a Condition of Liability

may not wear any insignia or uniform or similar clothing to the group [sic] and must wear a dirty grey rag tied around the left arm.
The formula of liability is:
1. Decide who are one's friends
2. Deliver an effective blow to the enemies of the group one has been pretending to be part of despite personal danger.
3. Make up the damage one has done by personal contribution far beyond the ordinary demands of a group member.
4. Apply for re-entry to the group by asking the permission of each member of it to rejoin and rejoining only by majority permission, and if refused, repeating (2) and (3) and (4) until one is allowed to be a group member again.[3]

The penalties attaching to the various Lower Conditions have varied since 1965 when they were instituted. The Condition of Enemy until late 1970 when penalties for Lower Conditions were said to have been abolished by the Org,[4] indicated that the individual was a 'Suppressive Person'. 'A Suppressive Person

[1] L. Ron Hubbard, *Introduction to Scientology Ethics* (Scientology Publications Organisation, Copenhagen, 1970), p. 23.
[2] Ibid., p. 33.
[3] Ibid., pp. 33–4; for a reconstruction of the experiences of an individual in Liability, see Kaufman, op. cit., pp. 164–7.
[4] Foster, op. cit., p. 128.

or Group is one that actively seeks to suppress or damage Scientology or a Scientologist by Suppressive Acts. Suppressive Acts are acts calculated to impede or destroy Scientology . . .'[1] Apart from the other penalties which included 'May be restrained or imprisoned',[2] a Suppressive Person became 'Fair Game',

> By FAIR GAME is meant, without right for self possessions or position and no Scientologist may be brought before a Committee of Evidence or punished for any action taken against a Suppressive Person or Group during the period that person or group is 'fair game'.[3]

> May be deprived of property or injured by any means by any Scientologist without any discipline of the Scientologists. May be tricked, sued or lied to or destroyed.[4]

In 1968 Hubbard issued a policy which ordered an end to the practice of declaring people 'fair game', on the ground that it caused 'bad public relations.' He added, however, that this order did not 'cancel any policy on the treatment or handling of an S.P.'[5]

Someone connected to a Suppressive Person was a Potential Trouble Source (PTS) and was required (until 1968) to 'handle' the S.P., which seems to have meant showing him the error of his ways, or to disconnect from him.[6] Disconnection involved cutting off all communication with the S.P. and declaring one's intention to do so publicly. Disconnections were at one time published in *The Auditor*. For example:

> I, Heath Douglas Creer, do swear that I do disavow and thoroughly disassociate myself from any overtly or covertly planned contact or association with J. Roscoe Creer and Isabell Hodge Creer or anyone demonstrably guilty of Suppressive Acts (as described in HCO Policy Letters, March 1965).
> I understand that any breach of the above pledge will result in my being declared immediately a suppressive person.
> signed H. D. Creer.[7]

[1] Hubbard, *Introduction to Scientology Ethics*, op. cit., p. 48.

[2] Foster, op. cit., p. 128.

[3] L. Ron Hubbard, *Introduction to Scientology Ethics* (Publications Organisation World Wide, Edinburgh 1968), p. 49.

[4] L. Ron Hubbard, *HCO Policy Letter*, 18 October 1966, cited in Foster, op. cit., p. 129. The exoteric interpretation of this presented by public relations officials of the movement is that it meant no more than that the individual no longer received the protection of the movement's ethical codes. This is an interpretation which employs an hermeneutics to which I am not privy, seeming to be contradicted both by the words on the page, and by actions taken against those regarded as enemies of the movement.

[5] Foster, op. cit., p 129.

[6] Although it was 'Policy' to require the PTS to handle *or* disconnect, I have copies of Ethics Orders (one of which appears to have been validated by Hubbard), which order disconnection *tout court*. This does not, however, appear to have been usual practice.

[7] *The Auditor*, 9, n.d., p. 8.

More usually, a brief note was sent to the S.P. by anyone who might be ordered or feel inclined to do so.

12.4.68

G—— H——
I hereby disconnect from you
A—— L——[1]
15.4.68

From M—— S——
To G—— H——
Dear G——
     I hearby disconnect from you.
               M—— S——.[2]

An individual could be required to disconnect from a relative, friend or a total stranger. Some interviewees who had been declared S.P. received as many as 200 disconnecting letters.[3]

Organizations or smaller sub-units could be assigned a Condition if they persistently manifested down-statistics,[4] employed 'out-tech' or 'out-admin'. When such a Lower Condition is assigned to an Org, its personnel are required to work longer hours, receive reduced pay and are liable for more severe ethics treatment. Practices similar to disconnection are relatively common among sectarian movements. Deviants or defectors from groups such as the Amish are 'banned', or 'shunned'. The Christadelphians practice 'disfellowshipment'.[5]

In each case, the practice involves the exclusion of the individual from effective interaction with the believers. He may not be allowed to enter the Church or to take communion, and believers in good standing may not be permitted to communicate with him. The ban usually extends even to members of his own family. When repentance has been appropriately signified and the elders or congregation agree, the individual may once again be accepted back into fellowship. Whole congregations might sometimes be 'disfellowshipped'.[6]

Conditions are normally assigned by an Ethics Officer. The Ethics Officers are located in the HCO Division, and their appointment is subject to approval by Hubbard on whose behalf they directly administer ethics.

> The actual authority on which Ethics operates, no matter who signs the order, is LRH.[7]

[1] Disconnection letters provided by an informant.
[2] Ibid.
[3] One formerly prominent figure in the movement received over 400.
[4] *OEC*, Vol. O, p. 195.
[5] On the Amish, see J. A. Hostetler, *Amish Society* (Johns Hopkins Press, 1968). On the Christadelphians, see Bryan R. Wilson, *Sects and Society* (Heinemann, London, 1961).
[6] Ibid.
[7] *OEC*, Vol. 1, p. 436.

> Ethics Officers are looked on by me as *my* Ethics Officers and none may be appointed without my okay with a review of their record by myself.[1]

The Ethics Officers act as an internal police force and a substantial body of such personnel are maintained by each Org.

> By recent experience and tests in the Sea Org it requires a ratio of one Ethics Officer for every 20 people being handled in or by an Org.[2]

As well as a police force, there exists an established judicial structure operated through 'Committees of Evidence' and 'Courts of Ethics', with Hubbard as the final court of appeal.

Ethics are administered on the basis of the movement's Ethics Codes which classify a wide range of acts as Errors, Misdemeanours, Crimes and High Crimes (Suppressive Acts). Among the Crimes are such offences as

> Not directly reporting flagrant departures from International Board policy in a section, unit, department, organization, zone or Division.[3]

By this means Org personnel are constrained to monitor and control each other.[4]

> Allying Scientology to a disrelated practice.[5]
> Organizing or allowing a gathering or meeting of staff members or field auditors or the public to protest the orders of a senior.[6]

Only *individual* petitions are permitted, thus atomizing the personnel and preventing organized opposition to, or constraint upon, the authority of the leadership.

> Heckling a Scientology Supervisor or lecturer.[7]

Among the High Crimes Hubbard specifies are:

> Proposing, advising or voting for legislation or ordinances, rules or laws directed towards the Suppression of Scientology.[8]
> Testifying hostiley [sic] before state or public inquiries into Scientology to suppress it.[9]
> Bringing civil suit against any Scientology Organisation . . .[10]
> Testifying as a hostile witness against Scientology in public.[11]
> Publicly resigning staff or executive position in protest or with intent to suppress.[12]

---

[1] Ibid. [2] Ibid., p. 482.

[3] L. Ron Hubbard, *Introduction to Scientology Ethics* (Second edition), Scientology Publications Organization, Copenhagen, Denmark, 1970, p. 42.

[4] Staff members are also encouraged to report on each other for idleness, error, failure to carry out policy, etc. See *OEC*, Vol. O, pp. 166–7.

[5] L. Ron Hubbard, *Introduction to Scientology Ethics,* op. cit., p. 45.

[6] Ibid., p. 46. [7] Ibid., p. 47. [8] Ibid., p. 49.

[9] Ibid. [10] Ibid. [11] Ibid.

[12] Ibid.

Anyone performing any of these acts is a Suppressive Person, and until 1968 was 'fair game'.

Ethics are administered by means of Ethics Orders. These may be issued for the most trivial or the most serious offences.

HCO Ethics Order

To: Those Concerned
From: Ethics Officer
Subject: Suspension from Staff.

Date 16 August 1965
No F–3

Mary Austin is hereby suspended from Foundation Staff for creating DEV T [Dev T – developed and unnecessary traffic] on August 13, 1965, by stopping ETHICS OFFICER, Anne Fewell, in her Route of Business to pay a personal compliment, and on the same date, distracting D. of T. [Director of Training] John Gillespie's attention from making out chits and other reports.

[Seal.]   Anne Fewell
                                       Ethics Officer, Foundation.[1]

HCO Ethics Order

To: Those Concerned
From: Ethics Officer
Subject: Disconnection Order

Date 6 September 1965
No 69

1. Dick Saunders is hereby ordered to totally disconnect from literature issued by the Food and Drug Administration as it is restimulative to him. The FDA literature he comes in contact with is not to be read by him at all.

[Seal.]   Anne Fewell
                                       Ethics Officer.

E.O. 3.7 AOLA   Date 7 December 1969

Harvey Thorpe is assigned a condition of Doubt for spreading false reports about the location of Flag. He is to apply the formula immediately.[2]

Writ of Expulsion   Date 7 December 1969

1. Maxine Johnson and Michael Childs, practitioners, New York City, no longer being in agreement with or willing to support the stated aims of Scientology, are on this date duly expelled from the Church of Scientology of California.

2. They have aided and abetted Bernard Green, who was duly expelled from the Church, and condoned his erroneous Counselling of parishioners when he was not ordained to do so.

3. All certificates and awards issued to them by the Church of Scientology are hereby cancelled.

4. Therefore, they are expelled from the Church of Scientology and may not receive spiritual counselling or training in any Church of Scientology until they

[1] *Clear News*, issue number unknown (1969), p. 5.
[2] *Clear News*, issue number unknown (1969), p. 5.

have performed an act of contrition and availed themselves of resources to re-enter the Church. They may not enter any Church of Scientology.

5. They are declared in no condition, as their actions indicate that they are below any condition currently assignable.[1]

While the sanctions for Ethics offences have been much modified in recent years, during the mid-1960s the leadership briefly flirted with the use of coercive sanctions. Provision existed within the Ethics codes for the restriction of movement of those who contravened ethics regulations[2] and former members have claimed that offenders were locked up for periods on Sea Org vessels and at the Edinburgh Offices of the movement.[3] A practice known as 'Instant Ethics' was employed at one time. This consisted of throwing an offender over the side of a Sea Org vessel sometimes with his hands or feet tied. On land organizations this practice was modified to throwing the offender in the lake at Saint Hill or throwing buckets of water over the offender elsewhere.[4]

Schismatics, seceders and social control
The most severe treatment appears to have been reserved for schismatics and seceders. Indeed an analysis of the development of social control within the movement clearly suggests that the threat of schism and secession was one of the major factors leading to the emergence of a severe formal machinery of social control. Until 1959 such formal control mechanisms were merely rudimentary. In this year, however, several of the leading executives in the movement defected, including Hubbard's eldest son L. Ron Hubbard Jr. ('Nibs'). Their defection was not accompanied by heresy, however. Hubbard's son left his Org office to take up more profitable private practice independent of the organization. Hubbard initially attributed these defections to lack of sufficient auditing of his executives[5] but he shortly came to the view that mere auditing was not sufficient to avert further serious defections. An attempt was made to isolate defectors by threatening to cancel the certificates of anyone giving them support[6] and the practice of 'security checking' was instituted. Security checking involved asking an individual a series of questions while watching for 'meter reads' on the E-meter, to locate questions which would not 'clear' indicating that the individual being checked was withholding something concerning that subject.

---

[1] Ibid.

[2] L. Ron Hubbard, 'Penalties for lower conditions', *HCO Policy Letter*, 21 July 1968. Those in a condition of Doubt may 'be confined in or be barred from premises'.

[3] The existence of a 'dungeon' at the latter was also alleged by Alexander Mitchell, *Sunday Times*, 12 February 1969.

[4] The practice of 'Instant Ethics' is portrayed photographically in *The Auditor*, 41 (1968).

[5] L. Ron Hubbard, 'Individuation', lecture 26 of the First Melbourne Advanced Clinical Course, 25 November 1959 (tape-recordings).

[6] L. Ron Hubbard, 'Cancellation of Certificates', *HCO Policy Letter*, 23 May 1960.

On a Security Check sheet you only note those questions that wouldn't clear. If something won't clear or cool off the person is a security risk. If he does tell you and clear it, if it's a heavy crime, note it.[1]

Remember as a security checker you are not merely an observer, or an auditor, you are a detective.[2]

Among the questions asked on 'Sec checks' were:

2. Are you a pervert?
10. Are you guilty of any major crimes in this lifetime?
11. Have you been sent here knowingly to injure Scientology?
12. Are you or have you ever been a Communist?[3]

A security check to be administered to students before acceptance on courses contained the following questions:

2. Do you or your close family currently have any connection with organisations violently opposed to L. Ron Hubbard?
3. Are you here purposely to upset or damage Scientology or Scientology organisations?
9. Do you intend to quit this course just as soon as you have achieved your own ends?[4]

During 1962, the Johannesburg HASI appeared unresponsive to Hubbard's orders[5] and among his efforts to restore control, he invented a particularly stringent security check known familiarly as the 'Jo'burg'. This security check contained 150 questions including:

Are you guilty of anything?
Do you have a secret you are afraid I'll find out?
Have you ever assaulted anyone, practised cannibalism, been in gaol?
Do you have any overts on L. Ron Hubbard, Mary Sue Hubbard?
Have you ever had any unkind thoughts about L. Ron Hubbard or Scientology?
Do you plan to steal a Scientology organisation?[6]

In 1964 a movement initially called Compulsions Analysis was founded by two individuals who had briefly been associated with Scientology in London, Robert and Mary Ann de Grimston. This movement, later known as The Process, and as the Church of the Final Judgement, began as an eclectic synthesis partly based on Scientology, employing the E-meter and many basic Scientology techniques. It later developed in altogether different

[1] L. Ron Hubbard, 'Security checks', *HCO Bulletin* 26 May 1960.
[2] Ibid.
[3] L. Ron Hubbard, 'HGC Pre-processing security check', *HCO Policy Letter*, 23 October 1961.
[4] L. Ron Hubbard, 'HCO WW Security form 5A', *HCO Policy Letter*, 1 November 1961.
[5] L. Ron Hubbard, 'Ron's Journal', *HCO Information Letter*, 27 October 1962.
[6] L. Ron Hubbard, 'The only valid security check', *HCO Policy Letter*, 22 May 1961, cited in Anderson, op. cit., pp. 138–9.

directions,[1] moving toward an hierarchical occult order with a flexible system of beliefs, practices, and location.[2]

Neither the defection of Hubbard's son, nor the appearance of Compulsions Analysis had any profound effect on Scientology. Independent practitioners could not, in the long term, compete effectively with Hubbard and the organization while they remained orthodox in their practice, since only in the Org could the client be assured of receiving the most recent techniques and training. Senior executives who defected could initially secure a sizeable clientele on the basis of the charisma they had acquired in office. When out of contact with the organization, this charisma typically faded rather rapidly, and the clientele declined – particularly in the face of the threat from Hubbard that those who supported non-approved practitioners would receive no future service from the organization. Compulsions Analysis never posed any serious threat to the organization. It has aimed its fluid and variable message at a particularly youthful, upper and upper-middle class following, and its leaders made no attempt to win over Hubbard's followers.

Precisely because it developed an heretical theory and practice and because its initial recruits were sought among Scientologists, Amprinistics, which emerged to prominence in 1965, posed a particularly acute threat. Amprinistics was the first major heresy to affect the movement since the days of Dianetics. Harry Thompson, its founder, had been a prominent Scientology practitioner. Early in the 1960s he began to formulate a set of theories and practices at variance with those of Hubbard, although these were not generally publicized until late in 1964.[3] Early in 1965, Thompson and his associates – many of whom were also prominent Scientology auditors – began offering professional training in Amprinistics (for 200 guineas in England and $1000 in the United States). Scientology mailing lists were employed to solicit support for the new movement.

The heresy was well-timed. Social control within Scientology was becoming increasingly rigorous, as the Ethics system was applied with increasing severity. Many of the Scientologists approached thought that Amprinistics might be worth trying. The incipient schism within the movement rapidly came to Hubbard's attention, and his response was draconian. Amprinistics was savagely attacked. Its leaders were characterized as thieves and sexual deviants.[4] The techniques were claimed to be composed of outmoded Scientological practices:

[1] *Daily Mail*, 8 December 1965; *News of the World*, 3 May 1970; *Sunday Telegraph*, 17 July 1966; *Mental Health* (Spring 1967).

[2] Interviews with Masters of The Process; 'The Process', *Mental Health* (Spring 1967), pp. 17–21; *Daily Mail*, 8 December 1965; *News of the World*, 3 May 1970. See also the movement's publicly distributed magazine, *The Processean*.

[3] George Malko, *Scientology: the Now Religion* (Dell, New York, 1970), pp. 156–67; I am indebted to Miss Sheila Hoad for making available to me a number of documents concerning Amprinistics, and detailed notes on the history and belief-system of this short-lived heresy.

[4] L. Ron Hubbard, 'Amprinistics', *HCO Executive Letter*, 27 September, 1965.

We don't object to Dianetics and Scientology being used. We prefer it to have its right name. But we like to have it in clean hands. There's been too much betrayal in this universe already and for fellows whose records include homosexuality and theft to start up a fuss with 14 year old technology is a bit thick.[1]

Loyal followers were enjoined to report to the Ethics Officer anyone they knew who was going to this group:

Treatment – They are each fair game, can be sued or harassed. H—— can be barred out of any Commonwealth Country or England as he was the subject of a deportation order from England and his file has come alive again in the Home Secretary's Office. H—— T——'s wives and victims are always looking for him to have him arrested. W—— is a set-up for arrest as a homosexual. Any meeting held by them should be torn up. The names of any persons attending should be collected and they should be labelled SP as they have left Scientology. These people are SP because they are seeking to avoid auditing and retain their withholds. Once labelled, these persons will not then be covered by amnesty and will never be admitted to further training or processing. Persons messing themselves up with Amprinistics self-audit and restim should be refused any assistance. If these persons move into your area act through any agency you can to have them deported or arrested on whatever grounds.[2]

Those who attended Amprinistics meetings claim that they found themselves spied upon by Scientology personnel, and shortly after were declared Suppressive Persons, Enemies and Fair Game.[3]

Amprinistics only remained a potential threat to Scientology for a very brief period. The central core of Thompson's disciples became disaffected when he began introducing elements into the belief system which accorded him a superior 'godly' status. He appears, moreover, to have lacked the requisite skills to institutionalize the movement's following. He relied to a great extent on direct personal communication and in his absence his dispersed following fell away. When Thompson's core disciples broke away they organized the New Principles Society and attempted to revive interest among the remaining followers of Amprinistics. This new group operated primarily through a correspondence course, but it progressively moved into financial difficulties. In 1971 one of the remaining core disciples of Amprinistics and its developments, Sheila Hoad, formed the Society for the Promotion of Principles. The belief systems of these developments from Scientology have moved increasingly far from their origins until the philosophy and educational system of Miss Hoad's Society bear little relation to Scientology. They have correspondingly proved progressively less of a threat to the Scientology organization.

Several other schismatic and heretical movements have developed from Scientology. One prominent secession was led by Charles Berner in 1965. He

[1] Ibid.

[2] Ibid. The names of the individuals have been omitted here since the statement is most probably libellous.

[3] Interviews.

initially split with Hubbard over the attempts of the movement leadership to exert greater control over his autonomous 'franchised' Church. Shortly after this schism, Berner began introducing new ideological elements and techniques and founded Abilitism.[1] Later he moved closer to Eastern philosophy and founded the Anubhava School of Enlightenment.

Dianology or Eductivism was started as an independent heresy by a formerly prominent Scientologist, Jack Horner.[2] It has developed relatively little from Scientology theory and practice, and it is perhaps for this reason that it has appealed to many Scientologists who have left the movement in protest against its severe internal controls.

Other secessionary practices have been started by former practitioners who have defected from the movement or who have been expelled from it. Many of these non-approved practitioners are in contact with, and occasionally co-operate with each other. However, despite some attempts to form a more organized alliance, no formal organization has emerged. Usually, while their initial form of practice is close to that of Scientology, it progressively diverges further according to the personal predilections of the leader. It would appear, however, that all of these marginal practices have a common antipathy to the severe social control employed by Scientology. None, as far as I have been able to determine, employs anything approximating to the Ethics system of Scientology. These movements display the re-emergence of cultic tendencies within Scientology, much like the New Thought Movement which burgeoned around Christian Science.[3]

It is undoubtedly the challenge that these schismatic and heretical movements represent to the sectarian, authoritarian, and dogmatic nature of Scientology that has led to the animosity visited upon them by the Org. The leaders of several of these movements have complained of harassment which they allege to stem from the Org. This harassment in some cases has been relatively trivial as in that of a practitioner who, until recently, continued to promote and practice Dianetics, and who often suffered from persistent spurious telephone

[1] On Abilitism, see Robert S. Ellwood, *Religious and Spiritual Groups in Modern America* (Prentice Hall, New Jersey, 1973), pp. 176–8.

[2] Jack Horner, *Eductivism and You* (The Personal Creative Freedoms Foundation, Westwood, California, 1971); Jack Horner, *Dianology a Better Bridge to Personal Creative Freedom* (The Association of International Dianologists, California, 1970); see also the movement's periodical, *Alternatives*.

[3] This cultic orientation is evident, for example, in the following statement of a schismatic who has moved some way from his Scientological origins in his current practice, incorporating Yoga and meditational techniques, as well as many of his own ideas:

> 'Millions of people have a role to play in the spiritual growth of the people of this planet. I don't have anything special. I prefer my own methods. I like them and they're good. If I see something that's better than mine, I take it and incorporate it.'

Interview.

calls from young people inquiring whether they were speaking to the Scientology Organization. These calls ceased when he complained to the Scientology leadership. In other cases, schismatic leaders have found the bookings for halls in which they were to speak mysteriously cancelled. Yet another case reported to me by several independent witnesses involved a false announcement in a California newspaper that a prominent defector was to give a public lecture. When the audience arrived they were subjected to a barrage of stereophonic cacophony and chanting which included what were construed as threats against a local schismatic leader. It is alleged by my informants that Sea Org personnel were the organizers of this event. Some schismatic leaders claim their offices have been broken into and mailing lists and pre-clear files stolen.

After the disappearance of mailing lists from the office of one schismatic leader, the individuals whose names were on the list were circulated with documents which were designed to suggest that this leader and his movement were close to bankruptcy, and which made other claims that would have been a source of embarrassment to him. His forged signature was appended to these documents. Copies of what appeared to be a page of the *Los Angeles Times* were also circulated, containing a story which reported the conviction of another schismatic for criminal sexual offences. This story was a complete fabrication and had never appeared in the *Los Angeles Times*.[1]

The existence of such independent leaders and their movements are seen as a threat by the Scientology leadership without regard to their size. The schismatic groups are numerically insignificant in relation to Scientology. For all its bureaucratic organization, Scientology is a *charismatic* movement. The doctrine is subordinate to the character of the leader who, since first introducing Dianetics, has modified the doctrine frequently without precipitating any significant opposition. Joseph Nyomarkay has argued that whereas in movements based around an ideology, such as Communism, factions within the movement seek to capture the ideology and in consequence effective schisms may develop around differing interpretations, this is not possible in charismatically led movements. In this case the belief-system is subordinate to the leader. Factions must therefore compete for the leader's support since only he, and not the belief-system, provides legitimacy. Hence in the Nazi party, factions appealed to the leader for support and legitimation. When Hitler supported one particular view, opponents either ceased their opposition or left the movement as individuals. In the case of Communism, however, appeal was to the legitimacy provided by the belief-system, and factions defended their own interpretation of the ideology against each other, leading to schisms in which the schismatic could claim to be offering the 'correct' interpretation.[2] Scientology's schismatics, unable to

[1] Letter to the author from Richard W. Smith, Assistant to the Editor, *Los Angeles Times*, 7 May 1973.
[2] Joseph Nyomarkay, *Charisma and Factionalism in the Nazi Party* (University of Minnesota Press, Minneapolis, 1967).

capture the leader, the Source, have never carried with them more than a handful of Hubbard's following.

The movement leadership has reacted violently against independent practitioners and movements competing on the basis of principles and practices drawn from Scientology, and to any threat to its exclusive control over the movement, its organization, or its belief-system. One clear example is the case of a group of Scientologists who were distributing 'Advanced materials' at a reduced price. A widely promulgated Ethics Order declared them the 'Enemies of mankind, the planet and all life' and ordered the following sanctions.

4. They are fair game.
5. No amnesty may ever cover them.
6. If they ever come to a Qual Division they are to be run on reverse processes.
7. Any Sea Org member contacting any of them is to use Auditing Process R2–45.
8. The Criminals Prosecution Bureau is to find any and all crimes in their pasts and have them brought to court and prison.[1]

Maintaining a watchful eye on heretics, schismatics and prominent defectors is among the duties of the Guardian's Office.[2]

Schismatics, heretics and defectors who publicize their disaffection present a challenge to Scientology, by indicating that the structure or beliefs of the movement have been found less than perfect by insiders who have experienced it sufficiently to have an authoritative view of its operation. Unlike the outside critic, they can not easily be shrugged off as merely ignorant. By criticizing the movement or establishing competing organizations or belief-systems, they offer a threat to the structure of power within Scientology, and to the validity of the social reality it maintains.[3]

Hubbard has exhibited a great deal of concern to ensure that senior executives within the movement do not become sufficiently powerful to challenge his own authority, or to lead away any substantial following on secession. Senior executives have been purged when they appeared to be opposing Hubbard on

[1] L. Ron Hubbard, 'Rackets exposed', *HCO Ethics Order*, 6 March 1968. Auditing process R2–45 refers to a joke Hubbard once made that there was only one *certain* way to produce a 'one-shot' clear!

[2] 'Enemies' of Scientology are the responsibility of the Guardian's Office. *OEC*, Vol. O, p. 260. Such enemies, as 'Suppressive persons' are construed as beyond the protection of the organization. See *OEC*, Vol. 1, p. 554:

> no Committee of Evidence may be called to punish any Scientologist for any offences of any kind against the suppressive person. . . .

> The homes, property, places and abodes of persons who have been active in attempting to suppress Scientology or Scientologists are all beyond any protection of Scientology Ethics. . . .

[3] Dwight Harshbarger, 'The individual and the social order: notes on the management of heresy and deviance in complex organisations', *Human Relations*, 26, 2 (1973) pp. 251–69.

organizational or ideological issues.[1] Frequently thereafter they would be casti-
gated in movement publications as criminals, Communists or sexual deviants.
Removing authority figures and charging them with deviance legitimated their
dismissal and provoked less questioning of the prevailing social order than
charging them with heresy alone.[2]

The tendency to impute immorality to defectors has also been characteristic
of Christian Science. Mrs Eddy had Daniel Spofford, a former close associate
who had turned against her, expelled from the Christian Scientists' Association
'for immorality and as unworthy to be a member', and a notice to this effect was
published in the Newburyport press.[3] Mrs Eddy equated any disloyalty with
'immorality', and was reported on one occasion to have charged a woman
prominent in the Boston Church with adultery, on the grounds, she later
discovered, that 'You have adulterated the Truth; what are you, then, but an
adultress?'[4] Defectors and heretics were accused of practising Mesmerism and
even witchcraft.[5]

Conclusions

After the collapse of Dianetics, Hubbard sought to exercise greater control over
his new movement. He organized it on centralized lines and arrogated authority
by eliminating the *lay* basis of the practice and instituting a *professional* basis.
Subsequently, professionals were transformed into organizational *functionaries* as
Hubbard undermined their independent authority and sought to eliminate
'private practice' independent of the Org.

An elaborate bureaucratic machinery was created and an internal disci-
plinary system developed, particularly in response to the emergence of heresy
and the defection of senior officials. Organizational controls were increased as
Hubbard sought to avoid the earlier individualism of Dianetics and its accompanying organizational fragility. A high degree of substitutability was built into
the bureaucratic posts of the organization, so that neither in the bureaucracy,
nor in the ranks of the professional practitioners of the movement, should there
be any locus of authority which might effectively challenge his own. As a further
safeguard, an elite corps, the Sea Org, was established with international
authority to which national leaders could be subjected. Dissenters within the

---

[1] For examples, see the cases of Helen O'Brien and Alphia Hart discussed earlier.

[2] For such attacks on former senior executives, see among the multitude of such
cases, *Ability*, mimeoed edition, no number, no date, p. 5, copy in the author's posses-
sion; Anderson, op. cit., p. 137; Ros Vosper, 'Subject: John McMaster – writ of
expulsion', *HCO Ethics Order*, 29 December 1969.

[3] Ernest S. Bates and John V. Dittemore, *Mary Baker Eddy: the Truth and the Tradition* (George Routledge & Sons, London, 1933), p. 185.

[4] Georgine Milmine, *The Life of Mary Baker G. Eddy and the History of Christian Science*
(Baker Book House, Grand Rapids, Michigan, 1971), p. 234.

[5] Ibid.; Bates and Dittemore, op. cit.

movement were expelled, and those who continued to challenge Hubbard's authority after leaving the movement were roundly attacked in its publications.

Scientology displays a fusion of charismatic and bureaucratic domination also evident in some other manipulationist sects. It was a notable feature of Christian Science during the lifetime of Mrs Eddy, and appears to be characteristic of the contemporary Soka Gakkai. The latter case differs from those of Scientology and Christian Science. In these two movements the charismatic leader gradually developed an elaborate bureaucratic machine to cope with the administration of large, widely dispersed movements. The Soka Gakkai, however, was bureaucratic from the beginning and charisma was only attributable to later Presidents of the movement, rather than to its founder.[1]

As Scientology has become institutionalized, Hubbard has been less obliged to rely on a highly centralized authority structure as a means of control. The implementation of a high degree of formalization of rules and procedures made it less necessary for him to maintain a direct personal command of operations, and permitted him to delegate authority to other family members and to members of his bureaucratic staff. Peter Blau has argued that

> Formalised procedures and centralised authority may not be two expressions of the same underlying emphasis on strict discipline, but they may rather be two alternative mechanisms for limiting the arbitrary exercise of discretion.[2]

Analysis of Scientology, however, supports the more familiar view that centralization and formalization may sometimes not only both be expressions of the same emphasis on strict discipline desired by the leadership of an organization, but may indeed be implemented sequentially as the leader relinquishes direct personal control over day-to-day operation of the movement or organization, and as his charisma becomes routinized.[3]

---

[1] James W. White, *The Sokagakkai and Mass Society* (Stanford University Press, Stanford, California, 1970).

[2] Peter M. Blau, 'Decentralisation in bureaucracies', in Mayer Zald ed., *Power in Organisations* (Vanderbilt University Press, Nashville, Tennessee, 1970), p. 152.

[3] On the routinization of charisma, see Max Weber, 'Charisma', in Hans Gerth and C. Wright Mills, eds, *From Max Weber: Essays in Sociology* (Routledge & Kegan Paul, London, 1970).

6. THE SCIENTOLOGICAL CAREER: FROM CASUAL CLIENT TO DEPLOYABLE AGENT

Scientology possesses an 'enrolment economy'. Its economic base is dependent upon the sale of services in the form of auditing and training, books, E-meters and memberships. Like any sales organization, therefore, Scientology is faced with the problems of marketing the available range of products – locating and attracting potential consumers, and creating 'brand loyalty' – in all, with mobilizing commitment. The movement leadership has always displayed a highly commercial orientation in its operations. The beliefs and practices of Scientology have been seen as a valuable commodity, worth whatever the market will bear, and to be distributed wherever a market can be found.

Recruitment
Recruitment has always been a major imperative for the organization in the view of its leadership.

> ... promote until the floors cave in because of the number of people – and don't even take notice of that, just keep on promoting.[1]

With the disappearance of the mass following generated by his article in *Astounding* and by his book *MSMH*, and after establishing internal control of the movement, Hubbard increasingly turned his attention to the problem of recruitment. In a *Professional Auditor's Bulletin* distributed to practitioners in 1956, Hubbard outlined 'Three methods of dissemination'. The first of these he labelled 'I will talk to anyone'.

> The gist of this plan is to place in newspapers an ad which says 'personal coun-selling – I will talk to anyone for you about anything. Phone Rev so-and-so between hour and hour' . . . If it is the purpose of the minister simply to solve the problem of the preclear thus phoning, he can of course cancel out his clientele with the

[1] *OEC*, Vol. O, p. 83.

greatest of ease. This however is not his purpose. His purpose is to get this individual into a weekly group processing unit . . . He should not talk to the person in such a way as to ease the problem. This may be the last problem this person has and it would be a disservice to simply solve it as easily as that. One makes something of the problem, not makes nothing of it . . . at the interview the minister places in the hands of the person material relating to the work of the church group which the minister is actually conducting every Sunday morning . . . Of course it stands to reason that any auditor who has a fairly good sized group which is undergoing free processing will get from the group many candidates for (1) personal auditing and (2) a basic course in Scientology for which charge can be made.[1]

The second method was labelled 'Illness researches'. This again required the placement of a newspaper advertisement as follows:

'Polio Victims. A research foundation, investigating polio, desires volunteers suffering from the after effects of that illness to call for examination at address'. When the people arrived, usually with a phone interview first, they were immediately given about three hours of auditing . . . We did this for polio victims, arthritics and were about to do it for asthmatics when the surging success of the project frightened various individuals who had other plans for Dianetics . . . He [the auditor] would not tell the person he was doing other than investigating the cause. He would tell them he was not interested in curing their polio but that educationally he could of course improve their ability to walk or breathe or whatever. . . . One would then follow up the same principles of group [sic]. He would compose a group of such people. . . . From this group he would tell them they could have free group processing and he would sell them individual auditing . . . .[2]

The Third method recommended by Hubbard at this time was called 'Casualty contact'.

One takes every daily paper he can get his hands on and cuts from it every story whereby he might have a preclear. He either has the address in the story itself or he gets the address as a minister from the newspaper. As speedily as possible he makes a personal call on the bereaved or injured person. . . . He should represent himself to the person or to the person's family as a minister whose compassion was compelled by the newspaper story concerning the person. He should then enter the presence of the person and give a nominal assist, leave his card which states exactly where church services are held every Sunday and with the statement that a much fuller recovery is possible by coming to these free services takes his departure.
Some small percentage of the persons visited or their families will turn up in his group. Thus he will build a group and naturally from that group he will get a great many individual preclears.[3]

---

[1] L. Ron Hubbard, 'Three methods of dissemination', *Professional Auditor's Bulletin, 73* (28 February 1956), pp. 1–3.
[2] Ibid., pp. 3–4. Helen O'Brien describes this practice in operation at the Wichita Foundation. Helen O'Brien, *Dianetics in Limbo* (Whitmore Publishing Co., Philadelphia, 1966), pp. 34–7.
[3] L. Ron Hubbard, 'Three methods of dissemination', op. cit., pp. 4–5.

As indicated earlier, however, Hubbard had begun to feel that group auditing was an ineffective means of gathering a permanent following. Individuals received group processing and ceased to attend or to devote further resources to Scientology.

> Auditors are pleaded with not to go on group processing people. Group processing people results in better individuals, but not better individuals for Scientology . . . It is not enough to make people feel better. What we're trying to do is to reach out into the public.[1]

Hence from the mid-1950s on, Hubbard advocated the establishment of Colleges of Personal (or Personnel) Efficiency which would offer basic courses in the more exoteric aspects of Scientology at a nominal fee, from the recruits to which paying preclears and students could be drawn.[2]

Hubbard realized that direct personal contact with prospective customers was not always necessary. Impersonal advertising might serve as well, if individuals could be located who were predisposed to purchase a commodity of this kind. In 1964, for example, Hubbard pointed out to the organization's executives the effectiveness of advertising by the Rosicrucians, and ordered a survey of all magazines and newspapers to find where the Rosicrucians placed advertisements. He then proposed that advertisements for his next book should be placed in the same locations.[3] He also advocated the purchase of mailing lists, which could be used for the distribution of promotional material. The kinds of mailing lists which he recommended for purchasing provide an indication of his own view of the market for Scientology:

> The mailing lists of most interest would be:
> 1. Those of mystical groups.
> 2. Those of self-betterment groups.
> 3. Those of self-study groups.
> 4. Those of health groups.
> 5. Those who subscribe to magazines of special interest to the above categories.
> 6. Recent buyers of books in the above categories.[4]

Addresses of prospective customers were also secured through writing the name and address of every purchaser of any Scientology item on the receipt and its duplicates, and through mail-back cards enclosed with every volume on Scientology or Dianetics published by the organization. Initially Scientology staff would write to all those whose names were collected in this way, to lapsed students and to preclears to try to interest them in further items or services. In more recent years the post of Letter Registrar has emerged, whose job it is to contact such individuals, and get them into communication and 'on

---

[1] Ibid., p. 1.
[2] *Professional Auditor's Bulletin*, 78/79 (April 1956).
[3] L. Ron Hubbard, *Executive Letter*, October 1964.
[4] L. Ron Hubbard, *Policy Letter*, 6 September 1966.

lines' for Scientology services. Once one's name is on a mailing list, one is generally subjected to a barrage of letters and promotional materials over many months. The letters are warm, friendly, 'personalized' by the use of first names, and often handwritten rather than printed or cyclostyled. For example:

> Dear Roy,
>
> Hello there! Do you remember who is writing to you. I signed you up for the communication course. Hope you are applying the data you learnt at college or whatever.
>
> Whatsoever meaning you everyday life! [sic!] As usual we are very busy here but do find time to enjoy the sun. Funny how the weather changes so often in England. One day you are roasting and the next day you know thick sweaters are needed.
>
> Today being the perfect example of what I mean. Well Roy, do drop me a line as I really would like to know what's happening your end of the line.
>
> Best wishes
M—— P——
Dist Exec Sec Fdn
>
> p.s. please excuse the terrible typing but this is the 73rd letter I have typed today and my fingers are aching.[1]

Students and preclears waiting for services – that is for an auditor, Ethics Officer, or some other official to become available – are often expected to stuff addressed envelopes with promotional material for mailing out to potential customers. Promotional activities are also carried out by entertainers committed to Scientology. The Incredible String Band, a pop group, have distributed mail-back cards at their concerts which suggested the sender would learn more about the group. A pamphlet is received in return telling how the group members came into Scientology and suggesting the inquirer also try out the practice at his nearest Org, the address of which is supplied.[2]

As well as advertising in local and other newspapers and magazines, and whenever possible in the telephone book Yellow Pages, the central organizations of the movement have also sought to attract the general public through subway advertisements (New York) or through the offer of a 'Free Personality Test'. The inquirer would be given a booklet and test sheet for the 'Oxford Capacity Analysis', an approximation to a schedule for the production of a personality profile. The inquirer would complete the schedule and after it has been processed, he would be shown an impressive graph divided into 'Desirable' and 'Unacceptable' states for a variety of dimensions: 'Stable'–'Unstable/Dispersed'; 'Composed'–'Nervous'; 'Capable'–'Inhibited'; 'Appreciative'–'Lack of Accord', etc. The sections of the graph falling into the 'Unacceptable' category would be pointed out to him. He would be told that he had a problem there, and that Scientology could help him. He would be encouraged to take the first

---

[1] Letter to the author.
[2] I am grateful to Gordon Marshall for bringing this to my attention.

course, available at a nominal fee, as quickly as he possibly could, or he might be encouraged to take individual auditing.

A further method of recruitment that has been used is personal dissemination. Hubbard established a 'Dissemination Drill' to facilitate this mode of recruitment, following four stages:

(1) *Contact* the individual

(2) *Handle* him '. . . handle any attacks, antagonism, challenge or hostility that the individual might express towards you and/or Scientology'.

(3) 'Find their ruin and *salvage*. Find out what is 'Messing them up? It must be a condition that is real to the individual as an unwanted condition, or one that can be made real to him'.

(4) *Bring to understanding* that Scientology can handle this problem.[1]

The promotional material of the movement has aimed at a variety of interests and concerns. Much of it shows bright, happy, young people jubilant after completing auditing or a course. A general promotional magazine, *The Auditor*, which has been widely distributed to potential customers, tends to lay a great deal of visual and textual emphasis on the successful and creative individuals who employ Scientology. Beneath a photograph of an attractive girl and the headline 'Top Model' is the following text:

Carlyn Ericksen is a beautiful photographic model and actress from New York City. She has been doing TV commercials for four years shown nationwide in the States and has also done magazine and fashion work. 'I love high randomity and doing-ness especially something truly creative.'

Carlyn, who was introduced to Scientology through a friend in 1968, as far as training goes, has done the HAS, the HQS and is now about to complete the Hubbard Standard Dianetics Course in New York.[2]

Beneath another photograph and the headline 'Jesus Christ Superstar':

Famous actor and musician Peter Winsnes is one of the most recent celebrities to enter Scientology.[3]

In another issue:

Dr Harry Wood, Professor of Art at Arizona State University has been applying Scientology concepts to his teaching of art.[4]

The successful businessman and the scientist have also been used as promotional material:

INDUSTRIALIST.
Unsure whether his business would expand and if he could handle the new problems growth implied, Ken Kirk of Adelaide, South Australia enrolled on the HCA Course in 1965 [. . .]

[1] L. Ron Hubbard, 'Dissemination Drill', *The Auditor*, 22 (1967), p. 3.
[2] *The Auditor*, 70 (1971), p. 5.
[3] *The Auditor*, 80 (1972), p. 5.
[4] *The Auditor*, 82 (1972), p. 8.

Since he became a Scientologist, the value of the company's equipment has jumped from \$5,000 to \$25,000.[1]

PHYSICIST
Research Associate at Hansen Physics Laboratory (Stanford University) near Palo Alto, California, Dr Hal Puthoff is very much a Scientologist. He is OT III Expanded and OT VII. An author and expert on laser beam technology, Dr Puthoff . . . considers Scientology an invaluable part of both his personal and professional life and is currently busy applying Scientology concepts to modern physics.[2]

Other promotional materials have been directed less to displaying the kind of individual that one might become, than to attracting individuals with problems.

We don't care what your problem is we can help you. Get some auditing.[3]

Wouldn't it help to know . . .
. . . how happiness happens?[4]

UNDERSTAND OTHERS
These books give you the keys to understanding the human mind and human nature. With them you have the Vital Knowledge necessary to understanding others, handling them, and establishing sane, growing relationships.[5]

BE A MEMBER OF SCIENTOLOGY.
The world has waited thousands of years for a technology to change conditions for the better. Scientology is the answer.[6]
If you have ever taken drugs of any kind you need L. Ron Hubbard's drug rehabilitation intensive.[7]

'Success stories' have often been reprinted in promotional publications. Hence the potential customer may be faced with material on the following lines:

Is my chronic illness handled? It is indeed. I've had it going more aeons than I can easily remember. And now it's gone. No more, finished, handled. And it feels great. Thanks to my Auditor for the application. Thanks to the Commodore for the Tech.
Expanded Dianetics Case B.[8]

The first thing I did on becoming Superliterate was pick up the most complicated book I could find. It was a dictionary of music – a subject I could never grasp at all. I started at 'scales' and eventually worked through most of the dictionary by cross reference. I sat back and gasped. I'd picked up the information of a whole technical subject in 40 minutes, and I understood it! I couldn't believe it. [. . .]
Vic Lyons (Superliterate)[9]

---

[1] *The Auditor*, 68 (1971), p. 7.   [2] *The Auditor*, 64 (1971), p. 5.
[3] *Certainty*, 19, 7 (1973), n.p.   [4] *Leaflet* (1972).   [5] *Change*, 62 (1974).
[6] *Change*, 55 (1973).   [7] *Leaflet* (1971).   [8] *Leaflet* (1973).
[9] Leaflet, n.d.

The second generation

As the movement has approached a quarter century of existence, provision has gradually emerged for recruitment from among the offspring of members. Separate courses of training and auditing have been available for children for some years in various Orgs, although the formalities surrounding auditing children have become greater in the face of public criticism. Increasingly, however, independent schools have appeared to educate the children of Scientologists, in a Scientological manner. In Hollywood, the Theta Power School has been established, primarily for the children of Sea Org members.

> Our purpose is to educate the children so that when they are old enough and ready for it they can then go into Orgs or Franchises and get their Scientology processing or training. We use Scientology study data, and also the codes, such as not forcing a child to communicate if they don't want to.
>
> We do not teach Scientology as such, but all the teachers are somewhere on the bridge, and most of our parents are Scientologists, so the children will probably be future leaders in it. Naturally we use all we know to see that the children learn and keep their ethics in.[1]

Another such school is the ARC School at Kollerod in Denmark. In 1968 this school was reported to have twenty-one pupils.[2]

Membership: background characteristics

Like their Dianetics precursors, Scientologists are overwhelmingly middle class. The occasional titled individual and the occasional manual labourer appear in the literature of the movement, but only rarely. This is reflected in the responses of thirty-seven practising or former Scientologists to my questionnaire. The educational level of the respondents was above average.

Secondary education	*No.*
Secondary modern/Elementary/Technical	6
Grammar	25
Public/Boarding/Other private	5
Unclassifiable	1
	—
	37

Further education	
Teacher training or other full-time professional	7
College of Advanced Technology	3
University[3]	11
None	16
	—
	37

[1] Julia Lewis Salmen, Principal, letter to the author, 5 December 1973.

[2] *The Auditor*, 43 (1968).

[3] It should be noted, however, that three respondents indicated that they had not *completed* their university courses, and there may have been others.

Age at the end of full-time education

Under 18	16
18 or over	18
Unclassifiable	3
	—
	37

The responses on a question concerning occupation indicated only one respondent to be a manual worker.

Occupation	*No.*
Housewife	4
White collar	32
Manual	1
	—
	37

Among the white-collar workers, there were relatively few engaged in lower level white-collar occupations. Thus there were no clerks among my questionnaire respondents. Among the occupations listed were: university lecturer, several teachers, two draughtsmen, two photographers, two copywriters, several branch and sales managers, two scientific research workers, two psychotherapists, a commercial artist, etc. As one might expect with such educational and occupational backgrounds, most of the respondents saw themselves as middle class. To a question on self-assigned class the following distribution of responses appeared.

Self-assigned class	*No.*
Upper	0
Middle	22
Working class	3
Do not recognize classes	11
No response	1
	—
	37

The data available, although not of a form to permit any rigorous correlational analysis, suggest a relatively low rate of inter-generational mobility. Most respondents had come from middle-class backgrounds.

Father's occupation when you were 15 years old	*No.*
Manual	8
White collar	23
Dead	5
No response	1
	—
	37

Most of those in the manual category had skilled occupations. Treating all the respondents as 'white collar'[1], it is evident that there is a considerable discrepancy between the rate of mobility for my respondents and the rates in the population of England found in four studies compared by McDonald and Ridge [2]

Father's occupation of non-manual sons: percentages[3]

	(a)	(b)	(c)	(d)	Scientology respondents
Non-manual	58	48	47	50	74
Manual	42	52	53	50	26
	100	100	100	100	100

The Scientology respondents display a very much lower rate of upward mobility than that exhibited in studies of the general population They are more solidly middle class in their social backgrounds.[4]

Given the small numbers of respondents in the Scientology study, however, it is not possible to have any great confidence in the validity of this finding.

A guide to the movement's sex distribution was obtained through classification of the first names of 823 individuals listed as 'clears' after 1966 in available issues of *The Auditor*. Of these 29 could not be allocated. Of the remainder, 446 were male (59 per cent) and 348 were female (41 per cent). Observation, promotional and other material suggest that the average age of the current following has dropped from that of the Dianetics following. This was confirmed in the case of my questionnaire respondents. The distribution of their ages on entry into the movement were as follows:

Age on entry	No.
Under 25	12
25–44	19
45 and over	6
	37

[1] A step not licensed by the data as the earlier table for *occupation* shows. The possibility of an analysis of rates of intergenerational mobility was pointed out to me by Richard Bland, but unfortunately by this stage the data were not in a form to permit the elimination of the four housewives and one manual worker.

[2] K. McDonald and J. Ridge, 'Social Mobility', in A. H. Halsey, *Trends in British Society* (Macmillan, London, 1972).

[3] Tables (a), (b), (c) and (d) are adapted from McDonald and Ridge, op. cit., p. 146. I am grateful to Richard Bland for recasting these tables in the form of percentages of fathers of non-manual sons.

[4] Even if the four housewives and the manual worker were withdrawn from the category for non-manual fathers, reducing the percentages to: non-manual fathers, 69 per cent and manual fathers, 31 per cent, it is still evident that the Scientology respondents are more solidly middle class in their social origins, and have therefore experienced a lower rate of upward mobility than has usually been discovered for the general population.

The average age of entry among these 37 respondents was 32 years. It is my impression, but not one that I can support, that the age distribution of members has been dropping since the early 1960s and particularly since 1965. If this is the case I suggest it can be accounted for in terms of the image of the movement gleaned from the mass media coverage by youthful potential recruits. Some younger former followers suggested that they were attracted in part by its anti-Establishment character and its message of 'Total Freedom'. Moreover, the 1960s was the period when a post-war generation of young people was growing to adulthood, a generation which was richer, more leisured, better educated, and more self-conscious than any which had preceded it.

Motivations for recruitment

As with followers of the early Dianetics phase of the movement, the motivations of recruits fall into three analytically distinct types: the career-oriented; the truth-seeker; and the problem solver.

The career oriented

Those who fall into this category saw Scientology as either providing a new or an alternative career, or as providing the means of advancing or developing a career in a psychological or therapeutic field in which they were already engaged.

One young man, for example, had attended university in Canada where he had not been satisfied by his psychology courses and had therefore failed to complete his degree. He had read widely in religious literature, including Buddhism and Theosophy, had tried meditation, and was interested in the work of Wilhelm Reich. Through his interest in Reich he became acquainted with Subud, since some of the Subudians in Canada were former disciples of Reich. He had tried psychoanalysis briefly when his studies were not going too well. On his return to England he took up a course of study in Osteopathy and Naturopathy, but found it too physically oriented. He had always wanted to work in the area of psychotherapy but found that a medical degree was generally required. He heard of Scientology and thought he would give it a try. He had no definite idea of practising as an auditor, but rather of acquiring skills that might be useful as a therapist in the future.[1]

The truth seeker

Some recruits identified their motivation for recruitment to Scientology in terms of a search for the truth:

> I've always studied comparative philosophy and comparative religion since as far back as I can remember . . . They've been my chief interest because there didn't seem much purpose living here and not having any purpose or any plan. Way back

[1] Interview.

in my teens I more or less threw out the orthodox religion that I was brought up in because it didn't seem logical. Quite frankly the first half of my life was seeking for logic, believing that logic held the whole answer to everything. I learned better later . . . One went through all the rather far south people like Gurdjieff, Ouspensky, and then after handling that quite a lot I went totally the other side – the didactic materialists, the logical positivists, and so on . . . Somewhere must come that leap forward which transcends reason . . . You can go along with logic so far and then you've got to just leap forward . . . or lateral thinking if you like, on a philosophical level. At this point I saw one must look a bit beyond logic. Of course that led naturally into studying extra-sensory perception . . . Then I thought, so many people much wiser than I have lived by some religion. The only way to study religion is to go back to the roots . . . the source. So I spent several years doing just that . . . It didn't lead one anywhere . . . I'd read *Isis Unveiled* and *The Secret Doctrine*. I read every word of *The Bible*.

After this intellectual journey of many years she read a copy of *MSMH* which her husband had been given.

I thought if part of this is true, only a little part, it's worth investigating. So I will investigate it. So I wrote and asked where my nearest Centre was.[1]

The problem-solver

The dominant motivational theme, however, was that provided by a problem-solving perspective. Many questionnaire respondents indicated that they had earlier sought solutions to the problems facing them through medicine, psychiatry, psychoanalysis, hypnotherapy, marginal and fringe religious movements, marriage guidance counselling, speech therapy and Pelmanism. Despite the reduced emphasis on healing after the transition to Scientology, some recruits were attracted to the movement by what they regarded as an implied claim to therapeutic efficacy for *physical illness and disability*. They entered the movement in pursuit of therapeutic methods to alleviate themselves or someone close to them of physical problems. (The Guardian's Office assert that: 'The Church does not attempt to handle physical illness and disability and ensures that all newcomers are made aware of this.')[2]

I had only been married less than six months, and my wife had contracted cancer. I was told she would live maybe 12 weeks to 12 months and that would be it . . . Prior to her operation I called the organisation because that was the only group I knew of that could be in some way of assistance to me and to her.[3]
[What attracted you to it?]
At first I was not attracted to it, but tended to argue with the ideas expressed about it by my friend. However at this time (and actually for most of my life) I had a rather bad speech impediment, and my friend suggested, on a number of occasions, that

[1] Interview.
[2] Personal communication, November 1974.
[3] Interview.

Scientology therapy might enable me to overcome this difficulty. Eventually I agreed to read one of the elementary books on Dianetics. I was particularly attracted by the scientific approach which appeared to have been made, in investigating the mind, and the behaviour of man. I was also attracted by the suggestion in that book, that the use of the therapy proposed would enable a person to overcome a stammer.[1]

Others saw the movement as a possible source of alleviation of problems they regarded as *psychosomatic* in character.

I was having a few psychosomatic ills at the time – things one got pills for but didn't really know what they were – one of which was a thyroid condition.[2]

Another suffered from migraine headaches for which he had received medication, but had come to the conclusion that they were of psychological origin. He therefore bought works of popular psychology from time to time in an attempt to find a solution to his problem. One day he came across *MSMH* in a bookstore and was excited by the prospect that this might solve his difficulty. Finding the book hard to follow he contacted the Org address given in the book and one Christmas in a fit of depression went in for auditing.[3]

The boundary between physical and psychological problems is obviously a fluid one. Some respondents identified their problems in unambiguously psychological terms. For example, one man who had first contacted the movement in his late twenties, and who was out of work when he first became interested in Scientology:

[What did you think it might be able to do for you?]
Well I knew damn well at the time I had to sort myself out. I'd had a nervous breakdown about nine months previous. Found out the medical profession were a load of charlatans and I had to find my own salvation.[4]

He saw an advertisement in a magazine inviting the reader to 'Come and have your personality tested'. He went along for a test and a lecture, found the lecture 'logical', and began to attend co-audit sessions. A questionnaire respondent indicated that he was attracted to Scientology by the hope 'that it might help to tackle my nervous trouble'.

Some recruits indicated that they were suffering from difficulties of a primarily *social or interpersonal* kind. One young man interviewed had had a very unhappy home life with a violent father and a large and inadequately provided for family. His father had been resentful of his staying on at a school until he was 19. He had no friends and heightened adolescent difficulties with girls. After being rejected by a girl whom he wished to marry and a final row at home, he left Glasgow for London. There, lonely and frustrated, he came across a sign: 'Solve your problems by increasing your mental ability. Phone D—— F——, Scientologist.' He arranged an appointment.[5] Similarly, a questionnaire

---

[1] Questionnaire respondent.
[2] Interview. [3] Interview. [4] Interview. [5] Interview.

respondent indicated that he was attracted to Scientology in the hope that it would 'solve my problem of loneliness'.

Most of those interviewed, from whom such information could be secured, had rather more mixed motivations. The following respondent displayed a combination of *seeker* and *psychological* themes.

> I was always interested in things like spiritualism. I went to one or two spiritualist meetings . . . From about the age of 13 I was trying to find the answer to the Mystery of Existence. I used to read anything I found on mysticism, philosophy, spiritualism, and so on.[1]

He and his wife would follow up advertisements in *Fate* and similar periodicals. His wife had a great deal of 'emotional trouble' and he now regards her as having been 'a borderline psychotic'. When he came across *MSMH* in a local library he had considerable hope that Scientology would help to alleviate her problems.

A large number of respondents displayed a combination of *psychological* and *social* themes. One respondent was 21 to 22 years old when his mother became interested in Scientology. He had dropped out of medical school because he felt that he wasn't 'cut out to be a doctor'. He was very shy at the time, felt unable to study, to communicate with people, or to make friends. He was suffering from lengthy periods of 'black depression', and felt that Scientology might be able to help him.[2]

Some displayed a combination of *psychological* and *career-oriented* themes, like the following respondent who was a qualified doctor of medicine and had been undergoing Jungian analysis for personal problems when a friend told him he was getting a lot out of Scientology:

> I had been interested in the field of mental health since my undergraduate days, having done a degree in psychology, and intending to do something in this line. I had got a bit dissatisfied with conventional approaches like hospital psychiatry. I thought I'd see what there was in it. There was no harm in going to a lecture. So there was this kind of professional interest. There was also a personal one in that I had some problems myself at the time which weren't being solved by conventional analysis.[3]

A number displayed more, sometimes all, of these themes in their accounts. The following individual exhibits at least a combination of seeker, problem-solving (psychosomatic illness), and social themes:

> I used to be an avid reader of almost every book I could get my hands on. I used to haunt the public libraries for books, which I read in an attempt to satisfy my thirst for knowledge. I would read of this and that and the other and would often feel I'd found something – only to follow it through and find it lead up a very interesting but quite blind alley. I could never find the answers to the questions I had been asking myself and others from childhood up.

[1] Interview. [2] Interview. [3] Interview.

I wanted to know what I was doing here, why I *was* here and what was the purpose behind this experience we called life. These were some of my questions. I searched and searched for the answers but with no real success.

I found my reading and searching was often interfered with quite considerably by the regular attacks of migraine headaches which used to lay me out completely for several days at a time. This, together with the frequent attacks of rheumatism to which I was subject, did not make my life particularly enjoyable. In fact, looking back to-day [sic], I would say that a large percentage of the reason why I was searching so avidly, was to take my mind off the reality of my own situation. Life was really a bit too grim for me, so I would lose myself in my books and long philosophical discussions which seemed to relieve the pressure of everyday living.

My job, which I did not care for particularly, was that of a 'white collar worker' and as I used to attend various evening classes for the study of psychology and related subjects, I did not have much time for feminine company. Anyway I was a little too shy to talk to girls very much.

Then one day, while browsing through the book-shelves in the public library – my usual shelves, those on philosophy, psychology and comparative religions – the librarian drew my attention to a book which the library had recently acquired at the request of another member. The title of this book was 'Scientology 8–8008' by an author called L. Ron Hubbard . . . I took it home with me to study.[1]

Twenty-nine of the 37 Scientology questionnaire respondents completed a question directed to ascertaining the kind of problems which they hoped Scientology would solve for them when they joined. Four indicated that they did not join in search of a solution to any problems. The remaining 25 displayed a wide range of problems (they could indicate more than one). The least important category was that of *marital problems*, while the most important was that of *psychological problems*. The distribution of problems to which responses were indicated, was as follows:

Problem		No.
(a)	Loneliness	8
(b)	Financial problems	4
(c)	Marital problems	5
(d)	Other problems of interpersonal relationships	14
(e)	Psychological problems	15
(f)	Physical illness	11[2]

Combining categories (d) and (c), it would seem that in general, problems of interpersonal relations were prominent sources of motivation to seek help through Scientology, particularly if combined with category (a). Over half of

[1] Frank Harding, 'How I became a Scientology Auditor', *Certainty*, 3, 7, n.d., pp. 2–3.

[2] A self-completion category elicited the further responses: philosophical; deafness; sexual inadequacy; speech impediment (2); problems with communication; smoking; 'enigma of life'; 'why people behave as they do'.

those who responded to this question acknowledged some form of *psychological* problem as a motivating factor, and over one-third, a *physical* problem.

Given its general style and teachings, it would be surprising were individuals to move into Scientology as a result of dramatic conversion experiences – although this sometimes occurred as a result of sudden cures. Those interviewed generally revealed that their association with the movement was the result of a progressive process rather than a sudden event. Few felt they had made any major commitment, that what they had entered embodied the complete truth from the beginning. Kaufman recounts the process of 'drift' by which he entered the movement, and his experience may not be untypical:

> If anyone had asked me 'Why would you be willing to join a cult?' I would have contended that I wasn't joining anything. I didn't even consider Scientology a cult – cults were peopled by the lonely, the alienated, the not-so-bright, not by comfortable, intelligent individuals like Felicia and her husband . . . I thought it the result of a combination of chance meetings, fortuitous circumstances, and the gentle suggestions of valued friends who believed that I had wanted auditing all along.[1]

Lofland and Stark and Gerlach and Hine argue that new social movements spread through networks of acquaintances on the basis of face-to-face interaction.[2] My own findings bear out this hypothesis to a considerable extent. Fifty-seven per cent of the respondents to my questionnaire had a friend or relative involved in the movement, and 68 per cent claim that they first came into contact with it by such means. Thirty per cent (2 per cent did not respond) claim first to have come into contact with the movement by impersonal means – through the medium of a book, magazine article, an advertisement, or a circular. In many cases, however, personal contact seems to have been slight and of only limited importance in their recruitment or their attachment to the movement.

Attachment

Once an individual has come into contact with Scientology, the organization brings to bear on him a great deal of pressure to affiliate himself further with the movement. As one Policy Letter states,

> When somebody enrolls, consider he or she has joined up for the duration of the universe – never permit an 'open-minded' approach.[3]

The individual who takes a 'Personality Test' is uniformly advised that Scientology can help him in some way, since that is the sincere belief of most

---

[1] Robert Kaufman, *Inside Scientology* (Olympia Press, London, 1972), p. 8.

[2] John Lofland and Rodney Stark, 'Becoming a world-saver: a theory of conversion to a deviant perspective', *ASR*, 30 (1965), pp. 862–75; Luther P. Gerlach and Virginia H. Hine, *People, Power, Change: Movements of Social Transformation* (Bobbs–Merrill, New York, 1970).

[3] *OEC*, Vol. O, p. 38.

Scientology personnel. Many recruits first attend a free public lecture or nominally priced Personal Efficiency Foundation Course. These courses are devised to interest the public in Scientology and draw them into further commitment.

> A PE Foundation is a programmed drill calculated to introduce people to Scientology and to bring their cases up to a high level of reality both on Scientology and on life. . . . A PE Foundation in its attitude goes for broke on the newcomers, builds up their interest with lectures and knocks their cases apart with comm course and upper indoc. . . . Never let anyone simply walk out. Convince him he's loony if he doesn't gain on it because that's the truth . . .[1]

Under the broad heading of *attachment* the factors which led to the emergence of some initial firm commitment on the part of those recruited to the movement will be examined. From the material available, three bases of affiliation can be discerned: cognitive, experiential and affective. By *cognitive* grounds are meant bases for further commitment of a primarily intellectual kind. For example, a doctor cited earlier attended an introductory Scientology lecture and found it stimulating, the lecturer

> was talking about practical life and relationships in simplified terms – about three concepts involved. I was tired of reading academic books containing 17 theories of learning which had no bearing on the way one actually lives. I was also tired of hospital psychiatry. I'd done psychiatric clinics myself in which one saw people for 30 minutes and prescribed a pill and never really had much contact with them. This at least seemed to be direct and immediate.[2]

Others indicated that they found the talks 'logical', that they were impressed by the explanations given for human behaviour, or that they found it made particular sense.

Many became committed to Scientology on *experiential* grounds. Some particular experience convinced them that Scientology was the key to something important. One questionnaire respondent indicated that he lost his doubts when his wife was cured of migraine by a 'touch assist'. An interview respondent indicated that he became convinced during his first auditing session when

> they did an assessment and the charged item was 'a child'. So then they ran me on a process – what have you done to a child, what have you withheld from a child. And the moment they asked those questions, something happened. Suddenly I was looking at the body of a little boy and I was recalling and suddenly I knew it was what I had done to this body when it was a child which had established the patterns for whatever happened later . . .[3]

Less dramatically, a number of individuals found that as a result of Scientology drills and techniques they were better able to communicate with others, or experienced other improvements, psychological or interpersonal.

[1] L. Ron Hubbard, 'The organisation of a PE Foundation', *HCO Bulletin*, 29 September 1959, cited in Kevin Victor Anderson, *Report of the Board of Enquiry into Scientology* (Government Printer, Melbourne, Australia, 1965), p. 103.

[2] Interview.   [3] Interview.

I found that [co-auditing with other beginning students] helped me tremendously, and it seemed to help the people I was auditing too.[1]

When I began having Scientology auditing I was impressed by the fact that it did work just as the books had said it would.[2]

The other major theme emerging from the interviews was that in which the motivation for affiliation developed on primarily *affective* grounds. The individual became emotionally committed to Hubbard, to other Scientologists in particular, or to the warm expressive atmosphere displayed in many Scientology organizations. One interview respondent cited earlier became emotionally involved with a committed Scientologist who discussed past lives with her and told her she was one of a group of thetans

who through all the centuries had been influencing people for good . . . I was . . . one of this fantastic group . . . At first I thought he was insane, and then I was slightly flattered of course.[3]

Others were attracted by Hubbard's 'magnetic personality'. Many were impressed by the immediate acceptance that they found among Scientologists. They were warmly welcomed into the group, greeted, and applauded. Every success was broadcast and congratulated. They were 'validated' in what they did.

Mine was the time of 'Quickie Release Grades' – a fairly short period – and people went around saying 'This is fantastic. This is a record'. Flinging their arms around me. 'Never been done before. What a fantastic thetan you must be'. Of course this puffed me up tremendously. With everybody congratulating me so much of course I had to write the most fantastic Success Story. I mean I owed it to these people who congratulated me.[4]

Many found themselves with a group of friends for the first time in years.

People come in and immediately they're enclosed in this atmosphere, which, when it first hits you seems a tremendously good and healthy atmosphere because everybody seems to be friends with everybody else.

An awful lot of lonely people go into it I think because they find this tremendous welcome . . . for the loner coming in . . . People need company. They want to be accepted and one thing the Scientologists did was accept people. They would tolerate an awful lot, because they had this thing, you must never invalidate anybody. For someone who's been pushed down, suddenly to find people coming up and saying, 'Well, look, you're a beautiful person in your own right. There are qualities in you which are likeable and lovable . . .; it's bound to do them good, to give them a lift, and then they come back and buy the courses.[5]

Socialization

Individuals enter Scientology with a multiplicity of goals of a personal kind which they wish to pursue. Socialization within the movement is oriented to the

[1] Interview.   [2] Questionnaire respondent.   [3] Interview.
[4] Interview.   [5] Interview.

progressive transmutation of such personal goals into Scientology goals, that is to ends permitted or preferred by the movement's leaders. Individuals also enter Scientology on a largely unselected basis. There is of course a differential appeal to certain categories of potential recruit, and no doubt considerable self-selection, but the movement does not require the display of any particular mark of merit nor the negotiation of any test of merit before an individual may join. Moreover, unlike other movements which proselytize widely, such as Jehovah's Witnesses, no extensive probationary period is required before full acceptance into the movement. Thus recruits are a potential source of disruption and must be socialized as quickly as possible into the movement's norms and values to neutralize this disruptive potential.

A major step is taken in the socialization of recruits once the individual comes to see the current level of training or auditing on which he is working as but the beginning of a journey through the increasing number of such levels that are available up to O.T.8 and Class XIII auditor (or whatever happens to be the number at any particular time). The recruit often appears to experience a considerable increase in self-confidence after the lower levels of training. After several hours of 'confronting' and 'bull-baiting' the individual may feel freer and more confident in interpersonal relations. After auditing in which he may have come to speak of or even think of things which he has repressed and hidden for many years and which he has probably never confided to anyone, he may experience a profound sense of relief. He has been released from some secret guilt or fear of many years standing, which will, he is assured, never trouble him again. The lectures which he attends provide him with a simple model of human behaviour which in the light of his confusions, uncertainties, and lack of comprehension of life's complexities, may appear as a sudden revelation. In a few simple but scientific-sounding terms he is offered an account of his own actions and those of others which is presented with absolute conviction. These insights and 'wins' provide the motivation to continue to the next course of training and auditing. If so much can be achieved at the lower levels, it is reasoned, what can not be achieved at those beyond?

Current doubts and dissatisfactions can be held in abeyance. Since one is only a beginner one cannot expect everything to be revealed at once. What one does not understand may be explained later. What one does not accept may merely be the consequence of some aspect of one's reactive mind, which will be resolved through future auditing.

The enthusiasm of others on the course, or of Scientology friends, is infectious. Group expectations lead the recruit to search for some gain, to achieve a success, to believe that it has worked.

> Everybody believed so firmly that it could work for me, so I couldn't *not* believe it because I so much wanted to believe that it would work. Everybody wants to believe that it's working . . . or the whole thing is meaningless. So there is this tremendous – what they call 'group agreement' that it does work. Instantly I was

caught up in this. I wasn't examining the thing, and it *did* work, or I felt that it worked. Now, I think to myself: I say it did work, but *what* worked? I can't think of anything that worked, but at the same time, yes, I thought, well Christ, I feel marvellous, this works.[1]

Having experienced that some aspect of the belief system 'works', having come to recognize his 'gains' as a consequence of Scientology, perhaps even having committed himself to this in writing in a 'Success Story', and having been applauded and congratulated and handed a certificate, the member would often willingly sign up for, and even pay a deposit or sign a cheque for, a further course of auditing and training.

Anderson suggests that more intensive 'hard-sell' tactics have sometimes been employed in some Orgs to ensure maximum financial commitment by pre-clears. After convincing and signing up a recruit for an amount of auditing, generally twenty-five hours, the Registrar would take the applicant and his form to the Director of Processing. The latter would talk to the applicant and endorse the form to the effect that he could not accept the applicant, since it was his considered opinion that only after some 250 to 300 hours of auditing could the individual achieve a 'stable result'. He would then return the matter to the Registrar. The applicant, aghast at his plight, would then often readily sign up for the greater number of hours of auditing recommended.[2] (The Church of Scientology assert that the Anderson Report contained many inaccuracies, and point out that the legislation which followed it has since [and in my view rightly] been repealed in some states of Australia, or effectively nullified by registration of the national Scientology church as a recognized denomination for purposes of the Federal Marriage Act.)[3]

A particularly important means of both enhancing commitment and social-izing the individual is that of convincing him to take an active part in Scien-tology by training as an auditor. When he has achieved some success with Scientology, the member may become convinced that this is something which he should not only benefit from, but the benefits of which he should carry to others. Scientology literature is studded with statements to the effect that nuclear war, communist revolution, and sundry other ills can be prevented only by the spread of Scientology. Thus appeal is made to the altruism of the pre-clear. However, he shortly learns that such altruism has concrete rewards. Taking the path to 'clear' by the Training or Professional Route rather than by the Pre-clear Route, that is taking courses to train as an auditor, while taking auditing to become a 'clear', will save him nearly one-third in total cost. In 1972, the Training Route to clear cost in total £1330 while the Pre-clear Route cost in the region of £1980.[4] Helping Ron to 'clear the planet' by becoming

[1] Interview.
[2] Anderson, op. cit., pp. 104–5.
[3] Personal communication, Guardian's Office, November 1974.
[4] *The Auditor*, 77 (1972), p. 4. The prices are higher today.

trained as a professional auditor also promises a further return since the individual will then be qualified to practise for a fee.

Those who are recruited to the movement without sufficient funds to pay for training and auditing are encouraged to join the Org staff where in return for long hours and low pay the member will receive auditing free, or at a reduced rate. The individual thereby commits himself as an employee as well as a follower.

By these means the recruit comes to identify his own goals with those of the movement.[1] Only within Scientology is he fully recognized and accepted as he is. Only Scientology has any real answer to his particular problem. As he becomes increasingly committed to the movement, he is increasingly alienated from features of the world beyond. The literature which he reads heaps invective on the medical profession, psychiatrists, politicians, and newspapers. He comes to learn that all of these, as well as a number of Scientology defectors, are involved in a conspiracy to silence Scientology through propaganda and legal attack, out of fear of its innovatory message. He comes to learn that inside Scientology individuals are sane and releasing all their abilities, while outside is a world full of people subject to their 'Banks'[2] and liable to engage in irresponsible and destructive behaviour at any time.

In the light of what he learns to see as the hostility of the outside world and the attempts by communists and 'squirrels'[3] to obtain Hubbard's 'data', he comes to recognize the need for strict internal control. The more closely he comes to see his own goals as linked to the avowed aims of the movement, the greater is the legitimacy with which he endows the movement's norms as embodied in the Ethics codes. The rigorous discipline of the movement, and the regimentation to which recruits are subjected in the central organizations, is accepted as necessary to achieving the goals the individual has set, or those which he is beginning to acquire:

> there was much that pleased me about the life at Saint Hill. I was being taught to crack down. It was one more burden lifted not to have to be rebellious anymore – rather, to be obedient. They were giving me the discipline I had lacked all my life, discipline which was going to be – in the long run – as beneficial as clearing . . . An almost imperceptible change was occurring in me: I no longer supposed that I was using Scientology for my own purposes. I liked the feeling; it was a clean one. My old ways had been grandiose – impure. Perhaps I was being affected by the lines, the strict regimen . . . If so, I appreciated the value of what I was getting, and was glad to see myself becoming less a wilful intruder and more one of the group at the Hill.[4]

---

[1] This process is central to Kanter's concept of commitment: 'Commitment thus refers to the willingness of people to do what will help maintain the group because it provides what they need.' Rosabeth Moss Kanter, *Commitment and Community* (Harvard University Press, Cambridge Massachussetts, 1972), p. 66.

[2] Reactive memory banks.

[3] Non-approved practitioners.

[4] Kaufman, op. cit., p. 101.

The group itself brings pressure to bear to secure conformity, in part because being associated with someone whose Ethics are suspect may lead to suspicion about their own.

> It is a truly illuminating experience to be assigned a Condition of Liability . . . Colleagues whom you regarded as friends, seem suddenly distant. They won't talk to you. They don't offer you cigarettes or suggest you take a swig out of their Coke bottle. In some really Eager Beaver cases, they even refuse your cigarettes when you offer them![1]

The recruit begins applying the Ethics codes to himself rather than waiting to have them applied to him by the Ethics Officer. Henceforth should he suffer any nagging scepticism he will realize that it is not a rational response but simply the consequence of his being in a 'Condition of Doubt'. Having assigned himself to this condition, he can then proceed to apply the Ethics formula and begin to work his way out.[2] The individual begins to conceive of the system of social control as central to the survival of the movement, hence Ethics sanctions are not merely something to submit to and suffer, they are to be welcomed as a source of Enlightenment.

> I have just completed three days of fabulous wins with Ethics. I really know what Ethics is all about now. Previously I'd had it confused with punishment, which it's not at all. Clarice has helped me to make my environment safer so that now I can be audited successfully. I really know what it means to be 'salvaged with Ethics' and it's great!
> Gloria Nickel, Clear No. 702.[3]
> So this is Ethics! It's beautiful. It's safe and helpful. I can really see for once how it makes things right so tech can go in.
> Janet Wiggins, Clear No. 1986.[4]

As the member begins to organize his daily life in terms of the Ethics Condition and formulae, he comes to embrace and internalize the norms of the movement.

> After receiving Integrity Processing and applying ethics to her situation as a writer, Ros Baws sat down and completed the script for her comedy screen play . . . 'I had been sitting there with thousands of blocks, knowing something was wrong', says Ros. 'After some auditing and looking at the formulas for the Conditions . . . I just did it. I had statistics on how many pages I had to do each day to be in a Normal Condition. It was amazing. When I set my mind to it I completed the entire script'.[5]

Progressively, the recruit comes to acquire a vocabulary peculiar to the movement through which he can articulate his thoughts and experiences, and in terms of which he can locate and define the behaviour of others. He is feeling 'banky' that day (under the restimulated influence of his reactive mind); an acquaintance is '1·1 on the Tone Scale', or 'covertly hostile'; while another

---

[1] Cyril Vosper, *The Mind Benders* (Neville Spearman, London, 1971), pp. 138–9.
[2] Kaufman, op. cit., p. 155.
[3] *Clear News*, number and date unknown, p. 5.
[4] *Clear News*, number unknown (1969), p. 5.
[5] 'Integrity Processing: a writer's win', *Celebrity Magazine*, Major Issue 6 (1972).

shows a high degree of ARC (Affinity, Reality and Communication). Locating his own situation and that of others in terms of this vocabulary carries with it as an almost automatic concomitant the identification of the movement as the means of improving or managing this situation. Only Scientology beliefs and practices prescribe means of coping with problems identified in Scientology language, or achieving a situation or state of mind that only Scientology reveals, and to which it alone offers access.

> The added lectures had their effect, however. I'd never paid much attention to the specific meaning of the individual grades, except for IV. After hearing about them repeatedly, I began to feel that I really was a Communications Release, a Problems Release, and the rest. It got so that I reveled [sic] in Gerald's speech. He was re-counting *my* gains; it was *me* he was describing, a Grade IV Release. . . . It was plain now that my recital had been the result of processing after all. I did owe it to Scientology. I was glad I had taken the course and gone to the added lectures. It wasn't until Gerald had given me a complete list of my gains that they became a reality to me.[1]

As the pre-clear accepts the first steps of the theory and technique he learns to see himself suffering from the restimulation of traumatic events. The model of mental and spiritual functioning on the basis of which he has achieved 'gains' in interpersonal relations or in relief from some hidden guilt, also prescribes the state of 'clear' as the only condition under which he would be fully free from such problems in future. From the relief of some particular pressing concern, the individual's goals are redirected toward achieving the state of clear.

The recruit, in the light of his new-found confidence, psychological relief, or enhanced ability, redefines his past biography as something to which he does not wish to return:

> I saw my old life as one big reactive mind. My moods had been affected by every-thing around me: weather, places, people. A person with a reactive mind was like a piece of lint blown about on a windowsill.[2]

Hence his current improvements can only be seen in the context of a sciento-logically-defined biography. His current condition is only the beginning, and can only be stabilized by continuing with training and auditing, at least to the state of clear. Clearing, he learns, is the only permanent means of maintaining his currently improved condition, and advancing beyond it. He acquires a 'vision' of clearing which motivates heightened commitment, and submission to the rigorous discipline of the movement:

> This vision represented fulfillment of all hope and escape from all aversions. The gains that I felt I owed to Scientology were based entirely upon a projection into the future. The aversions were mostly unknown to me until Scientology made me aware of them.[3]

[1] Kaufman, op. cit., p. 44.
[2] Kaufman, op. cit., p. 68.
[3] Ibid., p. 67.

By the time that he reaches this state he will have spent anything between six months and two years in the movement undergoing training and/or auditing, and have invested between £1300 and £2000. Having achieved clear, he learns that to be sure of maintaining his gains, and to achieve the spiritual abilities only a short distance beyond, he must take the OT levels. In the case of a number of those interviewed, on achieving the state of clear, they felt, after the initial exultation had subsided, that very little of any concrete kind had been gained. In the hope that the OT levels would provide more concrete demonstration of the efficacy of the theory and practice on which they had spent so much time and money, and in the pursuit of which they may have suffered indignity and embarrassment as a result of Ethics treatment, they invested sums in the region of £1100 to £1375 to secure the further knowledge and experience they had come to see as so vital to their personal development.[1]

The novice is rendered more malleable to this process of socialization by the injunction that he approach the material without a 'fixed opinion', that what he is being told is 'stable data' tested on many thousands of cases, and that he should only accept what is 'true for you'. The assumption, however, is that shortly it will all become true for him, since the entire system is an interlocking whole. The student is enjoined not to puzzle over possible sources of disagreement. 'Figure, figure', and 'Q & A' (Question and Answer) are not approved.

Maintaining reservations indicates that one is 'hung up on a maybe'.

> A person who's being impartial, conservative, etc. is hung up on a maybe so hard that it would take tugs to get him off.
> . . . figure, figure, figure is . . . very far from certainty.[2]

This condition is in need of remedy through auditing and 'cramming', before one proceeds further, and therefore slows one's progress to the goals one seeks to achieve (and is, moreover, a source of further expense).

> [Scientology] attains [its] aims in precise and definite ways, ways in which there is no room for 'maybes'.[3]

As one progresses further up the grades and levels of training it becomes increasingly difficult to admit disagreements or doubts, since to do so would endanger one's earlier achievements. Disagreement might suggest that one had 'falsely attested' to the earlier grades and levels, requiring that one retake them, have a 'review', or become subject to Ethics penalties. Doubts and disagreements, as matters for remedy, have costly consequences, and the incentives are therefore entirely in favour of easy acquiescence.[4]

[1] The cost of the OT levels is detailed in Sir John G. Foster, *Enquiry into the Practice and Effects of Scientology* (HMSO, London, 1971), p. 102. The higher of the two figures is that given in *Advance!*, issue 20 (August/September, 1973), p. 15.

[2] Both quotations are from *Professional Auditor's Bulletin*, 1 (10 May 1953), p. 4.

[3] Herbert Parkhouse, 'Scientology and religion', *Certainty*, 2, 9, p. 14.

[4] One of the characteristics of the 'Suppressive Person', for example, is that he does not 'respond to auditing'.

The further one progresses, the greater the commitment of time, money, and ego-involvement one has made, and the harder it is to admit that one has made a mistake. One's purpose in continuing involvement has become not the achievement of some particular improvement that, however nebulously, one had identified in oneself, but the achievement of a goal identified by the organization, by means which it alone provides. The *client* has become transmuted into a *follower*.[1]

Mobilization

Scientology is a movement with some totalitarian features. Its leadership seeks not merely to secure a clientele for its services, but to maximize the commitment of a large unselected membership and mobilize them in the service of the organization. Mobilization is directed to the end of transforming followers into active, deployable agents who see their own salvation intimately linked with the achievement of ends established by the organization leadership. Generally such ends are those of promotion and dissemination of Scientology, but others include staffing of Scientology Orgs, recruitment to the Sea Org, and the enhancement of the individual's commitment and dependency.

The members of the movement are early accustomed to submitting themselves to direction by Org personnel. On entry into an Org facility, the member has to 'go through lines', that is through an established routine of passage from one post to another collecting forms or other documentation, paying fees, awaiting an auditor, etc. While waiting for services he will often be expected to occupy his time on some clerical task for promotional purposes. After a day at the Org he may be asked to distribute leaflets to houses on his route home,[2] and when taking his training he will be required to secure a pre-clear from among the public, on whom he can demonstrate his competence and, if possible, recruit for Scientology. During later stages of his training he is required to undertake periods of 'internship' during which he audits full-time for the Org.

When not taking training or auditing, the follower is mobilized in the field. His increasing alienation from the rest of society, particularly from inter-

---

[1] When interviewed after having severed their connection with Scientology, some would refer to this process in which they were transformed into a following of the movement in terms which, if often less elegant than those of Fischer referring to his own commitment to Stalinism, mirrored his conclusions closely, on

'the lengths to which a man can go who, though neither stupid nor vicious, deliberately ceases to see, to listen, to think *critically*, subordinating his intellect to the "*Credo quia absurdum*" so as not to doubt the cause he serves and, having thus subordinated his intellect, proceeds to abuse it by clothing the resulting nonsense in threadbare syllogisms.'

Ernst Fischer, *An Opposing Man* (Allen Lane, London, 1974), cited in a review by George Steiner, *Sunday Times*, 17 March 1974.

[2] Kaufman, op. cit., p. 199.

personal relations with non-Scientologists is exploited to the end of proselytization for the movement:

LONESOME?
Have people who don't know Scientology stopped making 'sense' to you? Start a Group.
People don't bite. Ask them over to a sociable evening to discuss forming a mental health group. When they get there, don't ask them to join. Just elect them as officers. Get them to agree on future meetings and the programs.

Assume they want to know more about Scientology. Explain Scientology off-handedly as though it's sort of strange they don't know and get on with group organisation and business.[1]

He is encouraged to commit further resources to Scientology in order to maintain his advances. He receives promotional literature on the following lines:

Targets to Total Freedom
These targets have been designed to
assist you going Clear.
        Name————
Major Target   To go clear by————
                                (pick a date)

                 .   .   .   .

Decide on arrival date at
        ASHO/AOLA   (date)————
                [Etc.][2]

AOLA is your home for Clear and OT. The popular 'thetaccount' (the 'unbank' account) was designed for you so you can invest in your future self, Clear and OT, by sending regular advance payments to the AO. [Etc.][3]

He is encouraged throughout his association with Scientology to take not only auditing, but also training, to become an auditor rather than merely a pre-clear. Becoming an auditor offers the possibility not only of conducting the self-audit levels of processing more competently, but also of recouping some of the costs of auditing and training by auditing others professionally in private practice.

Those who have not committed themselves to a professional career as an auditor, or have not yet achieved the necessary qualifications, can be mobilized as part- or full-time Field Staff Members. These individuals act as recruiting agents for the Org, receiving a commission on the amount spent on Org services by the 'selected' individual. In recent years, the leadership have sought to mobilize a larger proportion of the membership as Field Staff Members, and to tie them more closely to official Orgs. Policy published in 1968 expressed an

---

[1] *Ability*, 50, p. 8.
[2] Promotional leaflet. ASHO is Advanced organisation, Saint Hill; AOLA is Advanced organisation, Los Angeles.
[3] Promotional leaflet.

aspiration 'to reclaim and enrol as staff members everyone we have ever trained'.[1]

The member is encouraged to attend Congresses and other mass membership events designed to increase promotional and disseminational activities in the field, such as a mass meeting early in 1974, which heralded the 'Battle of Britain'.

> The True Battle of Britain is Beginning. L. Ron Hubbard has sent Special Representatives to the United Kingdom. They have a message from him for each and every UK Scientologist . . . *It is imperative that you attend*!!! A Special tape from L. Ron Hubbard, will be played which you *must* hear. [Etc.][2]

Encouragement is also particularly strong for members to join the Org staff on a contractual basis or more permanently. The incentives for younger members to join are considerable. Without an established career to which they are committed and without adequate resources to finance training and processing, working for the Org often has considerable attraction. In particular, auditing and training are made available (in the evenings) at reduced rates or free.

> Staff Status Two, if on contract, is entitled to free processing up to Grade V, and 50% discount on training and further processing and uniforms.[3]

While pay is low and conditions often arduous, the young member without familial obligations may find this no great bar. The staff member is not tied to the Org by the mere formality of a contract. Should he break his contract, for example, by defection, he becomes liable for the full cost of all the training, processing and travel expenses that he has received.[4] Staff seconded for advanced training and auditing are required to sign promissory notes to the sum of $5000 on each occasion.

> Such a Note . . . must be legally binding in that if he breaks his Contract, he is automatically in debt to the Org for $5,000.[5]

The acme of Scientology involvement is membership of the Sea Org. Members at all levels of the movement are encouraged to join up.

> Come and work as part of Ron's expanding team of Sea Org members here at Saint Hill now! Contact me immediately!
> Love,
>   G—— [signed]
> G—— E——
> Area Secretary[6]

[1] L. Ron Hubbard, 'Field auditors become staff', *HCO Policy Letter* May 9 AD [After Dianetics] 15, revised and reissued 14 January 1968.

[2] Promotional Leaflet, emphasis in the original.

[3] *OEC*, Vol. O, p. 48.

[4] Ibid., pp. 48–9.

[5] Ibid., p. 52 One interview respondent received a bill for $14 000 for services rendered while on course at the Sea Org Flag ship, when expelled shortly after taking the course, and was threatened with civil suit for the collection of this sum.

[6] Letter to the author.

Dear Roy,

I note you have had some Scientology training. Here at St Hill we need people with some training to train further to hold vital Technical and Administrative posts within the Sea Org.

As a Sea Org member you would have no domestic worries as all accommodation and food is provided. This will free you up to really expand as a being on all the Dynamics. You would be helping to make this Planet a safe and sane place to be thus aiding the survival of all 8 dynamics.

The company and life in the Sea Org is very good, the Sea Org people are a dedicated team who can see that Planet Earth could be better and who are doing something to make it so.

The Clears and OTs leaving St Hill vouch for that.

So if you want to do something to help you are most welcome, I'd like you to call at St Hill to see me.

Love,

J—— P——[1]

Members are encouraged to become auditors, staff members, and Sea Org personnel in order to assist Ron to 'Clear the Planet'. On staff they become subject to remunerative as well as normative control.[2] Their commitment is increased in the sense that more and more resources are invested in the movement. 'Side-bets' are laid on continuing membership,[3] as the member increasingly withdraws from external social relationships, career, and financial involvements, centering all his resources and aspirations on the movement. Staff members become totally dependent financially on the Org, unless they possess independent incomes. Outside the Org they are forbidden to audit pre-clears for a fee. Their incomes are precarious, subject to the vicissitudes of Stats and Conditions. Indeed in some Conditions, for example, Doubt, they are not eligible for pay at all. Failure to fulfil the norms established by the movement leadership therefore raises the threat of sanctions of a far-reaching kind. The threat of financial liability at a punitive rate for courses taken while on staff, is a powerful incentive for subordination.

Expulsion and defection

In this section we are concerned with the reasons why people ended their association with the movement. Some, of course, had no choice in the matter. They were expelled, despite some continuing commitment to it. This commitment might be to other Scientologists – friends or relatives[4] – or it might be a

[1] Letter to the author, 28 October 1973.

[2] Amitai Etzioni, *A Comparative Analysis of Complex Organisations* (Free Press, Glencoe, 1961).

[3] Howard Becker, 'Notes on the concept of commitment, *American Journal of Sociology*, 66 (1960), pp. 32–40.

[4] See Vosper, op. cit.

continuing commitment to some of the beliefs and practices of Scientology. In these latter cases, however, generally a measure of alienation from the organisation had already occurred. A relatively high degree of antipathy toward the movement's mechanisms of social control could co-exist with a continuing and fervent belief in the theory and practise of auditing. Some time after his break with Scientology, one formerly prominent figure in the movement could still assert:

> If Ron said it was all a 'con', I would reply to him: 'I feel sorry for you that that is all you have got out of it'.[1]

Individuals interviewed were found to have left the movement at various points in their involvement with it, some after many years association, others after reading their first book on the subject.[2] Moreover, except for those whose association was decisively severed by expulsion, one could disassociate from Scientology in very varying degrees. A number of those interviewed, while out of touch with the movement for some time and conscious of aspects of it of which they strongly disapproved, had made no irrevocable break. Several expressed the feeling that when they had sufficient funds, or when the period of severe authoritarianism was over, they would return.

Reasons for disaffection with the movement fell generally into the following categories.

1. Disaffection emerged as a result of the application of particular practices of social control to oneself or to a close acquaintance or relative.

> I just wanted to know more about the auditing. But they made it hard. I was one minute late one morning on course, for a very good reason . . . I arrived just as the roll-call was ending and said sorry . . . but the Course Supervisor said, 'You must have overts against the Org'. She said, 'You have to write out what you've done against the organisation in order to have been late . . .' There were many occasions like that . . . Should I walk out, or should I learn more about this auditing from which I had had actual physical benefit. So I stuck it out. But I got less and less interested.[3]

Another interview respondent was asked to disconnect from his wife, who was declared an S.P. and, although he did so at first, he became disturbed by this demand and returned to her. This led to his also being declared an S.P. Others were also expelled for refusing to disconnect from a friend declared to be a Suppressive Person.

2. Others became disaffected, not as a result of any one specific application of

---

[1] Interview.

[2] To be fair to the movement and its following, one should perhaps stress the obvious point that many individuals do *not* leave even after many years' association. As far as an outside observer can tell, despite a very considerable turnover of membership, there are still a few individuals in the movement who first joined in the early 1950s.

[3] Interview.

harsh measures of social control, but rather as a result of what they viewed as the developing authoritarian atmosphere of the organization.

> . . . it became a crime to doubt any of Hubbard's statements, and I had always doubted a lot of Hubbard's statements, but when I went in, it wasn't considered a crime, even if one was given looks of incomprehension. I could not belong to any organisation which said you *must* believe this and that. Also there began to be strict codes of rules about Suppressive People . . . who were declared to be enemies of Scientology and one was not meant to have any contact with them . . . I was not willing to subscribe to this. It seemed to me to be a paranoid set-up and getting too fanatical, and I didn't want anything to do with this.[1]

Two former franchise operators in America also became disaffected largely as a result of the general tightening of control and the authoritarian imposition of Org practices. They both found that the official Orgs were increasingly interfering with the operation of the franchises, insisting that they employ Ethics Officers, use only prescribed techniques, and hand on their mailing lists of students and pre-clears to the Org.[2] A former senior Org executive found that organizational practices led to a *crise de conscience* which undermined his faith in Scientology.

> [Why did you leave?]
> Conscience . . . I just couldn't be a party to what was happening in the Organisation . . . I no longer had the same belief as when I started . . . I'd been embarrassed, humiliated, confused. It didn't serve any purpose for me to be part of it any longer . . . I looked back over my history in it and saw that I'd done a lot of good things . . . but I'd been party to things I'd much rather not have been party to.[3]

Harsh or indifferent treatment of people was the source of much dissatisfaction. Two respondents had received a severe blow to their faith in the movement when sick friends in hospital who had long been committed to Scientology were, despite requests, never visited or helped by Org personnel. Another became alienated, he said, when he saw a young girl being told she was not fit for Scientology because, only just having started work, she lacked adequate funds for training and auditing.

Several of those whose reasons for leaving Scientology fell predominantly into either or both of these first two categories commented on what they had seen as an increasing disparity between the ideology and the organizational structure of the movement, between the belief in 'Total Freedom' and the increasing authoritarianism of the organization.

3. A third important category of reasons for disaffection were what Gabriel Almond, et al. refer to as 'career-related dissatisfactions'.[3] These might occur to a student as well as to a staff member. One of the women who was interviewed had been committed to becoming a professional practitioner, but had failed her

---

[1] Interview.　[2] Interviews.　[3] Interview.
[4] Gabriel A. Almond, et al., *The Appeals of Communism* (Princeton University Press, Princeton, New Jersey, 1954), p. 300.

professional course, and felt very strongly that she had 'lost face' when another woman who had formerly been her pre-clear [patient] passed with flying colours. Another interview respondent failed the course twice and lost much of his enthusiasm for the movement in consequence. Yet another had believed himself capable of professional practice but had been unable to afford the course which would qualify him, and which the Org insisted that he take.

Some staff members, particularly in the leadership echelons of the movement, regarded themselves as virtually indispensable and able to assert their own views in independence of, or even in opposition to, Hubbard. They became disaffected when they were removed from authority, and were reduced to the same status as ordinary staff, and subjected to the same indignities. Others felt that their relationship with Hubbard, or their long-standing in the movement, entitled them to superior status and income, which they did not receive.

4. For some, dissatisfaction with Scientology was the result of their own metaphysical development. They gradually found that their own philosophies were diverging from that of the movement. Others, beginning to have doubts about the theory and techniques of Scientology, came to hear of one of the schismatic developments and pursued it, either dropping their association with the Org, or being expelled in consequence. One questionnaire respondent replied to the question 'Why did you leave?' as follows:

> I left because I met something far better, Truth itself I thought, which helped my understanding of anything to increase.[1]

A small proportion of those interviewed simply felt that the more they learned of Scientology, the less it had to offer them, or the more vacuous they found it to be. One woman found moral objections to some of the OT courses. The aim of the OT 7 course, which she described as attempting to implant a thought in another person's mind, she regarded as a form of 'Black Magic'.

5. Dissatisfactions for some were based on more practical considerations. A number of those interviewed claimed that the failure of the results they had expected to materialize was one cause of dissatisfaction. Some, for example, were thoroughly committed to the notion of Clear and were not convinced that some of those declared Clear in fact were so. One interview respondent said:

> You meet Clears and OTs who are meant to have tremendous abilities and you find them making little mistakes you don't expect them to make.[2]

Such considerations were sometimes a cause of growing doubt, which might be compounded when at times the techniques were not found to be successful when used on oneself or on those one was auditing. Some found that their 'gains' from auditing were very short-lived, or were disappointed when they found themselves to possess no significant new abilities after Clearing or the OT levels.

6. A number of those interviewed found the expense of training and auditing a barrier to increased commitment, or a source of alienation. They lacked the

[1] Interview.   [2] Interview.

resources to involve themselves deeply in Scientology and either gave up, or looked around for less expensive paths to salvation. A few had a stronger objection, regarding the leadership of the movement as largely oriented to the pursuit of profit – a conclusion which disillusioned them.

7. One important cause of defection that was reported in interviews and questionnaires occurred among followers who had had relatively little conviction of their own, but who were attached to other members whose conviction was stronger. A break with the close associate often led them to drop Scientology as well, since usually their involvement had been aimed at pleasing the more committed partner.

8. Finally, of course, there are a range of residual reasons for disaffection. One interview respondent dropped Scientology finally when it adopted the corporate structure of a church, since membership in a church was incompatible with his faith as a Baha'i. Others simply drifted away from the movement when they moved home and lost contact with distant acquaintances and the Org. Generally, most of those interviewed offered a range of such reasons in their accounts of why they left the movement.

For those who were expelled, or who walked out over some particular event, the break was sharp. More often defection from the movement was a process which took some weeks or months, or in some cases years, of mounting dissatisfaction and disillusionment. They would often find means of excusing practices they found objectionable, for example, by blaming Hubbard's lieutenants for them and arguing that he must be misinformed about what was going on at the Org's operational level. Or they excused their lack of results, as directed by Hubbard's writing, by blaming the lack of skill of particular auditors, rather than the 'technology' itself.

They might stifle doubts and confusions by concluding that these were a product of their reactive minds, or by following the injunction that they should not 'invalidate' the levels and 'gains' they had received:

> [Did being clear live up to what you had heard?] Yes and no. I put aside the doubts because I didn't feel that it was right to doubt it. Yet I was wondering why I couldn't do the things that I was supposed to be able to do.[1]
> ... one thinks, well, maybe all my doubts have been 'bank' ...[2]

Others continued in the movement out of a belief that this was the only answer available, or through attachment to others in the movement, or because they were unwilling to admit that they had been wrong, or because they had lingering suspicions that they might be wrong now.

> [... what kept you at it?]
> Well, the feeling that even though there were hold-ups and wrong decisions made, that it was still aiming towards a better thing than anything else that was offered. Also just the inertia or momentum of the whole thing. Once you're in a group like

[1] Interview.   [2] Interview.

that, its extraordinarily difficult to get out of it. How can you say to your friends you're a liar, a fraud and a charlatan? How can you say that, unless you are absolutely convinced? It's easier to keep in Scientology and have doubts than to go out of it with doubts.

It's a more positive thing. Doubts are negative and they're always seen as inferior to any positive drive. So you tend to swallow your doubts. And you say: 'Well, maybe next week . . .' Sometimes you have incredible successes. I had a top executive who came back from the Congo with a weird disease. Did 170 hours auditing on him and he walked out a changed man. There must be some good in Scientology if it can do this much for one individual, and it wasn't just one individual.

My wife, who is a highly intelligent and sane person and not easily conned was a totally dedicated Scientologist, and still is. I still feel, talking to her, maybe I have made a terrible mistake.[1]

Conclusions

Scientology appeals to people with very diverse motivations for affiliation. These motivations can be broadly classified in the categories: career-orientated, truth-seeking and problem-solving. We have aimed to describe and analyse the career of the typical recruit who becomes a core member of the movement. Such a recruit typically becomes associated with Scientology as a *client*, seeking some specific aid, knowledge or problem-solution. He becomes attached to the movement on cognitive, experiential, or affective grounds. He comes to view his biography in terms of a vocabulary and conceptual scheme provided by Scientology theory and practice, and to see his own goals as only attainable through the achievement of broader goals specified by the movement leadership. In the course of socialization he comes to internalize the movement's normative code. His association with the movement leads to the commitment of resources and ego-involvement which make withdrawal expensive and threatening to his own self-esteem. The recruit is transformed from a client to a *follower* and from a follower to a *deployable agent*.

A similar process would seem to be characteristic of most more-or-less totalitarian movements which seek to maximize the involvement and commitment of followers. Totalitarian movements seek to secure the total commitment of recruits rather than accepting partial or segmental commitment.

The processes outlined for typical recruits to Scientology are similar in many respects to those described by Gabriel Almond, et al., in their study of Communist defectors. The authors argue that 'at the point of entrance into the movement, the party is all things to all men'.[2] A range of 'images' are presented to different sections of the recruitment catchment area. These images are described as the 'public or exoteric images of the Communist movement', fashioned to have a broad appeal and 'to suit the susceptibilities of particular audiences'.[3] While

[1] Interview.
[2] Almond, et al., op. cit., p. 5.
[3] Ibid.

those who are to become party cadres are gradually inducted into the esoteric, power-seeking, goals of the Communist movement, a large proportion of recruits are not exposed to the esoteric doctrine and practice. Similarly, among recruits to Scientology, probably only a small proportion become employees or functionaries of the Org, and only a small proportion of these will be exposed to inner-movement decision-making, and strategy formulation. The majority of Scientologists, as of Communists, are only exposed to, and remain committed to, one or more of the movement's propaganda representations. Most Scientologists remain in full-time employment outside the movement, utilizing Scientology facilities only occasionally and limiting their involvement to a level compatible with their occupational and domestic responsibilities. In this respect they resemble the rank-and-file party member. As a result of their limited involvement and exposure, they remain unaware of the movement's esoteric, power-seeking orientation.

7. RELATIONS WITH STATE AND SOCIETY

During the period between the emergence of Scientology and the centralization of operations in Washington DC, the movement made little public impact. It grew very slowly after the loss of the early mass following, although from 1956 it began to grow at an accelerated rate.[1] While the reasons for the growth at this time are obscure, its consequences are more readily apparent.

After the disappearance of Dianetics, the movement only occasionally came to public attention, and this almost always only locally, when in the USA, Scientology practitioners were arrested for 'teaching medicine without a license'.[2] In 1958, however, the US Food and Drug Administration (FDA) seized and destroyed a consignment of 21 000 tablets of a compound known as Dianazene, marketed by an agency associated with the Founding Church of Scientology in Washington, the Distribution Center, claiming that they were falsely labelled as a preventative and treatment for 'radiation sickness'.[3] The Church of Scientology maintain that the product 'Dianezene [sic] was mis-labelled because the contents did not measure up to the contents quoted on the label (a fault in the manufacturer's process)'.[4] The Church of Scientology also later pointed out that the only labelling which referred to anti-radiation was on the manufacturer's bulk shipment, not on the bottles made up by Distribution Center Inc. However, the relevant federal legislation allows a wide interpretation of 'labelling'. In a book published by the Scientology organization,[4] part two of which is accredited to L. Ron Hubbard, Hubbard gives a formula for Dianezene which approxi-

---

[1] Figures cited during a later tax case indicate that the income of the Washington Church almost doubled between 1956 and 1957 ('Brief for the United States', Founding Church of Scientology v. USA in the US Court of Claims, Washington, DC., 1967, op. cit.).

[2] A schismatic publication, *The Aberree* reports that in 1955, two Scientologists were arrested on such a charge in Detroit, and placed on probation. *The Aberree*, 2, 6 (October 1955), p. 13.

[3] Personal communication, Food and Drug Administration, 21 January 1972.

[4] Personal communication, The Guardian's Office, November 1974.

[5] *All About Radiation*, by a Nuclear Physicist and a Medical Doctor (Publications Organisation [East Grinstead] 1957, 1967), pp. 121–4.

mates to that found in the FDA seized tablets. He asserts that 'Dianazene runs out radiation – or what appears to be radiation. It also proofs a person up against radiation in some degree. It also turns on and runs out incipient cancer.'[1]

The Dianazene seizure received little press publicity, but marks the beginning of active interest in the movement by federal agencies. The first serious adverse press reaction to the movement in Britain occurred as a result of the activities of the headmistress of an East Grinstead private preparatory school who was carrying out Scientology exercises on her pupils for a brief period each day.[2] Most of these exercises involved simple, repetitive, and rather innocuous commands such as 'stand up', 'sit down', etc., or communication exercises such as the teacher saying 'hello' and the children replying 'all right' for a few minutes. The exercise that led to the press outburst involved the pupils following the directions: Close your eyes. Concentrate. Now imagine you are dying. Imagine you are dead. Now you have turned to dust and ashes. Now imagine you are putting the ashes back inside yourself. The press reports referred histrionically to those periods as 'Death Lessons'.[3]

After conducting preliminary investigations into the E-meter during 1962, the FDA again raided the premises of the Founding Church of Scientology in Washington early in 1963 to seize examples of the E-meter, and associated literature.[4] On this occasion, unlike that of 1958, the FDA clearly saw an opportunity to exhibit their importance as agents of the public interest, meriting the appropriations of public funds which they received. The raid was accompanied by considerable publicity, the press, it was said, having been forewarned.[5]

> . . . recent hearings before the Subcommittee on Administrative Practice and Procedure exposed certain activities of the Food and Drug Administration to be disgraceful and completely contrary to the protective guarantees of our Constitution. Perhaps the most shocking of these exposures, involved the raiding of a premises here in the nation's capital. This raid was reminiscent of a bygone era when large numbers of Federal and local law enforcement officials set upon centers of gangland activity. True to form, this recent raid was preceded by intelligence from an FDA spy planted on the premises. In authentic Hollywood style, FDA agents and marshals descended on private property while local police roped off the street and held back the crowds. Press reporters and photographers accompanied the agents while they ran through the premises, banged on doors, shouted and seized what they viewed as incriminating evidence.[6]

[1] Ibid., p. 124.

[2] *Daily Mail*, 29 November 1960.

[3] *Daily Mail*, 28 November, 1960; Paulette Cooper, *The Scandal of Scientology*, (Tower, New York, 1971), p. 102.

[4] George Malko, *Scientology: the Now Religion* (Dell, New York, 1970), p. 75.

[5] Evidence before the Senate Subcommittee on Administrative Practice and Procedure, reprinted in Church of Scientology, *The Findings on the US Food and Drug Agency* (Department of Publications World Wide, Church of Scientology, East Grinstead, 1968), p. 32.

[6] Senator Edward Long, *Congressional Record*, 8 September 1965. This description of

The FDA seizures gave Hubbard cause to reaffirm the attitude of his organization to the press:

> The reporter who comes to you, all smiles and withholds [sic], 'wanting a story', has an AMA instigated release in his pocket. He is there to trick you into supporting his preconceived story.
> The story he will write has already been outlined by a sub-editor from old clippings and AMA releases.[1]

In the subsequent suit, the FDA charged that:

> . . . the labelling for the E-meter contains statements which represent, suggest and imply that the E-meter is adequate and effective for diagnosis, prevention, treatment, detection and elimination of the causes of all mental and nervous disorders and illnesses such as neuroses, psychoses . . . arthritis, cancer, stomach ulcers, and radiation burns from atomic bombs, poliomyelitis, the common cold, etc. and that the article is adequate and effective to improve the intelligence quotient . . . which statements are false and misleading . . .[2]

The seizure action led to the first serious press attention to Scientology in ten years in America. Much of it was hostile, and supported the FDA action. The Scientologists, however, reacted with considerable indignation, subsequently referring to the FDA with an uncharacteristic sense of irony, as 'an agency behaving as a sort of cult, with an almost fanatical urge – to save the world.'[3]

The FDA raid was reported throughout the English-speaking world, and in the state of Victoria in Australia it added fuel to a debate which had been taking place in the mass media over Scientology. In Victoria, Scientology had been under observation for some years by the Mental Health Authority, and the Australian Medical Association, which had sought to bring the activities of the movement to the attention of members of the government.

During the period 1960 to 1965, Scientology received a great deal of unfavourable publicity in Victoria. The Melbourne newspaper, *Truth*, attacked the movement in a series of feature articles. In November 1964 the Leader of the Opposition, the Hon. J. W. Galbally, in a speech to the Legislative Council of the Parliament of Victoria, referred to the FDA raid in Washington and alleged that Scientology was being used for blackmail and extortion and had seriously affected the mental well-being of undergraduates at Melbourne

---

[1] L. Ron Hubbard, *HCO Policy Letter*, 14 August 1963, cited in Kevin Victor Anderson, *Report of the Board of Enquiry into Scientology* (Government Printer, Melbourne, Australia, 1965), pp. 200–201.

[2] Cited in Malko, op. cit., p. 76.

[3] Church of Scientology, *The Findings . . .* , op. cit., p. 3.

---

the events was congenial to the Scientologists, who reprinted it in Church of Scientology, *The Findings on the U.S. Food and Drug Agency*, (Department of Publications World Wide East Grinstead, 1968), p. 27.

University.[1] On 26 November 1963, Mr Galbally introduced a Scientology Restriction Bill seeking to provide that fees should not be charged for Scientology services. Shortly afterwards the Victoria government agreed to establish a Board of Inquiry into Scientology.

The Hubbard Association of Scientologists International (HASI) in Australia initially co-operated with the Board of Inquiry but withdrew its representatives in November 1964. The Report published in 1965 presented an unmitigated condemnation of the movement. In the Report, Anderson, its author, formulated a number of phrases which were subsequently to be quoted throughout the world:

> Scientology is evil; its techniques evil; its practice a serious threat to the community, medically, morally and socially; and its adherents sadly deluded and often mentally ill.[2]
> The appeal of Scientology is at times deliberately directed towards the weak, the anxious, the disappointed, the inadequate and the lonely . . .[3]
> The principles and practices of Scientology are contrary to accepted principles and practices of medicine and science, and constitute a grave danger to the health, particularly the mental health of the community.[4]
> Scientology is a grave threat to family and home life.[5]

Anderson claimed to have

> been unable to find any worthwhile redeeming feature in Scientology. It constitutes a serious medical, moral and social threat to individuals and to the community generally.[6]

He described Scientology processes as having a 'brainwashing effect'. One disinterested commentator observed of the Report that it

> betrays a considerable lack of the objectivity and detachment necessary for proper scientific evaluation of evidence. The language is often highly emotive, and argument proceeds by the use of debating devices rather than by the scientific method.[7]

The immediate result of this Report was the passage, in December 1965, of the Psychological Practices Act (1965) which banned the practice of Scientology; banned the use of the E-meter except by a registered psychologist; and empowered the Attorney General to seize and destroy Scientological documents and recordings.

It was not until 1965 that mention of Scientology began to appear systematically in the British Press. The first reports indicated in *The Times Index* concern

---

[1] *Hansard* (State of Victoria), Vol. 273, 19 November 1963.
[2] Anderson, op. cit., p. 1.   [3] Ibid.
[4] Ibid., p. 2.   [5] Ibid.   [6] Ibid.
[7] Terence McMullen, 'Statutory Declaration', manuscript originally delivered to a Joint Meeting of the Sydney University Psychological Society and the Libertarian Society in 1968 – copy made available to me by Dr McMullen, but reprinted in *Whatever Happened to Adelaide? A Report on the Select Committee on Scientology (Prohibition) Act*, no publisher stated [The Church of Scientology] (1973), p. 50.

the Australian Inquiry and Hubbard's subsequent threats to sue the Victoria Government. Shortly afterwards, a number of other British newspapers discovered Scientology to be newsworthy. All cited the Victoria Report at length.[1] In January, the *News of the World* reported a young Scientologist's disconnection from her mother.[2] In February, Lord Balniel, MP, then the Chairman of the National Association for Mental Health, asked whether the Minister of Health would initiate an inquiry into Scientology in Britain, referring in his question to findings of the Anderson Inquiry.[3] The Minister replied that he would not, but the question itself roused the Scientology leadership to a vigorous reaction. In a series of documents issued in February 1966, Hubbard outlined a policy to be followed in the face of proposals to investigate Scientology.[4] The basic principle of this policy was that critics of Scientology should themselves be investigated and their past 'crimes' exposed with 'wide lurid publicity'.[5] A Public Investigation Section was established to pursue this end. In March, *The People*, under the headline: 'One man Britain can do without', published the story of a private investigator recruited by the Scientology organization to advise on setting up this section.[6] Lord Balniel, it appears, was to be the first person to be investigated.

Other newspapers developed these themes. The *Daily Mail* was one of the movement's most severe critics, publishing a front page story, in February, which challenged Hubbard's credentials,[7] and, in August, the story of Karen Henslow, a schizophrenic who had been working at Saint Hill Manor (which had by then become the headquarters of the movement), and who was returned to her mother's home one night in a deranged state.[8] This case became a *cause célèbre* when Peter Hordern, MP for Horsham, referred to it in the House of Commons in the adjournment debate of 6 March 1967.[9] Geoffrey Johnson Smith, MP also spoke, referring to the

> . . . many open-minded people in the town of East Grinstead, whose judgement on matters of this kind one can trust, [who] are seriously disturbed by the activities and objectives of this organisation . . .[10]

The Minister of Health, Kenneth Robinson, in his reply referred to a resolution sent to him by East Grinstead Urban District Council in December 1966, expressing 'grave concern' about Scientology and its effects on the town and its

[1] *News of the World*, 10 October 1965; *The Sun*, 6 October 1965; *Daily Mail*, 22 December 1965; *The Times*, 6 October 1965.

[2] *News of the World*, 16 January 1963.

[3] *Hansard*, House of Commons, Vol. 724, 7, February 1966.

[4] Sir John G. Foster, *Enquiry into the Practice and Effects of Scientology* (HMSO, London, 1971), pp. 140–5.

[5] Ibid., pp. 140–9; L. Ron Hubbard, *HCO Policy Letter*, 25 February 1966.

[6] *The People*, 20 March 1966.

[7] *Daily Mail*, 14 February 1966.

[8] *Daily Mail*, 23 August 1966.

[9] *Hansard*, House of Commons, Vol. 742.

[10] Ibid.

people. Liberal reference was made to the Anderson Report and Mr Robinson concluded of the Scientologists:

> What they do . . . is to direct themselves deliberately towards the weak, the un-balanced, the immature, the rootless and the mentally or emotionally unstable, to promise them remoulded, mature personalities and to set about fulfilling the promises by means of untrained staff, ignorantly practising quasi-psychological techniques, including hypnosis. It is true that the Scientologists claim not to accept as clients people known to be mentally sick, but the evidence strongly suggests that they do.[1]

During 1967 reports continued to appear concerning 'disconnections', and the growth of the Sea Org.[2]

Reactions to the Scientologists in the area of their headquarters had not improved and the East Grinstead Urban District Council refused planning permission for extensions to their premises. The ensuing inquiry by a Ministry of Housing Inspector, in July 1968, gave an opportunity for Scientology's neighbours to voice their feelings. The Scientologists were accused of accosting people in the streets; of boycotting East Grinstead shops and services; of visiting local schools in an attempt to give instruction in Scientology to pupils; of bringing foot-and-mouth disease to the district; and of allowing 'a mentally deranged member of your establishment' to range at large over a neighbouring barrister's estate.[3] The view adopted by the Minister of Housing was that these accusations had little to do with the subject of the inquiry. He permitted the Scientologists' appeal against the UDC in a decision finally rendered in 1969.[4]

In July 1968, Mr Robinson announced in a statement to the House of Commons that during the previous two years the Government had 'become increasingly concerned at the spread of Scientology in the United Kingdom'.

> The Government are satisfied, having reviewed all the available evidence, that Scientology is socially harmful. It alienates members of families from each other and attributes squalid and disgraceful motives to all who oppose it; its authoritarian principles and practices are a potential menace to the personality and well-being of those so deluded as to become its followers; above all its methods can be a serious danger to the health of those who submit to them. There is evidence that children are now being indoctrinated.[5]

The Government had therefore decided to take action to 'curb the growth' of the movement in Britain. Scientology organizations would no longer be recognized as educational establishments for the purpose of admission of foreign

---

[1] Ibid.

[2] *News of the World*, 19 November 1967.

[3] C. H. Rolph, *Believe What You Like* (André Deutsch, London, 1973). pp. 66–7; *The Times*, 19 July 1968.

[4] *Daily Telegraph*, 11 August 1969.

[5] *Hansard*, House of Commons, Vol. 769, 25 July 1968.

nationals; Scientologists would therefore no longer be eligible for admission to the UK as students, and no extensions to entry or work permits of foreign Scientologists would be allowed. Thereafter, up to June 1971, some 145 aliens were refused admission to Britain to study or work at Scientology establishments.[1]

In 1968, Acts were passed banning the practice of Scientology in the states of South Australia and Western Australia.[2] (The Act banning Scientology in South Australia was repealed on 21 March 1974, that in Western Australia was repealed in May 1973.) A petition was presented to the New Zealand Parliament asking for an Inquiry into, and Government action against, the movement there.[3] In South Africa, Scientology had been criticized in Parliament during 1966, and in 1968 became the defendant in an action for defamation initiated by Dr E. L. Fisher, the MP most active in Parliamentary criticism of the movement, who had been libelled in a Scientology publication.[4] In the USA the FDA won a decision ordering the destruction of the seized E-meters and in the same year, 1967, the tax-exempt status of the Washington Church of Scientology was revoked.

In the face of fierce criticism in the press and various national parliaments, the Church of Scientology, in November 1968, promulgated a *Code of Reform*, including:

1. Cancellation of disconnection as a relief to those suffering from familial suppression.
2. Cancellation of security checking as a form of confession.
3. Prohibition of any confessional materials being written down.
4. Cancellation of declaring people Fair Game.[5]

These reforms the Church of Scientology claimed were a response to public criticism of the practices concerned. This action was too late, however, to prevent the British government establishing an Inquiry into Scientology in January 1969[6] and the South African government from doing so in April 1969.[7] Already by mid-1968, however, the severe British government action against Scientology had begun to cause some doubts to appear about the justifiability of these actions. Questions were raised as to why Scientology had been singled out for such treatment when various other cults and sects which seemed to

---

[1] Ibid., Vol. 820, 29 June 1971.

[2] Scientology Act, 1968 – Western Australia; Scientology (Prohibition) Act 1968 – South Australia.

[3] Sir Guy Richardson Powles and E. V. Dumbleton, *Report of the Commission of Inquiry into the Hubbard Scientology Organisation in New Zealand* (Government Printer, Wellington, New Zealand, 1969), p. 8.

[4] G. R. Kotzé et al, *Report of the Commission of Enquiry into Scientology for 1972* (Government Printer, Pretoria, South Africa [1973]), p. 119.

[5] Ibid., p. 153.

[6] Foster, op. cit.

[7] Kotzé, et al., op. cit., pp. 2–3.

behave in a similar fashion were not.[1] MPs questioned the logic of banning people

> coming to this country to study something which we now admit we know so little about that we have to set up an inquiry.[2]

The New Zealand Commission of Inquiry reported in June 1969 in mild tones, recommending no changes in legislation and observing that if Scientology kept to its Code of Reform there should be 'no further occasion for Government or public alarm . . .'[3] Such a finding must have been heartening to the Scientologists who, in October 1970, further modified their practices by dropping the various penalties which attached to the assignment of an individual to a 'lower condition'.[4]

In 1969, the Scientologists also scored a success in the United States, when they appealed against the decision of a federal jury in 1967 in favour of the FDA, which directed that seized E-meters and literature should be destroyed. The US Court of Appeals reversed this decision in February 1969, on the ground that the Founding Church of Scientology had made out a prima facie case that it was a bona fide religion and that the E-meter was related to its religious dogma, and therefore not subject to the Court's condemnation.[5] The FDA retained the items seized pending a decision on appeal. In a final action in which the FDA sought condemnation of the E-meter in 1971, the Federal Judge ruled that the E-meter had been misbranded and its secular use was condemned. However, he further ruled that it might continue to be used in bona fide religious counselling if labelled as ineffective in treating illness.[6]

The Report of the British Inquiry conducted by Sir John Foster was published in December 1971. This Report also contained passages of undoubted comfort for the Scientology organization. Among these, Sir John observed that he disagreed:

> profoundly with the legislation adopted in both Western and South Australia, in turn based on part of that adopted in Victoria, [sic] whereby the teaching and practice of Scientology *as such* is banned. Such legislation appears to me to be discriminatory and contrary to all the best traditions of the Anglo-Saxon legal system.[7]

He advocated the establishment of a Psychotherapy Council to control the practice of psychotherapy, whose ranks Scientologists should be allowed to join provided they could satisfy the Council's requirements. The Report argued that it was wrong for the Home Secretary to exclude foreign Scientologists

---

[1] C. H. Rolph, 'Why pick on Scientology?' *New Statesman* (23 August 1968), p. 220; Quintin Hogg, 'Political parley', *Punch* (14 August 1968), pp. 230–1.

[2] *Hansard*, House of Commons, Vol. 776, 26 January 1969.

[3] Powles and Dumbleton, op. cit., p. 58.

[4] Foster, op. cit., p. 128.

[5] Malko, op. cit., pp. 76–7; *Psychiatric News*, March 1969.

[6] *Washington Post*, 31 July 1971; *Denver Post*, 14 August 1971.

[7] Foster, op. cit., p. 181 (emphasis in the original).

when there was no law against Scientology being practised by their British colleagues.

The South African Commission of Enquiry reported in June 1972. It recommended the passage of legislation to provide for the registration and control of psychotherapists; to make illegal 'disconnection', 'public investigation', 'security checking' and similar Scientology practices; and to control psychological testing, and the dissemination of 'inaccurate, untruthful and harmful information in regard to psychiatry and the field of mental health in general'.[1] Assuming that these recommendations were implemented, the Commission held that 'no positive purpose will be served by banning the practice of Scientology as such'.[2]

In Australia, it would appear that an attitude of increased tolerance for Scientology had begun to prevail. The electoral victory of the Labour party resulted in the registration of the Church of the New Faith, a Scientology organization, as a recognized denomination for the purposes of the Marriage Act, and the authorization of its nominated personnel to undertake the lawful solemnization of marriage.[3] In May 1973 the Western Australia Scientology Act was repealed.

Social involvement

While the movement developed no active programme of involvement with the wider society during its Dianetics phase, the emergence of Scientology produced a progressive transformation of this situation. Increased involvement by such means as the establishment of 'front organizations' and infiltration, can be seen as an attempt to achieve two distinct goals on the part of the movement leadership. First, increased involvement was seen as a propaganda and promotional activity designed to spread the name and basic beliefs of the movement to a wider potential clientele. Hence one prominent goal was that of recruitment. Second, particularly as sections of the public became increasingly hostile toward Scientology, increased involvement by various means appears to have been seen as a method of control (creating a 'safe space for Scientology'). The similarity of these apparent goals to those suggested by students of the Communist Party as rationales for aspects of its social involvement, give grounds for some expectation that there might also be similarities in the means employed in the pursuit of these goals.[4]

Shortly after the incorporation of the Church of American Science and the Church of Scientology in New Jersey late in 1953, a Freudian Foundation of America was established in Phoenix, Arizona. While the Churches offered degrees as Doctor of Divinity, the Freudian Foundation offered certification as

---

[1] Kotzé, et al., op. cit., p. 232. No such legislation has yet materialized.
[2] Ibid., p. 232.
[3] *Commonwealth Gazette*, 15 February 1973, p. 20.
[4] Philip Selznick, *The Organisational Weapon* (Free Press, Glencoe, 1960).

'Psychoanalyst', or 'Freudian Analyst'.[1] Hubbard proposed that the Foundation be established, but it was run by a prominent Scientologist, Burke Belknap. It appears to have been less successful as a marketing device than the Church, however, and was shortly abandoned.[2]

With removal to Washington DC, a number of new organizations were started. The Society of Consulting Ministers provided a useful business-card title for harassed Scientology Ministers. The American Society for Disaster Relief was also listed on the Founding Church of Scientology letter paper, although it does not appear to have been activated. Among Hubbard's projects in Washington was the formation of a political party, the Constitutional Administration Party, in which his wife held executive office. Its manifesto, circulated to Scientologists, contained much high-minded rhetoric appealing to the Constitution and the rights of the individual against the unconstitutional behaviour of the Department of Internal Revenue and the

> . . . Supreme Court Justice who does not recognize the rights of the majority, but who stresses the rights of the minority and who uses psychology textbooks written by Communists to enforce an unpopular opinion . . .[3]

At the same time, Hubbard had plans for establishing a corporation, the Citizens of Washington Inc., with much the same programme except that it emphasized an additional item, namely that members should mount a campaign demanding that citizens of the federal capital should have the same voting rights as other Americans. Hubbard had a rather grandiose view of the role this organization was to play:

> The ground in the District of Columbia at this time is ripe for subversion and only the Citizens of Washington Inc is capable of exercising a power of restraint upon the citizens. Should a depression strike which is extremely likely in view of the Republican withdrawal of funds we may find ourselves in the role of not only protecting [sic] the citizens of the city from the wrath and carelessness of the Federal Government, but the Federal Government from the wrath and forthright vengefulness of the citizens of this area.[4]

Hubbard planned to establish a newspaper through the sale of bonds, and later buy radio and television 'facilities'. As in the case of the Constitutional Administration Party, no direct link with Scientology was to be displayed, but their activities were to be monitored by a further corporation, Scientology Consultants Inc. None of these plans seems to have gone far beyond the drawing board.

[1] See the *Ghost of Scientology*, 16, April 1954, p. 2.

[2] Interview.

[3] 'The Campaign of the Constitutional Administration Party of America', circular (1956), p. 2.

[4] L. Ron Hubbard, from a dictation tape provided by an informant, dictated some time during 1956.

Another project was that of establishing United Survival Action Clubs. This project was promoted on the basis of fear about the possibility of nuclear attack:

> ... Survival Clubs will permit a large section of the American public to survive a national disaster ... The United States is the only country in the world which is organised to be destroyed by an atomic bombing [sic] ... Yet, our leaders act as though they were safe and secure in the possession of 'defences against atomic weapons'. There are no defences against atomic weapons except the defences which will be erected by the Survival Clubs.[1]

Scientologists were therefore encouraged to begin organizing such clubs, although the purpose of promoting Scientology was evidently more important than civil defence:

> The real and actual reason we want these people organised in clubs is not to protect them from atomic bombing, although this is a very worthwhile reason, but to raise their individual capabilities.[2]

During the late 1950s, the movement leadership also began more vigorously to attack orthodox medical and psychiatric practice. One agency for this assault was the National Academy of American Psychology founded at a Scientology Congress in 1957.

> 'It is time', Ron said at the Congress, 'that we cleaned up the entire field of psychotherapy'. He explained that we were impeded by the barbaric conduct of psychotherapy in the United States.
>
> One of the main dangers is government fear of psychological subversion. In that vested psychotherapy in the United States is Euro-Russian, and in that the government will sooner or later discover this, it is time we took the initiative in reforming the practice of psychology, psychiatry and psychoanalysis.[3]

The 'National Academy' was established with an executive board of Scientology personnel. It proposed to circulate a loyalty oath 'to all psychologists, psychiatrists and psychoanalysts, as well as ministers of various denominations who engage in mental practice'.[4] The loyalty oath contained the following clauses to which such individuals were expected to swear:

> (2) To refuse to practise 'Brainwashing' upon American citizens.
> (3) To actively prevent the teaching of only foreign psychology in public schools and universities.
> (9) To refuse to contribute money, dues or my services to organisations which knowingly impede American scientific research programmes or which work to discredit American psychologists to the public.
> (18) To accept as fellow psychologists only the psychologists adhering to this code and to speak no word of criticism in public of them.[5]

[1] L. Ron Hubbard, 'Survival Clubs', *Certainty*, 5, 3 (1958), p. 7.
[2] Ibid., p. 6.
[3] 'National Academy of American Psychology', *Certainty*, 5, 5 (1958), p. 1.
[4] Ibid   [5] Ibid., pp. 4–5.

Having circulated the loyalty oath, the NAAP then proposed to maintain a register on which all those who signed and returned the oath would be declared 'safe', while

> those who ignore it or refuse to sign it before witnesses are listed as 'potential subversive'. Those who rail against it are listed as 'subversive'.[1]

Signatories were to be 'offered an opportunity to have the National Academy verify their credentials' for a charge.[2] Newspaper advertisements were to be run asking the public to patronize only practitioners with an NAAP Certificate, which Scientologists were to be offered for $25.00 (others having to pay $80.00 for 'verification of credentials' and certification).[3]

As well as establishing peripheral organizations, the movements' leaders advocated the infiltration of organizations and political agencies as a means of promoting Scientology and extending control over its social environment. Generically, this was known as the 'Zone Plan'. It could be operationalized in a variety of ways:

> See this: a housewife, already successfully employing Scientology in her own home, trained to professional level, takes over a woman's club as secretary or some key position. She straightens up the club affairs by applying comm practice and making peace, and then, incidental to the club's main function, pushes Scientology into a zone of special interest in the club – children, straightening up marriages, whatever comes to hand, and even taking fees for it. . . .[4]

Government could also be infiltrated[5] on the same basis.

> . . . a nation or a state runs on the ability of its department heads, its governors, or any other leaders. It is easy to get posts in such areas . . . Don't bother to get elected. Get a job on the secretarial staff or the bodyguard, use any talent one has to get a place close in, go to work on the environment and make it function better. Occasionally one might lose, but in the large majority, doing a good job and making the environment function will result in promotion, better contacts, a widening zone.[6]

Anderson reported that one Australian Scientologist who had affiliations with the Australian Labour Party proposed to infiltrate and win over the Labour Party leadership for Scientology.[7]

[1] Ibid., p. 7.   [2] Ibid.   [3] Ibid., p. 8.

[4] L. Ron Hubbard, 'Special Zone Plan', *Comm Mag*, 2, 6 (June 1960), cited in Anderson, op. cit., p. 154.

[5] The Scientologists point out to me that 'advised' would be a more neutral word than 'infiltrated'. 'Advice' provided by such means seems to me to be part of what is involved in infiltration.

[6] L. Ron Hubbard, 'Special Zone Plan', op. cit.

[7] Ibid., pp. 154–5. An interview respondent indicated that he had proposed a similar plan. Infiltration tactics have also been employed for recruitment purposes by a new religious movement, The Unified Family. See John Lofland, *Doomsday Cult* (Prentice-Hall, Englewood Cliffs, New Jersey, 1966). I have myself seen this tactic in operation by Unified Family Members at the meetings of other cults. The tactic is also not

Another technique employed from time to time was that of establishing a committee or society, whose leading personnel would always, covertly, be Scientologists, which would concern itself with public morality, mental health, the state of the nation, or some other public issue. An Australian example was the formation of a Citizen's Purity League in Melbourne inaugurated by a Scientologist who heard of the idea on one of Hubbard's tapes.[1] Its executive committee was composed of HASI members, but the links with Scientology were not publicized. A campaign was started to secure public membership and support on morality issues.

> The aim of this Citizens' Purity League would be to reach a point of prestige and influence in the community that would enable it to carry out a plan of clearing, first the State Police Force, and then those engaged in the governing of the State of Victoria.[2]

Such tactics are said to have been employed in more recent years. Informants allege that the Scientology leadership indirectly organized a 'Loyalty Petition to Parliament' in the late 1960s which advocated that psychiatrists, psychologists and psychotherapists declare before a Justice of the Peace that they were neither in the pay of foreign governments nor members of any movement or party which aimed to subvert the Constitution and Parliament of Great Britain. Several thousand signatures of members of the public were secured, but it was found that the Petition was not drawn up in a form proper for parliamentary presentation.[3]

Interview respondents have also alleged that they were encouraged to form committees with high-minded titles for promotional purposes. The aim of such committees was to create a political lobby to promote the publication of material in the press related to such issues as the 'evils of psychiatry', 'brutality in mental hospitals', 'communism', and other issues on which the Scientology leadership had expressed a position. Whenever possible, prominent public figures unconnected with Scientology were approached to join the roster of patrons for such committees and associations. One such body, known as the Association for Health Development and Aid, among whose patrons, executive and consultant doctors were a number of Scientologists, managed briefly to secure the support of the Bishop of Southwark.[4]

Other committees and associations clearly have a more specific and ad hoc purpose. One explored by the *News of the World* was entitled the Citizens' Press Association. The group was established after reports concerning Scientology appeared in the *News of the World,* and sought to secure the support of other

[1] Mary Sue Hubbard, *HCO Newsletter*, 14 April 1961.
[2] Ibid.
[3] Interview.
[4] Rolph, op. cit., pp. 53–4; Letter to the author from the Bishop of Southwark.

unfamiliar from the history of the Communist party. Nathan Leites, *Operational Code of the Politburo* (McGraw-Hill, New York, 1951).

'victims' of this paper for the introduction of legislation to 'cope with these papers and prevent any further wrongs being committed'.[1] No association with Scientology was indicated in the letter from the Citizens' Press Association, although a spokesman for Scientology later admitted to *News of the World* reporters, 'that this was one of our ideas . . .'[2]

As well as such covert organizations, Scientology openly sponsors or assists a variety of organizations engaged in pressure-group or welfare activities.[3] A major pressure group openly supported by the Church of Scientology and predominantly composed of Scientologists is the Citizens' Commission for Human Rights. This organization seeks to bring pressure to bear on administrators of mental hospitals and members of government, by direct means and through press reports, to improve conditions in mental hospitals, protest against involuntary committal, physical and psychopharmacological modes of treatment, psychosurgery, and what are referred to generically as 'psychiatric atrocities'.

A prominent welfare organization sponsored by the Church is Narconon, which operates a drug programme employing Scientology techniques. It claims a very high rate of success, and official support in America and Scandinavia. Letters from various addiction facilities and prisons, in reply to my requests for information, indicated that Narconon was generally admitted to such facilities on the same basis as other community-based, volunteer, self-help groups. Replies were received from eight facilities in the USA listed in a Scientology publication as 'supporting' the Narconon programme. Four indicated that the programme was in operation and received unqualified support, as did most other volunteer self-help groups. Three indicated that the programme had met with little success and had died of attrition, while the final reply indicated that the programme had been cancelled some time previously by the prison director.[4] (This may not, however, be a true reflection of the status of Narconon. The City of Los Angeles, for example, recognized Narconon's contribution in a 'Resolution' which highly commended its efforts in twenty-five programmes, half of which were in penal institutions, and which had 'achieved remarkable success, in that 85 per cent of those in the program released on parole have no further involvement in the criminal justice system . . .')[5]

[1] Letter from Citizens' Press Association cited in *News of the World*, 24 August 1969.
[2] Ibid.
[3] Such front groups and organizations are not uncommon among more recent sectarian movements. On the front groups of the Japanese manipulationist sect Soka Gakkai, see James W. White, *The Sokagakkai and Mass Society* (Stanford University Press, Stanford, California, 1970), p. 113. On those of the Communist Party, see Philip Selznick, *The Organisational Weapon* (Free Press, New York, 1952), pp. 27, 114. On those of the Nazi Party, see William Ebenstein, *The Nazi State* (Farrar & Rinehart, New York, 1943), p. 59.
[4] Letters to the author.
[5] 'Resolution' adopted by the Council of the City of Los Angeles, 1 March 1974, copy made available by the Church of Scientology.

A further welfare organization associated with the Church is Applied Scholastics Inc, the aim of which is said to be to provide an educational programme for slow learners or potential educational dropouts. This programme also employs Scientology techniques.[1] The Church of Scientology supplied, in a letter to the author, the names of a number of US educational establishments in which the programme was said to be operating. Not all of these could be traced. Of five such institutions approached, four could not trace any programme in association with Applied Scholastics – although the programme may have been operating on an unofficial basis. The fifth institution located 'an informal program'.[2]

Scientology's most vocal social involvement is in its campaign against orthodox psychiatry and the methods which it currently employs. To promote this campaign, a 'newspaper', *Freedom*, was established in 1968. It concentrated on vilifying psychiatrists; attacking the practices of mental hospitals; and impugning the motives of supporters and leaders of the mental health movement and its organizations, such as the National Association for Mental Health.[3]

The Scientology movement secured a great deal of publicity when its members began demonstrating outside the offices of the National Association for Mental Health with banners reading, 'Psychiatrists maim and kill' and 'Buy your meat from a psychiatrist'[4] during early 1969, and when later that year it was discovered that between 200 to 300 Scientologists had secured membership in the NAMH.[5] The enormous increase in applications to the NAMH does not appear to have merited attention until, shortly before the scheduled Annual General Meeting in November, nominations began arriving for office in the NAMH which included known Scientologists such as David Gaiman, an Assistant Guardian of the Church, who was nominated for the office of Chairman of the NAMH. The Association hastily insisted on the resignation of over 300 recently admitted members, rendering them ineligible for attendance at the Annual General Meeting, and a lengthy period of litigation ensued, in which the Scientologists sought reinstatement. Their actions to this end proved unsuccessful.[6]

Recourse to the law courts has been a frequent occurrence for the Scientolo-

[1] See the *Basic Study Manual*, compiled from the works of L. Ron Hubbard (Applied Scholastics Inc, Los Angeles, 1972).

[2] Letters to the author.

[3] Such attacks led to the settlement of a libel action in favour of Kenneth Robinson as a result of his suit over a *Freedom* article.

[4] C. H. Rolph, *Believe What You Like* (André Deutsch, London, 1973), pp. 52, 102.

[5] Ibid., p. 102.

[6] Ibid., passim. The Scientologists' version of these events is the subject of David R. Dalton, *Two Disparate Philosophies* (Regency Press, London, 1973). See also my review of this work 'Convert or Subvert', *The Spectator* (29 December 1973). The Scientologists' arguments are also rehearsed in Omar V. Garrison, *The Hidden Story of Scientology* (Arlington Books, London, 1974).

gists. Often this recourse has been pursued in reaction to criticism of the movement by individuals, newspapers or books. At one time at least thirty-six libel writs were outstanding in Britain against newspapers.[1] Writs have also been issued against East Grinstead Councillors who expressed disapproval of the movement,[2] and recently against a number of senior police officers alleging libel in an Interpol report.[3] Probably the most significant libel action in which the movement was involved was in respect of a television broadcast in July 1968, in which Mr Geoffrey Johnson Smith MP stated, in reply to a question, that the Scientologists

> direct themselves towards the weak, the unbalanced, the immature, the rootless and the mentally or emotionally unstable.[4]

This action was decided against the Scientologists.

Books critical of Scientology have often been the subject of extensive litigation.[5] At one stage in the litigation connected with Cyril Vosper's *The Mind Benders*,[6] a High Court Judge was reported as saying of applications by the Church of Scientology that its author and a newspaper editor be committed to prison for contempt of court, that these actions were deliberately taken 'to try to stifle any criticism or inquiry into their [the Church of Scientology's] affairs'.[7]

Models of deviance

Scientology is a deviant religious movement. Its deviance lay initially in its rejection of the 'facilities . . . culturally provided for man's salvation . . .'[8] In this respect it is not unique. Scientology shares characteristics with other forms of sectarianism – Christian Science, Jehovah's Witnesses, Soka Gakkai, etc., but among the many contemporary deviant forms of religion, Scientology appeared for a while to become something of a bête noir, an object of special attention in the mass media, the courts and national legislatures. Scientology was publicly portrayed as 'an evil cult',[9] and a 'serious threat to the community'.[10] Laws were passed prohibiting its practice in three states of Australia, and aliens were prohibited from entering Great Britain to pursue its study. The pejorative and stigmatizing terms which were often employed to describe it, and the relative severity with which Scientology was treated on occasion, suggest that this

[1] Rolph, op. cit., p. 63.

[2] Ibid., p. 62.

[3] *Evening Standard*, 11 December 1973; *The Times*, 18 December 1973.

[4] Rolph, op. cit., p. 75.

[5] I discuss five such works in my article 'Religious sects and the fear of publicity', *New Society* (7 June 1973), pp. 545–7.

[6] Cyril Vosper, *The Mind Benders* (Neville Spearman, London, 1971).

[7] *Daily Telegraph*, 4 March 1972.

[8] Bryan R. Wilson, *Magic and the Millennium* (Heinemann, London, 1973), p. 21.

[9] *The People*, 19 March 1967.

[10] Anderson, op. cit., p. 1.

movement might fruitfully be examined from the theoretical perspective of the sociology of deviance.

The nature of the debate surrounding Scientology, and some of the rhetoric that appeared during its course, suggest that at times Scientology was viewed in a manner approaching *moral panic*. Stanley Cohen has defined moral panic as

> a condition, episode, person or group of persons [which] emerges to become defined as a threat to societal values and interests; its nature is presented in a stylized and stereotypical fashion by the mass media . . .[1]

Drawing on Neil Smelser's definition of panic, we may add that it can be understood as involving a collective sense of an immediate, powerful, but ambiguous threat to deeply held norms or values, for the preservation of which it is seen as urgent to take some action.[2]

This section is specifically concerned with the question of the relationship between the development of Scientology and the reaction to it from state agencies and society at large, particularly in the way this was portrayed in the mass media. The relationship between deviance and societal reaction has been an important focus of endeavour in the sociology of deviance, and three simplified models of the nature of this relationship may be extracted from the literature.

The first model which we may call the *classic model* relates deviance and societal reaction as a simple matter of undirectional causation:

Deviance————————→Societal reaction

Deviance, on this view, is essentially unproblematic. It lies in the infringement of social norms which are consensually held. Deviance develops as a result of processes internal to the deviant, and in due course provokes reactions of disapproval from conforming groups and individuals, and the mobilization of agents of social control.

This view informed most early speculation and theorizing concerning criminality. Due to differences in physiology, psychology, or early life-experience, criminals were held to have some differentiating characteristic(s) which led them to violations of the law. The reaction of agents of social control was seen as a relatively straightforward process of identifying and dealing with norm violators. Hence the accounting procedures and official statistics generated by social control agents could be employed by social scientists with some conviction that they reflected, more or less directly, occurrences of deviance in the 'real world'. This view of the nature of the relationship between deviance and societal reaction has tended to be the 'official' view. It generalizes the account of this

[1] Stanley Cohen, *Folk Devils and Moral Panics* (MacGibbon & Kee, London, 1972), p. 9.
[2] Neil Smelser, *Theory of Collective Behaviour* (Routledge & Kegan Paul, London, 1962).

relationship typically held by agents of social control, moral entrepreneurs and the mass media. The assumptions upon which this model rests, however, have come under considerable criticism during the last fifteen years from proponents of the second model.

We can refer to the second model as the *labelling model*.[1] Deviance on this view is seen as essentially problematic. Social norms and values are regarded as having at best sub-cultural rather than general cultural acceptance, and infringements of norms are seen as regular and widespread. Deviance is therefore a characteristic attributed to another, or a label assigned to him, which he is led to accept by public degradation and stigmatization, and coercive control. In Becker's oft-quoted words:

> . . . *social groups create deviance by making the rules whose infraction constitutes deviance* and by applying those rules to particular persons and labelling them as outsiders . . . The deviant is one to whom the label has successfully been applied; deviant behaviour is behaviour that people so label.[2]

In its more extreme formulations, this model relates deviance and societal reaction as a similarly simple matter of unidirectional causation, but in the reverse direction to the classic model:

$$\text{Societal reaction} \longrightarrow \text{Deviance}$$

Such an extreme formulation is not altogether a 'straw man', Lemert, for example, states that:

> . . . older sociology tended to rest heavily upon the idea that deviance leads to social control. I have come to believe that the reverse idea, i.e. social control leads to deviance, is equally tenable and the potentially richer premise for studying deviance in modern society.[3]

This model is evident in David Cooper's notion of schizophrenia, which he defines as:

> . . . a micro-social crisis situation in which acts and experience of a certain person are invalidated by others for certain intelligible cultural and micro-cultural (usually familial) reasons, to the point where he is elected and identified as being 'mentally ill' in a certain way, and is then confirmed (by a specifiable but highly arbitrary labelling process) in the identity 'schizophrenic patient' by medical or quasi-medical agents.[4]

[1] Since what I am seeking to do here is to erect three models for heuristic purposes, rather than to characterize accurately the way this perspective has generally been employed, I shall draw it in extreme terms, ignoring particularly those sociologists who combine, or draw no distinction between, this model and the following one, and I shall create a distinction where they would not.

[2] Howard S. Becker, *Outsiders: Studies in the Sociology of Deviance* (Free Press, New York, 1963), p. 9.

[3] Edwin M. Lemert, *Social Pathology* (McGraw-Hill, New York, 1951).

[4] David Cooper, *Psychiatry and Anti-Psychiatry* (Paladin, London, 1970), p. 16.

In order to define or dramatize the normative boundaries of society, moral entrepreneurs and social control agents select among a range of available norm-violators those suitable for labelling. On some accounts, the labelling model provides a conspiracy theory of deviance-generation. A 'victim' is selected who is 'scapegoated' by others and forced into a deviant role, more or less coercively, from which he may not be permitted to escape. Appeal is frequently made to this model by those identified as deviant, as an account of their own situation.[1]

The third model can be referred to as the *deviance-amplification model*. This model, elaborated initially by Leslie Wilkins to account for gang delinquency,[2] has since been employed to explain among other things, the development of 'Mods and Rockers' as a social problem,[3] and the nature of the societal reaction to drug-taking.[4] In its simplest form the deviance-amplification model suggests the possible sequence:

1. Initial deviation   from valued norms
                        leads to
2. Punitive reaction
                        which leads to
3. Further alienation of the deviants
                        which leads to
4. Further deviation
                        which leads to
5. Increased punitive reaction
                        which leads to (3) . . . etc., in an amplifying spiral.

Cohen discusses this process as it affected the identification of the Mods and Rockers as a social problem and the subsequent attempts to control them.

Minor acts of rowdy and irritating behaviour at a seaside resort during Easter Weekend 1964 were exaggerated and distorted enormously by the press, which presented the incidents as episodes of uncontrolled vandalism and violence. The media reports were instrumental in the creation of a stereotype accepted and reinforced by social control agents on subsequent occasions. Future bank-holiday weekends were viewed with fearful anticipation by residents, business-men, and police in seaside communities, leading to a propensity to over-react to the behaviour of the young people. The latter in turn were attracted to the resorts in increased numbers by the possibility of a repetition of the previous incidents,

[1] Gresham Sykes and David Matza, 'Techniques of neutralisation', *American Journal of Sociology*, 22 (December 1957), pp. 664–70; Miriam Siegler, Humphry Osmond and Harriet Mann, 'Laing's models of madness', *British Journal of Psychiatry* 115 (1969), pp. 947–58.

[2] Leslie T. Wilkins, *Social Deviance* (Tavistock, London, 1964), pp. 87–94, reprinted in W. G. Carson and Paul Wiles, eds, *Crime and Delinquency in Britain* (Martin Robertson & Co., London, 1971), pp. 219–26.

[3] Cohen, op. cit.

[4] Jock Young, *The Drugtakers* (Paladin, London, 1971).

and identified themselves with one of the two stereotypical factions portrayed by the media.

The inevitable friction between police and Mods and Rockers was further dramatized in the mass media, and by the courts, and sanctioned by heavy fines and some cases of imprisonment. De-amplification, Cohen suggests, finally set in as a result of the severity of social control. Potential deviants were

> frightened off or deterred by actual or threatened control measures. After being put off the train by the police before arriving at one's destination, and then being continually pushed around and harassed by the police on the streets and beaches, searched in the clubs, refused service in cafes, one might just give up in disgust. The game was simply not worth it . . . the amplification stops because the social distance from the deviants is made so great, that new recruits are put off from joining.[1]

The models of the relationship between deviance and social control outlined above are suggested as competing hypotheses to account for developments in the relationship between Scientology and society. While empirically rather than normatively directed, they have clear implications for the attribution of responsibility for the process, and those involved therefore tend to have an interest in promoting one theory rather than another. The Scientologists themselves are clear that model two best characterizes their brief history:

> To understand why the Church of Scientology ever needed stiff internal discipline in the past to defend a perimeter against overwhelming odds – it is necessary to look at the situation which existed at those times, *which forced the Church to develop policies to handle outside threats*. Which came first, the strict internal ethics policies, or the threat which they were designed to cater for?[2]

The implication here, and elsewhere, is that Scientology has been the victim of a concerted campaign ultimately sponsored by the World Federation for Mental Health for its 'forthright' stand against 'psychiatric atrocities':

> An analysis of 21 years of attacks shows a very plain pattern. First, several extremely vicious newspaper and magazine articles are published. Investigation by Church officials has shown these often to be commissioned articles. Reprints or copies are then made of these articles and are sent to every government or private agency which might be in a position officially or unofficially to censure or take action against the Church. After a period of time in which several articles have been sent, these agencies then receive a letter basically expressing the following; 'See how public opinion is against this group. Don't you think something should be done?'[3]

The moral entrepreneurs and social control agents who have opposed Scientology may be assumed to regard the situation in something like the terms

---

[1] Cohen, op. cit., p. 202.

[2] Anonymous, 'Attacks on Scientology and "attack" policies – a wider perspective', photocopy of manuscript, n.d., made available to me by the Church of Scientology. (My emphasis.)

[3] Anonymous, '*Scientology: the Now Religion:* false report correction', mimeo, n.d., made available by the Church of Scientology.

proposed in the first of the foregoing models, although I have found no explicit statement which propounds this view of events, and reconstruct their position from the course of official action. In contrast to both these views I shall argue that model three most adequately characterizes the process that developed.

Howard Becker and others have stressed that social problems are in part at least a consequence of *moral enterprise*. Some individual, or group of individuals, must generate public concern and mobilize public opinion or the opinion of legislators and law enforcers that 'something needs to be done', about the object of concern.[1] This moral enterprise may be exhibited by any number of individuals and agencies, variously motivated. Gusfield has described[2] how the Woman's Christian Temperance Union originally formed part of the general progressive, humanitarian movement for social reform in the late nineteenth and early twentieth centuries. Its adherents were members of socially dominant groups whose secure social position permitted them to feel sympathy for the plight of immigrant workers, and led them to organize to seek the conversion of individual drinkers.

After the repeal of prohibition, the WCTU found itself in a changed situation. Abstinence was no longer a norm of the dominant middle class. As drinking became increasingly acceptable, the total abstainer became a figure of ridicule, and the WCTU lost its upper-middle-class members. The movement increasingly adopted an attitude of moral indignation and a policy of coercive reform toward drinking as lower-middle and lower-class members found their values repudiated by the upper and middle classes.

Donald Dickson offers a persuasive account of the role of the Bureau of Narcotics in the passage of Federal legislation against marihuana,[3] suggesting that the primary motivation was to improve the position of the narcotics Bureau as a bureaucratic agency in a period of declining appropriations. Generating anxiety about marihuana use was a means of impressing upon the public and Congress that the Bureau was an important agency which should be maintained, even expanded.

The generation of moral panic may therefore be motivated in some cases by status anxiety or bureaucratic insecurity, or 'empire-building'. It may, of course, also arise from sincerely felt conflicts of values. Whatever its sources, the mass media are usually central to its propagation. As various studies have suggested, the operation of the mass media is to some extent constrained by commercial objectives. Fulfilment of these objectives may lead to exaggeration and distortion in the presentation of news concerning 'social problems'.

[1] Howard Becker, op. cit., Chapter 8.

[2] Joseph Gusfield, *Symbolic Crusade* (University of Illinois Press, Urbana, Illinois, 1963); and 'Social structure and moral reform: a study of the Woman's Christian Temperance Union', *American Journal of Sociology*, 61 (1955), pp. 221–32.

[3] Donald T. Dickson, 'Bureaucracy and morality: an organisational perspective on a moral crusade', *Social Problems*, 16 (1968), pp. 143–56.

The mass media operate with certain definitions of what is newsworthy. It is not that instruction manuals exist telling newsmen that certain subjects (drugs, sex, violence) will appeal to the public or that certain groups (youth, immigrants) should be continually exposed to scrutiny. Rather there are built-in factors ranging from the individual news-man's intuitive hunch about what constitutes a 'good story' through precepts such as 'give the public what it wants' to structured ideological biases, which predispose the media to make a certain event into news.[1]

The media typically build upon labels imputed to individuals and groups, elaborating a stereotype which will render the phenomenon intelligible and predictable to the readership in terms of general cultural images.

The moral crusaders

Those who have filled the ranks of the anti-Scientology crusade have fallen into a number of discrete categories, with distinct motivations for involvement:

1. State agencies – such as the FDA in America and the Mental Health Authority in Victoria
2. Doctors and psychiatrists (and to a lesser extent ministers of religion) and their professional bodies
3. Disgruntled ex-Scientologists
4. Relatives of Scientologists
5. Neighbours of Scientology
6. Members of Parliament
7. The Press.

While one would not wish to impugn the motives of any of those involved in demanding action against Scientology, it is clear that however righteous their moral indignation, such a crusade had useful and desirable consequences for each group. Characterizations of Scientology as a 'fraud', 'brainwashing', 'hypnosis', or 'quackery', served to legitimate attitudes adopted by the crusading groups and individuals, and their demands for social control of the movement. The interests of several of these groups directly conflicted with those of Scientology. Doctors and psychiatrists have persistently attacked Dianetics and Scientology, tending to resent the therapeutic claims made by their adherents particularly in respect of fields, such as severe psychological disorder, in which they had themselves experienced little concrete success. They also scorned the brief and unorthodox training of its practitioners in comparison with their own lengthy and arduous process of qualification. State agencies appear sometimes to have seen in Scientology an opportunity to impress legislators and the public with their zeal for the public protection, and the good use to which they put public funds.

Former Scientologists and relatives of members may sometimes have seen in

[1] Cohen, op. cit., p. 45.

stigmatization and government action against the movement a means of self-justification. If Scientology was a form of hypnosis or brainwashing, then this could justify and explain their involvement in, and devotion of considerable resources to, a movement which they now repudiated. Similarly relatives could explain the involvement of spouses or children in the movement as a result of fraud or brainwashing, and thereby excuse what might otherwise have been conceived as a failure on their own part. Some of Scientology's neighbours in East Grinstead appear to have found the presence of the movement in a respectable middle-class township a source of irritation and embarrassment.

The Press and Members of Parliament have an institutionalized interest in taking up a moral crusade of concern to customers or constituents. The two MPs most active in the British criticism of the movement were the MP for East Grinstead, the constituency containing the movement's headquarters, and the MP for a neighbouring constituency, Horsham. The Press found sensational copy in Scientology and the allegations made about it, and as Young has pointed out:

> The mass media in Western countries are placed in a competitive situation where they must attempt constantly to maintain and extend their circulation. A major component of what is newsworthy is that which arouses public indignation. Thus the media have an institutionalised need to expose social problems, to act as if they were the personified moral censors of their readership.[1]

Reality conflict

Scientology confronts the conventional world with a deviant reality of massive proportions. Unlike a belief-system such as spiritualism, it does not merely add another level to existing reality with only marginal implications for conventional life.[2] Rather, it offers a total *Weltanschauung*, a complex meaning system which interprets, explains and directs everyday life by alternative means to conventional, common-sense knowledge. Particularly in the area of the psychological life of man, it offers a radically competing theory to those prevailing in orthodox scientific circles and among those which look to them for the authority for their beliefs. The somewhat precarious status of the sciences of the person, and the therapeutic arts dependent upon them, have led their practitioners to be particularly sensitive to belief systems and practices which challenge their authority. The proponents of orthodox psychological healing practices have managed to secure no more than a tenuous claim to public legitimation as possessors of some unique professional expertise.[3] Like many radical belief

---

[1] Jock Young, *The Drugtakers*, (Paladin, 1971), p. 103.

[2] On Spiritualism, see Geoffrey K. Nelson, *Spiritualism and Society* (Routledge & Kegan Paul, London, 1969).

[3] Harold L. Wilensky, 'The professionalization of everyone?', *American Journal of Sociology*, 70 (1964), pp. 137–58, reprinted in Oscar Grusky and George A. Miller, eds, *The Sociology of Organisations* (Free Press, New York, 1970), p. 489.

systems, and in this respect no more than early Christianity, Scientology also presented a competing claim to the loyalty typically owed to the family. Unlike early Christianity, however, Scientology emerged in an era when the family had become a somewhat fragile institution,[1] and its claim to a higher loyalty under some circumstances was thus peculiarly threatening.

A further important feature of Scientology's challenge to prevailing reality lay in its ambiguous status.[2] Western conceptions of religion, grounded in the Christian experience, identify religious institutions and practices in terms drawn from that tradition and its vicissitudes. Religious institutions are distinguishable from secular institutions. The boundaries between church, business, science, and to a lesser extent psychotherapy, are relatively clearly drawn. Scientology infringed these boundaries and, refusing to recognize any necessity of occupying one category rather than another, behaved in ways characteristic of them all. It was thus a source of cognitive anomaly and psychological anxiety.[3] Since it behaved as a business as well as a religion (and that of a singularly alien form), many argued that its religious claim must be purely 'a front', and Scientology 'a confidence trick'.

Scientology's challenge to conventional reality remained unimportant while the movement itself was insignificant. However, there are indications that during the late 1950s and early 1960s Scientology began to grow rapidly. Figures cited during the American tax case indicate that the income of the Washington Church almost doubled between 1956 and 1957.[4] The Victoria Report shows a steady growth at least from 1958 through 1962:

Income of Scientology Organizations in Melbourne[5]

Year ended 30 June	£
1958	12 150
1959	30 500
1960	47 075
1961	57 640
1962	71 977
1963	54 071

[1] Talcott Parsons, 'The American family: its relations to personality and the social structure', in T. Parsons and R. F. Bales, *Family Socialisation and Interaction Process* (Free Press, Glencoe, 1956), pp. 3–21.

[2] Mary Douglas, *Purity and Danger* (Routledge & Kegan Paul, London, 1966).

[3] This anxiety seems evident, for example, from the almost audible sigh of relief uttered by the American Psychiatric Association when Scientology was legally declared a religion in a Federal Court, and they could henceforth regard it as beyond their domain. *Psychiatric News*, 4, 3 (March 1969), p. 2.

[4] Founding Church of Scientology v. USA in US Court of Claims, Washington, D.C. 1967, 'Brief for the United States'.

[5] Anderson, op. cit., p. 38.

The Foster Report indicates that in Britain, the movement's income roughly doubled every year between 1965 and 1968.[1]

Scientology was clearly having a considerable impact, recruiting individuals away from conventional reality. Moreover, the individuals recruited were not by any means *marginal* in conventional terms. Many were prosperous. Businessmen and professionals were converted as well as the less successful.

For some, particularly Anderson, Scientology's conflict with conventional reality was a *moral* affront. The Victoria Report reverberates with Anderson's indignation that anyone could believe such a 'weird idea',[2] such 'nonsense',[3] so much that was 'entirely contrary to conventional learning and experience',[4] 'irrational and perverted'.[5] He appears to have found it perverse and indeed 'incredible that a witness with such high academic qualifications, could voice such nonsense . . .'[6] and was forced to conclude that Hubbard's followers were 'deluded',[7] or in the grip of 'some inescapable compulsion'.[8] How otherwise could one account for the fact that apparently rational men could come to hold such bizarre and alien beliefs, than that they were 'hypnotized' or 'brainwashed'? Scientology posed a threat not only to the precarious domains of psychological treatment and family life,[9] but to the fabric of conventional reality itself.

Deviance-amplification and Scientology

Since its early days Scientology has been an authoritarian movement with only one source of authoritative definition of reality, its founder Ron Hubbard. The débâcle of Dianetics in the early 1950s convinced Hubbard that two major dangers threatened the survival of his organization – attacks from outside the Scientology community inspired by medical and psychiatric interests, and threats from within, in the form of heresy, 'individualism' and schism. Both these perceived dangers need to be considered to understand the movement's development. While the response of the movement's leadership to the latter was *sectarianization*, its response to the former appears to have been a complex combination of strategies involving the generation of peripheral organizations, infiltration, and undercover tactics designed to secure some control over the external environment. One important means of securing greater control over

---

[1] Foster, op. cit., p. 36.   [2] Anderson, op. cit., p. 48.
[3] Ibid., p. 59.   [4] Ibid., p. 48.   [5] Ibid., p. 12.   [6] Ibid., p. 52.
[7] Ibid., p. 51.   [8] Ibid., p. 52.
[9] One of the most persistent complaints against Scientology during this period was that it broke up families. The evidence in support of these claims, however, does not appear very strong. Scientology does not appear to cause familial disruption to a greater extent than other systems of beliefs to which one family member holds with great conviction but the rest reject. Indeed, it is my impression that it causes less familial disruption than some contemporary communitarian groups, and perhaps less than the early Christian church.

the movement's environment was through a more aggressive use of the techniques of public relations. This could be directed to the dual end of increased mobilization of recruits to the movement, as well as increased control.

> Unless you have control of the Public, driving the Public into the Org becomes a difficult task. This is why PR control is so important. Once you have the control, it is easy to bring in the public, in the thousands and millions! It is also needed to protect org expansion from attacks by opposition groups. PR is a social technique of control.
>
> How do you do this? Well, you get all the people who COUNT in the area – the VIPs, the community group, news media, under YOUR control. Then you USE these public control points to get the raw public in. Simple![1]

(The Scientologists point out to me in a private communication that 'the authenticity of the quote is doubtful'.)

One response of the movement to a hostile environment appears to have been a process of *deviance-amplification*. In the late 1950s and early 1960s, the gradual growth of the movement and its quasi-therapeutic claims brought it to the attention of a variety of state and professional agencies. In the pursuit of largely bureaucratic ends, the Food and Drug Administration in America, the Medical Health Authority in Victoria, the American Medical Association, the British Medical Association, the American Psychological Association, and similar agencies maintained a certain surveillance over Scientology, and occasionally issued public comment upon it. This led to defensive and offensive action by the Scientology organization in response. Critics were attacked, and internal security tightened. The FDA raid in 1963 inevitably led to further alienation from, and hostility towards, the state, press, and professional bodies, for what was felt by many Scientologists to be, and what was characterized by its leadership as, religious persecution.[2]

It was, however, the developments in Victoria which led to an international moral panic. There, press, medical and psychiatric agencies, professional bodies and disgruntled former Scientologists joined forces to promote government action against Scientology. The grounds for such action – alleged blackmail, extortion, and adverse effects on the mental health of local university students, were generally unsubstantiated by the Anderson Enquiry.

However, Anderson's Report presented, often in emotive terms, a highly negative stereotype of the movement. It instituted a *moral passage* in public designations of Scientology, leading to a transformation of the prevailing stereotype. The former conception of the movement as a relatively harmless, if 'cranky', health and self-improvement cult, was transformed into one which portrayed it as 'evil', 'dangerous', a form of 'hypnosis' (with all the overtones

---

[1] Diana Hubbard, April 1971, cited in *St Louis Post-Dispatch*, 6 March 1974, original source not indicated.

[2] This is the tenor of Church of Scientology, *The Findings . . .* , op. cit., for example.

of Svengali in the layman's mind), and 'brainwashing'. The symbolization of the movement rested largely on the *putative* features of its deviation, that is:

> that portion of the societal definition of the deviant which has no foundation in his objective behaviour. Frequently these fallacious imputations are incorporated into myth and stereotype and mediate much of the formal treatment of the deviant.[1]

Much play was made of Scientology practices which were *likely* to cause harm;[2] the '*potentiality* for the misuse of confidences';[3] and activities that were '*potentially* very dangerous to the mental health of the community'.[4] Exaggeration and distortion appear throughout the Report, probably the most notorious example of which occurs where Anderson asserts that he realized he had observed a woman being 'processed into insanity' when nine days after a demonstration auditing session in which she participated, she was admitted to a mental hospital.[5]

The Anderson Report provoked not only a legal ban on Scientology in Victoria, but a reaction in many other English-speaking countries. In 1966 Scientology became the subject of a question in the House of Commons, as well as of numerous unfavourable press reports, many of which drew directly upon Anderson's rhetoric and stereotyping. Hubbard was also requested to leave Rhodesia where it appears he may have hoped to settle.[6] In 1967 Scientology came under the scrutiny of the Ontario Committee on the Healing Arts.[7] The process described by amplification theorists began accelerating:

> . . . when society defines a group of people as deviant it tends to react against them so as to isolate and alienate them from the company of 'normal' people. In this situation of isolation and alienation, the group . . . tends to develop its own norms and values which society perceives as even more deviant than before.[8]

What Scientologists regarded as their 'persecution', experienced at a personal and not merely at an organizational level, resulted in the rapid development of a severe sense of alienation from the surrounding society, and the development among core members of new norms conceived to be essential for the movement's survival, although regarded by the conventional society as further evidence of Scientology's deviance. This alienation is evident in passages such as the following:

[1] Edwin M. Lernert, *Social Pathology*, McGraw-Hill, New York, 1951, pp. 55–6.

[2] Anderson, op. cit., p. 4.   [3] Ibid., p. 1. (My emphasis.)

[4] Ibid., p. 108. (My emphasis.)   [5] Ibid., p. 135.

[6] This is suggested in Christopher Evans, *Cults of Unreason* (Harrap, London, 1973), p. 85; *Daily Mail*, 14 July 1966.

[7] John A. Lee, *Sectarian Healers and Hypnotherapy: a Study for the Committee on the Healing Arts* (Queen's Printer, Toronto, Ontario, 1970).

[8] Jock Young, 'The role of the police as amplifiers of deviance, negotiators of reality and translators of fantasy, [etc]', in Stanley Cohen, ed., *Images of Deviance* (Penguin Books, Harmondsworth, 1971).

Scientology regards ordinary society as something akin to[a] dense jungle of intrigue, lies, confusion, illness, violence and sudden death covered with a thin social veneer of mildness.[1]

This sense of alienation and imminent threat led to more severe policies of internal control, and led the leadership to draw further away from contact with the Society, geographically as well as symbolically, with the creation of the Sea Org. The trend towards sectarianism was heightened, and sectarian practices such as *disconnection* led to further hostile commentary. In response to this hostile and threatening environment, Scientologists began to take what they construed as defensive action by more vigorous attacks on critics through legal actions, and investigation for past 'crimes'.[2]

Some of the individuals and organizations which have been critical of Scientology, or have commented on it in a fashion which the Scientologists disapprove, have found themselves the victims of various, often unexplained misfortunes. The South African Report describes the case of Dr E. L. Fisher, MP, who on several occasions requested the appointment of an inquiry into Scientology in the South African parliament.[3] Fisher in due course became the object of attack in a Scientology broadsheet 'teeming with baseless defamatory innuendoes of and concerning Dr Fisher'.[4] As a result of a subsequent action for defamation Dr Fisher received 'substantial damages', and an apology.[5] The Commission of Enquiry also indicate that in 1967, Dr Fisher became the object of a stratagem designed to induce him to procure an illegal abortion. The Scientology leadership argued that the responsibility for this subterfuge lay with the proprietor of an investigation agency whose services they had employed to uncover Fisher's 'past crimes'.

The Dutch Mental Health Centre (National Centrum Voor Geestelijke Volksgezondheid) in Utrecht suffered a theft of its files relating to Scientology. The two young men who committed the theft were caught by accident in a police check on driving licences. Because of their frightened behaviour, the car

---

[1] Anonymous, 'Scientology ethics policies and handling of attacks on Scientology', photocopy of manuscript, n.d., p. 16, made available by the Church of Scientology.

[2] Roy Wallis, 'Religious sects and the fear of publicity', *New Society*, 34, 557 (7 June 1973). Such behaviour might be characterized as 'secondary deviation'. Lemert defines secondary deviation as:

'deviant behaviour, or social roles based upon it, which becomes [a] means of defense, attack, or adaptation to the overt and covert problems created by the societal reaction to primary deviation. In effect, the original "causes" of the deviation recede and give way to the central importance of the disapproving, degredational and isolating reactions of society'.

Edwin M. Lemert, *Human Deviance, Social Problems and Social Control* (Prentice-Hall, New Jersey, 1967), p. 17.

[3] Kotzé, et al., p. 117.

[4] Ibid., p. 119.

[5] Ibid.

was searched, and the files found. A letter which was later received by the NCGV from Scientology headquarters in Holland, admitted that the two young men had been Scientologists, but suggested that the theft was undertaken on their own initiative and 'with the highest motivation'.[1]

A psychiatrist, Dr Russell Barton, found a private investigation agency to be conducting an investigation into his career, after he had criticized Scientology in a radio broadcast in 1970. The head of this agency was known to have had a close association with the Church of Scientology in California. Dr Barton became the object of a campaign which employed, out of context, a statement that he had made on conditions in Belsen, in an attempt to discredit him.[2]

Kenneth Robinson, a former Minister of Health, who had criticized Scientology in Parliament, found himself the object of defamatory attacks in the Scientology newspaper, *Freedom*. In November 1972 a forged letter bearing his name was published by *Management in Action* suggesting that the cause of strikes was 'a severe mental illness' and advocating psychiatric screening of workers.[3]

The National Association for Mental Health and its leadership were the object of what they took to be a concerted campaign of harassment. Circulars alleging misuse of NAMH funds and scandalous behaviour at NAMH hostels, purportedly written by a staff member who had resigned, were circulated to members of the Association. Documents were alleged to have continually disappeared from NAMH files.[4] Patrons of the NAMH and other prominent public figures (including members of the Royal family) received offensive forged letters which appeared to have been written by officers of the Association.[5]

Forged letters and documents have proved a source of embarrassment to others who have criticized or commented on Scientology. Paulette Cooper, author of a work hostile to Scientology,[6] was the subject of a thoroughly defamatory circular, allegedly written by 'a concerned neighbor', which sought to mobilize the tenants of her apartment block to secure her 'removal from our residence, and if possible, have her put under appropriate psychiatric care'. (Representations by the Church of Scientology make it incumbent upon me to indicate that Miss Cooper's writings on Scientology have been the subject of

---

[1] Letters detailing these circumstances from NCGV officials to the author.

[2] Letter and documents sent to the author by Dr Barton.

[3] *Management in Action* (November 1972). For Mr Robinson's repudiation of this letter see *Management in Action* (December 1972).

[4] Among such documents were letters of a private nature between Dr David Clark, Vice-Chairman of the NAMH, and its General Secretary Miss Mary Appleby. Dr Clark's letters and the carbons of Miss Appleby's replies are said to have disappeared from the Association files. Sections from these letters appear in a book highly favourable to Scientology, Omar V. Garrison, op. cit., pp. 210–13.

[5] Interviews with officers of the NAMH; see also *The Observer*, 29 July 1973.

[6] Cooper, op. cit.

much litigation. Sums in settlement and apologies from the publishers concerned, have been received by the Church of Scientology in respect of an article in *Queen* magazine, and the book *The Scandal of Scientology*.)

Olympia Press, the publishers of Robert Kaufman's, *Inside Scientology*, were also attacked by means of forged documents. These documents, circulated to newsagents and booksellers, were written on headed Olympia notepaper. They suggested that in the light of litigation in which Olympia was involved, all stocks of the firm's books should be returned for cash refunds. A further forged letter purportedly emanating from Olympia's accountants, claimed that Olympia was going into liquidation. The officers of Olympia have also alleged that illegal entry was made to their premises, that galley proofs of Kaufman's book were stolen from the printers, and that their files were tampered with.[1] (Representations by the Church of Scientology again lead me to note that Maurice Girodias, the principal figure in Olympia Press, is a flamboyant and controversial individual, whose methods of book promotion are not always entirely orthodox. Whether this has any bearing on Olympia's misfortunes is a matter for conjecture.)

Following the distribution of an article by the present writer, commenting on Scientology,[2] a young man, later discovered to have been a Scientology staff member, visited the author at the university at which he was employed. He used a false name and sought to win the author's confidence. He was later found to have made personal inquiries of students and others concerning the author. Shortly following this visit, forged letters bearing official letter headings were received by various individuals, designed to be a source of inconvenience and embarrassment to the author.[3] The young man who visited the university later appeared in Scientology publications as a graduate of a Saint Hill course.

Miss Cooper and Robert Kaufman both allege that they have been systematically spied on.[4] The author of another work on Scientology, Cyril Vosper, alleges that a copy of his manuscript disappeared from his lodgings and, while on holiday in Spain, he was questioned by the police when they opened a parcel addressed to the place in which he was staying, containing obscene caricatures of General Franco. Kaufman, who is also a musician, found that his booking for a concert hall was cancelled mysteriously prior to a performance.[5] While he was appearing on a 'phone-in' radio programme, a man telephoned, alleging that he had been a male nurse in a psychiatric hospital in which Kaufman had been a patient. He claimed to have seen Kaufman's psychiatric records and alleged

[1] See particularly *The Observer*, 29 July 1973.
[2] Roy Wallis, 'The sectarianism of Scientology', in Michael Hill, ed., *A Sociological Yearbook of Religion in Britain* (SCM Press, London, 1973).
[3] This and similar cases are discussed in Roy Wallis, 'Religious sects and the fear of publicity', *New Society* (7 June 1973), pp. 545–7.
[4] Interviews; 'Statement of Complaint', Paulette Cooper v. Church of Scientology of New York, Inc.; etc., 21 June 1972.
[5] Interviews.

that Kaufman had been diagnosed as a 'paranoid schizophrenic with castration fears and homosexual tendencies.'[1]

A further case concerns a Canadian family, the Mcleans, who became dis-affected with the movement.[2] The mysterious and unpleasant events from which they suffered began to occur after the Mcleans publicized some of the reasons for their dissatisfaction with Scientology in the local news media.

Mr Mclean claims that he shortly afterwards suffered from telephone calls to the school where he worked, of a kind which seemed designed to cause embarrassment. The family also assert that compromising Christmas cards and telephone calls were received at their home, and neighbours received telephone calls inquiring into the Mcleans' credit-worthiness and suggesting domestic problems in the family. The local Board of Education, Mr Mclean's employers, are said to have received anonymous telephone calls implying that he was misusing Board property and student labour for his own profit. They believe that their house was kept under surveillance by men in cars using binoculars. The Scientology Org's Assistant Guardian was instrumental in securing the prosecution of Mr Mclean for allegedly harassing him by repeated telephone calls. (The case was dismissed.) When Canadian Television (CTV) planned to make a film on Scientology, including the Mcleans, the television company was threatened with an 'inevitable suit which must follow should the show be aired'.[3] In the ensuing action the Mcleans were named among the co-defendants. Members of the Scientology organisation in Toronto held a 'mock funeral' for 'lost souls' in the Mcleans' home town, carrying a coffin and handing out leaflets charging 'that the Mclean family had "betrayed all God-fearing Canadians" and was "succumbing to the mysteries of evil".'[4] When Mr Mclean became an official of the Ontario high school teachers' federation, Scientologists are said to have picketed a federation meeting at which he was to speak on professional matters.

(The Scientologists assert that the Mclean's major source of disaffection concerned the refund of fees or donations paid to the organization. These were repaid to the family. The Scientologists also argue that undertakings in respect of the terms on which these payments were made, were broken by the Mcleans. Various legal actions are still in process.)

The Royal College of Psychiatry and the World Federation for Mental Health have also suffered from circumstances which appear similar in some respects to those which involved the Dutch Mental Health Centre.

During the Whitsun Bank Holiday in 1973 the offices of the Royal College of

---

[1] Robert Kaufman, letter to the author 2 April 1973.

[2] I am grateful to the Mclean family for making available to me ample documentation on which the following account is based.

[3] Letter from S—— S—— of the Church of Scientology to the President of CTV, 22 April 1973.

[4] *Mcleans Magazine*, (June 1974), p. 27.

Psychiatry were burgled. While nothing of value was touched, a file concerning Scientology, and associated correspondence, were removed. Some time earlier, in 1969, the headquarters of the World Federation for Mental Health, then situated at the Royal Edinburgh Hospital, were also burgled. Documents and headed note-paper were removed. Participants in a world mental health conference, to be held shortly after this event, were mailed a letter telling them that the venue for the conference had been changed from Washington to Havana.[1]

The cases briefly described above display a striking pattern in the nature of the events which transpired in these varied and dispersed settings (spying; theft of documents; forgery; anonymous or pseudonumous defamatory allegations), and in the character of the victim. In every case, those who suffered from these untoward circumstances, were individuals or organizations believed by Scientologists to be actively hostile to the movement.

Reports during late 1974 and early 1975 suggested that the Scientologists believed they could prove that they had become the object of a campaign to discredit them, sponsored by the Nixon administration, the FBI and the CIA.[2]

De-amplification

By 1968 external threat had reached such proportions as to render multi-national ban an imminent possibility. It appears that the combination of vocal public criticism and severe internal control measures increasingly employed by the movement may have caused a loss of committed membership. The only figures available are those for successful completion of the 'clearing course'. This was not developed in its current form until 1966, at which point it was the most advanced course available. This course was in effect demoted later, when even more advanced courses were introduced. (This should, if anything, have increased the number of students taking the course.)

Period	Number declared 'clear'[3]
March–December 1966	131
January–December 1967	475
January–December 1968	901
January–December 1969	774
January–December 1970	441
January–December 1971	385
January–December 1972	359
January–December 1973	383

With the announcement of clearing in 1966, recruitment to the clearing course expanded rapidly. The publicity that Scientology received during the early and

---

[1] The Observer, 29 July 1973.

[2] The Guardian, 7 January 1973; Washington Star-News, 21 December 1974; Evening Standard, 6 January 1975.

[3] These figures were calculated from lists of clears published in The Auditor.

middle 1960s drew new adherents to the movement, particularly among late adolescents and young adults, attracted by the anti-establishment image which it was gaining. Recruitment to, and completion of, the clearing course increased through 1968, but then declined, although this decline may have ceased since 1971, and a rise may have occurred since then. Clearing is a relatively advanced stage of achievement in the movement's structure and indicates a level of considerable commitment. It is not possible to say how lower-level training and auditing have been affected. Indeed the only figures published by the movement suggest that in the United Kingdom, membership in Scientology has continued to increase rapidly.[1] Since it is quite unclear how these membership figures are calculated, it is difficult to be certain of their validity. Six-months free 'membership' is given to any inquirer who wishes it.[2] Thus membership itself does not imply any high degree of commitment. But at the advanced levels, the rate of growth apparently declined for several years after 1968.

These figures suggest the first stages in a process of 'de-amplification'. Publicity had become so unfavourable by 1968, and the internal regime so repressive ('puritanical' is the term preferred by the Scientologists themselves to describe this period), that new members were either not being recruited at the same rate as during the early and middle 1960s or were becoming alienated from the organization earlier – or both. The gap between society and extensive Scientological commitment may have become too wide for many to cross. A 'field staff auditor' and former 'franchise operator' (that is, a semi-autonomous practitioner of Scientology) confirmed that a considerable drop in recruitment had been experienced at least at the local level, following the government statement in the House of Commons in 1968,[3] and a former Org Exec Sec claimed that by 1968 'stats were dropping all over the planet'.[4] In an effort to correct this situation, the Scientology leadership attempted a major modification in policy. Between 1968 and 1970, the most severe social control measures were publicly dropped as part of a campaign to change the movement's image.

A Policy Letter issued in March 1969, for example, states:

> We are going in the direction of mild ethics and involvement with the Society. After 19 years of attack by minions of vested interest, psychiatric front groups, we developed a tightly disciplined organisational structure.
>
> . . . We didn't know it at the time, but our difficulties and failures were the result of false reports put out by the small, but rich and powerful group of individuals who would deny man freedom.
>
> Now that we know . . . we will never need a harsh spartan discipline for ourselves.[5]

[1] *Freedom*, 37 (March 1972), p. 2.
[2] This offer is made in most Scientology publications.
[3] In an interview.
[4] Interview.
[5] *HCO Policy Letter*, 7 March 1969, as cited in 'Scientology ethics policies . . ', op. cit., p. 25.

Early in their history Scientologists had realized the advantages of being recognized as a religion. They now saw the advantages of being regarded as a denominational rather than as a sectarian form of religion. The stabilization and possible increase of recruitment to advanced courses suggest that this policy may have been successful.

De-amplification appears to have occurred on the part of agents of control as well. In Britain and Australia particularly, commitment to 'freedom of thought' and 'freedom of religion' led to uneasiness concerning the severity of state action against Scientology, and a willingness to reconsider earlier, possibly precipitate, decisions. (For example, the accreditation of Scientology in Australia by the federal government as a recognized denomination for purposes of the Marriage Act, which effectively nullified the discriminatory state government legislation.)

In the period after 1968, the organization opened its premises at East Grinstead on Sundays, invited doctors and ministers of all denominations to take courses, and developed its social reform programmes. It particularly publicized its stand as a radical opponent to institutional psychiatry, and emphasized the drug rehabilitation scheme Narconon, which the Church sponsors, The Church of Scientology had therefore a strategy of de-amplification open to it which is generally unavailable to the illicit drug-user or the delinquent. That is, it had the means to promote a change of the stereotype of Scientology which had grown up. (The delinquent or drug-user can, of course, change his own appearance and behaviour, but there is relatively little he can normally do to change the stereotype regarding delinquents and drug-users as a whole.) Whether or not this strategy will be successful remains to be seen. During the period 1970 to 1973, Scientology has been the subject of a number of books and articles by former Scientologists and others which have continued to publicize its more deviant features. In the reaction to critics, both in the courts and beyond them, there is evidence to suggest that the attempt by its leaders to present Scientology as a denomination, and as having accommodated to conventional reality, is still only an attempt to manipulate public relations.

Conclusion

The deviance-amplification model appears to be supported by the development of Scientology and the reaction to it within the wider society. Initial deviation by this movement led to hostile societal reaction which in turn led the movement to adopt strategies of defence towards, and attack upon, its detractors, construed in turn by the press and by agents of social control as confirmation for their initial diagnosis. A set of generalized beliefs and a stereotypic characterization of the movement were formulated and disseminated by the mass media and moral crusaders, leading to a panic reaction issuing in changes in the law.

It should be stressed, however, that amplification is not a deterministic process.

The Scientology movement *chose* to adopt an increasingly hostile stance towards critics and the wider society. Deviance-amplification and de-amplification were the results of strategies adopted and implemented by the movement's leaders, as a means of coping with a hostile environment.

Some drop in the *overt* hostility of the movement's attacks on outsiders appears to have occurred as a result of the severity of governmental action, and a decline in the growth rate of committed membership. However, this 'de-escalation' may be primarily a public-relations exercise, since despite a considerable drop in moral panic and in the severity of societal reaction, the movement continues to react to criticism and commentary in a manner that suggests some persisting alienation from conventional norms of behaviour.

8. REALITY MAINTENANCE IN A DEVIANT BELIEF SYSTEM

The manner in which members of social groups sustain 'definitions of the situation', and a sense of meaningful social order has been a prominent focus in recent sociological theory. A central thrust of this work has been to demonstrate that the conceptions of reality which prevail in human groups are socially constructed. The 'objective' character and moral validity – the 'taken-for-granted' status – of the prevailing institutional and cultural order and the conception of reality incorporated within it, are seen by such theorists as an accomplishment of social actors.[1]

Definitions of the situation and the sense of social order are seen as precarious constructs vulnerable to disruption. Their status as unproblematic, common-sense knowledge is sustained through reaffirmation in the course of conversation and social interaction. Despite their subjective origins, however, the symbolic constructs which order the social environment come, through socialization, reification, and habituation, to be seen as objective facts limiting and constraining the behaviour of social actors. Social groups evolve mechanisms for managing, eliminating, or accommodating challenges to widely-accepted definitions of the situation. Nevertheless, they remain susceptible to such challenges

---

[1] This theme has been developed from various theoretical points of view. Perhaps the most prominent work in this area has been that of Peter Berger and Thomas Luckmann, *The Social Construction of Reality* (Allen Lane, London, 1967). The work of Erving Goffman is also relevant: *The Presentation of Self in Everyday Life* (Doubleday Anchor, New York, 1959); *Behavior in Public Places* (Free Press, New York, 1963); *Relations in Public* (Penguin Books, Harmondsworth, 1972). Ethnomethodological writers have also contributed to this area: Harold Garfinkel, *Studies in Ethnomethodology* (Prentice-Hall, Englewood Cliffs, New Jersey, 1967); Aaron V. Cicourel, *The Social Organisation of Juvenile Justice* (Wiley, New York, 1967); Peter McHugh, *Defining the Situation: the Organisation of Meaning in Social Interaction* (Bobbs-Merrill, New York, 1968). Also relevant are Peter L. Berger and Hansfried Kellner, 'Marriage and the construction of reality', Joan Emerson, 'Behavior in private places: sustaining definitions of reality in gynaecological examinations', and Arlene K. Daniels, 'The social construction of military psychiatric diagnoses' – all in Hans Peter Dreitzel, ed., *Patterns of Communicative Behavior* (Collier-Macmillan, London, 1970).

emanating from alien cultures, or from deviant individuals and groups within the society.[1]

Such deviant groups not only challenge the social world in which they exist; they are, in turn, challenged by it. The very existence of a 'conventional' world inhabited by a majority which does not share their beliefs and practices is itself a major challenge to the legitimacy or validity of their definition of reality. The world of the deviant suffers from a discontinuity less characteristic of the world of the conventional. The deviant finds no taken-for-granted articulation between the various spheres of his life while he continues to inhabit the conventional world. His job, his bank, the bus company, etc., are not organized on principles derived from his belief system. They present a potential challenge to these beliefs rather than a reinforcement of them. The major legitimating agencies of the conventional world: the mass media, the educational institutions, the political parties, and the churches are oriented to the dissemination and support of a set of beliefs and assumptions at variance with – and perhaps sometimes in direct conflict with – those of the deviant minority group. The power institutions of the society which can be mobilized to enforce a particular definition of reality – the police, the courts, the military, and the state bureaucracy – are directed by those who are usually firmly committed to the prevailing hegemony.[2]

One strategy for coping with this problem is that of insulation or isolation from the surrounding society. Some deviant groups are able to accomplish this with greater ease than others. Communitarian groups such as the Hutterites and some Doukhobors maintained a distinctive style of life and a system of beliefs and practices radically at variance with those prevalent in the host society over several generations.[3] They were particularly successful in this respect, in part because neither of these groups sought to recruit converts from outside the community. They also preserved an agrarian way of life which permitted their members to fulfil their work roles largely within the confines of the collectivity. Contact between believer and conventional society was minimized further by geographical isolation, an alien language, and by bans on marrying non-believers, or participating in voluntary associations or forms of entertainment beyond the confines of the collectivity.

These methods of insulation are less readily available to Scientologists. Scientology is the product of a highly industrialized and technological culture.

[1] Robert A. Scott, 'A proposed framework for analysing deviance as a property of social order', in Robert A. Scott and Jack D. Douglas, eds., *Theoretical Perspectives on Deviance* (Basic Books, New York, 1972), pp. 9–35; H. Taylor Buckner, *Deviance, Reality and Change* (Random House, New York, 1971).

[2] Ralph Miliband, *The State in Capitalist Society* (Weidenfeld & Nicolson, London, 1969).

[3] On the Hutterites, see Victor Peters, *All Things Common* (Harper, New York, 1965); John W. Bennett, *Hutterian Brethren* (Stanford University Press, Stanford, 1967). On the Doukhobors, see George Woodcock and Ivan Avakumovic, *The Doukhobors* (Faber, London, 1968).

It finds its major support in the urban centres of advanced industrial societies. It is highly dependent upon recruitment from the general population. The high cost of its services has the consequence that the largest part of its membership must hold occupations outside the movement which secure a substantial income. Scientology also has no developed communal orientation. Members are relatively atomized and isolated from each other. Hence the movement is highly involved in conventional society, and the validity of the conception of reality which it purveys is therefore open to constant challenge.

For members this may pose a persistent problem of being required to justify the movement's world-view to others and, in consequence, to themselves. One mode of coping with this problem is to limit one's contact with non-believers by gradually dropping their acquaintance and replacing unbelieving friends and marital partners by Scientologists. A more general means of coping with the problem is one encouraged by the degree of differentiation of advanced industrial societies. Such societies display marked differentiation between the realms of work, home and other leisure activities. A high level of mobility results in the dispersal of friends and acquaintances across the ecology of the urban environment. Thus the various spheres of the individual's life may be located in distinct ecological areas with only relatively low visibility between them. The member may therefore minimize any challenge to the validity of his unconventional beliefs by simply not exposing them in conventional domains. He compartmentalizes and segregates his beliefs and behaviour.

> Experience has taught me never to tell one set of friends what I'm doing in another direction with another set of friends. I use one of the local pubs and you couldn't speak about anything to do with the occult there. . . . You've got to have separate compartments.[1]
>
> . . . I had a lot of friends who hardly knew I was a Scientologist. I didn't discuss Scientology much outside.[2]

The movement leaders have also established a variety of mechanisms to cope with this problem. The rigorous practice of socialization incorporated in the practice of auditing and the training programmes, and the stringent social controls embodied in the Ethics system serve to render new recruits less disruptive of the status of the movement's definition of reality. These features of Scientology produce a set of structural and motivational constraints on the articulation of criticism of its practices and presuppositions. (A number of the factors which we shall consider here have been alluded to briefly in earlier chapters.)

Structural and motivational constraints on criticism

Notable in this respect is the atomization of members. The bulk of the members have formal contacts with each other only in situations structured by the

[1] Interview.
[2] Interview.

leadership: on course, at Sunday services, or at Congresses. Such meetings are arranged almost entirely to facilitate the downward flow of communication, rather than to foster general discussion or debate. They are opportunities for the mobilization of members rather than opportunities for democratic decision-making. Hubbard has expressed his disenchantment with democratic forms of organization.

> A totally democratic organisation has a bad name in Dianetics and Scientology. . . . It has been found by actual experiment (L.A. 1950) that groups of people called on to select a leader from among them by nomination and vote routinely select only those who would kill them.[1]

> . . . a democracy is a collective-think of reactive banks. Popular opinion is bank opinion.[2]

(The more committed core members do have more frequent opportunity for formal and informal contact in the context of the various social reform activities of the movement, and on such occasions as concerts by Scientology entertainers. These events are either largely expressive, or are again opportunities for the mobilization of members, rather than for debate or democratic formulation of policy.)

Collective discussion and criticism is also inhibited by the Ethics codes which specify as a 'general crime', 'Organising or allowing a gathering or meeting of staff members or field auditors or the public to protest the orders of a senior'.[3] There is also an absence of established channels for the public expression of criticism. The movement's periodical publications ceased to publish critical letters and articles from members in the early 1950s.[4]

(The Church of Scientology points out to me that the following channels exist for the expression of criticism: 1. the Examiner; 2. the Chaplain; 3. the auditing session; 4. the petition line; 5. the Committee of Evidence line; 6. the Review Committee of Evidence line. Three points occur to me about these channels. They are individual rather than collective occasions for criticism; they are private rather than public; they exist to remedy deviations from policy and doctrine, not to provide means of challenging or critically debating points of policy or doctrine.)

Hubbard is accepted as possessing privileged access to the truth with regard to matters of doctrine and organization. His revelations are final and complete. Hence there can be no ground upon which they could be challenged or

---

[1] *OEC*, Vol. O, p. 32. Originally a *Policy Letter* published in 1962.

[2] *OEC*, Vol. O, p. 29. Originally a *Policy Letter* published in 1965.

[3] L. Ron Hubbard, *Introduction to Scientology Ethics* (2nd edition) Scientology Publications Organization, Copenhagen, Denmark, 1970, p. 46.

[4] The *Journal of Scientology* ceased publication of criticism after the removal of Alphia Hart as editor in 1953. No subsequent *official* publication has published commentary by members critical of the movement, to my knowledge. The 'independent' newspaper, *Freedom*, occasionally publishes critical letters.

criticized. When a new technique or belief is propounded, those which it supercedes are simply dropped from use, with only rare admission that they may ever have been less than perfect. Doubt or criticism would therefore involve 'invalidating Scientology'; 'public disavowal of Scientology or Scientologists in good standing with Scientology Organisations'; 'inciting to insubordination'; or one of the many other Ethics offences which can be mobilized against internal critics. The member is also isolated by the Ethics codes from other institutional sources of criticism. Among the 'High Crimes' of the movement are:

> Dependency on other mental or philosophical procedures than Scientology (except medical or surgical) after certification, classification, or award.[1]
> Continued membership in a divergent group.[2]

(The Scientologists point out to me that a 'divergent group is a group which uses Scientology technology in a messed up fashion, not repeat not a group different from Scientology'.)[3]

The 'hierarchy of sanctification' that has been erected within the movement is a further institutional barrier to criticism. The member is made to realize that there is a graded progression of enlightenment and insight into the gnosis. Those on the lower rungs of this hierarchy therefore shortly recognize that much information is not yet available to them and come to believe that as more is revealed in the progression upwards, so any lingering queries, doubts and criticisms will be dealt with. The belief system also has an interesting open-ended quality. Since it is believed that everything has been revealed, at least to Hubbard, the belief system is not open-ended in the sense that new knowledge may be discovered and contributed by others. It remains open-ended, however, in the degree to which it rests on mystification. Hubbard's literary output contains large portions which it is evident that even committed and long-serving adherents find thoroughly mysterious. One witness before the Victoria Enquiry, although a Scientologist of many years' standing, admitted that he still did not understand some of Hubbard's writings, such as the 'axioms',[4] of which the following is an example:

> The static, having postulated as-is-ness, then practises alter-is-ness, and so achieves the apparency of is-ness and so obtains reality.[5]

Other Scientologists of long-standing whom I have approached for explication of passages such as the following, also admitted that their comprehension of Scientology was not yet sufficiently developed for them to understand everything that Hubbard has written.

[1] L. Ron Hubbard, *Introduction to Scientology Ethics*, op. cit., p. 51.
[2] Ibid.
[3] Personal Communication, November 1974.
[4] Kevin Victor Anderson, *Report of the Board of Enquiry into Scientology* (Government Printer, Melbourne, Australia, 1965), p. 68.
[5] L. Ron Hubbard, *The Creation of Human Ability* (Scientology Publications, London, 1955), p. 15.

Self-determinism is entirely and solely the imposition of time and space upon energy flows. By imposing time and space upon objects, people, self, events, and individuals, is Causation. [sic] The total components of his self-determinism is the ability to impose time and space. His energy is derived from the discharge of high and low or different, potentials to which he has assigned time and space. Dwindling sanity is a dwindling ability to assign time and space. Psychosis is a complete inability to assign time and space. This is, as well, will power. [1]

Such passages convince the member that he has a great deal more to discover before he will be in a position to criticize the beliefs and practices of the movement. They also provide an area of 'mystery' upon which Hubbard can draw in the articulation and legitimation of modifications to the currently accepted corpus of Scientological knowledge.

The authoritarian nature of the movement's epistemology entails that modification or elaboration of doctrine or practice is not something in which the individual member can participate. It is his place to *receive* the doctrine, not to question it. Hence, the movement's literature warns against doubt, questioning, criticism, and open-mindedness. 'Persons who "have an open mind"' are regarded as 'threatening sources' and 'the policy in general is to cut communication' with them.[2] Criticism is regarded as impeding the movement's progress:

> If you find something wrong with the organisation of the HASI, its personnel or people, and if you criticise this weakly or strongly, remember you are criticising your own organisation . . . and if you criticise constantly and continually about the various ills to which any human organisation is subject, allowing of course that the HASI is a human organisation – you're making it just that much tougher to get this job done.[3]

Scientology is the 'science of certainty', therefore doubt can only be a product of the reactive mind, and a lower Ethics condition. Each of these offences may result in penalization. They will be seen as indicating that the individual is making poor progress; and that he needs further auditing before continuing with his training. Should he persist, he is likely to be seen as 'suppressive' and to be expelled. Even private criticism to friends in the movement is dangerous, since in the course of Ethics inquiry they may confess that someone has 'invalidated' Scientology, or their 'gains', and hence is 'PTS' (Potential Trouble Source), and this may lead to the exercise of sanctions.

Criticism, however, is inhibited not only among members. The movement's leaders have attempted to constrain criticism by non-members. Those who

[1] L. Ron Hubbard, *Scientology 8–80* (The Distribution Center Inc., Silver Springs, Maryland, 1952), p. 44.
[2] L. Ron Hubbard, 'Policies on physical healing, insanity and troublesome sources', *HCO Policy Letter*, 27 October 1964.
[3] L. Ron Hubbard, 'Ownership: special PAB', *Professional Auditor's Bulletin*, 53 (27 May 1955), p. 2.

publicly voice their disapproval of the movement are liable to defamation;[1] to legal action;[2] and to threatened investigation of their private lives.[3]

Language

Language is the basic building material for the construction and repair of social reality. Language 'marks the co-ordinates of my life in society and fills that life with meaningful objects'.[4] Scientology displays an acute preoccupation with language. Hubbard has invented several hundred neologisms, for example: 'Randomity', 'itsa', 'opterm', 'midruds', 'expanded gita', 'disenturbulate', and 'as-isness'. In his writings and those of his followers, verbs and adjectives are often employed as nouns ('a withhold', 'a static') and nouns are transformed into verbs ('squirrelling', 'short sessioning'). Prepositions are used in unfamiliar ways ('at cause'), and numerous contractions and acronyms are employed ('MEST', 'D of P', 'Exec Sec', 'Qual', 'Org'). The net effect of this extensive reorganization of the English language is to render Scientological conversation and internal documentation all but unintelligible to the uninitiated.

The language of Scientology also serves to support the validity of its beliefs and practices. The existence of an extensive technical vocabulary impresses newcomers who see it as a proof of the scientific character of the enterprise. It serves to maintain the faith of those who may be inclined to doubt. Since, it is believed, the words must mean something, failure to understand or unwillingness to accept some statement in the movement's literature can be attributed to the student having 'misunderstood' some word used in the text. Any disagreement with, or disinclination to pursue the study of, Hubbard's work is a consequence of failure fully to understand the meaning of some term that one has passed over, that, is of a 'misunderstood'. Most books currently issued by the Org now contain an 'Important Note'.

> The only reason a person gives up a study or becomes confused or unable to learn is that he or she has gone past a word or phrase that was not understood.

One is enjoined to go back, locate this word, ensure that one understands it and can apply it, and then continue. If one finds there is still some point of disagreement, doubt, or incomprehension, the cause of the problem is that one has either

---

[1] For example Kenneth Robinson and Dr E. L. Fisher, discussed in Chapter 7.

[2] After publicly commenting on Scientology, numerous individuals and newspapers have had writs for libel served on them by the movement's solicitors. The movement is so litigious that many editors are extremely wary of publishing articles on Scientology. See Omar V. Garrison, *The Hidden Story of Scientology* (Arlington Books, London, 1974), p. 80. Hubbard has stated that '. . . we should be very alert to sue for slander at the slightest chance so as to discourage the public presses from mentioning Scientology'. L. Ron Hubbard, 'Dissemination of material', *Ability*, Major 1 (1955), p. 5.

[3] For example Lord Balniel, see above, p. 194.

[4] Peter Berger and Thomas Luckmann, op. cit., p. 36.

missed some *other* word in the text; or one has failed to understand the meaning of a word in the dictionary definition of the word one originally sought to understand; or misunderstood some word in earlier study (academic or Scientology).

A dictionary of Scientology terms has been compiled, and students are obliged to check non-Scientology words in standard English (or American) dictionaries until they are able to make sense of any statement. 'Making sense' seems to be accomplished by searching for a dictionary definition which conveys some meaning in the context of that statement. Thus, for example, in the case of the phrase: 'One can only do those things with which he can exchange communication',[1] the student might have to scour several dictionaries to locate some definition of 'communication' which will permit him to gloss this phrase as: you can only do things if you can make contact with/face up to/engage with/ gain some response or reaction from whatever is necessary to/is involved in/is an adjunct to doing them. If some such acceptable (albeit trivial) gloss is not achieved, the student may have to seek definitions of further words either in the definitions of 'communication' or of words he has earlier misunderstood. He may be required to read the passage while being checked on the E-meter to see if some reaction occurs on another word. He may be required to 'demonstrate' the word, or even his misunderstanding of it, by using various bric-a-brac to provide a visual model. Finally an appeal may be made to the student not as a human being but as a thetan. He may not be able to exchange communication with running/reading/parachuting or whatever, as a human being, but he could as a thetan.[2]

The logic of this process is that one disagrees with, doubts, or fails to comprehend Hubbard, not because he is talking nonsense, but because of 'misunderstoods'. The individual learns to doubt his own judgement; to locate some meaning in the undoubted mystification of much of Hubbard's writing; or to acquiesce to some half-comprehended and yet half-incomprehensible statement in the hope that all will be made clear to him at some later point. There is now an elaborate 'Study Technology' employed to assist those who are slow in grasping the principles of the movement.

'Word-clearing' currently forms an important part of the lower level courses. Unless the student quickly finds an acceptable gloss for 'misunderstoods', the process is extremely tedious. Failure to make sense of the material leads to delays before the student is allowed to begin the courses on general Scientology theory and practice for which he has come to the Org. If, as is often the case, students are renting accommodation near the Org, such delays are also a source of further expense. Hence there is considerable motivation to repress doubts and difficulties. The student learns to observe in the text or to elicit from the

[1] Course 'pack' for the Communications Course.
[2] This was the sequence of events which transpired when the author failed to make sense of this phrase while engaged on the Communications Course.

instructor, cues as to what will constitute an acceptable interpretation. The process of 'word clearing' therefore leads to a further suspension of the individual's critical faculty, or to its inhibition, and to the ready acceptance of Hubbard's formulations as intrinsically meaningful.

Interpretation

Under the label of *interpretation* we shall explore the processes by which Scientology deals with challenges to its validity by referring them to its ideology and identifying them as predictable deviations. Berger and Luckmann discuss two aspects of this process, *therapy*, and *nihilation*.

> Therapy entails the application of conceptual machinery to ensure that actual or potential deviants stay within the institutionalised definitions of reality, or, in other words, to prevent the 'inhabitants' of a given universe from 'emigrating'. It does this by applying the legitimating apparatus to individual 'cases'.[1]
>
> Since therapy must concern itself with deviations from 'official' definitions of reality, it must develop a conceptual machinery to account for such deviations and to maintain the realities thus challenged. This requires a body of knowledge that includes a theory of deviance, a diagnostic apparatus, and a conceptual system for the 'cure of souls'.[2]

Like psychoanalysis, Scientology contains conceptual machinery for the interpretation of failure and opposition. The application of the belief system in terms of therapy[3] has been touched on earlier. Doubt, disbelief, and deviance are attributable to 'Bank', to the 'Reactive Mind'. They are believed to manifest themselves through 'down-statistics' and through 'failure to make case gains'. People who are in contact with suppressives, for example, are said to 'roller coaster'. That is, their 'case' may improve for a while and then deteriorate. The remedy in such a situation may involve Ethics action and further auditing. Dissatisfaction with the results of auditing is also attributable to 'withholds', or to a faulty auditor. Since the practice is held to be uniformly effective if properly applied, it follows that failure to achieve some 'gain' from auditing might be a consequence of 'withholds' on the part of the individual being audited (that is, failure to disclose some thought or deed which should have been reported); or a consequence of the auditor employing 'out-Tech' (that is, some practice not approved, or in a manner not approved, by Hubbard). The responsibility for lack of success from auditing lies always with either the pre-clear or the auditor, never with the theory and technique.[4] Remedies are again available through Ethics action or further auditing.

---

[1] Berger and Luckmann, op. cit., p. 130.

[2] Ibid., pp. 130–1.

[3] In Berger and Luckmann's rather than the medical sense.

[4] 'There are no auditing failures. There are only errors in auditing.' *Professional Auditor's Bulletin*, some time in 1968.

Nihilation is the application of conceptual machinery to the management of challenges emanating from outside the collectivity. It involves endowing the sources of any such challenge with a negative cognitive status,[1] and accounting for it in terms of concepts drawn from the accepted ideology.[2] Nihilation in Scientology rests mainly on the application of a general conspiracy theory to any criticism of, or hostility toward it.

Psychiatrists and supporters of the mental health movement are the leading figures in the conspiracy against Scientology. Psychiatrists are inhuman beings who seek to rule the world. Politicians, state and international agencies are pawns in their strategy to subvert the free world, a strategy that only the Scientology movement is capable of resisting.

> These psychiatric front groups have a very thorough programme of Western destruction.
> 1. Destruction of the Constitution.
> 2. Eradication of boundaries.
> 3. Easy seizure of anyone.
> 4. The 'right' to torture or kill.
> 5. Eradication of all churches.
> 6. Destruction of sexual morality.
> 7. Deprivation of future leaders by the creation of dope addiction in schools.
> All those things and more are to be found throughout their campaign literature, their advices to members and their little puppet political supporters.[3]

> We're playing for blood. The stake is Earth. If we don't make it nobody will. We're the sole agency in existence today that can forestall the erasure of all civilization or bring a new better one.[4]

The leaders of the psychiatric profession and mental health movement are claimed to have had close links with the emergence of Nazism.

> We have traced their origins to two years *before* Hitler and have traced the *Nazi death camps and Nazi philosophy* to this group.[5]

Psychatrists have infiltrated positions of political power and influence. They seek to promote the rise of fascism in order to encourage a communist reaction which will, in the resulting disorder, take over the free world.

> The psychiatrist has masters. His principle organisation, World Federation of Mental Health [sic], and its members, the National Associations of Mental Health, the 'American' Psychiatric Association and the 'American' Psychological Association are directly connected to Russia.
> Even the British Broadcasting Company has stated that psychiatry and the KGB (Russian Secret Police) operate in direct collusion.
> A member of the WHMF, [sic] sits on every 'Advisory Council' of the US Government, to name one government.

[1] Berger and Luckmann, op. cit., p. 132.
[2] Ibid., p. 133.
[3] *Freedom*, 5 (1969). [4] *OEC*, Vol. O, p. 72.
[5] L. Ron Hubbard, 'Enemy finances', *Flag Orders of the Day*, 4 April 1971.

Ministers of Health or Health Authorities are members of the National Association of the WFMH. The psychiatrist has masters.[1]

Since 1938 the psychiatrists and psychologists have advanced a long way toward their goal of power seizure.

They employ terrorism, corruption and blackmail to cow political henchmen. They have taken over education not only in Universities but even in the lesser schools, and are producing a submissive degraded generation over which to rule.[2]

Only Scientology is 'working for the salvage of western civilisation, working effectively . . .'.[3] Hence it is the only barrier to the psychiatric-communist take-over, and therefore subject to attack.

Every single lie, false charge and attack on Scientology has been traced directly to this group's members. They have sought at great expense for 19 years to crush and eradicate any new development in the field of the mind.[4]

Of twenty-one persons found attacking Dianetics and Scientology with rumours and entheta, eighteen of them under investigation were found to be members of the Communist Party or criminals, usually both.[5]

Attacks on Scientology can be explained by Scientology theory through the concepts of 'overt' and 'withhold'.[6] Critics of Scientology have committed crimes which they have not admitted (that is, which they have withheld). Such individuals fear the ability of Scientologists to discover the truth.

Unfortunately the person who does not want you to study Scientology is your enemy as well as ours.

When he harangues against us to you as a 'cult', as a 'hoax', as a very bad thing done by very bad people, he or she is saying 'Please, please, please, don't try to find me out'.

Thousands of such protesting people carefully investigated by us have been found to have unsavoury pasts and sordid motives they did not dare (they felt) permit to come to light. The wife or mother who rails against a family member who takes up Scientology is, we regret to have to say, guided by very impure motives, generated in the morass of dread secrets long withheld. The father, husband, or friend who frowns upon one knowing more about the mind is hiding something that he feels would damage him.[7]

Thus, all criticism of Scientology can be discounted as a product of fear and guilt which is being displaced on to the movement.

[1] L. Ron Hubbard, 'The psychiatrist at work', *HCO Bulletin*, 16 July 1970, reprinted in *Certainty*, 18, 11 (1972). It is not always clear from such polemic whether it is the psychiatrists or the communists who are the 'real' masters.

[2] *Freedom*, 5 (1969).

[3] L. Ron Hubbard, 'The future of Scientology and Western Civilization', Lecture 6 of the *Lectures on Clearing*, London Congress, 1958 (Hubbard Communications Office, London, 1958).

[4] Ibid.

[5] L. Ron Hubbard, *Manual of Justice* [probably HCO, no location, c. 1959]. See also Appendix 3.

[6] See above, p. 108.

[7] L. Ron Hubbard, *Why Some Fight Scientology* (HCO, Washington DC, 1960), p. 5.

There is, however, a further reason to discount the criticisms of Scientology by doctors and psychiatrists. Nihilation may also take the form of a claim that the practice and research of such men itself belatedly supports the revealed truths of Scientology (or of Dianetics, which is now conceived as a kind of preliminary to Scientology).

> The following cutting from a recent 'Time' Magazine was sent to Ron by an auditor in the U.S.A.
> 'Surgeons and Nurses must be careful of what they say even when a patient is anaesthetized, said San Francisco's Dr D——. Even when the patient seems completely "out", he can still hear, and may remember disturbing or embarrassing indiscretions'.
> The auditor adds a comment: 'Thought you might be amused by someone's ten year communication lag'.[1]
> Just as 'medical science' has accepted PRENATAL EXPERIENCE according to their best heralds, the popular magazines such as CORONET and READER'S DIGEST [sic], prenatals fade into the obscurity of curiosa in Dianetics.[2]

Nor is this always entirely accidental. It is further argued that doctors and psychiatrists are in fact acting entirely in bad faith in criticizing Dianetics and Scientology, since they *know* that they work; secretly employ their methods; or have them employed on family members.

> This unreasoning attack on the part of a few has resulted in bad publicity for dianetics. There is some reason to believe that the principles and techniques of dianetics are being used, in some part, by people who have been writing publicly against it.[3]
> Out of 21 psychiatrists in Washington DC, none of whom would use dianetics in their practice, 18 gave me quiet places to audit their wives who through various practices had become intensely neurotic and could not be rescued by psychiatric techniques. This tells us why dianetics gets nowhere in the psychiatric world, brutal as the fact may be.[4]
> On a recent graduate course at Saint Hill on the practise of Dianetics, there were six medical doctors . . . in London, 17 psychiatrists visited our bookshop and bought copies of the standard work on Dianetics.[5]

The technique of nihilation then can serve not only to counter criticism and undermine its cognitive status, it can be used to display that such criticism actually supports and demonstrates the truth of Scientology. As Berger and Luckmann suggest in another context, 'the devil unwittingly glorifies God . . . even . . . the atheist is *really* a believer'.[6]

[1] L. Ron Hubbard, 'Quick on the uptake', *Professional Auditor's Bulletin* (June 1960), p. 10.
[2] L. Ron Hubbard, *A History of Man* (HASI, London, n.d.), p. 12.
[3] 'Editorial', *Dianetic Auditor's Bulletin*, 1, 9 (1951).
[4] Letter from L. Ron Hubbard, *The Ghost of Scientology*, 10 (April–May 1953), p. 4.
[5] *Freedom*, 18 (1969).
[6] Berger and Luckmann, op. cit., p. 133.

Legitimation

The term *legitimation* will here be employed to label the means by which the prevailing social order and institutional practices of the movement are symbolically represented as historically necessary and morally right.[1] Legitimation involves the elaboration of an exoteric ideology which employs a rhetoric acceptable to the bulk of the members to explain and justify tactics of the leadership. Such an ideology should also provide a means of mobilizing sympathy and support from non-members as part of a strategy of 'creating a safe space for Scientology'.

The conspiracy theory outlined above is clearly central to the process of legitimating the organizational behaviour of Scientology. In the face of a world conspiracy to crush the movement, rigorous internal control and 'harsh Ethics' were a necessary defence to prevent infiltration and maintain the organization. 'Attacking the attackers' could also be legitimated by the seriousness of the threat. 'In that, self-defence is an apposite defence. One is not obliged to wait for the first blow to be struck.'[2]

The rhetoric of the wider society can also be deployed for the defence of the movement's beliefs and practices. Scientology could be defined as a 'science'[3] and also as a 'religion'.[4] Whatever the objective merits of these seemingly incompatible claims, they had the useful consequence of providing two alternative sets of imagery for display through the movement's propaganda. Until the early 1960s the rhetoric of Scientology as a 'science' was the more prominent throughout its literature. After the FDA raid in 1963 the public relations apparatus of the movement increasingly stressed the nature of Scientology as a religion.[5] Hence, the FDA seizures and subsequent government actions throughout the world could be characterized as 'religious persecution'.

Since 1968, the movement has also shown a greater concern for social welfare and reform. In that year, the newspaper, *Freedom* was founded which polemicized against psychiatry and the mental health movement claiming to be

---

[1] For the related use of this term by Berger and Luckmann, see ibid., pp. 110–22.

[2] Anonymous, 'Attacks on Scientology and "attack" policies – a wider perspective', photocopy of manuscript, n.d., made available to me by the Church of Scientology, p. 40.

[3] Scientology is an organised body of scientific research knowledge concerning life, life sources and the mind and includes practices that improve the intelligence, state and conduct of persons.' L. Ron Hubbard, 'Definition of Scientology – written by LRH for legal [department] when setting up HASI Ltd', *HCO Bulletin* (9 July 1959).

[4] Anonymous, *Scientology: Twentieth Century Religion* (Church of Scientology World Wide [East Grinstead], 1972).

[5] The movement's Washington publication, *Ability* began printing lists of Sunday services after the FDA raid. See *Ability*, 149 (March 1963).

concerned about the plight of mental patients, and employing the rhetoric of 'Human Rights for Mental Patients'. *Freedom*'s scope broadened progressively in later years. The American Internal Revenue service became the subject of Freedom exposés following the revocation of the tax-exempt status of the Church of Scientology in Washington;[1] and Interpol and the police became the subject of a campaign after the Church of Scientology had instituted proceedings for libel against a number of senior police officers.[2] These campaigns were presented as motivated by a general reformist concern for human rights rather than as a response to particular events involving Scientology and the agencies concerned.

The social reality of Scientology can also be legitimated by reference to its power, its size, its ability to achieve results, and its success as a movement in terms of its wealth. The movement's propaganda generally numbers Scientologists in the millions, and its income and property is a source of considerable pride.

> We own quite a bit of property over the world. We will be acquiring more, as well as some countries.[3]

Comparing Scientology to psychiatrists and supporters of the Mental Health movement, Hubbard stresses these legitimating features:

> There were not 200,000 at their peak. So over the world we outnumber even their rank and file 25 to 1 at a very low estimate. We could buy all they own out of a week's income and never miss it. Although a few skirmishes or even battles are still ahead of us, there is no slightest question as to who is winning this war. The Nazi psychiatrists and Nazi psychotherapists will most surely to the way of the dinosaur [sic]. No, there is no question as to who will win this war. We will.[4]

An aspect of the same public relations exercise is the practice of publicizing the names of any individuals who enter the movement who may have any claim to status or prestige. In the early 1950s an Archbishop of the American Catholic Church, Archbishop Odo Barry was often mentioned as a supporter of Scientology. In recent years a titled former Colonial Governor and his wife, and a titled doctor and his wife (also a doctor) have often been referred to in Scientology publications. Academics, entertainers and artists also frequently appear in the movement's magazines.[5] Such figures can be utilized to provide the basis for a claim that Scientology is successful since even the most prominent people are taking it up.

[1] See *Freedom Reports: The Internal Revenue Service* (Freedom Editorial Offices, Los Angeles, California, 1973).

[2] *Freedom*, early issues in 1974.

[3] L. Ron Hubbard, *Flag Order of the Day*, 20 February, 1971.

[4] L. Ron Hubbard, 'Enemy finances', op. cit.

[5] Disproportionately often for their numerical representation in the movement membership as a whole, as far as one can tell.

Celebrities are taking up Scientology. That's the sign. Remember 20 years ago when artists were taking up psychoanalysis? It is always the beginning of the big win when celebrities – song writers, actors, artists, writers, begin to take something up.[1]

Conclusions

Scientology maintains an extensive public-relations apparatus, the purpose of which is to publicize an image of the movement which will attract new followers, stimulate sympathy and support from non-members for Scientology policies and practices, and rouse antagonism towards Scientology's opponents. This public-relations apparatus aims to legitimate the tactics and hostilities of the movement's leaders by elaborating an exoteric ideology which draws on contemporarily acceptable rhetorics of justification. For example, the esoteric ideology states that:

> We should attack with the end in view of taking over the whole field of Mental Healing.[2]

The exoteric formulation of the movement's motivation is rather differently represented.

> The Scientologists claim that they are in the 'traditional mainstream' of religious reform movements: they state categorically that reforms are needed urgently in the field of mental health, and they make it quite clear that they are not wanting to provide their own technology as a substitute to current psychiatric therapy, but rather, that the psychiatrist should reform his own house . . .[3]

That the published humanitarian aims of the movement's leaders in connection with these wider social issues, are post hoc rationalizations of a power-seeking strategy is suggested by two facts. First, the movement's social reform campaigns have generally *followed* what its leaders regarded as hostile acts or statements by the individuals or agencies concerned. The movement declared itself to be concerned with the rights of mental patients only after psychiatrists and mental health agencies became prominent in the public controversy surrounding Scientology in the early and mid-1960s.[4] It displayed a concern about the rights of those criticized in the press only after it had itself been the victim of such criticism. The Internal Revenue Service of the US government was not attacked until after the revocation of the Church of Scientology's

---

[1] *The Auditor*, 44 (1969), p. 4.

[2] *OEC*, Vol. O, p. 319.

[3] David R. Dalton, *Two Disparate Philosophies* (Regency Press, London, 1973), p. 86.

[4] Although Hubbard has displayed an antipathy towards psychiatrists since the early days of Dianetics, he and Dr Joseph Winter did initially seek the acceptance of the medical and psychiatric professions for Dianetics. It is at least a plausible hypothesis that Hubbard's hostility towards psychiatrists stems from their rejection of his 'science of the mind'.

tax-exempt status. Nor did the movement mount a campaign against 'police abuse' by means of 'falsified records', police corruption, and infringements of the rights of the citizens, until after it had issued writs for libel against a number of senior policemen in connection with Interpol files.

Second, the movement's social reform and social welfare campaigns are usually very short-lived. Allied Scientists of the World, United Survival Clubs, the National Academy of American Psychology, Citizens of Washington Inc, the Constitutional Administration Party, and the Citizen's Press Association, did not prove effective in the pursuit of the goals of the movement leadership, and were dropped very quickly.[1] (It is worth noting that the Citizen's Commission on Human Rights [founded in 1968], and Narconon [founded in 1966] persist and seem to indicate a trend toward more durable social reform activity.) However, while the motivation of the movement's leaders for such propaganda activities may be that of 'securing a safe space for Scientology' and extending its control over its social environment, there can be no doubt that many, perhaps all, of the ordinary members who involve themselves in these propaganda exercises do so out of genuine conviction. As in the case of the Communist movement, the specific reformist programmes of Scientology may be a source of appeal to lower-echelon members who are not privy to the esoteric, power-seeking strategy of the leadership.[2]

The propaganda and public-relations activities of the movement are important reality-maintaining devices, the objects of which are to increase the respectability of the movement and its public acceptance as a new religious denomination unjustly persecuted by an insidious and sinister conspiracy. They form part of a battery of techniques that defends the movement against internal challenges and supports the validity of the view of social reality which it embodies.

(The increased social reform activity of the movement has been represented to me rather differently by an executive of Scientology. He argued that the movement leadership became increasingly aware after 1968 that the problems which the movement had faced up to that time were in large part a result of their prior failure to take sufficient responsibility for social reform. This conflicts with my own interpretation that such activity was strategically motivated. I should stress, however, that while I see no necessary implications for social reform in the individualistic theory and practice of Scientology, reformist concerns appear to have been a persistent feature of Hubbard's thought since the

---

[1] One of his early associates recalled that Hubbard was prolific in the generation of organizational ideas which he would institute on a trial basis. His attitude to these tactics was expressed by the phrase: 'Run it up the flagpole, and see who salutes it' my informant recollects. (Interview.)

[2] Gabriel A. Almond et al., *The Appeals of Communism* (Princeton University Press, Princeton, New Jersey, 1954), Philip Selznick, *The Organizational Weapon* (Free Press, Glencoe, 1960).

earliest days of Dianetics. They are also of undoubted importance to many followers of the movement who have sincere convictions regarding the plight of the hospitalized mental patient, drug-addicts, and the educationally deprived. The sincerity of those involved is less at issue than the character of the circumstances in which such feelings are mobilized as part of an organized programme of reformist activity.)

Part IV
CONCLUSIONS

CONCLUSIONS

Scientology is a manipulationist movement. It offers a set of theories and techniques which explain the situation of the individual in this life, and provide
means of improving that situation. While these techniques may be directed
ultimately to the liberation of man's spiritual nature, this ultimate end is not a
well-elaborated condition, the virtues of which are clearly explicated in doctrinal literature. This literature concentrates upon more proximal goals. Salvation is envisaged in terms of the alleviation of psychosomatic ills, relief from
psychological disabilities, remedies for lack of success or loneliness, or means of
improving one's efficiency and competence in the world as we know it. No
radical challenge is offered to prevailing values. Rather means, held to surpass
any other means available, are provided for achieving these culturally valued
ends. Salvation is this-worldly in character, and achieved by the individual
through a client relationship with the dispensing organization rather than as a
collective or communal achievement. Communication within the movement is
relatively impersonal; relationships are role-articulated; and the organization is
bureaucratic.

Scientology and the contemporary religious climate

While Scientology may, at first glance, appear to mark a radical discontinuity
with the Western religious tradition, the characteristics summarized above and
described in detail in earlier chapters, identify it, in fact, as a logical outcome
and extension of certain central features of that tradition.

The roots of the progressive secularization of western societies, particularly
Protestant western societies, have been traced back to Old Testament Judaism.
The God of Ancient Israel, unlike those of neighbouring societies, was a radically transcendent God who made severe ethical demands upon his followers
and was immune to magical manipulation. Hence, there was a polarization
between Man and God, with a thoroughly demythologized cosmos between
them.[1]

This conception of God and the universe was carried over into Christianity,
although Catholicism implemented a progressive remythologization of the

[1] Peter L. Berger, *The Social Reality of Religion* (Faber, London, 1969), Chapter 5.

cosmos in important respects. Angels and saints as semi-divine beings peopled the universe. Mary was elevated as a mediator and co-redeemer with Christ. The divine could be manipulated through ritual, confession and penance, undermining the trend toward ethical rationalization. Hence, the Reformation marked the re-emergence of the rationalizing potential of Judeo-Christianity.

On Weber's account of the relationship between religious and social change in this period, the predestinarianism and ethical rigorism of Calvinist Protestantism led to a fundamental rationalization of the believer's way of life and thought.[1] Without objective indicators of salvational status, the believer sought a subjective conviction of salvation through the practice of asceticism and methodical planning in his vocation, and in his life beyond. Rational calculation became a central component of the methodology of securing this conviction, leading to increased productive efficiency and industrial acceleration.

The consequence of this process, however, was the subversion of the religious aims and motivations which caused its emergence. Industrial and economic rationalization led to industrialization and urbanization, social mobility, and social differentiation. The rationalization of man's relationship with the universe between him and God led to the development of science.[2] These trends in turn led to further secularization.

The efficacy of science and technology in producing viable explanations of, and improvements in, the world pushed back the domain into which religion could authoritatively offer insight. The state and other political institutions faced with the integration of a differentiated mass citizenry increasingly became organized on bureaucratic lines. As in the economic sphere, so in the political sphere, the need to organize and control a massive administrative machine and enormous investments, and to satisfy the diverse interests of a mass clientele, led to increasing reliance on empirical, pragmatic, and scientific rather than religious bases for state action and political decision.

Social differentiation led to the emergence of distinctive social groups and strata whose world-views might overlap with those of neighbouring groups only marginally. New religious movements emerged to provide religious rationales and direction more immediately suited to the needs of the members of such groups. Thus in advanced industrial societies a situation of religious pluralism prevails, in which religious institutions and collectivities are in competition for a clientele.[3]

As Peter Berger has argued, pluralism tends to lead to a religious *market*, in

---

[1] Max Weber, *The Protestant Ethic and the Spirit of Capitalism* (Unwin, London, 1930).

[2] On Merton's account: Robert K. Merton, *Science, Technology and Society in Seventeenth Century England* (Harper, London, 1970); although the matter is much debated. See the papers on this issue in George Basalla, ed., *The Rise of Modern Science: Internal or External Factors?* (D. C. Heath & Co., Lexington, Mass, 1968).

[3] Peter L. Berger, 'Secularisation and pluralism', *International Yearbook for the Sociology of Religion*, 2 (1966), pp. 73–84.

which supplying organizations may become subject to the same mechanisms constraining survival as organizations in any other consumer commodity market. Maintaining the viability of the organization requires the generation of consumers. The desire by organizational leaders to expand the market can lead to the tailoring of products to fit consumer demand. Public-relations and salesmanship may come to take on a central importance in maintaining the prominence and acceptability of the religious brand-name. Religious organizations may experience pressures to rationalize budgeting and 'production' in order to compete in the market, and hence, may tend to become increasingly bureaucratized in order to increase operating efficiency. In order to attract consumers in a mass market, competing 'products' may tend to become only marginally differentiated, with more or less the same characteristics but different labels, to maintain brand loyalty. To minimize the costs of free competition, deals may be entered into with competitors, sometimes leading to a restriction of territory by each supplier or, more recently, to the familiar market process of merger, or ecumenicalism.[1]

In these circumstances, shifts in market demand will tend to be reflected in the character of the products supplied, to meet consumer preference. Thus the average consumer today may be less in need of a cosmology than of a solution to anxiety and other sources of psychological concern.[2] Some religious institutions have increasingly seen their role as the provision of these goods, shifting their attention from the provision of heavenly salvation to that of psychological reassurance.

The situation of religious pluralism may be seen as a severe blow to claims of absolute validity for any given church's doctrine, particularly as it is obliged to modify it in the face of changing consumer demand. The view of its beliefs as timeless and irrefutable truths may become increasingly hard to sustain. Religious belief may tend to lose any self-evident objective plausibility that could be maintained in a situation of religious monopoly. Religion in this situation may increasingly move away from being an objective reality to become a purely personal and primarily individual reality, and a solely *inner* experience.[3]

In this light, it is evident that Scientology emerged as a religious commodity eminently suited to the contemporary market. It provided assurance of fundamental ability and competence within every consumer, and offered to resolve all the major psychological problems of modern man. It was packaged in a rhetoric of science which had a widespread popular appeal. Its organization, and the production of the commodity it purveys were thoroughly rationalized. It

[1] Ibid.

[2] This seems to be the implication of Louis Schneider and Sanford M. Dornbusch, 'Inspirational religious literature: from latent to manifest functions of religion', *AJS*, 62 (1957), pp. 476–81; and idem, *Popular Religion: Inspirational Books in America* (University of Chicago Press, Chicago, 1958).

[3] Peter L. Berger, 'Secularization and pluralism', op. cit.

developed to a level far in advance of most other contemporary religious movements and institutions the techniques of salesmanship and public relations.

Rather than the traditional church, Scientology has drawn its organizational model from institutions more appropriate to its market situation. The mass political party and the mass educational institution have clearly been important influences on the organization's development. More important than these, however, is the institution which has proved most successful in the contemporary market economy. Scientology is organized on lines similar to those of multi-national enterprises such as the Ford Motor Company, Coca Cola, or International Telephone and Telegraph.[1]

Scientology represents a logical outcome of the incorporation of the Protestant Ethic into Western culture. Rationalization of life in the world has led to the rationalization of the institution through which salvation is secured. Rational calculation has led to the provision of salvation as a standardized and differentiated commodity available at a set rate per unit (with discounts for cash in advance, plus Value Added Tax).

L. Ron Hubbard: the generation and institutionalization of charisma

Ron Hubbard, after a varied career in the course of which he came to puzzle over the operation of the mind and the explanation of mental phenomena, established himself as a thaumaturge. On the basis of a set of techniques with which he was experimenting, and a half-formulated rationale, he practised as a magical healer. In Hollywood and Bay Head, New Jersey, he gathered a small clientele. After a period of probably no more than a few months, Hubbard desired to broadcast his practices to the world, and steps were taken through the establishment of the New Jersey Foundation to institutionalize the practice and organize his clientele.

Acquaintances of Hubbard recall him, even before Dianetics, as a man of powerful personality. His early followers commented that 'he was able to make you feel things that you had never felt before'.[2] Hubbard was always completely convinced of the validity of what he was doing. He possessed a sense of absolute certainty of his own ability and the truth of what he said, or at least he was able to convey such a conviction to others. I have been able to trace no occasion on which Hubbard ever admitted to making a mistake, or apologized in any way. He seemed to lack the capacity to doubt, and in his personality and self-assurance others were able to see the strengths that they lacked, and thereby found him easier to believe.

Joseph Nyomarkay notes that

---

[1] Charles J. McMillan, 'Corporations without citizenship: the emergence of multi-national enterprise' in Graeme Salaman and Kenneth Thompson, eds, *People and Organisations* (Longman, London, 1973), pp. 25–44.

[2] Interview.

. . . no matter how extraordinary he may be, a person will not become a charismatic leader unless his extraordinariness is recognised by others. The transformation of extraordinariness into charisma depends on the political skills and magnetism of the potential charismatic leader and on his conviction of his historical role.[1]

The Dianetics following accorded Hubbard a superior status as the founder of the science, but for many he remained only primus inter pares. While he was generally acknowledged to be the leader of the movement, this gave him no permanent claim to authority. Others believed themselves equally competent to develop the movement's theory and practice and to challenge Hubbard's decisions and behaviour.

His situation was highly insecure. The revelation which he had made public was open to subversion by innovators. The movement's following was fluid and fickle, with only limited commitment to a healing and self-improvement cult, and even less to its leader. His status as leader was open to frequent, albeit somewhat tentative, challenge from local leaders in the field; and his income seemed likely to decline drastically with the slump in Dianetics by the beginning of 1951.

In response to this situation, Hubbard developed as a separate enterprise Scientology, a new gnosis, which provided a transcendental legitimation for his authority. He had penetrated the realm of the supernatural and there secured knowledge which would restore to men their long lost spiritual abilities. On the basis of this new doctrine, Hubbard began to organize his following as a congregation responsive to his charismatic authority. He had transformed himself from a *magician*, to a *mystagogue*.[2]

His extraordinary character was transformed into charismatic authority by a process of subordinating other potential leaders, and expelling those who refused to accept his sole authority. Through control of the movement's publications he determined what was to be represented as correct doctrine and practice, and hence secured a virtual monopoly of the means of revelation. In these publications he skilfully promoted an image of himself as a superior human being.[3] Hubbard's was the only name to figure prominently in movement publications. Even when he later withdrew from active personal involvement in the daily operation of the Orgs, his photograph and other symbols of his presence continued to be widely displayed in Scientology buildings. Members were enjoined

---

[1] Joseph Nyomarkay, *Charisma and Factionalism in the Nazi Party* (University of Minnesota Press, Minneapolis, 1967), p. 11.

[2] Max Weber, *Sociology of Religion* (Methuen, London, 1965), pp. 47, 54, 55, 61.

[3] One of the means by which he achieved this end was through writing eulogistic articles about himself under the name of Tom Esterbrook. See Helen O'Brien, *Dianetics in Limbo* (Whitmore Publishing Co., Philadelphia, 1966), p. 69. (The Scientologists point out to me that 'Tom Esterbrook' was a 'house name in the magazine. Anyone in the understaffed organization with writing ability would write an article under the house name.' Personal Communication, November 1974).

to write to 'Ron' personally with problems they might have, and students were encouraged to study hard lest one day they meet Ron and he query them on some aspect of theory or practice.[1]

The attitude of Hubbard's following towards their leader justifies the description of him as charismatic. Scientologists see Hubbard as having privileged access to supernatural knowledge of a kind never before revealed, which rendered established disciplines such as psychology and philosophy obsolete. Hubbard had located a means of transcending human limitation and the downward spiral of man's spiritual nature. Like Buddha, he had made available a route to Total Freedom.

Indeed recently Hubbard has been presented, in publications for advanced students, as the Maitreya Buddha supposedly prophesied to appear by Gautama Buddha.[2] The Maitreya would, it is believed by some Buddhists, appear when corruption and spiritual degeneration had proceeded apace, at some point in the 5000 years after Gautama Buddha's translation to Nirvana. The Maitreya would herald a new spiritual and world order, and is the object of millennialist aspiration among some sectors of Buddhists.[3] Hubbard's identification as the Maitreya may mark his transformation from mystagogue to *exemplary prophet*:

> an exemplary man who, by his personal example, demonstrates to others the way to religious salvation, as in the case of the Buddha. The preaching of this type of prophet says nothing about the divine mission or an ethical duty of obedience, but rather directs itself to the self-interest of those who crave salvation, recommending to them the same path as he himself traversed.[4]

Weber's distinction between the mystagogue and the exemplary prophet is largely a matter of degree. The mystagogue does not proclaim an ethical doctrine, distributes primarily magical salvation, and normally makes a living from his practice. Over the past decade or so, Hubbard has insisted that he derives little or no income from Scientology. The movement has adopted a much more self-consciously religious character, and laid increasing stress upon its ethical content, marking itself off from the degeneration and corruption of the surrounding world. Moreover, it has correspondingly stressed the character of Scientology as a *philosophy of life* rather than merely a set of techniques for therapeutic or self-improvement purposes. In this context, Hubbard may now appropriately be seen as an exemplary prophet.

[1] Notices to this effect were displayed in the Org classrooms.

[2] *Advance!* issue 26 (November 1974); issue 27 (December 1974). I am grateful to Mr Beau Kitselman for bringing these to my attention.

[3] Winston L. King, *A Thousand Lives Away* (Bruno Cassirer, Oxford, 1964); Melford E. Spiro, *Buddhism and Society: Great Tradition and its Burmese Vicissitudes* (Allen & Unwin, 1971).

[4] Max Weber, 'The Prophet', in his *The Sociology of Religion* (Methuen, London, 1966), p. 55.

Sectarianization

The Dianetics movement contained within it the possibility of development in a number of directions. There were those among its following who sought to develop the theory and practice as a science. They wished to subject it to rigorous empirical test under controlled conditions, and to refine its theory and practice on the basis of such public procedures. There were those among its following who saw Dianetics as an 'added blessing', one further methodology and set of techniques by which salvation could be secured. They wished to select from its beliefs and practice those which they regarded as suitable to combine with the corpus of 'truth' already possessed; or to advance new theories and techniques, developing the foundations Hubbard had laid. There were, finally, those who saw salvation as available only through Hubbard's relevation, which constituted an exclusive path. They wished to preserve the beliefs and practices from dilution and contamination, permitting only those additions and modifications which Hubbard sponsored or invented.

Dianetics could conceivably have developed into a science, or at least a 'respectable' therapeutic practice, as have psychoanalysis or gestalt psychology. It could have persisted as a diffuse cultic movement with many organizations, leaders, and variations on a central core of shared belief and practice, as has New Thought. Ron Hubbard its founder, however, was among those who viewed the movement in sectarian terms. To secure his own position as a mystagogue, Hubbard broke with the leaders who defined the movement in more 'cultic' or 'scientific' terms.

On the basis of his new gnosis he centralized authority within the movement, distinguished its doctrine and practice from competing belief systems, and sought through the erection of an increasingly elaborate hierarchy of sanctification, to mobilize greater commitment and involvement on the part of his following. The earlier individualism of the movement now became something to denigrate:

> Obsessive individualism and a failure to organise were responsible for our getting into the state we got into.[1]

The radical shift towards a more sectarian stance did not occur, however, until the movement was threatened internally by schism and defection, and externally by hostility from press and state. Defections by senior executives and the potential for schism led Hubbard to institute tighter social control measures. The boundary between the movement and the world became less fluid. Less tolerance was shown toward nonconformity by members. Greater bureaucratization was implemented to increase control over operations. As criticism was voiced and sanctions introduced against the movement by outside agencies, the movement became increasingly hostile to the surrounding society, its organization became tighter, and expulsions became more frequent.

[1] L. Ron Hubbard, *HCO Policy Letter*, 17 January 1967.

Beliefs and practices

The belief-system of the movement developed from a lay psychotherapeutic system to a religious doctrine. Although this transformation may also have secured other ends such as legitimating Hubbard's authority, it can be seen as primarily an attempt to rationalize the movement's beliefs.

Dianetics provided a secular solution to the problem of theodicy. Suffering, guilt, inadequacy, disability, lack of success, the apparent arbitrariness of the distribution of favour and fortune, were accounted for in terms of the tone-scale and the theory of engrams. Whatever its practical success in alleviating these conditions, it failed in this more ultimate enterprise. Learning that the individual's abilities were the consequence of engramic trauma failed to resolve the issue of why a particular individual suffered the trauma and hence the disabilities. Scientology offered a solution to this problem through a metaphysics of the thetan and transmigration. The thetan had become bored with his omniscience, permitted limitations upon his abilities, and allowed himself to become increasingly the effect rather than the cause of the environment which he had created. Thus ultimately the thetan was responsible for everything that happened subsequently. More directly, the disabilities suffered in this life were a consequence of things he had done in previous lives. Hence the problem of theodicy was resolved by a quasi-karmic theory of sin and retribution.

The belief-system and practices of the movement developed in part as a result of empirical phenomena: the 'past life' material produced by pre-clears in Dianetic sessions, and the failure of the techniques (directed to engrams sustained in this life) to clear all the cases attempted. However, these only further heightened the problem of meaning which rationalization aimed to resolve. The explanation of such phenomena was sought in more ultimate realms. The problem of theodicy was shifted back, even if no final or complete solution to it could be provided.

The practice of Scientology was also rationalized. The E-meter represented a substantial development away from subjective and intuitive methods of auditing. A calculated and measurable score indicated in an objective way marked the progress and success of auditing. From a skilled technique requiring diffuse professional abilities, auditing became a semi-skilled occupation, which effectively anyone could learn. Training was rationalized on the basis of an established, standardized body of knowledge available entirely on an impersonal basis through Hubbard's writings.

The organization of Scientology

As we argued earlier, Scientology has more in common organizationally with mass political parties, institutions of mass education, or multinational corporations, than with traditional churches. Its followers are drawn into no collective communion but rather into an atomized mass, differentiated only by their level of attainment in the theory and practice of the gnosis. With few institution-alized links among the members, communication and authority flow downwards from the leaders to the member who faces the authority-structure of the move-ment as an isolated individual. The only collective means of influencing the decision-making process is that in which the members 'vote with their feet' through defection or apathy.

The movement's earlier patrimonial administration exercised by a band of functionary-disciples has gradually been supplanted by an imposing bureau-cratic machine. Autonomous and independent sources of authority or organiza-tion outside the bureaucracy have been progressively eliminated, or brought under its direct administration. Professional practitioners have been reduced to organizational functionaries. Members are increasingly brought under organi-zational control as leaders seek to mobilize their resources for organizational ends.

Beyond the jurisdiction of the bureaucracy and possessing superior authority, exists an elite corps, the Sea Org, which acts as the direct executive arm of the charismatic leader of the movement. The Sea Org provides an international executive force insulated from local commitments, and mobilizable to secure conformity from the bureaucratic administration and to prevent it acquiring any independent authority to challenge Hubbard's own.

Scientology and society

Emerging in America as a therapeutic movement, Dianetics was the object of hostility from the established healing professions. The movement and its leader were criticized and ridiculed in the press and subjected to legal action instigated by medical agencies. In the light of his developing theory these attacks upon Hubbard and his science could only be interpreted as a consequence of the fact that the critics had 'something to hide'.

With the submergence of Dianetics and the disappearance of the mass following, Hubbard and his movement rarely came to the attention of state and medical agencies. The gradual growth of Scientology during the late 1950s and early 1960s brought it once again under surveillance. The severe actions taken by these agencies in the form of the FDA raid, the virulence of the Anderson Report, and the British Home Office ban on foreign students, convinced Hub-bard that Scientology had become the victim of an immense conspiracy aimed at its extermination. Behind every hostile act seemed to lurk the figure of a psychiatrist or a Mental Health Association, all connected in more or less 'mysterious' ways with the World Federation for Mental Health. This con-spiracy became linked in Hubbard's mind with that of many another populist American, the international Communist conspiracy.

Determined to fight what had become systematized in his mind as a concerted campaign to crush Scientology, Hubbard and other leaders of the movement sought to defend it against the onslaught, and even to counterattack. In the belief that the tactics of their opponents were immoral and that the end was so vital as to justify the means employed, Scientologists may at times have felt called upon to defend the movement by tactics that may have seemed extreme to outsiders.

The deviance-amplification model suggests that when relatively unsystematic and transient deviant behaviour becomes the object of moral crusading and severe stigmatization, one possible outcome is that those so stigmatized experience a sense of outrage and injustice which alienates them from conventional norms and from the agents of the conventional order, and leads to the elaboration of new norms in defence against attack. The new norms and the behaviour to which they give rise are seen by the moral crusaders as further evidence of deviance and justification of their initial diagnosis. Such a process appears to characterize the development of Scientology in its relations with the wider society in the 1960s.

Particularly since the mid-1960s, however, the movement has begun to present itself in a different light. It has officially dropped a number of its practices which were subject to public criticism. It has become more actively involved in programmes and campaigns for social reform. These reform campaigns have been initiated in such areas as drug rehabilitation, the human rights of mental patients, educational programmes for school and college dropouts and, latterly, campaigns against abuses of their powers by the police and other state agencies.

At the same time, there are beginning to appear signs that Scientology is coming to be recognized as a legitimate and valid religious collectivity. It has been accorded a measure of recognition in Australia through legal authorization as a body permitted to solemnize marriages. Those states which have passed discriminatory legislation against the practice of Scientology have revised, or are in the process of revising, this legislation, and various legal decisions have accepted the movement's claim to religious status. Hostile press reports on Scientology are now rare.

In terms of the typology outlined in Chapter 1, this may signify a transition of Scientology from a collectivity regarded by members of society at large as 'deviant' to one regarded as 'respectable'. Christian Science perhaps acquired its respectable status as a consequence of its church structure and religious practice, rather than as a result of any acceptance of its therapeutic system.[1] Scientology has, similarly, increasingly stressed its religious character and subdued its claims to therapeutic efficacy. It may therefore come, in time, to be accorded the same sort of status as is accorded Christian Science today.

There are also signs that Scientology is adopting a more tolerant attitude toward other belief-systems. The movement's criticisms of psychiatry have lost

[1] I am indebted to Dr Bryan Wilson for this point.

some of their earlier virulence in their more recent publications. The compatibility of belief in Scientology and continued membership in other religious denominations has been much publicized in movement literature. From some future perspective it may appear that Scientology is undergoing a clear process of denominationalization. From the perspective of the present time, however, it is impossible to be certain if what we are viewing is a genuine process of accommodation with the surrounding society and competing systems of belief, or whether it is merely a public-relations facade, an exercise in impression-management, designed to convey that image, while masking persistent sectarian aims. The question that remains, perhaps to be determined by research at some future time, is whether Scientology is in fact undergoing a process of denominationalization or whether it is undergoing a process of '*pseudo*-denominationalization', in which it is merely *presented* as denominational in character in order to defend the movement against further attack, to mobilize support, and to retain an appeal to a mass clientele which might otherwise seek salvation from less controversial sources.[1]

[1] Similarly, whether Scientology is undergoing *institutionalization* in the sense employed by Hans Toch, is also an interesting question to which only time can provide the answer, that is:

'a process . . . characterized by the tedency to relegate ideology more and more to a position of a means to ends. Whenever a belief becomes an impediment to public acceptance, it is modified or abandoned. Changes in belief may even represent anticipations of future inconvenience for the adapting movement.'

Hans Toch, *The Social Psychology of Social Movements* (Methuen, 1971), p. 215.

APPENDICES

APPENDIX 1: SPECIAL LETTER FROM RON HOWES[1]

The following is addressed to all optimum and pre-optimum humans:
The primary step in the production of an optimum race is the invention of a higher tone reality.

> To be optimum this reality must have self-corrective machinery determined by firm, dynamic goals. The inventor of a suitable reality is forced by the race life-cause and assisted by race-intelligence to communicate the invention.

The second step toward optimum-race-purpose is the acceptance of the invention by units of the race.

> Within a given race each unit possesses basic endowments. From unit to unit these endowments remain similar. Each unit acceptance of the invention implies nearly complete capabilities necessary to full use of the invention.

The third step for optimum-race-production is the formation of true groups.

> A true group is an assemblage of units whose efforts are coordinated aligned for the basic goals of the invention. A true group is formed by units of the race.

The fourth step is establishment of true communication among all groups and units of the race.

> Race dynamics insure the integrated results of all steps.

To aid in the progress necessary for application of the above principles certain mechanical features may be brought into use. Since the second month, tenth day, of this year, there has been in existence a field of psycho-mechanical structure. This field is directional and can be beamed through an area three thousand miles in radius. The source of this field will stand unknown. The field produces the following:

1. Amplifications of causative factors in the race.
2. Temporary enrichment of mind-reality applied to desire and need.
3. Communication enhancement among units of the race.

The above has been written in basic American.
As of the fourth month, first day, this field will extend to maximum radius and continue through the third day.

---

[1] Gordon Beckstead, ed., *Prologue to Survival*, Part I (Psychological Research Foundation, Phoenix, Arizona, 1952).

Following this test signal, the writer will be appreciative if persons interested communicate subjective and objective data to the address given.

In so far as possible, use the principle of minimum effort in reports. Some data has been gathered concerning items of extreme interest to optimum persons. If the optimum person wishes, this data will be communicated. The optimum person can request the data.

The method of request is available to these persons.

Editor's Note: Postmark date of the above, March 5. A field test occurred March first through third. Data are requested for observations (positive, null, or negative) during this period. Ron assured me by telephone that the machine producing the field, though crude at this time, exists. A large number of reports for both March and April should enable him to make allowances for the influence of suggestion. Send reports to Ron Howes, 3020 Rawleigh Ave., Apt. 102, St. Louis Park, Minneapolis 6, Minn.

APPENDIX II: HCO ETHICS ORDER

To: Those concerned   Date: 29 June 1965
From: A/HCO EXECUTIVE SECRETARY
       FOR OFFICE OF LRH

Subject: Suppressive Person

I. RALPH GLASER is declared a Suppressive Person for the following reasons:

A. He failed to handle or disconnect from his wife as ordered by Natalie Fisher on May 5, 1965. By his own testimony, 'The more I gain, the more she natters,' his wife is Suppressive to him; three weeks elapsed from the time of the order from Natalie until his next interview with Ethics, which might have been construed as rescinding Natalie's order.

B. He has repeatedly done the Crime of heckling Scientology instructor or lecturer. For example:

1. Donna Fisk, Night Theory Instructor, was discussing questions on the cancellation of Student Rules and Regulations with the class; in particular, a question concerning the use of alcoholic beverages. Ralph introduced the question as to whether tobacco was more harmful than other drugs and alcohol; Donna replied she had never seen deleterious technical effects of it, but had seen these on alcohol; Ralph pressed the question, she replied she did not know; he pressed it further, and required finally a statement that that was all on that point before he would stop.

2. Pem Wall was explaining to class the no-checkout system in Theory. Ralph questioned the reason for this. Pem said he could not give Ron's reasons, any he could give would be his own. Ralph pressed for these, Pem said one would be to make the student take responsibility for learning the material, himself, rather than leaving it to an instructor to determine. Ralph remarked that, then the next logical step would be for students to not come in at all.

3. Wayne Rohrer was discussing Ethics with the class, and stated that it was a kindness to a Suppressive Person to declare him as such. Ralph remarked, sarcastically, that there was such a thing as killing a person with kindness.

4. Wayne Rohrer was introducing the policy of the Free Scientology Center to the class. Ralph objected to this, causing student Marie Page to cringe, and Bill Gibbons to attempt to counter the objections. Ralph stated that he could not attend the FSC, Wayne acknowledged, Ralph said he needed more than an acknowledgement, Wayne said, then he would send Ralph to Ethics.

5. Wayne Rohrer was discussing policy on Suppressive Persons with the class, Ralph presented a series of far-fetched circumstances such as, what if the phone company were declared suppressive, which Wayne explained; finally, Wayne said that Ralph could keep mocking these up and he, Wayne, handling them, but it was not going to get them anywhere, Ralph persisted still further, Wayne finally dismissed him with an 'example' of, what if one were trapped in an elevator with a Suppressive Person.

(The above are given as specific examples, not to be construed as the totality of repetitions of this Crime; many more exist.)

II. That, before the label 'Suppressive Person' is removed, Ralph must also discontinue his project of correspondence with and concerning the FDA, the AMA; since these groups are Suppressive and his continued communication with them would make him immediately a Potential Trouble Source and then if continued, again, a Suppressive Person.

John H Higginbottom, Jr.
A/HCO EXECUTIVE SECRETARY
FOR OFFICE OF LRH

(SEAL)

APPENDIX III. EXECUTIVE DIRECTIVE FROM L. RON HUBBARD

LRH ED 55 INT   Date 29 November 1968

The War

You may not realize it staff member but there is only one small group that has hammered Dianetics and Scientology for 18 years.

The press attacks, the public upsets you receive and all those you have received for all your time in Scientology were generated by this one group.

For eighteen years it has poured lies and slander into the press and government agencies.

Last year we isolated a dozen men at the top. This year we found the organisation these used and all its connections over the world.

They are as red as paint. Their former president was a card-carrying Communist and they have four on their Board of Directors, yet they reach into International Finance, Health Ministries, Schools, the press. They even control immigration in many lands.

Psychiatry and 'Mental Health' was chosen as a vehicle to undermine and destroy the West! And we stood in their way.

They knew we had the answers. We were over $2,000,000 dangerous to them. That's about what they've spent to try to get rid of us.

Well, today, the World Federation of Mental Health (which pretends to be part of the United Nations and isn't) and their 'National' Mental Health organisations (which pretend to be part of each national government and aren't) in every western nation have been spotted by us and proven to be the ones responsible.

If a platoon of Russian soldiers landed in your country and started shooting down people, the military or the citizens would wipe them out.

But if several regiments landed in small groups, with phoney passports, dressed in dark business suits, each one vouched for as a professional doctor by the 'best people', they could (and do) select out everyone they wish to kill, get him behind closed doors in an institution and de-personalise or kill him.

They have infiltrated boards of education, the armed services, even the churches.

They hold the wives or daughters of a great many politicians and keep them 'under treatment'.

They appoint Ministers of Health by pretending they are already part of the government.

They collect millions.

Their 'technology' is the same as that used by Intelligence Services. Electric shock. Brain operations. These were used in Lubenka Prison in Russia but are not allowed on Russians!

Anyway, this was the live wire we got across by being *able to undo their effect on the West*.

None of this is fiction. There are too many dead men around for that.

We have the goods on them and right this minute more art is being rolled up by us from more quarters than they could predict.

We've made a beach head. We are slamming in closer.

You aren't standing alone. There is more ammunition being flung at them right this minute than they could ever duck.

They made a few gains. They could even make one or two more.

But they made a bad mistake. They attacked us. And we weren't even in the same line of country.

For eighteen years we have had constant sniping at us over the world. They did it.

We've got to fight this one on through and we will.

Think of what it would be like to have no such opposition!!!! My, how we would expand. And will.

You just carry on your job well, do it very well. Keep the show on the road. Get the stats up.

A lot of good guys amongst us are taking care of *them*. We are using only legal means over the world. *We* don't stoop to murder and rough house. But man, the effectiveness of our means will become history.

It is a tough war. All wars are tough. It isn't over.

But if the enemy knew all that was heading in his direction this minute from how many quarters he'd faint.

Let him lah-de-dah with the socialites and 'best people' a little longer. Let him pose as part of the government yet a little while. And then he's had it.

Our error was in failing to take over total control of all mental healing in the West. Well, we'll do that too.

You never did understand his treatments? Well so the psychiatrist acts like a Russian storm trooper after all.

L. RON HUBBARD
Founder

APPENDIX IV. ON ROY WALLIS' STUDY

J. L. Simmons Ph.D.[1]

Roy Wallis has written some interesting passages and he has expounded some knarly conceptual schemes. Unfortunately, his study has little to do with Dianetics and Scientology, his subject matter.

Wallis might have done a lot of things. An objective study of Scientology as a social movement in our time would have been interesting. A no-nonsense statistical analysis of psychological and intelligence test scores before and after Scientology experiences, with a carefully matched control group who had no contact with Scientology would have been quite informative. An analysis of the growth of Scientology as a world-wide organization would have yielded invaluable 'challenge and response' data to the social scientist. A 'Sociology of Religion' study of Scientology might have proved enlightening to both author and reader. An anthropological field study of how people get into Scientology and how it then affects their lives and their environment might have had all the excitement of a Margaret Mead book on exotic civilizations. Wallis has regrettably done none of these things.

What has he done? He has produced a piece of work that would probably fetch him a critical mark in any traditional university Research Methods class. When I taught Research Methods and Statistics classes at the University of Illinois I demanded – and got – better, less biased work from my undergraduate students.

Since Wallis has credentials I can only assume that his violations of the scientific method are indicative of either a decline in scholastic method or are deliberate and malicious.

I will document specific violations and biases a bit later but first I would like to speculate on *why* they might have occurred. The answer might lie in the sociological concept of 'culture lag', which is the almost inevitable time lag between the development of an invention, a new idea, a new viewpoint, and its general acceptance by the surrounding society. This period is almost always accompanied by resistance, harassment, and debunking of the new by Authorities. Often as not, violence is perpetrated upon the heads of the originators and their early followers. Virtually every new development in the history of the

---

[1] Formerly, Department of Sociology faculty, University of Illinois and University of California, Santa Barbara.

world has had to survive (if it did indeed survive) in the teeth of such a culture lag.

Dianetics and Scientology technology contain more than enough discoveries to have set the culture-lag mechanism in motion. As one small example, the press widely ridiculed L. Ron Hubbard's breakthrough plant researches where he demonstrated with full scientific rigor that plants are directly affected by the emotional outflows of the people in their vicinity. A dozen years later the same press excitedly told the world about the new discoveries that plants are affected by the emotions of the people around them, with no mention of Hubbard's earlier work.

Now social scientists themselves sometimes fall prey to culture-lag mechanisms so that they end up dramatizing this phenomenon rather than studying it. It is only my speculation, but I suspect this to be the case with Wallis. It is my impression from his description that he found the Scientology Communications Course he had enrolled in, filled with ideas and concepts that were new and different enough to jar his preconceived worldview. And so a 'culture lag' was created on the spot. My supposition would explain why Wallis sought so diligently for ulterior motives in the movement and why he listened so eagerly (and almost exclusively) to Scientology dropouts. Some such mechanism must have occurred – I cannot believe that Roy Wallis is simply dishonest.

Wallis has every right to reject Scientology personally, and indeed Scientologists themselves would defend his right to do so. But does he have the right to disguise his opinions and feelings as an honest sociological inquiry? Let's go to specifics.

Wallis' failings are both theoretical and empirical. At the level of theory Wallis simply plays games with words and their meanings. As one major example his use of the concept 'totalitarian' bends and twists through the pages of his manuscript to the point where virtually any leadership and any movement that is not utterly anarchistic would fit his conceptualization of totalitarian. As I read the theory sections, 'totalitarianism' and 'organization' become, for Wallis, tautological (circular) and synonymous. The word fails to differentiate categories and so becomes meaningless. In personal correspondence with Church of Scientology officials (11 November 1974), Wallis writes 'Totalitarianism can mean whatever I choose to make it mean . . .' And pig means pot and sixpence is a crown.

At the level of Wallis' actual empirical research, we find sampling errors so blatant that the entire book is suspect from then on to the conclusions. To put it oversimply, 'sampling' is the precise technology of selecting and examining a *representative* small number of items from a large 'population' of items in order to estimate the character of the large population. A biased sample gives one a false picture – for example, a study of US Presidents based only on researching the ones who were impeached. *All of Wallis' samples are grossly biased.*

In his sampling of respondents, Wallis focuses throughout his study almost exclusively on people who had left the movement for one reason or another. As a specific example, Wallis deals extensively with six dissident Clears but does not take up an offer to interview a sampling of over four thousand Clears who have not become dissident. Convenient for his theories perhaps but not intellectually honest. It is an endeavour very like studying the modern University by speaking only to school dropouts.

Another instance which reveals sampling bias on Wallis' part. From twenty-five years of written books, policy, and technical bulletins, Wallis has chosen a 'sample' of only a few statements, out of context, to support his theories. Again this would fetch a failing mark in any elementary statistics course. Content analysis of a random sampling of, say, a thousand statements written by Hubbard would have been legitimate and would have yielded a quite different picture.

And in the area of documents Wallis' sampling errors become grave. Wallis' account is conspicuous for all the data *left out*. There are on file thousands upon thousands of statements of people who have improved their lives through Scientology, test scores of raised I.Q. and personality improvement, X-ray verified medical recoveries, validations of the effectiveness of Scientology technology by prison wardens, educators, and government officials, sworn statements of remorse and retraction by hostile witnesses, Hubbard's Honors from the Explorers Club, the Key to the City of Long Beach, etc., etc. Where are the lengthy quotes from these documents? The fact that Narconon has a phenomenal success rate with hard-core drug-users (verified in Arizona State Prison), should be splashed on the front dust jacket of the book, not buried in a footnote.

The above are heavy methodological points against Wallis. But the most telling criticism of his work is to what extent does it have any real correspondence with Scientology as it is actually practised and as it actually developed?

Wallis paints a bleak picture indeed of the Scientology organizational network and of daily life within it. So bleak is this picture that if it were actually the situation only a devout masochist could endure it. If this *were* the situation I certainly would not be involved, nor would many of my friends.

The further one goes into the manuscript the more sweeping become the inaccuracies and distortions of fact of the development, practice and training of Dianetics and Scientology in order to conform with Wallis' preconceived model. For example, I have spoken at length with many early Dianeticists, including some that are not active in Scientology and some that have actively broken with Hubbard. Their stories are quite different from the Wallis account. Even the most outspoken apostates have not described Hubbard (whom they knew personally) as a manipulator or a dark-motived man. The common portrait which emerges, then and now, is of a man who has been trying for twenty-five years to *give away* any control he has so that he can devote himself to further research and writing. And one of the commonest complaints among the

Scientology dissidents is that Hubbard left the running of affairs in the hands of others.

Another instance. We are told (page 125) 'Aspects of the theory and practice most closely linking the belief system to the cultic milieu were abandoned. Dianetic "reverie" with its clear links to hypnosis and the concern with the trauma of early childhood and birth, with clear links to psychoanalysis and its developments, were abandoned.' A sound backing to the Wallis theory if true. But what if not true? Wallis points out earlier that *Dianetics Modern Science of Mental Health* embodied these ideas and was the basis for the 'cultic movement'. Has it been abandoned? The United States sales figures for the month of November 1974, according to Publications Organization shipping invoices for Scientology books, run as follows. First, *Dianetics Modern Science of Mental Health*, eight thousand eight hundred and thirteen copies. Next best seller, *Evolution of a Science*, eight hundred and ninety copies. *DMSMH* is still far and away the best selling Scientology book and is a required basic text for all professional auditors. And it is the book most often sold to new people.

To speak to each of Wallis' contentions and misdirections would require a book the length of his own. In his portrayal of field auditors, professional training, the Sea Org, the aims of Scientology, the credentials and personal life of L. Ron Hubbard, the social reform activities of the Church, its legal history, and the reasons people are in Scientology instead of real estate (or sociology), Wallis is simply wrong. I am reminded of Bob Dylan's 'Ballad of a Thin Man', about a man who knows something is happening here, but he does not know what it is. (For a quite different account, also written by a non-Scientologist, see Omar V. Garrison's *Hidden Story of Scientology*, Arlington Books, London, 1974.)

Wallis' fundamental weakness is that he converts his theories into fact by seeking only data which support them. This is true in his interpretation of the socialization process of Scientology's membership, in his conception of the Sea Org as a para-military organization, in imputing Machiavellian motives to L. Ron Hubbard and other Scientology leaders. Again and again and again he selectively ignores the genuine results of Scientology, admitted even by a great many of the dissidents he quotes. The Australian and South African inquiry reports and transcripts, for instance, are filled with statements of witnesses who had received great personal benefit from Scientology. But, again, where are these statements in Wallis' book?

Wallis does not believe that there is such a thing as a genuine result. It is all 'coaching' and 'indoctrination'. Perhaps Wallis believes an engineer produces a bridge by 'indoctrinating' the motorists that it is there.

Wallis does not grant any moral sensibility to the Scientology leadership whatsoever. Nor does he believe that they believe they can and do produce genuine results. He ignores the Guarantee of Refund if not fully satisfied (displayed in every Scientology organization). This guarantee of refund is more than any other profession offers, either in the therapeutic or religious fields. A doctor does not return his fees when he fails to cure a patient, a lawyer does not return his fees when he loses a case, a psychiatrist does not return his fees when he has made a nervous individual into a drug addict. And a sociologist does not return his grant when he fails to produce a work dealing with social facts.

I am sorry, I cannot take Wallis' work seriously. I have had seven years of intensive experiences in Scientology. And I came into Scientology as a practising, and widely published, sociologist. What I have found within the movement is a wealth of valid data, a battery of technology which works, hundreds of new friends, a return of a boyish lightheartedness that I had feared lost forever, and almost more adventure than I can handle.

It has not always been a primrose path. Scientology is not perfect and has never claimed to be. I personally made a baker's dozen mistakes last week that I already know of. But I have personally seen hundreds upon hundreds of beings move from death toward life. L. Ron Hubbard is not infallible nor has he ever claimed to be. In the *Aims of Scientology* he writes 'We may err, for we build a world with broken straws'.

But we *do* build. There is a Bridge to Freedom. I know because I have walked it. One *can* stand on the underside and complain about the paint job or the fact that there is no hot-dog stand yet, as Wallis does. Or one can walk over to the other side and try the view.

It would be true to say that there are areas of social problems wherein Scientology is, or has the potential of being, indispensable as a solution.

At this point the reader is probably in doubt about *both* Wallis and Scientology. I would invite you to do your own investigation. Get a copy of *Dianetics Modern Science of Mental Health* and read it along with this book. See for yourself which is more alive and hopeful *and scientifically objective*. And decide on the basis of your own comparison whether you wish to favor the Wallises of the world or the Scientologists, or to remain in doubt for now and wait for the historical dust to settle.

And as a final note, Wallis' thesis and my rebuttal are both a bit irrelevant. History will decide for both of us – and indeed, I suspect, already is. The behavioural sciences and universities in general are being more and more abandoned by a whole generation, while Scientology, according to the *Encyclopedia Britannica Yearbook*, is 'the largest of the new religions'.

Elting Memorial Library
93 Main St.
New Paltz, N. Y.

BIBLIOGRAPHY

(Only the more important titles are listed here. For other works, see the footnotes in the text.)

1. *'Official' literature*
ANONYMOUS. *Ceremonies of the Founding Church of Scientology.* Department of Publications World Wide, East Grinstead, 1967.
ANONYMOUS. *The Findings on the U.S. Food and Drug Agency.* Department of Publications World Wide, East Grinstead, Sussex, 1968.
ANONYMOUS. *Whatever Happened to Adelaide?.* [Church of Scientology, East Grinstead, Sussex], 1973.
HORNER, J. F. *A New Understanding of Life.* HCO, Auckland, New Zealand, 1961.
HUBBARD, L. RON. *A History of Man.* HASI, London, n.d. (originally titled *What to Audit*).
Electropsychometric Auditing Operator's Manual. HASI, London, n.d.
Advanced Procedure and Axioms. Central Press, Wichita, Kansas, 1951.
Dianetics: the Original Thesis. HDRF, Wichita, Kansas, 1951.
Science of Survival. Hubbard Dianetic Foundation Inc, Wichita, Kansas, 1951.
Scientology 8–80. The Distribution Center, Silver Springs, Maryland, 1952.
How to Live Though an Executive. Department of Publications World Wide, East Grinstead, 1953.
The Creation of Human Ability. Scientology Publications, London, 1955.
E-Meter Essentials 1961. HCO, East Grinstead, 1961.
Notes on the Lectures of L. Ron Hubbard, Edited by the staff of the California Foundation. HCO Ltd, East Grinstead, Sussex, 1962.
Scientology: a New Slant on Life. The American Saint Hill Organisation, Los Angeles, California, 1965.
Scientology 8–8008. Hubbard College of Scientology, East Grinstead, Sussex, 1967.
Dianetics 55!. Department of Publications World Wide, East Grinstead, 1968.
Dianetics: the Evolution of a Science. Publications Organisation, World Wide, 1968.
Dianetics: the Modern Science of Mental Health. Hubbard College of Scientology, East Grinstead, 1968.
Have You Lived Before This Life?. Department of Publications World Wide, East Grinstead, 1968.

The Fundamentals of Thought. Publications Organisation World Wide, Edinburgh, 1968.

Introduction to Scientology Ethics. Scientology Publications Organisation, Copenhagen, 1970.

The Book Introducing the E-Meter. Publications Organisation World Wide, Edinburgh, 1968.

The Organization Executive Course. Scientology Publications Organisation, Copenhagen, 1970 (8 volumes).

HUBBARD, JR, L. RON, HALPERN, GEORGE RICHARD and HALPERN, JAN (compilers). *ACC Preparatory Manual for Advanced Students in Scientology*. The Academy of Scientology [Washington D.C.] 1957.

HUBBARD, MARY SUE (compiler). *The Book of E-Meter Drills*. Hubbard College of Scientology, East Grinstead, 1967.

MINSHULL, RUTH. *How to Choose Your People*. Scientology Ann Arbor, Michigan, 1966.

Miracles for Breakfast. Scientology Ann Arbor, Michigan, 1968.

SILCOX, VICTOR and MAYNARD, LEN. *Creative Learning: a Scientological Experiment in Schools*. Scientology Publications, London, 1955.

Periodicals
Ability Major
Ability Minor
Advance!
Celebrity Magazine
Certainty
Change
Clear News
Dianetic Auditor's Bulletin
Freedom
Group Newsletter
Journal of Scientology
Professional Auditor's Bulletin
The Auditor
The Dianamic
The New Civilization

2. Independent, heretical and schismatic literature

BECKSTEAD, GORDON. *Prologue to Survival* (Parts I, II and III). Psychological Research Foundation, Phoenix, Arizona, 1952.

BERNER, H. CHARLES and WILLIAMS, RICHARD. *Abilitism: a New Religion*. Adams Press, Chicago, 1970.

HORNER, JACK. *Jack Horner Speaks*, Transcription of a lecture at the New York Dianetic Association, November 1952. The Eidetic Foundation, Alabama, 1952.

Dianology: a Better Bridge to Personal Creative Freedom. The Association of International Dianologists, California, 1970.

Eductivism and You. The Personal Creative Freedoms Foundation, Westwood, California, 1971.

MCPHEETERS, WOODWARD R., trans. *Scientologie 1934.* Causation Press Lucerne Valley, California, 1968.

SULLIVAN, FRANK S. *Adventures in Reincarnation.* CSA Press, Clayton, Georgia, 1971.

TOOLEY, MARCUS. *People Are Human.* Graham Ltd, Auckland, New Zealand, 1955.

WINTER, JOSEPH A. *A Doctor's Report on Dianetics: Theory and Therapy.* Julian Press, New York, 1951.

Periodicals
Auditor and Philosopher
Bristol Dianetic Review
CADA Bulletin
California Association of Dianetic Auditor's Journal
Dianetics Today
Dianotes
Dunbar's ARC
Epicentre
International Dianetic Society Letter
Introductory Bulletin of the Central Pennsylvania Dianetic Group
Life Preserver
The Aberree
The Arc Light
The Communicator
The Dianeticist
The Dianews
The Ghost of Scientology
The Preclear

3. *Other literature cited*

ADAMS, ROBERT LYNN and FOX, ROBERT JON. 'Mainlining Jesus! the new trip'. *Society*, **9**, 4, 1972, pp. 50–6.

ALDISS, BRIAN W. *Billion Year Spree.* Weidenfeld and Nicolson, London, 1973.

ALMOND, GABRIEL A., et al. *The Appeals of Communism.* Princeton University Press, Princeton, New Jersey, 1954.

AMIS, KINGSLEY. *New Maps of Hell.* New English Library, London, 1963.

ANDERSON, KEVIN VICTOR. *Report of the Board of Enquiry into Scientology.* Government Printer, Melbourne, Australia, 1965.

BASALLA, GEORGE. *The Rise of Modern Science: Internal or External Factors?* D. C. Heath & Co., Lexington, Mass., 1968.

BATES, ERNEST S. and DITTEMORE, JOHN V. *Mary Baker Eddy: the Truth and the Tradition.* George Routledge, London, 1933.

BAUDOUIN, CHARLES. *Suggestion and Autosuggestion.* Allen & Unwin, London, 1920.

BECKER, HOWARD. 'Notes on the concept of commitment', *AJS*, **66**, No. 1 1960, pp. 32–40.
Outsiders: Studies in the Sociology of Deviance. Free Press, New York, 1963.

BENNETT, JOHN W. *Hutterian Bretheren*. Stanford University Press, Stanford, 1967.

BERGER, PETER L. 'Secularization and pluralism', *International Yearbook for the Sociology of Religion*, 2, 1966, pp. 73–84.
The Social Reality of Religion. Faber, London, 1969.

BERGER, PETER and KELLNER, HANSFRIED. 'Marriage and the construction of reality', in Hans Peter Dreitzel, ed., *Patterns of Communicative Behaviour*. Collier-Macmillan, London, 1970.

BERGER, PETER and LUCKMANN, THOMAS. *The Social Construction of Reality*. Allen Lane, London, 1967.

BLAU, PETER M. 'Decentralisation in bureaucracies' in Mayer Zald, ed., *Power in Organisations*. Vanderbilt University Press, Nashville, Tennessee, 1970.

BRADDESON, WALTER. *Scientology for the Millions*. Sherbourne Press, Los Angeles, 1969.

BRADEN, CHARLES S. *Christian Science Today*. Southern Methodist University Press, Dallas, Texas, 1958.
Spirits in Rebellion: the Rise and Development of New Thought. Southern Methodist University Press, Dallas, Texas, 1963.

BRENMAN, MARGARET and GILL, MERTON M. *Hypnotherapy: a Survey of the Literature*. International Universities Press, New York, 1947.

BREUER, JOSEPH and FREUD, SIGMUND. *Studies in Hysteria*, Vol II of the Standard Edition of the Complete Psychological Works of Sigmund Freud. Hogarth Press, London, 1955.

BROWN, J. A. C. *Freud and the Post-Freudians*. Penguin Books, Harmondsworth, 1964.

BUCKNER, H. TAYLOR. 'The flying saucerians: a lingering cult'. *New Society*, 9 September 1965.
'The flying saucerians: an open door cult', in Marcello Truzzi, ed., *Sociology and Everyday Life*. Prentice Hall, Englewood Cliffs, N.J., 1968.
Deviance, Reality and Change. Random House, New York, 1971.

BURIN, FREDERIC S. 'Bureaucracy and National Socialism: a reconsideration of Weberian theory', in R. K. Merton, et al., *Reader in Bureaucracy*. Free Press, New York, 1952.

BURRELL, MAURICE C. *Scientology: What It Is and What it Does*. Lakeland, London, 1970.

CALLEY, MALCOLM J. C. *God's People*. Oxford University Press, London, 1965.

CAMPBELL, COLIN. 'The cult, the cultic milieu and secularization', in Michael Hill, ed., *A Sociological Yearbook of Religion in Britain*, No. 5. SCM Press, London, 1972.

CASSEE, E. TH. 'Deviant illness behaviour: patients of mesmerists'. *Social Science and Medicine*, **3**, 1970, pp. 389–96.

CICOUREL, AARON V. *The Social Organization of Juvenile Justice*. Wiley, New York, 1967.

COHEN, STANLEY. *Folk Devils and Moral Panics*. MacGibbon & Kee, London, 1972.

COLBERT, JOHN. *An Evaluation of Dianetic Therapy*. Thesis for the degree of Master of Science in Education. School of Education, The City College, New York, 1951.

CONN, JACOB H. 'Hypnosynthesis: III Hypnotherapy of chronic war neuroses with a discussion of the value of abreaction, regression, and revivification', *Journal of Clinical and Experimental Hypnosis*, **1**, 1953, pp. 29–43.

COOPER, DAVID. *Psychiatry and Anti-Psychiatry*. Paladin, London, 1970.

COOPER, PAULETTE. *The Scandal of Scientology*. Tower, New York, 1971.

DAKIN, EDWIN FRANDEN. *Mrs Eddy: the Biography of a Virginal Mind*. Charles Scribner's Sons, London, 1929.

DALTON, DAVID R. *Two Disparate Philosophies*. Regency Press, London, 1973.

DANER, FRANCINE J. 'Conversion to Krishna Consciousness: the transformation from hippie to religious ascetic', in Roy Wallis, ed., *Sectarianism: Analyses of Religious and Non-Religious Sects*. Peter Owen, London, 1975.

DANIELS, ARLENE K. 'The social construction of military psychiatric diagnoses', in Hans Peter Dreitzel, ed., *Patterns of Communicative Behaviour*. Collier-Macmillan, London, 1970.

DATOR, JAMES A. *Soka Gakkai: Builders of the Third Civilization*. University of Washington Press, Seattle, 1969.

DICKSON, DONALD T. 'Bureaucracy and morality: an organisational perspective on a moral crusade'. *Social Problems*, **16**, 1968, pp. 143–56.

DOHRMAN, H. T. *California Cult: the Story of Mankind United*. Beacon Press, Boston, 1958.

DOUGLAS, MARY. *Purity and Danger*. Routledge & Kegan Paul, London, 1966.

EEMAN, L. E. *Co-operative Healing*. Frederick Muller, London, 1947.

EISTER, ALLAN W. *Drawing-Room Conversion*. Duke University Press, Durham, North Carolina, 1950.

ELIADE, MIRCEA. *Yoga: Immortality and Freedom*. Routledge & Kegan Paul, London, 1958.

ELLWOOD, ROBERT S. *Religious and Spiritual Groups in Modern America*. Prentice Hall, New Jersey, 1973.

EMERSON, JOAN. 'Behaviour in private places: sustaining definitions of reality in gynaecological examinations' in Hans Peter Dreitzel, ed., *Patters of Communicative Behaviour*. Collier-Macmillan, London, 1970.

ENGLAND, R. W. 'Some aspects of Christian Science as reflected in letters of testimony'. *AJS*, **59**, 5, 1954, 448–53.

ENROTH, RICHARD, ERICSON, EDWARD and BRECKINRIDGE PETERS, C. *The Story of the Jesus People*. Paternoster, Exeter, 1972.

ERICKSON, MILTON H. 'Hypnotic treatment of acute hysterical depression: report of a case'. *Archives of Neurology and Psychiatry* **46**, 1941.

ERICKSON, MILTON and KUBIE, LAWRENCE S. 'Successful treatment of a case of acute hysterical depression by return under hypnosis to a critical phase of childhood'. *Psychoanalytic Quarterly*, **10**, 4, 1941, pp. 585–609

ESSIEN-UDOM, E. V. *Black Nationalism: a Search for Identity in America*. Penguin Books, Harmondsworth, 1962.

ETZIONI, AMITAI. *A Comparative Analysis of Complex Organizations*. Free Press Glencoe, 1961.

EVANS, CHRISTOPHER. *Cults of Unreason*. Harrap, London, 1973.

FESTINGER, LEON, RIEKEN, HENRY W. and SCHACHTER, STANLEY. *When Prophecy Fails*. Harper, New York, 1964.

FISCHER, HARVEY JAY. *Dianetic Therapy: an Experimental Evaluation*. Unpublished Ph.D. dissertation. School of Education, New York University, 1953.

FODOR, NANDOR. *The Search for the Beloved*. Hermitage Press, New York, 1949.

FOSTER, SIR JOHN G. *Enquiry into the Practice and Effects of Scientology*. HMSO, London, 1971.

FOX, JACK, DAVIS, ALVIN E. and LEBOVITS, B. 'An experimental investigation of Hubbard's engram hypothesis (dianetics)', *Psychological Newsletter*, Vol. 10, 1959, pp. 131–4.

FRANK, JEROME D. *Persuasion and Healing*. Johns Hopkins Press, Baltimore, 1961.

FRAZER, JAMES G. *The Golden Bough*. Macmillan, New York, 1922.

FREUD, SIGMUND. *The Future of an Illusion*. Hogarth, London, 1962.

FULLER, R. BUCKMINSTER. *Nine Chains to the Moon*. Southern Illinois University Press, 1938.

GARDNER, MARTIN. *Fads and Fallacies in the Name of Science*. Dover Publications, New York, 1957.

GARFINKEL, HAROLD. *Studies in Ethnomethodology*. Prentice-Hall, Englewood Cliffs, New Jersey, 1967.

GARRISON, OMAR V. *The Hidden Story of Scientology*. Arlington Books, London, 1974.

GERLACH, LUTHER P. and HINE, VIRGINIA H. *People, Power and Change: Movements of Social Transformation*. Bobbs-Merrill, New York, 1970.

GERTH, HANS. 'The Nazi Party: its leadership and composition'. *AJS*, **45**, 4, 1940, pp. 517–41.

GILL, MERTON M. 'Spontaneous regression on the induction of hypnosis'. *Bulletin of the Menninger Clinic*, **12**, 2, 1948, pp. 41–8.

GLOCK, CHARLES Y. and STARK, RODNEY. *Religion and Society in Tension*. Rand McNally, Chicago, 1965.

GOFFMAN, ERVING. 'Symbols of class status', *BJS*, **2**, 1951.
Presentation of Self in Everyday Life. Doubleday Anchor, New York, 1959.
Behaviour in Public Places. Free Press, New York, 1963.
Relations in Public. Penguin Books, Harmondsworth, 1972.

GRANT, KENNETH. *The Magical Revival*. Muller, London, 1972.

GREENACRE, PHYLLIS. 'The predisposition to anxiety', *Psychoanalytic Quarterly*, **10**, 1941, pp. 66–94.

GUSFIELD, JOSEPH. 'Social structure and moral reform: a study of the Woman's Christian Temperance Union'. *AJS*, **61**, 1955, pp. 221–32.
Symbolic Crusade. University of Illinois Press, Urbana, Illinois, 1963.

HANDLIN, OSCAR. 'Science and technology in popular culture', in Gerald Holton, ed., *Science and Culture*. Beacon, Boston, 1967, pp. 184–98.

HARSHBARGER, DWIGHT. 'The individual and the social order: notes on the management of heresy and deviance in complex organisations', *Human Relations*, **26**, 2, 1973, pp. 251–69.

HERBERG, WILL. *Protestant–Catholic–Jew.* Doubleday Anchor, N.Y., 1960.

HOEKEMA, A. A. *The Four Major Cults.* Eerdmans, Grand Rapids, 1963.

HOSTETLER, J. A. *Amish Society.* Johns Hopkins Press, Baltimore, 1968.

ISICHEI, ELIZABETH. 'From sect to denomination among English Quakers' in Bryan Wilson, ed., *Patterns of Sectarianism.* Heinemann, London, 1967, pp. 161–81.

JOHNSON, BENTON. 'A critical appraisal of the church-sect typology', *ASR*, **22**, 1957, pp. 88–92.
'On church and sect', *ASR*, **28**, 1963, pp. 539–49.
'Church and sect revisited', *JSSR*, **10**, 2, 1971, pp. 124–37.

JONES, KENNETH. 'The Catholic Apostolic Church: a study in diffused commitment', in Michael Hill, ed., *A Sociological Yearbook of Religion in Britain*, No. 5. SCM Press, London, 1972, pp. 137–60.

JUDAH, J. STILLSON. *The History and Philosophy of the Metaphysical Movements in America.* Westminster Press, Philadelphia, 1967.

KANTER, ROSABETH MOSS. *Commitment and Community.* Harvard University Press, Cambridge, Massachussetts, 1972.

KAUFMAN, ROBERT. *Inside Scientology.* Olympia Press, London, 1972.

KOTZÉ, G. R. C. et al. *Report of the Commission of Enquiry into Scientology for 1972.* Government Printer, Pretoria, South Africa, 1973.

LEE, JOHN A. *Sectarian Healers and Hypnotherapy.* Queen's Printer, Toronto, 1970.

LEITES, NATHAN. *Operational Code of the Politburo.* McGraw-Hill, New York, 1951.

LEMERT, EDWIN M. *Social Pathology.* McGraw-Hill, New York, 1951.
Human Deviance, Social Problems and Social Control. Prentice Hall, New Jersey, 1967.

LEVY-BRUHL, LUCIEN. *Primitive Mentality.* Allen & Unwin, London, 1923.

LINCOLN, ERIC C. *The Black Muslims in America.* Beacon, Boston, 1961.

LOFLAND, JOHN and STARK, RODNEY. 'Becoming a world-saver: a theory of conversion to a deviant perspective', *ASR*, **30**, 1965, pp. 862–75.

LOFLAND, JOHN. *Doomsday Cult.* Prentice-Hall, Englewood Cliffs, New Jersey, 1966.

LUCKMANN, THOMAS and BERGER, PETER. 'Social mobility and personal identity'. *European Journal of Sociology.* Vol. **5**, 1964, pp. 331–43.

MAHOLICK, LEONARD T. 'The infant in the adult'. *Psychosomatic Medicine*, **11**, 1949, pp. 295–337.

MALKO, GEORGE. *Scientology: the Now Religion.* Dell, New York, 1970.

MARTIN, DAVID. 'Secularisation', in Julius Gould, ed., *Penguin Survey of the Social Sciences* **1965**. Penguin Books, Harmondsworth, 1965.
The Sociology of English Religion. SCM Press, London, 1967.
The Religious and the Secular. Routledge & Kegan Paul, London, 1969.

MASSERMAN, J. H. 'The dynamics of hypnosis and brief psychotherapy'. *Archives of Neurology and Psychiatry*, **46**, 1941, pp. 176–9.

MCDONALD, K. and RIDGE, J. 'Social mobility' in A. H. Halsey, *Trends in British Society.* Macmillan, London, 1972.

MCFARLAND, H. N. *The Rush Hour of the Gods.* Macmillan, New York, 1967.

MCHUGH, PETER. *Defining the Situation.* Bobbs-Merrill, New York, 1968.

MCMILLAN, CHARLES. 'Corporations without citizenship: the emergence of multinational enterprise', in Graeme Salaman and Kenneth Thompson, eds, *People and Organizations.* Longman, London, 1973, pp. 25–44.

MILIBAND, RALPH. *The State in Capitalist Society.* Weidenfeld & Nicolson, London, 1969.

MILMINE, GEORGINE. *The Life of Mary Baker G. Eddy and the History of Christian Science.* Baker Book House, Grand Rapids, Michigan, 1971.

NIEBUHR, H. R. *The Social Sources of Denominationalism.* Holt, Rinehart & Winston, New York, 1925.

NELSON, GEOFFREY K. 'The analysis of a cult: Spiritualism', *Social Compass*, **15**, 6, 1968.

'The concept of cult', *Sociological Review*, **16**, 3, 1968, pp. 351–62.

Spiritualism and Society. Routledge & Kegan Paul, London, 1969(a).

'The Spiritualist movement and the need for a redefinition of cult', *JSSR*, **8**, (Spring) 1969(b).

NORDENHOLZ, A. *Scientologie, Wissenschaft von der Beschaffenheit und Der Tauglichkeit des Wissens.* Ernst Reinhardt, Munich, 1934.

NYOMARKAY, JOSEPH. *Charisma and Factionalism in the Nazi Party.* University of Minnesota Press, Minneapolis, 1967.

O'BRIEN, HELEN. *Dianetics in Limbo.* Whitmore Publishing Co., Philadelphia, 1966.

OFFNER, C. B. and VAN STRAELEN, H. *Modern Japanese Religions.* Brill, Leiden, 1963.

PARSONS, TALCOTT. 'The American family: its relations to personality and the social structure', in Talcott Parsons and R. F. Bales, *Family Socialisation and Interaction Process.* Free Press, Glencoe, 1956.

PAYNE, MURIEL. *Creative Education.* William Maclellan, Glasgow, 1958.

PETERS, VICTOR. *All Things Common.* Harper, New York, 1965.

PETERSON, DONALD W. and MAUSS, ARMAND L. 'The Cross and the Commune: an interpretation of the Jesus People' in Charles Y. Glock, ed., *Religion in Sociological Perspective.* Wadsworth, Belmont, California, 1973, pp. 261–79.

PODMORE, FRANK. *Modern Spiritualism: a History and Criticism.* Methuen, London, 1902.

POWLES, SIR GUY RICHARDSON and DUMBLETON, E. V. *Report of the Commission of Inquiry into the Hubbard Scientology Organisation in New Zealand.* Government Printer, Wellington, New Zealand, 1969.

PRATT, VERNON. *Religion and Secularisation.* St Martin's Press, London, 1970.

PUGH, D. S. and HICKSON, D. J. 'The comparative study of organisations' in Graeme Salaman and Kenneth Thompson, eds, *People and Organisations.* Longman, London, 1973.

RANK, OTTO. *The Trauma of Birth.* Harcourt Brace & Co., New York, 1929.

ROBBINS, THOMAS and ANTHONY, DICK. 'Getting straight with Meher Baba', *JSSR*, **11**, 2, 1972, pp. 122–40.

ROBERTSON, ROLAND. *The Sociological Interpretation of Religion.* Blackwell, Oxford, 1970.

ROLPH, C. H. *Believe What You Like.* André Deutsch, London, 1973.

SARGANT, WILLIAM. *Battle for the Mind.* Pan Books, London, 1959.

SCHNEIDER, LOUIS and DORNBUSCH, SANFORD M. 'Inspirational religious literature: from latent to manifest functions of religion', *AJS*, **62**, No. 5, 1957, pp. 476–81.
Popular Religion: Inspirational Books in America. University of Chicago Press, Chicago, 1958.

SCOTT, ROBERT A. 'A proposed framework for analysing deviance as a property of social order' in Robert A. Scott and Jack D. Douglas, eds, *Theoretical Perspectives on Deviance.* Basic Books, New York, 1972.

SELZNICK, PHILIP. *The Organisational Weapon.* Free Press, Glencoe, 1960.

SEMON, RICHARD. *Mnemic Psychology.* Allen & Unwin, London, 1923. *The Mneme.* Allen & Unwin, London, 1921.

SIEGLER, MIRIAM, OSMOND, HUMPHRY and MANN, HARRIET. 'Laing's models of madness'. *British Journal of Psychiatry*, **115**, 1969, pp. 947–58.

SMELSER, NEIL. *Theory of Collective Behaviour.* Routledge & Kegan Paul, London, 1962.

SPELT, DAVID K. 'The conditioning of the human foetus *in utero*'. *Journal of Experimental Psychology*, **38**, 1948, pp. 338–46.

STARK, RODNEY and GLOCK, CHARLES. *American Piety: the Nature of Religious Commitment.* University of California Press, Berkeley, 1968.

STEINER, LEE R. *Where Do People Take Their Troubles?* Houghton Mifflin, Boston, 1945.

SYKES, GRESHAM and MATZA, DAVID. 'Techniques of neutralisation', *ASR*, **22**, No. 6 1957, pp. 664–70.

TEENER, JAMES. *Unity School of Christianity.* Unpublished Ph.D. dissertation. University of Chicago, 1939.

THOMSEN, H. *The New Religions of Japan.* Tuttle, Rutland, Vermont, 1963.

TUCKMANN, JACOB and KLEINER, ROBERT J. 'Discrepancy between aspiration and achievement as a predictor of schizophrenia'. *Behavioral Science*, **7**, 1962, pp. 443–7.

VOSPER, CYRIL. *The Mind Benders.* Neville Spearman, London, 1971.

WALLIS, ROY. 'The sectarianism of Scientology' in Michael Hill, ed., *A Sociological Yearbook of Religion in Britain*, No. 6. SCM Press, London, 1973, pp. 136–55.
'Religious sects and the fear of publicity'. *New Society*, 7 June 1973, pp. 545–7.
'A comparative analysis of problems and processes of change in two manipulationist movements: Christian Science and Scientology' in *The Contemporary Metamorphosis of Religion?* Acts of the 12th International Conference on the Sociology of Religion. The Hague, Netherlands, August 1973, pp. 407–22.
'The Aetherius Society: a case study in the formation of a mystagogic congregation'. *Sociological Review*, **22**, 1, 1974, pp. 27–44.
'Ideology, authority and the development of cultic movements'. *Social Research*, **41**, 2, 1974, pp. 299–327.

WEBER, MAX. 'Bureaucracy' in Hans H. Gerth and C. Wright Mills, eds,

From Max Weber: Essays in Sociology. Routledge & Kegan Paul, London, 1970.
'Charisma' in Hans Gerth and C. Wright Mills, eds, *From Max Weber: Essays in Sociology.* Routledge & Kegan Paul, London, 1970.
The Protestant Ethic and the Spirit of Capitalism. Unwin, London, 1930.

WHITE, JAMES W. *The Sokagakkai and Mass Society.* Stanford University Press, Stanford, California, 1970.

WHITEHEAD, HARRIET. 'Reasonably fantastic: some perspectives on Scientology, science fiction and occultism' in Irving I. Zaretsky and Mark Leone, *Religious Movements in Contemporary America.* Princeton University Press, Princeton, 1974.

WILENSKY, HAROLD L. 'The professionalization of everyone?', *AJS*, **70**, 1964, pp. 137–58.

WILKINS, LESLIE T. *Social Deviance.* Tavistock, London, 1964.

WILSON, BRYAN R. 'The Origins of Christian Science: a survey', *The Hibbert Journal*, 57, 1959, pp. 161–70.
Sects and Society. Heinemann, London, 1961.
Religion in Secular Society. Penguin Books, Harmondsworth, 1969.
Religious Sects. Weidenfeld & Nicolson, London, 1970.
Magic and the Millennium. Heinemann, London, 1973.

WINTER, JOSEPH A. *Are Your Troubles Psychomatic?* Messner, New York, 1952.

WOLBERG, LEWIS R. *Hypnoanalysis.* Grune & Stratton, New York, 1945.

WOODCOCK, GEORGE and AVAKUMOVIC, IVAN. *The Doukhobors.* Faber, London, 1968.

YINGER, J. MILTON. *The Scientific Study of Religion.* Collier-Macmillan, New York, 1970.

YOUNG, JOCK. 'The role of the police as amplifiers of deviance [etc]' in Stanley Cohen, ed., *Images of Deviance.* Penguin Books, Harmondsworth, 1971.
The Drugtakers. Paladin, London, 1971.

YOUNG, PAUL CAMPBELL. 'Hypnotic regression – fact or artifact?' *Journal of Abnormal and Social Psychology*, **35**, 1940, pp. 273–8.

ZABLOCKI, BENJAMIN. *The Joyful Community.* Penguin Books, Baltimore, Maryland, 1971.

INDEX